William-R. Brownlow, Giovanni Battista de Rossi

Roma Sotterranea

Some Account of the Roman Catacombs, Especially of the Cemetery of San Callisto

William-R. Brownlow, Giovanni Battista de Rossi

Roma Sotterranea
Some Account of the Roman Catacombs, Especially of the Cemetery of San Callisto

ISBN/EAN: 9783744692779

Printed in Europe, USA, Canada, Australia, Japan

Cover: Foto ©ninafisch / pixelio.de

More available books at **www.hansebooks.com**

ROMA SOTTERRANEA

OR

SOME ACCOUNT OF THE ROMAN CATACOMBS

ESPECIALLY OF THE

CEMETERY OF SAN CALLISTO

*COMPILED FROM THE WORKS OF COMMENDATORE DE ROSSI
WITH THE CONSENT OF THE AUTHOR*

BY

REV. J. SPENCER NORTHCOTE, D. D.
PRESIDENT OF ST MARY'S COLLEGE, OSCOTT

AND

REV. W. R. BROWNLOW, M.A.
TRINITY COLLEGE, CAMBRIDGE

LONDON
LONGMANS, GREEN, READER, AND DYER
1869
[*All rights of Translation reserved*]

EDINBURGH
PRINTED BY BALLANTYNE AND COMPANY,
PAUL'S WORK.

PREFACE

THE interest which the Roman Catacombs have excited in the minds of our countrymen, especially of those who have visited the Eternal City, has long made us wish to present them with that most full and accurate information upon the subject which is contained in the ROMA SOTTERRANEA of De Rossi.

Two courses were open to us; either to bring out a translation from the Italian original, or to embody in a work of our own the most interesting and important facts which those volumes contain. The first would have been incomparably the easier, and in some respects the more satisfactory course. But the size and cost of such a work would have put it entirely beyond the reach of many whom we were most anxious to benefit. We therefore decided on the plan adopted in the volume which we now introduce to our readers, and which, we believe, will be found to contain as fair a summary as its dimensions would allow—not only of De Rossi's two volumes of *Roma Sotterranea*, published in 1864 and 1867,—but also of many articles in his bi-monthly *Bullettino di Archeologia Cristiana*, of papers read by him before learned societies in Rome and elsewhere, and of his occasional contributions to works published by others, such as the *Spicilegium Solesmense* of Cardinal Pitra, &c.

It was our intention at one time to have drawn up a tabulated statement, showing the exact portion of De Rossi's works from which each part of this had been compiled; but as those works are unhappily without indices, and the intention referred to was not entertained when first this volume was taken in hand, some three or four years ago, it was found that the benefit to be derived from such a statement would not be likely to repay the labour of drawing it out. Nevertheless, it has been thought worth while to retain a number of references in the notes, wherever they happened to have been preserved in our MSS., and either related to some mere *obiter dicta* which might easily have been overlooked even by persons who had studied the original, or belonged to some of those minor works which we have enumerated, and which are not so generally known as the larger works of our author.

A more important omission, which will be regretted by many of our readers, requires a word of explanation. We allude to the Inscriptions on the grave-stones of the Catacombs. But this was too large a subject to be disposed of satisfactorily at the end of a volume already longer than was desired. Moreover, it would hardly be fair, either to the subject or to our author, to handle this question until the second volume of *Inscriptiones Christianæ*, on which he is at present engaged, shall have been published. That volume will contain all the Christian inscriptions of Rome which bear upon Christian doctrine and practice; and should the present attempt to put the fruit of De Rossi's wonderful discoveries in the Catacombs within the reach of English readers meet with sufficient encouragement, a similar epitome—already begun—of his labours in the fields of Christian epigraphy will soon follow.

In the arrangement of this volume, we have followed, in the main, the order of De Rossi himself; but to those to whom the subject is altogether new, we should recommend a certain departure from this order. They would do well to postpone the perusal of the Introduction, or Literary History of the Catacombs, until they have first read Books I. and II., which contain an account of their origin and *real* history. Then the Introduction would form a suitable link between the general treatment of the subject in Books I. and II., and the more minute examination of one particular cemetery (San Callisto), which forms the subject of Book III. Book IV., on Christian Art, is, of course, complete in itself. The last two chapters of it are, in great part, taken from the works of Bosio and of Padre Garrucci. Even here, however, we are indebted for many important additions and corrections to the works of De Rossi. Book V. is compiled from that part of the Commendatore's volumes which was contributed by his brother. It is a development, partly of the last chapter in Book I., and partly of the second chapter in Book III., of this volume. We suspect that to many of our readers this Book will seem dry and tedious, in spite of the assistance of the numerous plans and sections by which we have illustrated it; yet, the study of it is certainly indispensable to those who would go thoroughly into the matter, and satisfy themselves as to the solidity of the foundation on which De Rossi's conclusions rest. Its special value lies in the fact of its being an examination of the subterranean excavations themselves, which are made to bear testimony to the successive periods of their own construction, and thus its conclusions are drawn from a source quite independent of those historical documents which have been the main guide of Gio. Battista de Rossi in all his labours in this field of Christian archæology.

We have prefixed a chronological table and a list of the Catacombs according to their ancient appellations and their position on the various roads out of Rome, which we hope may assist our readers in forming a clearer notion both of the history and geography of the cemeteries referred to in the course of the work.

Finally, it may be well to add that, although both Editors are jointly responsible for the whole volume, the first portion, to the fifth chapter of Book IV., is mainly the work of Dr Northcote; the remainder of the text, and Note C in the Appendix (on St Peter's Chair), is the work of Mr Brownlow.

EASTER TUESDAY, 1869.

LIST OF PLATES

AT THE END OF THE VOLUME.

———✦———

The pages refer to the passages where they are described or alluded to.

Plate.   Page

I. Damasine Inscription found in Papal Crypt (See Plan L[1] Atlas B*e* 4), ... 147

II. Copy (probably by Pope Vigilius) of Damasine Inscription to St Eusebius, found in his Crypt (Atlas, D*e* 1), . 170

III. The same, as originally set up by St Damasus, . . 170

IV. Fresco of Moses, from a *cubiculum* near to Area VI., . 248

V. Fresco of Saints Cornelius and Cyprian in the Crypt of St Lucina (Atlas D*h* 3), ... 181

VI. Ceiling of *cubiculum* near the above; painting of Second Century; representing in the centre Daniel between the lions, and in the corners the Good Shepherd alternately with a female *orante*, which is probably the Blessed Virgin (on the walls of this same chamber are painted Plate XIV. 1, and Figs. 14 and 19), . . . 255

VII. Fresco of Jonas, ... 244

VIII. Frescoes from Bosio : (1) Good Shepherd and the Blessed Virgin with Birds (Bosio, p. 387) from *cubiculum* in Cemetery of Saints Peter and Marcellinus, . . 255

(2) Noe, from Cemetery of St Agnes (Bosio, p. 449), 241

IX. Do. : (1) Lazarus from Cemetery of Saints Peter and Marcellinus (Bosio, p. 359), ... 247

(2) Three Children from Cemetery of St Hermes (Bosio, p. 565), ... 245

X. (1) The Blessed Virgin Mary and the Prophet Isaias, Fresco of Second Century in a *cubiculum* of St Priscilla, . 258

(2) The Adoration of the Magi, from Cemetery of Saints Peter and Marcellinus, a Fresco of the Third Century, . 257

List of Plates.

Plate.		Page
XI.	(1) Sacrifice of Isaac, from *cubiculum* A_3, Fresco of Second Century,	270
	(2) Our Lord under the symbol of Orpheus, from ceiling of *cubiculum* L^2, same age,	199
	(3, 4) Fossors painted on either side of the doorway of *cubiculum* A_4, Third Century,	272
XII.	(1) The Smitten Rock and the Fisher of Souls, from *cubiculum* A_2, Second Century,	265
	(2) The same subjects, from *cubiculum* A_3,	ib.
	(3) Paralytic carrying his Bed on the same wall with 2,	ib.
XIII.	The Eucharistic Feast, from *cubiculum* A_3, where it is painted between XI. 1 and XIV. 3, forming one composition with them,	269
XIV.	(1) Symbol of Holy Eucharist, from the same *cubiculum* in Cemetery of St Lucina as Plate VI.,	224
	(2) Eucharistic Symbols, from *cubiculum* A_2,	214
	(3) Sacrifice of the Mass symbolically depicted in *cubiculum* A_3 (see XIII.),	266
XV.	Papal Crypt, as it must have appeared in the time of St Damasus, restored by De Rossi from fragments found in the Crypt itself,	147
XVI.	Christ and the Apostles under symbol of Good Shepherd, painted in the lunette of an *arcosolium*, probably towards end of Third Century, in the same *cubiculum* with Plate IV. (see Atlas, Area VII. 3),	237
XVII.	(1) Bronze Medal of Saints Peter and Paul, of First or Second Century, found in Cemetery of St Domitilla,	284
	(2) Gilded Glass of St Peter as Moses, in Vatican Library,	287
XVIII.	Gilded Glasses from the Catacombs :—	
	(1) Blessed Virgin between Saints Peter and Paul, in Propaganda Museum,	285
	(2) St Agnes with two Doves, in Vatican Library,	286
XIX.	Sarcophagus found at St Paul's on Via Ostiensis, now in Lateran Museum,	300
XX.	Sarcophagi with Pagan Sculptures used by Christians in ages of persecution :—	
	(1) Dolphins, Epitaph of *Longlianus, buried on the 6th of April*,	297
	(2) Orpheus and Fisherman ; *my sweet Furia, holy soul*,	300

ATLAS—A description will be found at the end of the Volume.

LIST OF WOODCUTS.

Fig.		Page
1.	General view of the Gallery of a Catacomb with Graves,	26
2.	Plan of *arenaria* immediately above the Catacomb of St Agnes,	28
3.	Plan of part of that Catacomb from Padre Marchi,	29
4.	General appearance of an *arcosolium*,	30
5.	Table-tomb, called also *sepolcro* or *loculo a mensa*,	30
6.	Chamber in Catacomb of St Agnes, with Chairs and Bench cut out of the solid tufa,	31
7.	A *luminare* giving light to two Chambers in Catacomb of Saints Marcellinus and Peter,	34
8.	Sepulchral Stone found in a Catacomb on Via Latina, having engraved upon it the Monogram, the Fish, and Good Shepherd,—explained in page 213,	55
9.	View of entrance to Cemetery of St Domitilla, Via Ardeatina,	71
10.	Fresco of Vine on Ceiling of Cemetery of St Domitilla, First Century,	72
11.	Remains of Fresco of Daniel in Cemetery of St Domitilla, First Century,	73
12.	Painted Chamber in Cemetery of St Pretextatus, Second Century,	79
	Epitaph of St Januarius by Pope Damasus,	80
13.	Stone (having a Lamb, Dove, and Anchor engraved on it) which still closes a *loculus* in a very ancient part of the Lower Gallery of Area of St Lucina,	82
14.	Two Sheep with Milk-pail, in *cubiculum* of St Lucina, (described in p. 225),	103
15.	Sarcophagus, with inscription, *O Blastianus, peace with thee!* a form of Epitaph similar to the very ancient ones in St Priscilla, found in very ancient *cubiculum* of St Lucina, adjoining that described in p. 225,	109
	Epitaph of Pope Cornelius,	118
16.	Fresco of the Baptism of our Lord in the *cubiculum* described under Fig. 15,	119
	Epitaphs of Popes St Antherus, St Fabian, St Lucius, and St Eutychianus,	137

List of Woodcuts.

Fig.		Page
17.	Statue of St Cecilia, by Maderna, who had seen her body incorrupt in 1599, ...	157
18.	Inscription (with Monogram and Doves) on an *arcosolium* in the Cemetery of St Soteris, ...	166
19.	Fresco of Doves from the *cubiculum* in which is Fig. 14, First or Second Century, ...	185
20.	Fresco of Good Shepherd in centre of Ceiling of the adjoining Chamber, ...	201
21.	Epitaph from very ancient part of Catacomb of St Priscilla, .	207
22.	Another Epitaph from the same, ...	213
23.	Frescoes of Gospel Stories illustrating the Holy Eucharist, from Catacombs of Alexandria, ...	221
24.	Sepulchral Stone from ancient Christian Cemetery at Modena, .	223
25.	Fresco of Lamb with Palm and Milk-pail, being one of those in each of the four corners of a *cubiculum* in Saints Peter and Marcellinus, ...	225
26.	Fresco of Lamb with Shepherd's Crook and Milk-pail, from very ancient part of Catacomb of St Domitilla, . . .	225
27.	Different forms of the Cross and Monogram of Christ, . .	230
28.	Sarcophagus found in Crypt of St Lucina, with Monogram of *Tyranio*, and Sculpture representing Ulysses and the Syrens, ...	232
29.	Inscription found in Crypt of St Lucina, with Doves plucking at Grapes. There is an error towards the end, of N for II, as the original runs SABBATIAOVEVIXI IANNIIIAENSV, evidently the work of a stone-cutter ignorant of letters, and intended for *Sabbatia quæ vixit ann. iii., mens. v.;* "Sabbatia, who lived three years and five months,"	238
30.	Sculpture of Elias being taken up into Heaven, in Lateran Museum, ...	250
31.	Fresco of the Madonna and Child in Catacomb of St Agnes, early part of Fourth Century, ...	257
32.	Sarcophagus with Pagan Good Shepherd, and Cupid and Psyche found beneath the floor of *cubiculum* Q¹ (Atlas, B*e* 7), in San Callisto, described in p. 298, ...	261
33.	Gilded Glass, with Saint Peter as Moses, in Vatican Museum, .	287
34.	Fragments of Glass Paten found at Cologne, A.D. 1864, .	290
35.	Sarcophagus, still containing the body of a man, ornamented with unfinished figure of the deceased, veiled and clothed in tunic and pallium, with a roll of a book in his hand, and a box of books at his feet—described in p. 299. At either end is a shepherd with a dog. This and two other sarcophagi, likewise containing bodies, were found in the *cubiculum*, where they now are, close to the staircase in Area VII. (Atlas, C*e* 2), ...	294

List of Woodcuts.

Fig.		Page
36.	Sarcophagus representing the Passion, in Lateran Museum, of Fourth or Fifth Century, ...	307
37.	Spandrils of arches on Sarcophagus of Junius Bassus, A.D. 359, .	312
38.	Glass in the Vatican Library, representing Christ between Sts. Peter and Paul; also Christ as the Lamb, and the Faithful as Lambs—Jews and Gentiles coming from Jerusalem and Bethlehem (*Bécle*) to Mount Sion, whence flow the four Evangelical Streams, united in the Mystical Jordan, .	316
39.	Part of Wall of Gallery of St Hermes, ...	323
40.	Section of Gallery in St Hermes, ...	323
41.	Section of Gallery supported by brickwork, . . .	324
42.	Plan of part of Catacomb of St Priscilla, . . .	329
43.	Gilded Glass in the Louvre Collection, representing St Callixtus,	332
44.	Section of the Cemetery of St Callixtus, ...	336
45.	Plan of principal Area of St Callixtus, in the First Period of Excavation, ...	340
46.	Elevation of outer Wall of Ambulacrum C in it, . .	341
47.	Elevation of inner Wall of Ambulacrum A, . . .	342
48.	Second Period of Excavation, ...	343
49.	Third Period : Connexion with Arenarium, . . .	345
50.	Section of Secret Staircase into Arenarium, . . .	347
51.	Fourth Period of Excavation : Union with a second Area, .	349
52.	Fifth Period : Galleries made when old ones were filled with earth, ...	353
53.	Section of Galleries, ...	353
54.	Last Period of Excavation : Works of St Damasus, . .	354
55.	St Peter's Chair, ...	389

ERRATUM.

In page 37, Note (*), *for* Tacitus Hist. iii. 65, 75, *read* Dio Cass. Hist. lxxii. 4.

CHRONOLOGICAL TABLE.

The dates of the Popes' accession are given, and the place of their burial according to the *Liber Pontificalis;* the dates of the Emperors are only proximately exact.

ROMAN EMPERORS.	A.D.	POPES.	PLACE OF BURIAL.
NERO. *First Persecution,* .	67	PETER, .	*In Vaticano juxta Palatium Nerouianum.*
GALBA, OTHO, VITELLIUS, VESPASIAN. *Fall of Jerusalem,*	70	LINUS, . .	*Juxta corpus B. Petri in Vaticano.*
TITUS, ...	79		
DOMITIAN, ...	81	CLETUS, . .	*Juxta corpus B. Petri in Vaticano.*
	93	CLEMENT, . .	*In Græcia,* (*i.e.,* in the Crimea.)
NERVA, . .	96		
TRAJAN, . .	98		
	103	ANACLETUS, .	*Juxta corpus B. Petri.*
	110	EVARISTUS, .	*Juxta corpus B. Petri in Vaticanum.*
HADRIAN, . . .	117	ALEXANDER, .	*Via Nomentana, milliario VII.*
	120	SIXTUS I., . .	*Juxta corpus B. Petri in Vaticanum.*
	127	TELESPHORUS,	*Juxta corpus B. Petri in Vaticano.*
ANTONINUS PIUS, . .	138	HYGINUS, . .	*Juxta corpus B. Petri in Vaticano.*
	142	PIUS I., . .	*Juxta corpus B. Petri in Vaticano.*
	156	ANICETUS, . .	*In cæmet. rio Callixti* (?) see page 141.
M. AURELIUS, .	161		
	163	SOTER, . . .	*In cæmeterio Callixti Via Appia* (?) see page 141.
	177	ELEUTHERUS, .	*Juxta corpus B. Petri in Vaticano.*
COMMODUS, . .	180		
SEPTIMIUS SEVERUS, .	193	VICTOR, . .	*Juxta corpus B. Petri in Vaticano.*
	197	ZEPHYRINUS, .	*In cæmeterio suo juxta cœm. Callixti Via Appia.*
CARACALLA, . .	211		
MACRINUS, . .	215	CALLIXTUS, .	*In cæmeterio Calepodii, via Aurelia, milliario III.*
HELIOGABALUS, .	218		
ALEXANDER, . .	222	URBAN I., . .	*In cæmeterio Prætextati, Via Appia.*
	230	PONTIANUS, .	*In cæmeterio Callixti,* after being brought back from Sardinia.
MAXIMIN, . . .	235	ANTHEROS, .	*In cæmeterio Callixti, Via Appia.*
	236	FABIANUS, . .	*In cæmeterio Callixti, Via Appia.*
GORDIAN, . . .	238		
PHILIP, ...	244		
DECIUS, ...	250	CORNELIUS, .	*In crypta, juxta cœmet. Callixti, in prædio B. Lucinæ.*
GALLUS, . . .	253	LUCIUS, . .	*In cæmeterio Callixti, Via Appia.*
VALERIAN, . .	254	STEPHEN, . .	*In cæmeterio Callixti, Via Appia.*
	257	SIXTUS II., . .	*In cæmeterio Callixti, Via Appia.*
GALLIENUS, . . .	259	DIONYSIUS, .	*In cæmeterio Callixti, Via Appia.*
CLAUDIUS II., . .	268	FELIX, . . .	*In basilica Via Aurelia milliario II.*
AURELIAN, . . .	270		
TACITUS, FLORIAN, PROBUS.	274	EUTYCHIANUS, .	*In cæmeterio Callixti, Via Appia.*
NUMERIAN CARINUS, .	283	CAIUS, . . .	*In cæmeterio Callixti, Via Appia.*
DIOCLETIAN, . .	284		
	290	MARCELLINUS,	*In cæmeterio Priscillæ, Via Salaria, in cubiculo claro.*
GALERIUS MAXIMIAN, .	303	MARCELLUS, .	*In cæmeterio Priscillæ, Via Salaria.*
CONSTANTINE MAXENTIUS, ...	309	EUSEBIUS, . .	*In cæmeterio Callixti in crypta.*
	311	MELCHIADES, .	*In cæmeterio Callixti in crypta.*
Edict of Milan, . .	312	Peace given to the Church.	
CONSTANTINE, .	314	SYLVESTER, .	*Via Salaria, milliario III., in cæmeterio Priscillæ,* [*in basilica.*]

LIST OF CEMETERIES, MENTIONED IN ANCIENT HISTORICAL RECORDS, ON THE VARIOUS ROADS.

ROADS.	GREATER CEMETERIES.		LESSER CEMETERIES;	CEMETER
	Primitive Names.	Names in 4th Century, Time of peace.	Or, Isolated Tombs of Martyrs.	Constructed the Peace o Church
APPIA,	1. Callixti {Lucinæ, Zephyrini, Callisti, Hippolyti,	{ S. Xysti. S. Cæciliæ. SS. Xysti et Cornelii.	27. Soteridis.	
	2. Prætextati,	{ S. Januarii. SS. Urbani, Felicissimi Agapiti, Januarii, et Quirini. SS. Tiburtii, Valeriani, et Maximi.		
	3. Ad Catacumbas,	S. Sebastiani.		
ARDEATINA,	4. Domitillæ,	{ S. Petronillæ. SS. Petronillæ, Nerei, et Achillei.		38. Balbinæ S. Mai 39. Damasi.
	5. Basilei,	SS. Marci et Marcelliani.		
OSTIENSIS,	6. Commodillæ,	SS. Felicis et Adaucti	28. Sepulcrum Pauli Apostoli in prædio Lucinæ. 29. Cœmeterium Timothei in horto Theonis. 30. Ecclesia S. Thec'æ. 31. Ecclesia S. Zenonis	
PORTVENSIS,	7. Pontiani ad ursum pileatum,	{ SS. Abdon et Sennen. S. Anastasii, pp. S. Innocentii, pp.		40. Julii via tuensi, iii, S. cis via tuensis 41. S. Felic Aureli
AURELIA,	8.	S. Pancratii.		
	9. Lucinæ,	{ SS. Processi et Martiniani. S. Agathæ ad Girulum.		
	10. Calepodii,	{ S. Callisti via Aurelia. Julii via Aurelia.		
CORNELIA,			32. MEMORIA Petri Apostoli et sepulturæ episcoporum in Vaticano.	
FLAMINIA, CLIVUS CUCUMERIS,	11.	S. Valentini.		
	12. Ad Septem Columbas,	Ad caput S. Joannis.		
SALARIA VETUS,	13. Basillæ,	{ S. Hermetis, SS. Hermetis, Basil'æ Proti, et Hyacinthi.		
	14.	S. Pamphyli.		
SALARIA NOVA,	15. Maximi,	S. Felicitatis.	33. Ecclesia S. Hilariæ in horto ejusdem. 34. Crypta SS. Chrysanti et Dariæ. 35. Cœmeterium Novellæ.	

List of Cemeteries, &c.

LIST OF CEMETERIES—Continued.

ROADS.	GREATER CEMETERIES.		LESSER CEMETERIES;	CEMETERIES
	Primitive Names.	Names in 4th Century, Time of Peace.	Or, Isolated Tombs of Martyrs.	Constructed after the Peace of the Church.
	16. Thrasonis,	S. Saturnini.		
	17. Jordanorum,	S. Alexandri. SS. Alexandri, Vitalis et Martialis et VII. Virginum.		
	18. Priscillæ,	S. Silvestri. S. Marcelli.		
NENTANA,	19. Ostrianum vel Ostriani,	Cœmeterium majus. Ad Nymphas S. Petri. Fontis S. Petri.	36. Cœmeterium S. Agnetis in ejusdem agello. 37. Cœmeterium S. Nicomedis.	
URTINA,	20.	S. Hippolyti.		
	21. Cyriacæ,	S. Laurentii.		
		S. Gorgonii.		42. In Comitatu sive SS. Quatuor Coronatorum.
ICANA,	22. Ad Duas Lauros,	SS. Petri et Marcellini. S. Tiburtii.		
	23.	S. Castuli. S. Gordiani. SS. Gordiani et Epimachi.		
INA,	24.	SS. Simplicii et Serviliani, Quarti et Quinti, et Sophiæ.		
	25.	S. Tertullini.		
	26. Aproniani,	S. Eugeniæ.		

CONTENTS.

INTRODUCTION.

PART I.

MODERN AUTHORS.—Roma Sotterranea—Its discovery—Visited in fifteenth century by Franciscan friars—and by Pomponio Leto and his companions—In 1578 visited by Baronius—Researches of Ciacconio, De Winghe, and Macarius—Bosio—His life and labours—Immense learning and industry—His labour in the Catacombs and its danger—Posthumous publication of his *Roma Sotterranea*, and its success—Its value and general arrangement—Sad destruction of antiquities in Catacombs—At length prevented by the Popes—Protestant notices of Catacombs—John Evelyn—Burnet and Misson—Fabretti *custode* of Catacombs—Succeeded by Boldetti—Works of Boldetti, Buonarrotti, Marangoni, and Bottari in eighteenth century—Christian Museum in the Vatican—D'Agincourt, his work and devastations—Padre Marchi—De Rossi—Follows system of Bosio—His sources of information, . . 1

PART II.

ANCIENT RECORDS.—The Martyrologium Hieronymianum—Its value and antiquity—Almanac of Furius Dionysius Filocalus—Inscriptions of Pope Damasus—Liber Pontificalis—Martyrologies—Acts of martyrs, their importance even when of doubtful authenticity—Itineraries of pilgrims in seventh century—Papyrus list of *olea* at Monza in time of St Gregory the Great, . . . 17

BOOK I.
ORIGIN OF THE CATACOMBS.

CHAPTER I.—GENERAL DESCRIPTION.—Position and extent of Catacombs—Their number and names—Their origin and purpose, and distinctions from sand-pits or *arenariæ*—Explanation of terms

—Different kinds of tombs—The Catacombs as places of pilgrimage until the relics were removed—Their abandonment and rediscovery in sixteenth century, ... 25

CHAPTER II.—SOCIAL AND RELIGIOUS POSITION OF THE FIRST ROMAN CHRISTIANS.—The Roman Church in Apostolic times comprised among its members persons of noble rank, Greeks and Jews—Scattered notices of them in Pagan authors—The Flavii—Flavius Clemens, the consul and martyr—Flavia Domitilla—Pomponia Grecina—Their political position—At first confused with the Jews, and protected as a sect of a legalised religion—Proscribed by Nero—First persecution—Domitian—Nerva—Trajan and Pliny—Insecure position of Christians even under tolerant princes, ... 35

CHAPTER III.—ROMAN LAWS AND CUSTOMS AFFECTING BURIAL. —Christian sepulchres protected by the ordinary privileges of Roman tombs—Even in times of persecution—Roman burial-places readily adapted for Christian cemeteries—Their size and appurtenances—Catacombs originally limited by the size of the superincumbent area, as in St Lucina—Funeral confraternities in Rome, their rules and customs—Might easily have been made use of by Christians as a safeguard—Instance of this having been done —First edict expressly against Christian cemeteries by Emperor Valerian, ... 45

CHAPTER IV.—BEGINNING OF THE CATACOMBS.—Roman burial-places, extra-mural—Their character as contrasted with Christian cemeteries—Jewish Catacombs—Christians did not burn their dead, but buried them entire—First Christian cemeteries small and private—Examples of these very early cemeteries, . . . 56

BOOK II.

HISTORY OF THE CATACOMBS.

CHAPTER I.—THE CATACOMBS IN THE FIRST AGES.—Apostolic origin of some of the Catacombs—Papal crypt on the Vatican—St Paul's on the Via Ostiensis—St Priscilla on the Via Salaria—Cemetery of Ostrianus or Fons Petri—Signs of antiquity—Cemetery of St Domitilla—Its description—Entrance and arrangement —Character of its paintings—Evidences of Apostolic antiquity— Description of the very ancient cemetery of St Pretextatus on the Via Appia—Its architecture—Tomb of St Januarius—His epitaph in Damasine characters—Tomb of St Quirinus—Catacomb of St Alexander on the Via Nomentana, ... 63

b

Contents.

CHAPTER II.—FROM THE BEGINNING OF THE THIRD CENTURY TO CONSTANTINE'S EDICT OF PEACE, A.D. 312.—Public Christian cemeteries—Cemetery of St Callixtus—Under the pontificate of St Zephyrinus—Burial-place of the popes—Other public cemeteries—Edict of Valerian against the Christian cemeteries—Martyrdom of St Sixtus II. and St Laurence—Cemeteries restored to Pope Dionysius—Necessity of concealment—Christians attacked in cemeteries—Martyrdoms in them—Used as hiding-places—Their condition from Aurelian to Diocletian—Confiscated by the latter, and restored by Maxentius to St Melchiades—Parishes or *titles* of Rome—Each had its own cemetery—Their ecclesiastical administration—Reflections upon this portion of their history, . 83

CHAPTER III.—FROM THE EDICT OF MILAN TO THE SACK OF ROME BY ALARIC, A.D. 410.—Gradual disuse of subterranean cemeteries—Basilicas of the martyrs—Care of St Damasus for the Catacombs—His labours and inscriptions—Catacombs as places of pilgrimage—Described by St Jerome—Also by Prudentius—Scene on the *festa* of a saint—Damage caused by indiscreet devotion and private interment—Rapid disuse of Catacombs as burial-places—Total cessation after A.D. 410, ... 95

CHAPTER IV.—FROM A.D. 410 UNTIL THEIR FINAL ABANDONMENT.—The Catacombs abandoned as burial-places—Still frequented as shrines—Profaned by the Goths under Vitiges, A.D. 537—Repaired and cared for by the popes—First translation of relics from Catacombs, A.D. 756, by Paul I.—Afterwards by Paschal I. and other Popes—Final abandonment of Catacombs—Origin of the name *Catacomb*, ... 104

BOOK III.

CATACOMB OF ST CALLIXTUS.

CHAPTER I.—ITS DISCOVERY AND IDENTIFICATION.—Pre-eminence of the Via Appia, both in Pagan and Christian Rome—Its cemeteries and shrines described by ancient writers—Those in or near the Catacomb of St Callixtus—Basilica of St Sebastian—The temporary resting-place of the bodies of St Peter and St Paul—Their translation—Erroneous medieval inscriptions in the Catacomb beneath this basilica—Proof that the Catacomb of St Callixtus is not there—Discovery of the crypt of St Cornelius—And of the Papal crypt, ... 110

CHAPTER II.—DISTINCTION OF THE SEVERAL PARTS OF THE CATACOMB OF ST CALLIXTUS.—Difficulties of mapping the Catacombs—Overcome by Michele de Rossi—Several different *area* of cemeteries originally independent—Crypt of St Lucina—Belonged originally to the Gens Cæcilia—Who was St Lucina?—Characteristics of this *area*—The central *area* of St Callixtus—Another *area* subsequently added to it—Cemeteries of St Soteris and of St Balbina, ... 120

CHAPTER III.—THE PAPAL CRYPT.—Its entrance—*Graffiti* on the plaster—Of three kinds—Mere names—Prayers and pious ejaculations—Invocations of saints—Their antiquity—Examination of the crypt itself—Ancient altar—Original epitaphs of popes of third century—Burial of bishops at that period—Rarely, but sometimes away from their own churches—Popes buried in this cemetery—Zephyrinus—Urban I.—Pontianus—Anteros—Fabian—Lucius—Eutychianus—Sixtus II. martyred in Catacomb of St Pretextatus—Inscription of Pope Damasus concerning it—Has been erroneously applied to St Stephen—Caius—Traces of Diocletian persecution in this cemetery—Tomb of St Melchiades—Inscription by Pope Damasus in Papal crypt—Vast number of martyrs mentioned in itineraries not improbable, ... 130

CHAPTER IV.—CRYPT OF ST CECILIA.—General appearance of this chamber—History of St Cecilia—Her martyrdom and burial—Her body discovered and translated by Paschal I.—Found incorrupt, A.D. 1590—Examined by Cardinals Baronius and Sfrondrati—Statue by Maderna from the body itself—Critical examination of the crypt—Its discovery and excavation—Its paintings and other decorations—Identification of the tomb of St Cecilia, by inscriptions and *graffiti*—Verification and correction of the Acts of St Cecilia—Alterations made in the crypt—Saints depicted on its *luminare*, ... 151

CHAPTER V.—EPITAPH OF ST EUSEBIUS.—Crypt of St Eusebius—Fragments of a Damasine inscription found there—Which had been restored in the sixth or seventh century—Inscription explained—Its importance as supplying a lost page of history of the pontificate of St Eusebius, ... 166

CHAPTER VI.—THE SEPULCHRE OF ST CORNELIUS.—Inscription to Saints Parthenius and Calocerus—Labyrinth connecting the cemetery of St Callixtus with the crypts of St Lucina—Family of St Cornelius—How his epitaph came to be in Latin instead of Greek—His sepulchre described—Damasine inscription there, and also one by Pope Siricius, restored by De Rossi—Fresco of St Cornelius and St Cyprian, its date and peculiarities—Another of St Sixtus and St Optatus—Pillar near tomb of St Cornelius—*Graffiti* on the plaster, ... 175

BOOK IV.

CHRISTIAN ART.

CHAPTER I.—ANTIQUITY AND ORIGINAL TYPES OF CHRISTIAN ART.—Opinions of D'Agincourt, Raoul Rochette, and others on the antiquity of Christian paintings—De Rossi claims a very high and even apostolic antiquity for many of the frescoes in the Catacombs—Protestant testimony to the same effect—The birth of Christian art—Its progress checked by persecution—Explanation of the canon of the Council of Elvira against pictures in churches—Means of distinguishing the dates of paintings—The *nimbus*, its introduction and prevalence—Letters on garments—The monogram—Evidence from style, and choice of subject, locality, &c.—Sketch of early history of Christian art—In apostolic times—Christian artists by no means confined themselves to Pagan models, as was supposed, from the discovery of two Gnostic cemeteries—Christ represented as Orpheus and the Good Shepherd—Division of our subject, ... 186

CHAPTER II.—SYMBOLICAL PAINTINGS.—Symbolism explained—Rules for interpreting symbolical representations and their abuse—The anchor a symbol of hope—Sheep and dove of living and deceased Christians—Dove joined with other symbols—The fish: its symbolical use confined to ages of persecution—A symbol both of Christ and of a Christian—Origin of its use as symbol of Christ—Instances of its use by the Fathers in this sense and in monuments of art—Used with a ship, a dove, or an anchor—Fish and bread (St John xxi.) explained of the Holy Eucharist by St Augustine and the rest of the Fathers—Confirmed by epitaphs of St Abercius and of Autun, and by monuments of art—Similar paintings in a Catacomb of Alexandria—Summary of evidence on this subject, and importance of conclusion—Holy Eucharist symbolised by milk in very ancient frescoes, as in acts of St Perpetua and by St Augustine—The cross: its different forms and disguises—The monogram: its successive modifications, ... 202

CHAPTER III.—ALLEGORICAL PAINTINGS—Parables of our Lord give the key to many of these paintings—*e.g.*, The vine—The wise and foolish virgins—The Good Shepherd: its frequency and various forms—Explanation of Plate XVI., . . . 233

CHAPTER IV.—BIBLICAL PAINTINGS.—Subjects taken from holy Scripture are but few in number, and confined in mode of treatment; being, in fact, symbolical rather than historical—Noe in the ark typical of baptism, not copied from Pagan type—Jonas and the fish a type of the resurrection—The ivy or gourd—Daniel

Contents. xxi

Page

in the den of lions, and the three children—Adoration of the Magi—Moses striking the rock, and the resurrection of Lazarus —Moses taking off his shoes—These subjects probably chosen by ecclesiastical authority, ... 239

CHAPTER V.—PAINTINGS OF CHRIST, HIS HOLY MOTHER, AND THE SAINTS.—Historical paintings extremely rare in Catacombs— No real portrait of Christ, or of the Blessed Virgin—A bust of our Lord described by Kügler—The saints generally represented praying—The Blessed Virgin as an *orante* in Catacomb paintings, sculptures, and glasses—Sometimes, perhaps, as a figure of the Church —Remarkable fresco of her in Catacomb of St Agnes—She is frequently represented with the adoration of the Magi, who are nearly always three—Very ancient painting of the Blessed Virgin and Child with Isaias, in Catacomb of St Priscilla—Its date of the second century—Other paintings of Our Lady, St Joseph, &c., . 251

CHAPTER VI.—LITURGICAL PAINTINGS.—Liturgical paintings are necessarily very rare—Remarkable series of them in *cubicula* near the papal crypt—Made in second and third century—Description of them—Explained by Tertullian—Baptism under figures of smitten rock, a fisherman, and the paralytic carrying his bed— Holy Eucharist—Consecrating priest clothed in *pallium* only— Church represented by a woman praying—Answers to objections —Sacrifice of Isaac explains the companion scene—Resurrection of Lazarus forms a conclusion to the series—Jonas—Painting of teachers and of fossors—Series probably drawn out by authority —Other liturgical paintings in Catacomb of St Priscilla, . . 262

CHAPTER VII.—GILDED GLASSES FOUND IN THE CATACOMBS.— Various articles found in the Catacombs—Gilded glasses in Vatican Museum—In England and elsewhere—Description of these glasses —Their discovery by Bosio and others—Two found recently at Cologne—The art of making them known only in Rome, and practised there only in the third and fourth centuries—Subjects depicted on them—Pagan—Social and domestic—Jewish—But most frequently Christian—Description of some of these—Biblical subjects—Figures of saints—Most favourite subject is Saints Peter and Paul—Probably used at the feast of these apostles, which was very solemnly observed at Rome in the fourth century —Eighty glasses have these apostles on them—Inscriptions round them—Ancient portraits of the apostles—Valuable bronze medal of them found in cemetery of St Domitilla—They are variously represented on glasses—Sometimes to symbolise the Roman Church with St Agnes and other saints—St Peter under the type of Moses, illustrated by sarcophagi and fresco paintings—Large *patenæ*, with small medallions let into the glass—Whether these glasses have been used for chalices?—Glass patens and their use in the third century, ... 275

CHAPTER VIII.—CHRISTIAN SARCOPHAGI.—Christian use of sarcophagi dates from apostolic times—Tomb of St Petronilla and of St Linus—It was not a common mode of burial—During the ages of persecution, Christian subjects were not sculptured on sarcophagi, for obvious reasons—But Christians selected from Pagan shops those subjects which suited them—Pastoral scenes—The Good Shepherd—Instances of such subjects as Cupid and Psyche, and Ulysses and the Syrens--Orpheus, &c.—The sarcophagi in the Lateran Museum—Large one from St Paul's described and explained: representation of the Holy Trinity—The fall—The adoration of the Magi—Christ giving sight to the blind—Eucharistic symbols—Resurrection of Lazarus—St Peter in three scenes—Daniel among the lions, and the prophet Habacuc—Small statues of the Good Shepherd—Sarcophagus, with history of Jonas, Noe, and other subjects—Sarcophagi, with Cain and Abel, the fall, and St Mary Magdalene—Cover with sheep carrying *ciambelle*—Sarcophagus which once contained the relics of the Holy Innocents, having figures of Mary and Lazarus, St Peter's denial, Moses receiving the law, the sacrifice of Isaac, St Peter as Moses, Daniel, healing of the blind and paralytic, and Zaccheus—Sarcophagus with *labarum*, and scenes from the Passion—Sculpture of the *Agape*—Sarcophagus under a canopy, representing Christ in glory, surrounded by the apostles, St Peter's denial, the smitten rock, and *Noli me tangere*—Sculpture of Elias ascending into heaven—The *pallium*—The Nativity—Sarcophagus of Junius Bassus, its date, and the subjects on it, especially the lambs in the spandrils of the arches—Statue of St Hippolytus—Of the third century—His *canon paschalis*—Note on the comparative frequency of the various subjects sculptured, ... 293

BOOK V.

THE TESTIMONY OF THE CATACOMBS THEMSELVES.

CHAPTER I.—TESTIMONY OF THE CATACOMBS TO THEIR CHRISTIAN ORIGIN.—Scope of this part of the work—Catacombs used as burial-places by none but Christians—Pagan inscriptions in them accounted for—Their Christian origin first vindicated by Padre Marchi—First proof: the nature of the rock in which the Catacombs are excavated—The various volcanic strata of the Roman

Contents. xxiii

Page

Campagna—Second proof: the form of the Catacombs as contrasted with that of pozzolana quarries—Instance of *arenarium* converted into the Catacomb of St Hermes—Grounds of the theory of their Pagan origin stated and examined—Meaning of the term *cryptæ arenariæ*—Examination of passages in ancient records which seem to identify the *arenariæ* with the Catacombs, viz., in the case of—1. St Cornelius—2. The Quattro Coronati—3. Saints Chrysanthus and Daria—4. St Crescentianus in cemetery of Priscilla—5. St Hippolytus, &c., on Via Appia.—These apparent exceptions prove the rule, ... 317

CHAPTER II.—TESTIMONY OF THE CATACOMBS TO THE MODE OF THEIR CONSTRUCTION AND DEVELOPMENT.—Scope of this chapter—Locality of Christian cemeteries, and distance from the city—On high ground—Excavated in *tufa granulare*—Systems of galleries, each horizontal, though in different flats, one below another—Section of geological strata—Mode of excavation—Different periods to be distinguished in the *area* in which are the crypts of the Popes and of St Cecilia—First period—Second period: level of galleries lowered—Third period: a deeper *piano* tried, signs of necessity for concealment, connexion with *arenarium*—Union with a second *area* previously distinct—Fourth period: *arcosolia*—Fifth period: earthing up of galleries during the Diocletian persecution—Sixth period: formation of small galleries upon this earth—Last period: works of St Damasus—Recapitulation and application to development of catacombs generally, . . 333

CHAPTER III.—ANALYTICAL DESCRIPTION OF THE PLAN OF THE MOST IMPORTANT AREA OF THE CATACOMB OF ST CALLIXTUS, 360

APPENDIX.

NOTE A.—The finding of the body of St Hyacinth (p. 15), . . 379
NOTE B.—The Acts of St Cecilia (p. 22), ... 387
NOTE C.—St Peter's Chair (p. 68), ... 388
   1. Description of the Chair in the Vatican.
   2. Historical Notices of it.
   3. Another Chair of St Peter in the Cemetery of Ostrianus.
   4. The two Feasts of St Peter's Chair.
NOTE D.—Burial near the sepulchres of saints (p. 102), . . 399
NOTE E.—Altars in the primitive church (p. 184), . . . 401
NOTE F.—The origin of the pallium (p. 310), . . . 404
NOTE G.—Description of the Atlas accompanying this volume, . 406

INDEX, ... 409

INTRODUCTION

TO

ROMA SOTTERRANEA:

ITS LITERARY HISTORY.

PART I.

MODERN AUTHORS.

ON the last day of May, A.D. 1578, some labourers, who were digging *pozzolana* in a vineyard (now the property of the Irish College) on the Via Salaria, about two miles out of Rome, came unexpectedly on an old subterranean cemetery, ornamented with Christian paintings, Greek and Latin inscriptions, and two or three sculptured sarcophagi. The discovery at once attracted universal attention, and persons of all classes flocked to see it. "Rome was amazed," writes a contemporary author, "at finding that she had other cities, unknown to her, concealed beneath her own suburbs, beginning now to understand what she had before only heard or read of:" and "in that day," says De Rossi, "was born the name and the knowledge of *Roma Sotterranea*."

<small>Discovery, A.D. 1578.</small>

<small>Of Roma Sotterranea.</small>

It is true that the man who was destined to be the first thoroughly to explore and describe this city of the dead, was as yet only three years old;* but even then there were not wanting men whose learning and industry sufficed to keep alive the

---

* Bosio, Rom. Sott., p. 511.

newly enkindled flame of love for Christian antiquities. Nearly one hundred and fifty years before, and at various intervals during half a century, the same, or at least precisely similar, objects had been seen in another vineyard on the opposite side of the city; but those who saw them were either men of religion, attracted by motives of piety, or men of learning, with enthusiasm only for what was Pagan. Among the first class must be reckoned certain Franciscan friars, whose visits to the Catacomb of St Callixtus between the years 1432 and 1482 are recorded by scribblings on the walls of two or three *cubicula* in one quarter of that cemetery. " Came here to visit this holy place," (*fuit hic ad visitandum sanctum locum istum*,) writes Brother Lawrence of Sicily, with twenty brethren of the order of Friars Minor, January 17th, 1451. Another visit was made in 1455, " in the week in which Pope Nicholas V. died," (*hebdomadâ quâ defuntus est pp. N. V.*) An abbot of St Sebastian's entered with a large party, (*cum magnâ comitivâ*,) May 19th, 1469; some Scotchmen in 1467, (*MCCCCLXVII. quidem Scoti hic fuerunt,*) &c. &c. Not one, however, of these numerous visitors seems to have thought of making any historical or antiquarian examination of the precious monuments of the past which were before them. The other class of visitors to whom we have alluded belonged to the same period, but were men of a very different character. The names of Pomponio Leto and other *litterati*, his associates in the famous Roman Academy, may still be read in several places of the same quarter of the Catacombs, written there by themselves, with the addition of their title as *Unanimes antiquitatis Amatores*, or *Perscrutatores*; yet not even one of these seems ever to have made any study of what he saw, certainly none ever wrote about it.

Those who are familiar with the literary history of the fifteenth century, will remember how these men fell into disgrace with the Sovereign Pontiff, Paul II., on suspicion both of being infected with heresy and of conspiring against the Government. One of the grounds for the first of these charges was their pedantic conceit of taking old Pagan classical names in place of their Christian ones; but it has always been a matter of controversy how far the charge of conspiracy was really supported by evidence; and Tiraboschi hardly mentions any appreciable ground for it at all.* We are not here concerned with the religious or political integrity of the Academy; yet, in elucidation of an obscure point in history, it may be worth while to mention that the name of Pomponio Leto is found in these newly-discovered memorials of him, with the title of *Pontifex Maximus*, and even *Pont: Max: regnans;* and that other titles are added to some of the names, showing the dissolute habits of the Academicians, and that they were not ashamed to perpetuate their own memories as lovers, not only of ancient names, but of ancient manners. We must also express both our regret and surprise, that men whose lives were devoted to the revival of learning, and of whose chief it is particularly recorded that he applied himself to the elucidation of Roman antiquities "which were then being disinterred," should have been familiar with these earliest monuments of the heroic age of Christianity, and yet never have felt sufficient interest to excite them to investigate their history, or to publish anything at all about them. Whatever, therefore, they may really have believed, we cannot wonder at the charge brought against them by their contemporaries, and which we find addressed to one of them by a bishop even after their acquittal, that they were more Pagans than Christians.

We fear, indeed, that this charge might at that time have been justly urged against many more than the members of the Roman Academy. Now, however, in the year of which we first spoke, A.D. 1578, Christian learning and Christian morality were in a far more hopeful condition in the Eternal City. It was the age of St Ignatius Loyola, St Charles Borromeo, and St Philip Neri. Baronius, the friend and disciple of the latter, was already engaged on his immortal work, the "Ecclesiastical Annals," in more than one page of which he shows the warmth of his interest in the new discovery, and his just appreciation of its importance. He was among the first to visit it; and had not his time been fully absorbed by his own gigantic work, he might, perhaps, have become its first explorer and historian. As it was, this labour and honour seems rather to have fallen to the lot of foreigners resident in Rome, than to Romans themselves. They were Alfonso Ciacconio, a Spanish Dominican, and two young Flemish laymen, Philip de Winghe, and

Baronius.

* Storia della Litteratura Italiana, tom. vi. part i. pp. 93-97.

Joannes Macarius, (the Grecised form of Jean l'Heureux;) and the labours, even of these, were not destined to be of much service in spreading a knowledge of the Catacombs among their contemporaries.

Researches of Ciacconio,   Ciacconio was a man who delighted in investigating and collecting curiosities of every kind, and possessed a valuable museum of Christian and Pagan antiquities. He also employed artists to copy for him some of the more remarkable paintings in the Catacombs. Their skill, however, appears hardly to have been equal to their good intentions, since we are told that Noe in the Ark, with the dove bringing him the olive-branch, was represented and explained as "Marcellus, Pope and Martyr, instructed by an angel whilst he is preaching."

De Winghe,   De Winghe, not unnaturally, was dissatisfied with his friend's performance, and had the paintings more faithfully re-copied for himself. These copies were seen and used both by Macarius and Bosio. All traces of them, however, have now been lost, unless De Rossi be correct in supposing that he has discovered a few in the Imperial Library at Paris; anyhow, they were never made public. Had De Winghe lived, he would, doubtless, have been the first author on Roma Sotterranea; Baronius, Frederic Borromeo, and other good and learned men set their hopes upon him, and his talents and industry seem to have been in every way worthy of their expectations. He died, however, at a very early age at Florence, in the summer of 1592; and his MSS., after having formed part of the famous library of the Bollandists, were sold in 1825, with the rest of that magnificent collection, and now remain unedited in the Royal Library at Brussels. The notes of Ciacconio, exceedingly voluminous and miscellaneous, appear never to have been prepared for publication, and still lie buried in various public and private libraries of Rome and Naples. The

and Macarius.   labours of Macarius were scarcely more fruitful; they were continued during a residence of twenty years in Rome, and the work in which they resulted was prepared for publication, and even licensed for printing on the 22d of June 1605. The author, however, although he lived until 1614, left his work still in MS. to a public library in Louvain. It was afterwards annotated by Bollandus, who announced its publication, but died before redeeming his promise; and it is only in our own day that Padre Garrucci, S.J., has given this precious manuscript to the public.*

The labours, however, of these and some others mentioned by De Rossi, great as they may have been, fade into insignificance when compared with those of Antonio Bosio, who has justly been called the true Columbus of this subterranean world. He was a man worthy to be had in remembrance. De Rossi seems unable to speak of him without a certain feeling of enthusiastic reverence and devotion, in which all lovers of Christian archæology can scarcely fail to sympathise. A Maltese by birth, an advocate by profession, Bosio had resided in Rome from his earliest years with his uncle, who was *Procuratore* or Roman agent for the knights of Malta. His attention was drawn to the subject of the Catacombs, while he was yet very young, and when once he had taken up its pursuit he never abandoned it. The earliest date recorded in his book, and found written on the walls of the Catacombs, is December 10, 1593, the year after the death of De Winghe, when Bosio himself was not yet eighteen; and his labours were continued both in the cemeteries themselves, and in studying the works of authors from whom he expected to derive information on the subject, for the six and thirty years of his subsequent life. His industry was prodigious; and the volumes of his MSS., still extant in the Bibliotheca Vallicelliana (the Oratorian Library) at Rome, are a wonderful monument of it. Two of these volumes, containing upwards of two thousand pages folio, besides fifty pages of index, all in his own handwriting, show that he had read carefully through all the fathers, Greek, Latin, and Oriental; all the collections of canons and councils, ecclesiastical histories, lives of the saints, and an immense number of theological treatises, including those of the schoolmen; in fact, every work in which he thought there was a chance of finding anything in illustration of his subject. In two other volumes of the same size he transcribed the "Acts of the Martyrs," especially of all those who suffered in Rome, together with other ancient records which bore upon the topography of the Christian cemeteries.

[margin: Antonio Bosio. His life and labours. Immense learning and industry.]

---

* HAGIOGLYPTA : *sive picturæ et sculpturæ sacræ antiquiores præsertim quæ Romæ reperiuntur, explicatæ a Joanne l'Heureux (Macario.)* Paris. 1856.

These were taken from MSS. in the Vatican and other libraries. And yet it is certain that even these volumes by no means represent the whole of his writings. He himself refers to other commonplace books of his which are now lost.

Labours in the Catacombs. Again, in making our estimate of the labours of this truly great man, we must never forget the anxious, fatiguing, and even dangerous nature of his subterranean researches. When, from his study of ancient records, he had ascertained something as to the probable position of a Christian cemetery on the Appian or other of the Roman roads, Bosio would explore with the utmost diligence all the vineyards of the neighbourhood, in order to discover, if possible, some entrance into the bowels of the earth; and often, after returning again and again to the same spot, his labour would be all in vain. At another time he would hear of some opening having been accidentally made into a Catacomb, by the digging of a new cellar or a well, and would hasten to the spot, only to find that the whole place was so buried in ruins that all ingress was impossible. Even when an entrance was once effected, he still had to force a *Dangers of his work.* passage, often by the labour of his own hands, through the accumulated rubbish of ages; or, if the galleries were tolerably clear, there was the danger of being drawn too far in the eagerness of discovery, and of being unable to retrace his steps through the intricate windings of these subterranean labyrinths. In fact, this danger was actually experienced on his very first visit to the Catacombs, in company with Pompeo Ugonio and others, on the 10th of December 1593. They had penetrated into a Catacomb about a mile distant from St Sebastian's, and having forced their way into a lower level, by means of an opening in one of the chapels, they incautiously proceeded so far, that, when they wished to return, they could not recognise the path by which they had come. To add to their perplexity, their lights failed them, for they had remained underground longer than they had intended; and "I began to fear," says Bosio, "that I should defile by my vile corpse the sepulchres of the martyrs." Taught by this experience, he always in future visits took with him a quantity of candles, and other requisites sufficient for two or three days.

This indefatigable examination of the Catacombs, and of all ancient documents connected with them, was continued, as we

have said, for six and thirty years, and then Bosio too paid the Publication of
debt of nature, without having either completed his work, or Bosio's *Roma Sotterranea,*
published any part of it. It seemed as though Roma Sotterranea A.D. 1632.
were never to be revealed to the world at large. The work of
Bosio was, however, too important to be allowed to lie buried
as had those of his predecessors in these researches. He had
also powerful friends, who would not suffer the fruit of so
much labour to perish. His papers and other property had
been bequeathed to the Order of the Knights of Malta, with
whom, as we have seen, his uncle had been officially connected.
The ambassador of the Order then at Rome, Prince Carlo
Aldobrandini, showed the MSS. to Cardinal Francesco Barberini, the librarian of the Vatican, the nephew of the reigning
Pontiff, the friend of Galileo, and the Mæcenas of those days.
The cardinal at once recognised their value, and lost no time
in engaging Padre Severano, of the Oratory, to put the finish-
ing-stroke to the work. An eminent architect and a mathema-
tician were employed to draw the plans and maps which were
still wanting; the Knights of Malta undertook the expense;
and in five years' time the magnificent volume which we now
possess was produced and dedicated to Pope Urban VIII.*
It was welcomed by the whole literary and archæological world Its success.
with the utmost eagerness, and the demand for it was such that
a Latin translation was begun almost immediately after its
appearance. Bosio himself had at one time intended to com-
pose the whole work in Latin, and a portion of it, written in
that language, may still be seen among his MSS., although
through some oversight this portion was not incorporated into
Severano's original edition. Something appears to have prevented the publication of Severano's translation; and it was
not until fifteen or sixteen years later that a new translation,
with considerable alterations and omissions, was published by
Aringhi, in 1651.†

Although Bosio's work was never completed according to his Value of
own original design, yet the omissions were for the most part Bosio's work.

* *Roma Sotterranea, opera postuma di Antonio Bosio composta disposta ed accresciuta da Giovanni di Severano, Sacerdote della Congregazione dell' Oratorio.* Roma, 1632.
† *Roma Subterranea novissima post Ant. Bosium et Joan. Severanum.* Romæ, 1651.

such as could be supplied from the works of other authors. Had his life been spared, he intended to have described and illustrated the practice of the earliest ages of the Church with reference to the administration of the sacrament of penance, the viaticum, extreme unction, prayers for the dying and the dead, and other matters connected with the death and burial of Christians. In these particulars his book was deficient, but in its detailed account of each cemetery which he had visited it was most complete; and the whole was admirably arranged on a very simple principle of topography. He took in order all the great consular roads which led out of Rome, and collected every historical notice he could find concerning the Christian cemeteries on each of them; their precise position, their names, their founders, and the martyrs or other persons of distinction who had been buried in them. He then by the light of this information examined all the Catacombs he had seen, and endeavoured to assign to each its proper name and history. That his conjectures were often erroneous, is only what might have been expected from the known inaccuracy and sometimes spuriousness of the Acts of the Martyrs and other authorities by which he was led; but these were the only guides which could then be had; and the system itself is quite unexceptionable, indeed, the only one that can be safely followed in laying a solid foundation for a scientific treatment of the whole subject.

Its general plan.

It is much to be regretted, therefore, that the work so wisely begun should not have been continued on the same plan and with the same diligence. But the re-discovery of the Catacombs was not a matter of merely archæological interest: the devotion of the faithful was excited by the report that in those dark recesses might still be lying concealed the remains of saints and martyrs; and the concessions made to the piety of individuals to search for and extract these relics proved in the end most disastrous to the cemeteries, as authentic records of the early Roman Church. Instead of the ecclesiastical authorities taking this matter into their own hands, as they have since happily done, and proclaiming themselves the watchful and jealous guardians of such precious treasures, they permitted a number of private persons, acting independently of each other, to make excavations. It is true, that rules were laid down, and

Destruction of antiquities in Catacombs since their recovery.

learned pamphlets were written to prove the value of these
rules, for the identification and translation of the relics, and we
have no reason to doubt that they were scrupulously observed.
But, in the interests of Christian archæology, we may justly *too long per-*
complain that those engaged in the search had no regard for *mitted,*
the preservation of monuments, whether of painting, sculpture,
or inscriptions, which came in their way. They did not even
care to keep a record of what they had seen, which would at
least have provided materials for future *litterati* to continue the
work of Bosio. Many of these permissions to extract relics were
given to religious communities; and all the explorers availed
themselves, in their researches, of some of the workmen who
had been employed by Bosio. None of them, however, followed any systematic and comprehensive plan; and soon afterwards the permissions were all revoked and vigorously repressed *stopped at*
by the Popes. We find traces of them for the last time during *Popes, about*
the pontificate of Urban VIII.; and under Clement IX., about *1688.*
A.D. 1668, the arrangements which still prevail were definitely
settled. The loss, however, sustained by Christian archæology
in the interval is incalculable; and all must heartily sympathise
with De Rossi, both in his lamentations, and his astonishment
that such ravages should have been tolerated in silence under
the very eyes, as it were, of such men as Holstenius, Allaccius,
and other antiquarians who were then living in Rome. We
learn something of the nature and extent of our loss from the *Lost treasures.*
incidental notices which occur in the writings of the archæologists of the seventeenth century; thus, we hear of a sepulchre
all covered with gold, of a superb cameo, a series of the rarest
coins and medals, various ornaments in crystal and metal, &c.,
besides a multitude of other objects which were secretly sold
by the labourers engaged in the excavations; but we are told
nothing as to the precise localities in which any of these things
were found. Had but an accurate record been kept of all
discoveries, the work of reconstructing the history and topography of these cemeteries would have been comparatively easy
and certain.

After the works of Bosio and Aringhi, the literary history of *Nothing new*
the Catacombs remains a blank for nearly half a century. They *from 1650 to*
had taken their place among the *mirabilia* of Rome, and as *1700.*
such were an object of curiosity to all intelligent travellers; but

those who wrote about them were generally more influenced by religious than by scientific motives. Bosio's work had been the means of recalling some learned Protestants to the bosom of the Church;* and thenceforward the subject became an arena for party strife. John Evelyn, indeed, who visited Rome in 1645, was content simply to record what he saw or heard, but not so those who came after him. Evelyn was first taken to the subterranean cemetery at St Sebastian's, "where the Fulgentine monks have their monastery." " They led us down," he says, " into a grotto which they affirmed went divers furlongs under ground. The sides or walls which we passed were filled with bones and dead bodies, laid as it were on shelves, whereof some were shut up with broad stones, and now and then a crosse or a palme cut in them. At the end of some of these subterranean passages were square rooms with altars in them, said to have been the receptacles of primitive Christians in the times of persecution, nor seems it improbable." By and by, being detained in Rome longer than he expected, he was persuaded to visit another Catacomb. He says, " We took coach a little out of towne, to visit the famous Roma Sotterranea, being much like what we had seen at St Sebastian's. Here, in a corn-field, guided by two torches, we crept on our bellies into a little hole, about twenty paces, which delivered us into a large entrie that led us into several streets or allies, a good depth in the bowells of the earth, a strange and fearefull passage for divers miles, as Bosio has measured and described them in his book. We ever and anon came into pretty square roomes, that seem'd to be chapells with altars, and some adorn'd with very ordinary ancient painting. Many skeletons and bodies are plac'd on the sides one above the other in degrees like shelves, whereof some are shut up with a coarse flat stone, having ingraven on them Pro Christo,† or a crosse and palmes, which are supposed to have been martyrs. Here, in all likelyhood, were the meetings of the primitive Christians during the persecutions, as Pliny the younger describes them.

* Bottari, Rom. Sott. t. i. pref. p. v.
† It would seem that neither Evelyn nor his guides knew Greek. This is clearly their misinterpretation of the monogram ☧, and we are afraid the same blunder is even now sometimes repeated by persons showing the Catacombs to strangers.

Modern Authors

As I was prying about, I found a glasse phiale, fill'd as was conjectured with dried blood, and 2 lachrymatories. Many of the bodies, or rather bones, (for there appear'd nothing else,) lay so entire as if plac'd by the art of the chirurgeon, but being only touch'd fell all to dust. Thus after wandering two or three miles in this subterranean mæander, we returned almost blind when we came into the daylight, and even choked by the smoke of the torches."* A very different tone pervades the letters of Bishop Burnet,† who visited the same scenes forty years later. He reckoned upon his countrymen's religious prejudices, on the one hand, and their ignorance of Rome, on the other, with such confidence, that he hazarded the astounding statement that "those burying-places that are graced with the pompous title of Catacombs are no other than the *puticoli* mentioned by Festus Pompeius, where the meanest sort of the Roman slaves were laid, and so without any further care about them were left to rot," and that the Christians did not come into possession of them until the fourth or fifth century. He was followed by some other writers in the same strain, as for example, Misson, who, being unable to deny that Christians had certainly been buried here in very ancient times, only insisted that "this was no reason for excluding others from being interred there also, in those holes that were set apart for the dregs of the people." ‡

<small>Burnet, 1685.</small>

<small>Misson, 1714.</small>

The controversies which arose out of ignorant or malicious falsehoods like these, contributed nothing to archæological science, and are not therefore worthy of any detailed mention in this place. We repeat, therefore, that there is a blank of half a century in the literary history of the Catacombs, from Aringhi to Fabretti, who, in the year 1700, deserves our gratitude for having preserved the account of two cemeteries unknown to Bosio, together with the inscriptions which they contained. He had been appointed, in 1688, *custode* of the Catacombs, and it belonged to his office to superintend the removal of any relics that might be discovered. In this post he was succeeded by Boldetti, who held it for more than thirty years.

<small>Fabretti's work on Inscriptions, A.D. 1700.</small>

<small>Boldetti on Christian Antiquities, A.D. 1720.</small>

---

* Evelyn's Memoirs, edited by Bray, 1819, pp. 153, 164.

† Some letters from Italy and Switzerland in the years 1685 and 1686. Rotterdam. P. 209.

‡ A new voyage to Italy, &c. London, 1714. Vol. ii. part i. p. 166.

years, but who, unfortunately, did not possess sufficient knowledge or love of archæology to enable him to make the most of the great opportunities he enjoyed. During his time, whole regions of *Roma Sotterranea* were brought to light, galleries of tombs that had remained apparently unvisited since the last corpse was buried in them, a vast number of inscriptions, medals, and other treasures came under his notice: and yet it is doubtful whether any account of these things would have come down to us had he not been commanded to write in the defence of religion. Mabillon's anonymous letter *de cultu sanctorum ignotorum* had attracted considerable attention, and the unfair use which had been made of it by Misson and other Protestant controversialists seemed to demand an answer. Boldetti was therefore desired to publish an account of the rules which had been followed by himself and his predecessors in the extraction of relics; and he accompanied this with a description of the discoveries that had been made in the Catacombs generally during his own time.* The object of his work, however, being not scientific, but religious and apologetic, its contents were arranged with this view, and its value as a contribution towards the complete history of the subterranean city of the dead was proportionably diminished.

Buonarrotti on the Gilded Glasses of the Catacombs.

Buonarrotti, who had assisted Boldetti in the archæological part of his work, himself wrote a valuable book on the vessels or fragments of gilded glass found in the Catacombs,†—a subject which has been handled afresh and with great erudition in our own day by Padre Garrucci, S.J. ‡ Another of Boldetti's assistants, Marangoni, who was officially associated with him for twenty years in the guardianship of the cemeteries, seems to have intended to carry out Bosio's plan of making a minute and faithful report of every new discovery arranged according to the historical and topographical outline of that great man, and corrected by any new light thrown upon the subject by later discoveries. After he had continued this plan for about

Marangoni, A.D. 1740.

---

* *Osservazioni sopra i cemeteri dei SS. Martiri ed antichi cristiani di Roma.* Roma, 1720.

† *Osservazioni sopra alcuni frammenti di vasi antichi di vetro ornati di figure trovati nei cimeteri di Roma.* Firenze, 1716.

‡ *Vetri ornati di figure in oro trovati nei cimiteri dei cristiani primitivi di Roma raccolti e spiegati da Raffaele Garrucci, D.C.D.G.* Roma, 1858.

sixteen or seventeen years, an accidental fire destroyed all his papers. "Truly," says De Rossi, "the history which I am relating seems to be but an Iliad of misfortune and irreparable losses." The little that remained from this fire, together with the results of his subsequent labours, Marangoni published in the *Acta Sancti Victorini* in 1740.

The *Roma Sotterranea* of Bottari,* published by command of Clement XII., was a mere republication of the plates from the work of Bosio, illustrated with great care and learning, but not arranged in any order, nor enriched by any additions, unless we reckon one which we could well have spared, viz., the paintings of a Gnostic sepulchre falsely attributed to the Christians. These have seriously perplexed and misled later authors, especially Raoul Rochette, who founded upon it in great measure his theory as to the origin of Christian art. Bottari's *Roma Sotterranea*, A.D. 1737.

The learned students of Christian archæology who flourished during the latter half of the last century, such as Mamachi, Olivieri, Zaccaria, Borgia, &c., made considerable use of the works of Bosio, Aringhi, Boldetti, and Bottari, in their treatises on various points of Christian antiquity, but do not appear to have explored for themselves, or even to have taken any notice of the new discoveries that were being made year by year in some part of the ancient cemeteries. Benedict XIV., by founding the Christian Museum in the Vatican Library, and collecting there the inscriptions that had hitherto been dispersed among the various churches, relieved antiquarians of the labour of examining the places where these inscriptions were found, and even such an archæologist as Marini does not appear to have thought it worth while to visit the Catacombs themselves. D'Agincourt, indeed, penetrated their recesses to find materials for his History of the decline of the fine arts; and, by attempting to detach the pictures from the walls of living rock on which they had been painted, taught the modern fossors the last lesson in the art of destruction. The attempt signally failed, and was not long persisted in, but it resulted in the ruin of many precious monuments which can never be replaced. Indeed, it is truly lamentable to see what Latter part of eighteenth century. Christian Museum founded by Benedict XIV. D'Agincourt, A.D. 1825. His devastations in the Catacombs.

---

* *Sculture e Pitture Sacre estratte dai Cimiteri di Roma, pubblicate gia dagli autori della Roma Sotterranea ed ora nuovamente date in luce colle spiegazioni.* Roma, 1734-1754.

a record of destruction the history of the Catacombs has been, almost ever since their re-opening in the sixteenth century. The paintings which were seen at that time in the crypts on the Via Salaria, by Baronius and others, had been destroyed when Bosio revisited the place fifteen years afterwards. Padre Mazzolari, S.J., the pious author of the *Vie Sacre*, was only just in time to traverse the gallery accidentally opened near San Lorenzo in 1779, before he saw the work of devastation ruthlessly accomplished under his very eyes. The lessons of destruction taught by D'Agincourt have been only too frequently followed even as recently as our own day. The vast extent of subterranean territory that has to be guarded from injury, and the facility with which access may from time to time be gained to the Catacombs in consequence of accidental openings in the soil, make it difficult for the authorities to prevent depredations; still we cannot but regret that there should not have been always a succession of antiquarians, able and willing to transmit to posterity a faithful record of each new discovery as it was made.

Padre Marchi, S.J., A.D. 1841. At the beginning of the present century, tokens of a reviving interest in the Catacombs may be traced in some of the proceedings of the Roman Archæological Society, and in a few other writings. It was reserved, however, for the late Padre Marchi, S.J., to give the first great impulse to that lively interest in the subject which is now so universally felt. In 1841, he commenced his great work on the Monuments of early Christian Art.* It is almost needless to enter upon any detailed examination of the labours of this learned Jesuit, since they were interrupted and finally abandoned, partly in consequence of the political vicissitudes of the times by which his own Order was especially affected; and also because he was conscious that the work of rehabilitating (so to say) these venerable monuments of antiquity, and setting them forth before the public in their original integrity, was necessarily reserved for one who should come after him. He had begun to publish prematurely; at most he had but broken the soil. He had, however, imparted his own enthusiasm to one of his scholars, who was at first the frequent companion

* *Monumenti delle arti Christiane Primitive nella Metropoli del Cristianesimo.* Roma, 1844.

of his subterranean exploring expeditions, whom he soon recognised as a valuable fellow-labourer, and whom he finally urged in the most pressing manner to undertake the work which he found too great for his own failing strength. This scholar was De Rossi, of whom it were hard to say whether De Rossi. his talent, learning, and industry have done more for the work of discovery in subterranean Rome, or the discoveries he has made done more for the increase of our knowledge of it. At any rate, the fruits of his labour speak for themselves; for whereas before his time only two or three important historical monuments* had been discovered in the Catacombs during more than two centuries of examination—and all of these the result of accident,—the excavations directed by the Commission of Sacred Archæology, of which De Rossi is one of the most active members, have brought to light within a few years six or seven historical monuments of the utmost value, and in every instance he had announced beforehand with more or less accuracy what was to be expected.

We are naturally led to ask after the cause of so great a contrast. From what new sources had De Rossi derived his information? or what was his new system for extracting ore from His system of old mines? The answer is soon given, and it is much more research. simple than we might have expected from the magnitude of the effects to be accounted for. He followed the same general plan as had been originally laid down by Bosio; he studied also the same ancient authorities, but with the addition of two or three more of considerable value which in Bosio's time lay buried in the MSS. of libraries. Father Marchi indeed had known these new authorities; but he had not adopted Bosio's topographical system. Moreover, the particular object which he had proposed to himself, led him precisely in the opposite direction from that to which these new guides offered to conduct him. They were, in fact, veritable guides—itineraries or guide-books—written in the seventh and eighth centuries by

---

* The baptistery and paintings of SS. Abdon and Sennen, and other crypts in the cemetery of San Ponziano, on the Via Portuensis, discovered by Bosio; the crypt of SS. Felix, Adauctus, and Emerita, discovered by Marangoni, behind the Basilica of St Paul's, on the road leading to St Sebastian's; and the tomb, the original epitaph, and the *body* of St Hyacinth, found in the cemetery of St Hermes, by Padre Marchi. (See Note A. in Appendix.)

pilgrims from foreign countries, who carefully put on record all the sacred places which they visited in Rome. Especially they enumerated all the tombs of the martyrs, as they lay each in his first resting-place in the different suburban cemeteries. Now these were the precise spots in the Catacombs where St Damasus and other popes had made many material changes. They had built spacious staircases to conduct the pilgrims immediately to the object of their pious search; opened more *luminaria* to supply light and air; widened the galleries, or added vestibules to the chapels; or raised small basilicas above ground; and for the support of these, solid substructions of masonry had been sometimes necessary in the crypts themselves. But when the Catacombs ceased to be used, not only were all these works left to perish by a process of natural decay, they also attracted the greedy hand of the spoiler, so that after the lapse of seven or eight hundred years every centre of historic interest had become a mass of ruins. Whereas, then, it was the special desire of Father Marchi to recover, if possible, galleries and chambers of the Catacombs in their primitive condition as first they were hewn out of the rock, any appearance of bricks and mortar in the way of his excavation was sufficient to turn him aside from that part of the cemetery altogether. De Rossi, on the other hand, shrewdly judged that the crypts which had been changed into sanctuaries contained the very key, as it were, to the history of each Catacomb. Wherever one of these could be recovered and identified, we had a certain clue to the name and history of the cemetery in which it was found. He hailed, therefore, every token of ruined masonry in the heart of a Catacomb with the keenest delight, as a sure sign that he was in the immediate neighbourhood of what he most desired to see; and the results have abundantly proved that he was not mistaken in his reasoning.

His sources of information. The importance of these results renders it worth our while to enumerate and give some short account of the authorities which have furnished the clue to their discovery. They are such as the rash criticism of the last century would have contemptuously condemned as worthless,—the old Calendars and Martyrologies, the Acts of the Martyrs, the Lives of the Popes, and the Itineraries of pious pilgrims of the seventh, eighth, and ninth centuries. Doubtless there has been need of great patience and ingenuity to disentangle the thread of truth from the web of confusion with which it has been sometimes interwoven in these documents. Nevertheless, they have proved themselves such efficient guides, that henceforward no account of Roma Sotterranea can be considered complete that should pass them over in silence.

PART II.

ANCIENT RECORDS.

PERHAPS the most ancient record of the Roman Church to be found is the so-called *Martyrologium Hieronymianum;* a work which, though not put together in its present form until the end of the sixth or perhaps even the seventh century, certainly contains many portions of far older martyrologies belonging to the ages of persecution. The exceeding care of the early Church in treasuring up both the acts and the relics of her martyrs, is too well known to require proof. It is sufficient to observe, that it is recorded of St Clement, before the end of the first century, that "he caused the seven regions [of Rome] to be divided among the faithful notaries of the Church, who should, each in his own region, with diligent care and zeal search out the acts of the martyrs;"* and of St Fabian, Pope in the middle of the third century, it is added that "he divided the regions among the deacons, and appointed seven subdeacons to superintend the seven notaries, that they might collect in all their details (*in integro*) the acts of the martyrs."† Most of these invaluable records perished in the terrible persecution of Diocletian. Still it was impossible but that some few of them should have escaped, and these furnished the first groundwork of the martyrology of which we are speaking. The most authentic copies of it, say the Bollandists,‡ make no mention of a single martyr after the time of the apostate Julian; not of any, for example, who suffered under the Vandals in Africa. In itself this is no sure criterion of its antiquity; but there are other internal evidences which warrant our assigning one portion, or perhaps we should rather say one edition, of it to the

<small>The *Martyrologium Hieronymianum*.</small>

<small>Its antiquity.</small>

* Lib. Pontif. c. iv.   † Ibid.
‡ Acta Sanct. Octob. tom. ix. p. 269.

earlier part of the third century, another to the beginning of the fourth, and a third to the beginning of the fifth century. An evidence of the first of these dates is, that the anniversary of St Antherus, who was Pope A.D. 235, appears on the 24th November, whereas in all later Martyrologies it is assigned to the 2d of January. Now, the *Liber Pontificalis* gives as the length of his pontificate "one month and twelve days," which is precisely the interval between the two above-mentioned dates; so that we feel confident that the 24th of November was really the date of his succession to the Chair of St Peter, not of his death. But the anniversary of the accession of a pope, as indeed that of any other bishop, is never celebrated except during his lifetime; whence it follows that this particular portion at least of this ancient Martyrology must have been drawn up during the pontificate of St Antherus. And it is not a little remarkable, that although his pontificate lasted for so short a time, yet the *Liber Pontificalis* expressly records of him that "he diligently sought out from the notaries the Acts of the Martyrs, and stored them up in the church;" it goes on also to say, "on account of which he received from the Præfect Maximus the crown of martyrdom." It is by observing similar notes, which only the keenness of modern criticism has taught men to appreciate, that archæologists have been able to detect the hand of a later compiler or copyist of this Martyrology, who must have lived in the time of Miltiades, or between A.D. 311 and 314; and a third in the time of St Boniface I., or between A.D. 418 and 422, since festivals are noted here of *Ordin. Miltiadis*, on July 2d, and *Bonifacii Epi de Ordinatione*, on the 29th of December, besides the *depositio* of each of these pontiffs on the days on which we still commemorate them. But it would occupy us too long to show in each case how the repetitions, and even the errors and contradictions, of these various copyists, have often proved of service in furnishing a clue by means of which the ingenuity and patience of learned antiquarians have succeeded in unravelling the truth. We must content ourselves with observing that this Martyrology is of inestimable value, as having preserved to us much that would otherwise have perished.

Almanac of Fur. Dion. Filocalus.

Next in chronological order comes the Christian Almanac, for we can call it by no more appropriate name,) the first edition of which appears to have been published in A.D. 336, and the latest, with highly ornamented illustrations, in A.D. 354, by Furius Dionysius Filocalus. This consists of lists of the deaths or burials of the popes from Lucius to Julius—*i.e.*, A.D. 255 to 352,—of the principal Christian festivals celebrated during the year, especially of martyrs, but including also Christmas-day, Cathedra Petri, and other immovable feasts; finally, a catalogue of the popes from St Peter to Liberius.* In this last catalogue the deaths of the popes begin to be registered from the time of St Antherus, which would seem to show that the earlier portion of the history had been probably compiled from some older work, such as the Chronicon of Hippolytus. But the most important of these documents is undoubtedly the first of the three. It follows immediately upon the list of prefects of the city, and this list, evidently compiled with great accuracy from contemporary registers, begins in like manner from the year 254. Is this synchronism purely accidental? or were the two lists really derived from state documents, the public registers of the government? At first sight it might seem an almost extravagant conjecture to suppose that the names of the popes should have been known to the civil governors of pagan Rome, and officially taken cognisance of. Yet it is certain, that even as early as the beginning of the third century, many churches used to pay a tribute to the government that they might escape from persecution, and for this purpose they were enrolled on the registers of the police (so to speak), where they found themselves, as Tertullian † takes care to remind them, in very strange company. Again, we read that, after the death of Fabian, Decius strictly forbade the election of a successor, and was greatly enraged when he heard of the appointment of Cornelius. In genuine Acts of Martyrdom the question is sometimes asked, to what church the prisoners belong. When the ecclesi-

* This catalogue is generally quoted as *Liberian*, or *Bucherian*: the latter name being taken from its first editor, Ægidius Bucherus, S.J. De Doctrinâ temporum. Antwerp, 1634.

† Non decet Christum pecuniâ constare. Quomodo et martyria fieri possent in gloriam Domini, si tributo licentiam sectæ compensaremus. . . . . Massaliter totæ ecclesiæ tributum sibi irrogaverunt. Nescio dolendum an erubescendum sit, cum in matricibus Beneficiariorum et Curiosorum, inter tabernarios et lanios et fures balnearum et aleones et lenones Christiani quoque vectigales continentur. *De fugâ in persec. cc. xii. xiii.*

astical property is restored after a persecution, it is to the bishops that the surrender is ordered to be made; from them the sacred books are demanded; against them and their clerics special edicts are issued. All this seems to indicate a certain knowledge and even recognition of their position in the ecclesiastical hierarchy.* And it is very curious to observe how some of the difficulties in this catalogue are immediately cleared up, if we suppose it to have been derived from civil and official sources. Thus, for instance, it is stated of the year 304, that at this time the episcopacy ceased for seven years, six months, and twenty-five days. This statement cannot be reconciled even with the dates given elsewhere in the same list; but it is observable that it was precisely during this very time that Diocletian confiscated the *loca ecclesiastica*, and that the hierarchy was (at least legally) suppressed. Again, we read in the *Liber Pontificalis* that Maxentius required of St Marcellus that he should deny that he was a bishop, (because he had not been recognised,) and his name accordingly does not appear in this list. However, be this as it may, from whatever source these lists may have been originally procured, it is certain that they have proved to be of the greatest use in the hands of De Rossi.

Inscriptions of St Damasus. To these we must next add the numerous inscriptions composed by Pope Damasus, engraved by the same Furius Filocalus, and set up by the Holy Pontiff at so many of the martyrs' tombs. Several of these monuments destroyed by the Goths, Lombards, and other sacrilegious barbarians, were restored, more or less correctly, by later popes: many are preserved to us only through the copies that were taken by learned ecclesiastics or pious pilgrims in the ninth or tenth centuries; some few yet remain in their original integrity, and some also have been recovered by De Rossi himself. These monuments, wherever they are found, are witnesses of the utmost value on questions relating either to the history or the geography of the Catacombs.

Liber Pontificalis. The *Liber Pontificalis*, or, as it is sometimes (less correctly) called, the Lives of the Pontiffs by the Librarian Anastasius, is our next authority. It was, from the first, formed out of documents more ancient than itself, like the *Martyrologium Hierony-*

---

* De Rossi does not hesitate to say, that the proofs of this new and unexpected fact are so strong that they amount almost to a complete demonstration. R. S. II. 372.

mianum, and there had been at least three versions or editions of it before the days of Anastasius. Two of these had been made at the beginning and about the middle of the eighth century, and another in the beginning of the sixth; but a portion of it may even be traced to the times of St Damasus, if not to a yet earlier period. Its statements are often at variance with those of the Almanac and the most ancient Martyrology, especially in the matter of dates; yet these very variations are sometimes useful, and enable us to detect the truth. Often they are accounted for by the fact that they record some translation of the popes' relics, instead of the day and place of their original burial. Certainly there could be no object in changing the dates without reason; the compiler can only have followed some other authority.

The Martyrologies of Bede, of Ado, Usuard and others, are sometimes useful; but they are inferior in importance to the Acts of the Martyrs, which, even when not authentic, often contain most valuable fragments of truth. Tillemont and other critics of his school have dealt with these venerable monuments of antiquity too summarily. Disgusted by the flagrant anachronisms, or the barbarous diction, or the tone of legendary exaggeration, or the historical difficulties which abound in them, they have found it easier to reject altogether than to criticise and distinguish; whilst a more learned and cautious examination not unfrequently succeeds in detecting many traces of a true and genuine story. The Acts of St Cecilia, for example, which were so thoroughly set aside by Tillemont that he questioned whether there had ever been such a virgin and martyr in Rome at all, and suspected that her history might perhaps have been a myth imported from Sicily, are certainly not, in their present form, a genuine and original document; they are not contemporary with the martyrdom itself; on the contrary, both in the preface and in the body of the Acts there are clear tokens of a writer in the time of peace, between the fourth and fifth centuries;[*] nevertheless it is equally certain that they must have been composed upon very minute and truthful records, since a number of circumstances which they narrate were most exactly confirmed on the rediscovery of her

Other Martyrologies.

Acts of the Martyrs.

---

[*] The liturgical prayers both of Leo and of Gelasius abound with allusions to them.

relics at the end of the sixteenth century, which relics were certainly hid from every human eye at the time of the compilation of the Acts. Moreover, on a critical comparison of the various readings even of the MSS. which still exist of these Acts, it is easy to detect the little additions and embellishments introduced by later writers.* They are precisely such as we might have anticipated; and it is probable that the original compiler did not use greater license in dealing with the materials before him, than his own successors used towards himself. In either case, it was not such as to destroy the substance of the story, nor to distort its principal features, historical or geographical; and as most of these spurious Acts (if they must still be branded by this opprobrious epithet) were written before the sacred deposits in the Catacombs had been translated from their first resting-place, they have been of great service in enabling De Rossi to reconstruct both the history and the geography of subterranean Rome. The same may be said also of some incidental notices in the ancient Liturgical Books of the Roman Church.

Itineraries of pilgrims in the seventh century.

All these documents, however, were accessible to the predecessors of De Rossi, and were freely made use of by them. To him belongs the credit of having demonstrated by argument, and still more by actual discovery, the immense importance of the information to be derived from the ancient Itineraries or local guide-books to the sanctuaries of Rome. One of these descriptions may be seen in the works of William of Malmesbury, where he records the visit of the Crusaders to Rome, A.D. 1095;† but as this description speaks of the Saints still resting in their subterranean sepulchres, it is manifest that the chronicler has copied it from some document written four or five centuries before his own time: and there is internal evidence that it was written between the years A.D. 650 and 680. Another of these Itineraries, about a century later, was published by Mabillon, in 1685, from a MS. in Einsiedlen; and a third, belonging to the tenth century, by Eckart, in 1729, from a MS. in the library of Wurtzburg. These, however, are all surpassed in value by two others which were discovered about a hundred years ago in the library of Salzburg, and published as an appendix to an edition of the works of Alcuin, with which the

* See Note B. in Appendix.
† In the excellent edition of Duffus Hardy, tom. ii. 539-544.

MSS. had been accidentally bound up. It is certain from internal evidence that one of these, and that the most exact, was written between the years 625 and 638, and the other is not many years later. The first is a genuine Itinerary, written on the spot, and abounds with topographical notices of all that the writer saw, above ground or below, on his right hand or his left, to the east or the west. He starts from the centre of Rome, and proceeds northwards through the Flaminian gate; and in visiting the various roads in order, he does not return to Rome and make a fresh beginning every time, but goes across from one road to another by by-paths, many of which still remain. The second, though following the same general plan and taking each road in succession, is not the real journal or description of what had been seen by the traveller himself; rather, it bears tokens of being an epitome of some larger work. However, both of them were written before the practice of translation of relics had begun, so that the minute topographical details which they record have reference to the original condition of the Catacombs before their sanctity had been profaned or their traditions obscured.

In the same category with these Itineraries may be classed the list of relics collected by the Abbot John, in the days of St Gregory the Great, and sent to Theodelinda, Queen of the Lombards. This list, written on papyrus, together with many of the relics themselves, and the little parchment labels attached to them, is still to be seen in the cathedral of Monza.* We must not, however, be misled by the word "*relics*," and picture to ourselves, according to modern custom, the bodies or portions of the bodies of saints. St Gregory himself specifies the only kinds of relics that in his day were permitted to be carried away by the faithful. He writes to the Empress Constantina: "When the Romans present the relics of the saints, they do not touch the bodies: their custom is only to put a piece of linen in a box, which is placed near the holy body, and which they afterwards take away.... In the time of the Pope St Leo, some Greeks, doubting of the virtue of these relics, brought scissors and cut the linen, from whence proceeded blood, as is reported by the ancient inhabitants."†

Papyrus list of olea at Monza.

---
* It has been published by Marini, Papir. Diplom., p. 327, No. CXLIII. See also p. 377.
† Epist. lib. iii. ep. 30. The pieces of linen were called *brandea*.

But besides these, drops of the oil from the lamps which burned before the tombs of the saints were frequently carried away as relics; and St Gregory often sent these *olea* in little glass phials to persons at a distance.* These latter were the relics collected by John the Abbot; and in the list of them he carefully records every shrine which he visited, and this (as was natural) in the order of his visits. By comparing this local order with the topographical notices in the Itineraries, De Rossi has been enabled to decide with accuracy many important questions concerning the localities of particular tombs. To follow him into these details would require us to transcribe many entire pages of his work, and would weary the unscientific reader. It is sufficient to say, that a careful study of them will amply repay all who are capable of appreciating the keenness of his criticisms, and the happy boldness with which he frequently seizes upon some fact, or hint about a fact, before unnoticed, but which eventually leads to valuable discoveries.

<small>This work an epitome of De Rossi's.</small> These are the principal sources of information of which De Rossi has made use in his *Roma Sotterranea;* and by the help of them he has constructed a very full and life-like narrative of its history. The labour which it has cost him to do this can only be appreciated by those who take the pains to follow him through the slow, deliberate, sometimes almost wearisome method of his operations, and examine in detail the mass of minute criticisms by which he insists upon justifying every step which he takes; and for this it is indispensable that the whole work should be read exactly as he has himself written it. Many threads of his argument are so subtle, yet so strong and so necessary to the establishment of his conclusions, that they can neither be omitted nor reproduced in any compressed form, without injury to their substance. These, therefore, we must perforce leave untouched; nevertheless, we hope to be able to extract from his pages sufficient matter to set before our readers an intelligible account of the history of the Catacombs, sufficiently supported both by the language of ancient documents, and by the remains which his researches have enabled us to see and examine for ourselves.

<small>* This custom may even now be observed in the Church of Sant' Agostino, where people take oil from the lamp that burns before the statue of the *Madonna del Parto*, and from other shrines.</small>

BOOK I.

ORIGIN OF THE CATACOMBS.

CHAPTER I.

GENERAL DESCRIPTION.

THE daily-increasing celebrity of the Roman Catacombs might almost seem to render a general description of them unnecessary; for who does not know, if not by personal observation, at least from the accounts of friends or from popular literature, the leading features of that marvellous city of the dead which has received the appropriate name of *Roma Sotterranea*, subterranean Rome? Nevertheless, so many errors are often mixed up with these popular accounts, and our knowledge of the subject has been so much improved of late, both in point of accuracy and of extent, that it will conduce to clearness, and the general convenience of our readers, if we set before them at once some outline at least of what is contained in the following pages. We shall make our statement as concise as possible, not strengthening it at present by any proofs or arguments, but leaving these to be supplied when we come to fill in the several parts of the picture in detail.

General description of the catacombs.

The Roman Catacombs—a name consecrated by long usage, but having no etymological meaning, and not a very determinate geographical one—are a vast labyrinth of galleries excavated in the bowels of the earth in the hills around the Eternal City;

Their position and extent.

not in the hills on which the city itself was built, but in those beyond the walls. Their extent is enormous, not as to the amount of superficial soil which they underlie, for they rarely, if ever, pass beyond the third milestone from the city, but in the actual length of their galleries; for these are often excavated on various levels, or *piani*, three, four, or even five, one above

FIG. 1.—*Gallery with Tombs.*

the other; and they cross and recross one another, sometimes at short intervals, on each of these levels; so that, on the whole, there are certainly not less than 350 miles of them; that is to say, if stretched out in one continuous line, they would extend the whole length of Italy itself. The galleries are from two to four feet in width, and vary in height according to the nature of the rock in which they are dug. The walls on both sides are pierced with horizontal niches, like shelves in a book-case or berths in a steamer, and every niche once

General Description.

contained one or more dead bodies. At various intervals this succession of shelves is interrupted for a moment, that room may be made for a doorway opening into a small chamber; and the walls of these chambers are generally pierced with graves in the same way as the galleries.

These vast excavations once formed the ancient Christian cemeteries of Rome; they were begun in apostolic times, and continued to be used as burial-places of the faithful till the capture of the city by Alaric in the year 410. In the third century, the Roman Church numbered twenty-five or twenty-six of them, corresponding to the number of her titles, or parishes, within the city; and besides these, there are about twenty others, of smaller dimensions, isolated monuments of special martyrs, or belonging to this or that private family. Originally they all belonged to private families or individuals, the villas or gardens in which they were dug being the property of wealthy citizens who had embraced the faith of Christ, and devoted of their substance to His service. Hence their most ancient titles were taken merely from the names of their lawful owners, many of which still survive: Lucina, for example, who lived in the days of the Apostles, and others of the same family, or at least of the same name, who lived at various periods in the next two centuries; Priscilla, also a cotemporary of the Apostles; Flavia Domitilla, niece of Vespasian; Commodilla, whose property lay on the Via Ostiensis; Cyriaca, on the Via Tiburtina; Prætextatus, on the Via Appia; Pontian, on the Via Portuensis; and the Jordani, Maximus and Thraso, all on the Via Salaria Nova. These names are still attached to various catacombs, because they were originally begun upon the land of those who bore them. Other Catacombs are known by the names of those who presided over their formation, as that of St Callixtus, on the Via Appia; or St Mark, on the Via Ardeatina; or of the principal martyrs who were buried in them, as SS. Hermes, Basilla, Protus and Hyacinthus, on the Via Salaria Vetus; or, lastly, by some peculiarity of their

Their number and names.

position, as *ad Catacumbas* on the Via Appia, and *ad duas Lauros* on the Via Labicana.

Their origin and purpose.

It has always been agreed among men of learning who have had an opportunity of examining these excavations, that they were used exclusively by the Christians as places of burial and of holding religious assemblies. Modern research has now placed it beyond a doubt, that they were also originally designed for this purpose and for no other; that they were not deserted sand-pits (*arenariæ*) or quarries, adapted to Christian uses, but a development, with important modifications, of a form of sepulchre not altogether unknown even among the heathen families of Rome, and in common use among the

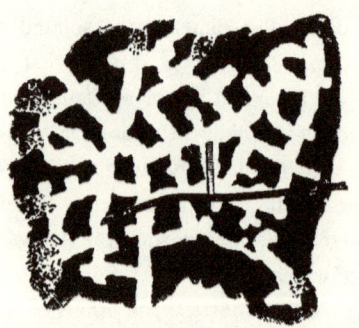

FIG. 2.—*Plan of Arenaria at St Agnes.*

Jews both in Rome and elsewhere. Our readers may judge for themselves, even from the miniature specimen here set before them, how easy it is to distinguish the galleries of an *arenaria* from those of a Catacomb. These plans represent a portion of the cemetery, commonly called of St Agnes, in the Via Nomentana, and of a sand-pit which lies over it, (both drawn to the same scale;) and the greater width of the passages excavated in the sand-pit, and the greater regularity of those in the Catacomb, are characteristics which at once arrest the attention, and suffice to impress upon our minds the essential difference between them.

At first, the work of making the Catacombs was done openly, without let or hindrance, by the Christians; the entrances to

General Description.   29

them were public on the high-road or on the hill-side, and the galleries and chambers were freely decorated with paintings of a sacred character. But early in the third century, it became necessary to withdraw them as much as possible from the public eye; new and often difficult entrances were now effected

FIG. 3.—*Part of Catacomb of St Agnes.*

in the recesses of deserted *arenariæ*, and even the liberty of Christian art was cramped and fettered, lest what was holy should fall under the profane gaze of the unbaptized.

Each of these burial-places was called in ancient times either *hypogæum*, i.e., generically, a subterranean place, or *cœmeterium*, a sleeping-place, a new name of Christian origin, which the Pagans could only repeat, probably without understanding;* sometimes also *martyrium*, or *confessio*,† (its Latin equivalent,) to signify that it was the burial-place of martyrs or confessors of the faith. An ordinary grave was called *locus* or *loculus*, if

Explanation of terms.

* Euseb. H.E. vii. 11.
† Hence the crypt under the high altar of the Vatican Basilica is called the *Confession*, i.e., the tomb, of St Peter.

it contained a single body; or *bisomum, trisomum,* or *quadrisomum,* if it contained two, three, or four. The graves were dug by *fossores,* and burial in them was called *depositio.* The galleries do not seem to have had any specific name; but the chambers were called *cubicula.* In most of these chambers, and sometimes also in the galleries themselves, one or more tombs are to be seen of a more elaborate kind; a long oblong *chasse,* like a sarcophagus, either hollowed out in the rock or built

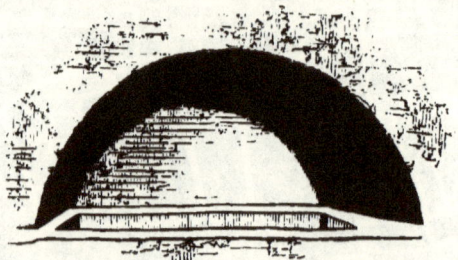

FIG. 4.—*Arcosolium.*

up of masonry, and closed by a heavy slab of marble lying horizontally on the top. The niche over tombs of this kind was of the same length as the grave, and generally vaulted in a semi-circular form, whence they were called *arcosolia.**

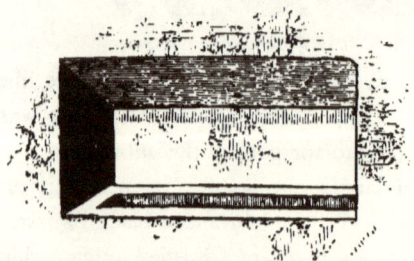

FIG. 5.— Sepolcro a mensa *or Table-tomb.*

Sometimes, however, the niche retained the rectangular form, in which case there was no special name for it, but for distinction's sake we may be allowed to call it a table-tomb.†

---

* *Solium* was used to denote the urn of marble or terra cotta, in which the Pagans sometimes buried their dead.

† De Rossi calls it *sepolcro a mensa.*

Those of the *arcosolia* which were also the tombs of martyrs were used on the anniversaries of their deaths (*Natalitia,* or birthdays) as altars whereon the holy mysteries were celebrated; hence, whilst some of the *cubicula* were only family-vaults, others were chapels, or places of public assembly. It is probable that the holy mysteries were celebrated also in the private vaults, on the anniversaries of the deaths of their occupants; and each one was sufficiently large in itself for use on these private occasions; but in order that as many as possible

FIG. 6.—*Interior of a Cubiculum in St Agnes, with chairs and bench hewn out of the rock.*

might assist at the public celebrations, two, three, or even four of the *cubicula* were often made close together, all receiving light and ventilation through one shaft or air-hole, (*luminare,*) pierced through the superincumbent soil up to the open air. In this way as many as a hundred persons might be collected in some parts of the Catacombs to assist at the same act of public worship; whilst a still larger number might have been dispersed in the *cubicula* of neighbouring galleries, and received there the Bread of life, brought to them by the assistant priests and deacons. Indications of this arrangement are not only to be found in ancient ecclesiastical writings; they may still be seen in the very walls of the Catacombs themselves, episcopal chairs, chairs for the presiding deacon or deaconess, and benches for the faithful, having formed part of the original design when the chambers were hewn out of the living rock, and still remaining where they were first made.

<small>Catacombs frequented as shrines,</small>

By and by, when peace was restored to the Church, the Catacombs were constantly visited as objects of pious interest, and of course the graves of the Popes and other principal martyrs became special centres of attraction. The number of the faithful who flocked to these shrines on the annual recurrence of their respective festivals was immense; so that it became necessary to provide more commodious means of entrance and exit, and in other ways to enlarge and improve the chapels within. Pope Damasus distinguished himself above others in his devotion to this work: he also set up a number of inscriptions at various places, generally written in verse, and all engraved by the same artist, in which he sometimes commemorates the triumphs of the martyrs, and sometimes his own work of restoration or decoration at the tomb. The festivals continued to be celebrated here as long as the bodies of the martyrs remained in their original resting-places.

<small>till the translation of relics, A.D. 750; then neglected and forgotten.</small>

But these having been desecrated, and sometimes plundered, by the Lombards and other invaders of Rome, all the principal relics were removed into the city-churches by the care of successive Popes, during a period of sixty or seventy years, beginning from the middle of the eighth century; and when this had been done, the catacombs were naturally neglected, and by degrees forgotten. They remained in oblivion for nearly seven centuries and a half, so that when Onuphrius Panvinius, an Augustinian friar, considered the marvel of his age for learning and industry, published a work in 1578 on the "Ceremonies of Christian Burial and the Ancient Christian Cemeteries," he

General Description. 33

could only gather their names from the Acts of the martyrs and other ancient documents. He expressly states that only three of them were at all accessible,—that at St Sebastian's, that at San Lorenzo, meaning (as is clear from his description) the single gallery which may yet be seen from the window of the chapel of St Cyriaca in the Basilica itself, and that of St Valentine on the Via Flaminia, which lay under property belonging to his own order. It happened, however, that in this same year, 1578, an accident brought to light another of the ancient cemeteries, far more interesting than either of these; and a desire was soon enkindled, both in the interests of religion and of learning, to know something more about such venerable monuments of antiquity. But this could only be the fruit of much time and labour; it was impossible to reconstruct their history, which had been lost, except by a careful examination of them, and a comparison of their contents with the notices to be discovered in ancient books. It has been already shown in our sketch of the Literary History of the Catacombs, how this work has been attempted by many authors, during the last two hundred years, with various degrees of success; and how, in our own day, the Commendatore de Rossi, having had his interest awakened to the subject from his earliest youth, having devoted to its study great natural abilities and untiring industry for more than twenty years, and having, moreover, enjoyed some advantages beyond most of his predecessors, has far outstripped them all both in the extent and importance of his discoveries. Hence the opportunity and the necessity for the present volume, which aims only at putting within the reach of English readers the fruit of De Rossi's labours. Treading faithfully in his footsteps, we propose first to trace the history of the Catacombs from their beginning, and then to describe the cemetery of St Callixtus in particular; after which we shall consider the light which they throw upon early Christian art and doctrine. But in order that this work may be done well, and that we may

Re-discovered in 1578.

satisfy our readers that the history we shall give rests on a sure foundation, it is necessary that we should go back to the first introduction of Christianity into Rome, and make a brief review of the legal and social position of its professors even from the days of the Apostles.

FIG. 7.- *Section of Chambers in Catacomb of Saints Marcellino and Pietro, showing lower end of the shaft of the luminare, with dove painted on it.*

CHAPTER II.

THE SOCIAL AND RELIGIOUS POSITION OF THE FIRST ROMAN CHRISTIANS.

THE first sowing of the seed of the gospel in the metro- Among the first Christians in Rome
polis of the ancient Pagan world is involved in some
obscurity. It is certain, however, that it must have been
almost simultaneous with the birth of Christianity. For we
know that among the witnesses of the miracle of Pentecost
were "strangers of Rome, Jews and proselytes;"* and on
the return of these strangers to their homes, the wonderful
sight they had witnessed would be at once communicated to
others, and the solemn tidings they had heard would be circu-
lated from mouth to mouth among the Jews of the capital.
Moreover, the Gentile converts in "the Italian band," † of
which Cornelius was a centurion, probably returned to their
native city soon after the appointment of Herod Agrippa to
the kingdom of Judea, at the accession of Caligula, and these
too would have given a fresh impulse to the movement; and
if St Peter, who had been about the same time miraculously
released from prison, accompanied them from Cæsarea, this
would agree with the tradition which assigns A.D. 42 as the
date of the coming of the Prince of the Apostles to Rome.
At any rate, the faith of the Roman Christians was "spoken
of in the whole world" ‡ as early as A.D. 57; and it is the
opinion of learned and impartial judges that, even from the were native nobles, Greeks, and Jews.
first, there were several of noble blood and high rank who
made profession of this faith. "From the time of Cæsar

* Acts ii. 10, 11.   † Ib. x. 1.   ‡ Rom. i. 8.

downwards," says Mr Merivale, "Jews had thrust themselves into every Roman society, and not least into the highest. . . Many citizens of every rank had more or less openly addicted themselves to Jewish usages and tenets; and when a Jewish sect ventured to transfer its obedience from the law of Moses to the gospel of Jesus Christ, the number of its adherents in the capital of the empire would seem to have embraced Jews, Greeks, and Romans in nearly equal proportions." *

Scattered notices of them,

We are not unmindful of the Apostle's testimony relative to the Church at Corinth—viz., that "there were not amongst them many wise according to the flesh, not many mighty, not many noble;" † nevertheless everything combines to show that the spread of Christianity among the higher classes, and even among the imperial families at Rome, was more extensive, from the very earliest times, than either the records of ecclesiastical history or the pious legends of the Church would have led us to expect. Indeed, it is easy to see how scanty and imperfect these are. Thus no memorial has reached us of the names or condition of those " of Cæsar's household " to whom St Paul sent a special salutation ; of Flavius Clemens, the consul and relative of Domitian, we know little beyond the fact of his martyrdom; of Apollonius, the senator and martyr under Commodus, we only know that little which Eusebius has told us, writing so long after the event, and at so great a distance from the scene of it. Ancient metrical inscriptions have been found, celebrating the praises of another noble patrician, named Liberalis, holding the highest office in the State, and laying down his life for the faith, whose memory in all other respects is buried in oblivion. Other inscriptions also have been found, in more recent times, recording the burial, by their husbands, of noble Roman ladies of senatorial rank (*clarissimæ*), in the common graves of the galleries in the most ancient parts of the Roman cemeteries. It was only

---

* History of the Romans under the Empire, vii. 380. See also vi. 436, *et seq.* † 1 Cor. i. 26.

Position of the First Roman Christians. 37

from the pages of a Pagan historian* that we knew of the profession of Christianity, or at least of a great interest in it and partiality towards it, by Marcia, concubine of Commodus, until, in our own day, this intelligence has been confirmed and enlarged by the newly-discovered *Philosophumena*. Tertullian,† again, writing at the beginning of the third century, tells us that Septimius Severus protected Christian senators and their wives, but says nothing as to their names or number, excepting indeed that in another place he says boldly, before the whole Pagan world, that not only were the cities of the Roman empire full of Christian people, but even the senate and the palace.

One cause of the extreme scantiness of our information as to the early Christians in Rome is doubtless the destruction of all ecclesiastical records during the last terrible persecution by Diocletian; and there was nothing in the temper or practices of Christianity to commend it as a special theme for Pagan writers. Nevertheless it was not altogether overlooked by them; and we know, from the testimony of Eusebius, ‡ that some at least wrote about it whose histories have not reached us. Indeed it is to Pagan rather than to Christian writers that we are indebted for our knowledge of some of the most interesting and remarkable facts in the annals of the early Church. One of these it will be well for us to dwell upon at some length in this place, as the history of a Catacomb depends upon it: we allude to the early conversion of some of the family of the Flavii Augusti, that is, of the family which gave Vespasian to the throne. His elder brother, Titus Flavius Sabinus, had been Prefect of the city in the year in which the Princes of the Apostles, Sts Peter and Paul, suffered martyrdom; and it is certain, therefore, that he must have been brought into contact with them, and heard something of the Christian faith. He is described by the great historian of the empire as a

chiefly in Pagan writers,

e.g., of the Flavii.

* Tacitus Hist. iii. 65, 75.   † Ad Scapul. c. 4.
‡ Hist. Eccl. iii. 18.

man whose innocence and justice were unimpeachable;* a mild man, who had a horror of all unnecessary shedding of blood and violence. Towards the close of his life, he was accused by some of great inactivity and want of interest in public affairs; others thought him only a man of moderation, anxious to spare the lives of his fellow-citizens; others again spoke of his retiring habits as the natural result of the infirmities of old age. Whilst we listen to all these conjectures as to the cause of a certain change which seems to have come over him in his declining years, the question naturally occurs to us, whether it is possible that he can have had some leanings towards the Christian faith, or even been actually converted to it? It is a question which cannot now be answered; but at least it is certain that charges of this kind were commonly urged against Christians;† and the fact that some of his descendants in the next generation were undoubtedly of this faith, gives a certain degree of probability to the conjecture. Flavius Sabinus seems to have had four children, of whom the most conspicuous was Titus Flavius Clemens, the consul and martyr. He married the daughter of his cousin, who was sister to the Emperor Domitian, and called by the same name as her mother, Flavia Domitilla. Flavia Domitilla the younger bore her husband, the consul, two sons, who were named respectively, Vespasian junior, and Domitian junior, having been intended to succeed to the throne; and the famous Quinctilian ‡ was appointed by the Emperor himself to be their tutor. At what time their parents became Christians, and what was the history of their conversion, we do not know; but the facts of Clement's martyrdom and Domitilla's banishment are attested by Dio Cassius.§ His words are, that "Domitian put to death several persons, and amongst them Flavius Clemens, the consul, although he was his nephew, and

Flavius Clemens.

---

* Tacitus Hist. iii. 65, 75.
† " Infructuosi in negotiis dicimur."—*Tertull. Apol.*, § 42.
‡ Instit. iv. 1, § 2. § Hist. lxvii. 13.

although he had Flavia Domitilla for his wife, who also was a relation of the Emperor's. The charge of atheism was brought against them both, on which charge many others also had been condemned, going after the manners and customs of the Jews; and some of them were put to death, and others had their goods confiscated; but Domitilla was only banished to Pandatereia," an island opposite the Gulf of Gaeta, half-way between Ponza and Ischia, now known by the name of Sta. Maria. Learned critics are agreed that the atheism and adoption of Jewish manners, here urged against Flavius Clemens and his wife, were in reality nothing else than a profession of Christianity, the charge of atheism never having been brought specifically against the Jews.* Both Christian and Pagan writers alike testify to the persecution which Domitian instituted against Christians towards the end of his life; and we cannot understand the motives which have led some modern writers to call it in question. However, we are not at present concerned with this fact. We only care to insist upon the Christianity of this branch of the imperial family, and the martyrdom of the consul, facts whose importance will soon be recognised. Had it been handed down in any Acts of the Martyrs that, immediately after the death of the apostles, Christianity was within an ace of mounting the imperial throne, that a cousin and niece of the Emperor not only professed the new religion, but also suffered exile, and even death itself, on its account, we can imagine with what vehemence the pious legend would have been laughed to scorn by many modern critics; but the testimony of Dio Cassius, to which we may add perhaps that of Suetonius also, is received with greater respect.†

St Domitilla. There was yet a third lady of the same noble family, bearing the same name of Flavia Domitilla, who was a granddaughter (on the mother's side) of Titus Flavius Sabinus, and consequently a niece of the consul. She, too, suffered banishment, like her aunt, and for the same cause—profession of the

* Merivale, vii. 381.   † He accuses the consul " *contemptissimæ inertiæ.*"

Christian faith. It is in speaking of this lady that Eusebius has that striking passage to which we have already referred, and which testifies so clearly to the marvellous spread of the Christian religion, even before the expiration of the first century. He has just had occasion to mention the latter part of Domitian's reign, and he says: " The teaching of our faith had by this time shone so far and wide, that even Pagan historians did not refuse to insert in their narratives some account of the persecution and the martyrdoms that were suffered in it. Some, too, have marked the time accurately, mentioning, amongst many others, in the fifteenth year of Domitian, (A.D. 97,) Flavia Domitilla, the daughter of a sister of Flavius Clemens, one of the Roman consuls of those days, who, for her testimony for Christ, was punished by exile to the island of Pontia." The same writer, in his " Chronicon,"* gives the name of one of the authors to whom he refers, and that name is Bruttius. It is worth remembering, for we shall meet it again in the cemetery of the very same St Domitilla whose exile he had recorded. He was a friend of the younger Pliny, and the grandfather of Crispina, wife of the Emperor Commodus.

Pomponia Grecina.

It is generally supposed that there is another still more ancient notice, by a Pagan writer, of the conversion to Christianity of a Roman lady of rank, which ought not, therefore, to be altogether omitted; we mean that by Tacitus, of Pomponia Grecina, the wife of Plautius, who conquered Britain under Claudius. We read that, in the year 58, this lady was accused of having embraced the rites of "a foreign superstition;" that the matter was referred to the judgment of her husband, in the presence of a number of her relations, who pronounced her innocent; that she lived afterwards to a great age, but "in continual sadness;" no one, however, interfered with her in this matter any more, and in the end

* St Hieronym. Interp. Chron. Eus. Pamph., A.D. 98, Opera, tom. viii., p. 605, ed. Migne.

Position of the First Roman Christians. 41

it was considered the glory of her character.* It must be confessed that the language in which this history is recorded is not so precise as what we have read from Dio about the Flavii, neither has the history itself so intimate a connexion with the Catacombs; nevertheless it has its point of contact with them, and the ordinary interpretation of the "foreign superstition," as having been intended for Christianity, has lately received considerable confirmation from an inscription found in the Catacomb of St Callixtus, showing that a person of the same name and family was certainly a Christian in the next generation, and buried in that cemetery.

These glimpses at the social condition of the first Roman Christians, slight and imperfect as they are, are valuable; and when we come to study the first period in the history of the Catacombs, they will be found to furnish some very interesting examples of "undesigned coincidences." A still more important subject, however, and one on which it is happily much more easy to throw sufficient light, is the political or religious position of Christians in the eye of the law, and consequently their freedom with reference to the rites and usages of burial. The political position of the first Christians.

It is certain that, at first, the Imperial Government looked upon the Christians as only a sect of the Jews. Gallio, the proconsul of Achaia, drove both Paul and his accusers from his tribunal, refusing to adjudicate upon "questions of a word and of names, and of your law."† Claudius Lysias wrote to Felix, procurator of Judea, saying that Paul had been accused before him "concerning questions of the Jewish law;"‡ and Festus explained to Agrippa that the clamours of the Jews against the Apostle were about "certain questions of their own superstition, and of one Jesus, deceased, whom Paul affirmed to be alive."§ The very terms in which Suetonius|| They were regarded as a sect of the Jews.

---

* " Mox in gloriam vertit."—*Annal.* xiii. 32. † Acts xviii. 12-17.
‡ Ib. xxiii. 29. § Ib. xxv. 19.
|| " Impulsore Chresto."—*Suet. in Claud.* xxv.

mentions the expulsion of the Jews from Rome under Claudius, and which we know included the Christians Aquila and Priscilla,* while they indicate a disturbance raised by the Jews against the faith, show at the same time that, in the eyes of Romans, both the Jews and the Christians were regarded as belonging to one and the same religion. Indeed it is not easy to see how the Romans could take any other view of the matter, since it was notorious that the Christians worshipped the God of Moses and the Prophets, and claimed that their religion was the fulfilment of all the promises, types, and figures of Judaism, and thus enjoyed the protection afforded to Judaism.

Now Judaism, both in its national customs and its distinctive religious rites, "even in Rome itself," was expressly recognised and protected by the Roman laws from the days of Julius Cæsar;† and though under Tiberius,‡ and (as we have just seen) under Claudius, the Jews were banished from the city, yet this was merely a temporary suspension of the decree of the same emperor, which permitted "the Jews, who are in all the world under us, to keep their ancient customs without being hindered so to do."§ This is proved by the fact of St Paul, a few years afterwards, finding at Rome very many Jews, and being allowed to assemble them at his lodgings, and preach to them without prohibition. ‖ From inscriptions on Jewish Catacombs, and from incidental expressions in Suetonius, it is evident that this protection extended to both classes of proselytes. As long, therefore, as the Christian Church continued to be confounded with the Jewish religion, the Christians would enjoy the protection of the law both in their assemblies and in the burial of their dead. They were *akin to* the Jewish religion, as Tertullian says,¶ "and lived

---

* Acts xviii. 2.   † Joseph. Ant. xiv. 10, 8.   ‡ Ib. xviii. 3, 5.
§ Ib. xix. 5, 3.   ‖ Acts xxviii. 17–31.
¶ "Nos quoque ut Judaicæ religionis *propinquos*, sub umbraculo insignissimæ religionis certè licitæ."—*Tertull. Ad Nationes*, i. 11.

Position of the First Roman Christians.   43

under the shadow of that most famous religion, about whose lawfulness there was no question."

The Jews, however, vigorously denounced their supposed co-religionists, and became, in Rome, as elsewhere, the first cause of the persecution of the Church.* Thenceforward it became necessary that the Roman Government should either legally recognise the Christian religion *as well as* the Jewish, or else proscribe it.† The burning of Rome by Nero, and his false accusations and unjust punishment of the Christians, decided between these alternatives. "This," says Sulpicius Severus, speaking probably with exact historical accuracy, "was the beginning of cruelties against Christians; afterwards, the religion was forbidden even by express laws, and decrees were published declaring it to be illegal to be a Christian."‡ It does not appear, however, that there was any further open persecution of Christians for a period of thirty years after Nero. Domitian, as we have seen, renewed it, banishing and putting to death even members of his own family. The same Emperor also persecuted the Jews and their proselytes for matters connected with the fiscal regulations.§ Both Jews and Christians, however, were protected by his successor, Nerva,‖ so that Lactantius, or whoever else may have been the author of the work "*De Mortibus Persecutorum*," even goes so far as to say (c. 3) that the Church was then restored to her former condition of liberty. This, however, must not be interpreted too strictly, for the statutes which created the distinction between the impiety or "atheism" of the Christians, and the "religion" of the Jews and proselytes, had never been repealed; and their operation, though for awhile suspended, could be revived at any time, as in fact it was on the death of Nerva. Pliny's famous letter to Trajan distinctly says that

margin notes: Christian religion proscribed by the Roman law, A.D. 64. First persecution. Domitian. Nerva. Pliny's letter to Trajan, A.D. 104.

* Merivale, vi. p. 449, note viii. p. 361 ; Mamachi Orig., tom. i. lib. vi. 5.
† "As soon as the Christians established their independence of Judaism, they fell under the ban of an illicit religion."—*Merivale*, vii. 381.
‡ Sulp. Sev. Hist. ii. 41.   § Sueton. in Domit. xii.
‖ Tertull. Apolog. 5.

the Christians worshipped Christ as God; and the Emperor's reply leaves no doubt as to the state of the law, for while he counsels Pliny not to originate active measures against them, nor to seek for them, yet he tells him that if they were denounced, and brought before the tribunal, the laws required that they should be punished, unless they consented to renounce their faith. *Non licet esse vos!* [*] was the cruel but plain letter of the Roman law against the very existence of the Christians, and their only means of escape were to be found in the hindrances put in the way of accusers by benevolent and tolerant princes.

And even this did not always prove a sufficient protection, when the malevolence of individuals insisted on pressing the execution of the law. Thus, when the Senator Apollonius, in the reign of Commodus, was accused of Christianity, the informer was condemned to be broken on the wheel; but Apollonius was required to defend himself before the Senate, and suffered martyrdom by decapitation, "as there was a law of long standing with them, that those who had been once led to trial, and would by no means change their purpose, should not be dismissed."[†] From the time of Nero, then, the sword was always suspended over the Church. "Sometimes it descended, and the disciples, always insecure, were made to suffer; for, whenever the jealousy of the State was awakened, no special edict was required to drag them before the altar of Jupiter, and invite them to sprinkle it with incense, and conceive a vow to the genius of the Emperor,"[‡] which, if they refused, they were at once liable to capital punishment as traitors and rebels. It is no part of our present purpose to pursue the history of the Church's fortunes through all its vicissitudes during the first three centuries. It is enough to have given this general outline, and to have pointed out the principle on which they depended. How this affected the origin and development of the Roman Catacombs will appear more clearly in the sequel.

[*] Tertull. Apolog. vi. 4.   [†] Euseb. H. E. v. 21.   [‡] Merivale, vi. 451.

CHAPTER III.

ROMAN LAWS AND CUSTOMS AFFECTING BURIAL.

IT does not follow, from the refusal of the Roman law to protect, or even to tolerate Christianity, that the sepulchres of those who professed it would be interfered with. Neither the correspondence of Pliny and Trajan, nor any other cotemporary document of the first two centuries, can be alleged in proof ot any difficulty attending Christian burial, or any necessity for concealment. In fact, it required a special decree against the Christian cemeteries, such as we first meet with in A.D. 203, to exclude them from the protection extended by law over all burial-places. No classical scholar need be reminded of the sacred character which attached to such places among the civilised peoples of antiquity. In Athens it entered into the preliminary examination of men chosen to fill the highest offices of the State, whether they had been negligent in the care of their father's sepulchre.* In Rome, land which had been once used for purposes of burial was protected by special privileges of the law. It did not, indeed, *ipso facto* become *sacer*, for this could only be effected by all the ceremonies of a ritual consecration; but it became, in the technical language of the time, *religiosus*;† and one of the chief consequences of this religious character, which henceforth attached to it, was its exemption from many of the laws which regulated the tenure or transfer of property. It could

Christian sepulchres protected by ordinary laws of burial.

Privileges of Roman tombs.

* Xen. Mem. ii. 2, § 13.
† "Religiosum locum unusquisque sua voluntate facit, dum mortuum infert in locum suum.—*Marcian. Digest.* i. 8, 6, § 4.

not become the lawful property of a man by *usucapio*, or prescription;* and it was inalienable, belonging exclusively and for ever to the families of those who had been buried in it. In times of war, and during any prolonged period of civil disturbance, those rights were probably not always strictly observed; but the law, at least, remained always the same. Hence the frequent recurrence on ancient Roman monuments of these letters, or something equivalent to them—H.M.H.EX.T.N.S., (*Hoc monumentum hæredes ex testamento ne sequatur;*) in other words, "This tomb and all that belongs to it is sacred: henceforth it can neither be bought nor sold; it does not descend to my heirs with the rest of my property; but must ever remain inviolate for the purpose to which I have destined it, viz., as a place of sepulture for myself and my family," or certain specified members only of the family; or, in some rare instances, others also, not of the same family. Thus, without any desire on his part, the Christian, by the mere fact of burying his dead, put his sepulchre under the protection of the Roman laws, and though he himself might be an outlaw, yet his burial-place was secure from disturbance, and under the guardianship of the *Pontifices*, who from time to time inspected the tombs, and without whose permission no serious alteration could be made.†

Christian martyrs allowed the honours of burial.

The Roman Government also permitted the bodies of those who had forfeited their lives to the law to be delivered up for burial to any who asked for them.‡ Diocletian and Maximin distinctly confirmed, by a new edict, this merciful provision;

* Cic. De Legibus, ii. 24.

† De Rossi [*Bullettino*, 1865, pp. 89, 90] shows that this permission was only necessary as far as the portion of the sepulchre above ground was concerned, and that there was a regular system of fees which removed all difficulties. In fact, so insignificant were these, that the Christian Emperor Constans confirmed the Pagan Pontifices in their authority over Roman sepulchres.

‡ "Corpora animadversorum *quibuslibet petentibus* ad sepulturam danda sunt."—*Digest.* xlviii. 24, 2. This law illustrates the fact of "Joseph of Arimathea going in to Pilate and begging the Body of Jesus."

Roman Laws and Customs affecting Burial. 47

and it was only under very special circumstances, says Ulpian, that this permission was ever refused. Of course, we know from ecclesiastical history that some of the Christian martyrs were precisely among the few who were excepted, and the reason of the exception is expressly mentioned, viz., that the faithful who survived might not have the consolation they so highly prized, of preserving and honouring the sacred relics. Still there is no trace in the first two centuries of such prohibition ; and, as a matter of fact, some of the most ancient Catacombs had their origin from this very circumstance, that a pious Christian, generally a Roman matron of noble rank, buried the remains of some famous martyr on her own property.

The extent to which the private burial-places of Roman Christians could be made available for the necessities of their brethren in the faith, will appear more clearly if we consider that not only was the sepulchre itself invested with a sacred character, but the Roman law included in its protection also the *area* in which the monument stood, the *hypogeum*, or subterranean chamber, which not unfrequently was formed beneath it, and perhaps even the buildings, gardens, and other possessions attached to it. Letters inscribed upon most of the sepulchral monuments which line the public roads leading into Rome tell us how many feet of frontage, and how many feet backwards into the field, belonged to the monument. IN · FR · P. [so many] ; IN · AG · P. [so many] : *In fronte, pedes* — ; *In agro, pedes* —. From these inscriptions it appears that quite a moderate-sized *area* for a Roman sepulchre might have extended 125 Roman feet, more or less, each way. The classical example in Horace* gives us 1000 feet by 300. Sometimes of course it was very much less, *e.g.*, 16 feet square, 24 feet by 15, &c. Sometimes also it was very much larger; for instance, 1800 feet by 500 is the measurement given on a marble slab, once a part of the monument

Size of Roman burial-places adapted for Christian cemeteries.

Ancient plan of sepulchral area.

* 1 Sat. viii. 12.

48 Roman Laws and Customs affecting Burial.

itself, which was dug up many years ago on the Via Labicana, and given to the museum at Urbino. On this slab, not only are the usual measurements of frontage and depth carefully recorded, but also the private or public roads which crossed the property, the gardens and vineyards of which it consisted, the swampy land on which grew nothing but reeds, (it is called *Harundinetum*,) and the ditch by which, on one side at least, it was bounded. Unfortunately the slab is not perfect, so that we cannot tell the exact measurements of the whole. Enough, however, remains to show that the property altogether was not less than twelve Roman *jugera*, or nearly 350,000 square feet; and other inscriptions are extant, specifying an amount of property almost equal to this, as belonging to a single monument (*e.g.*, *Huic monumento cedunt agri puri jugera decem*).* The necessity for so large an assignment of property to a single tomb was not so much the vastness of the mausoleum to be erected, as because certain funeral-rites were to be celebrated there year by year, sacrifices to be offered, feasts to be given, &c.; and for these purposes semicircular recesses (*exedræ*) were provided, with sofas, and all things necessary for the convenience of guests. A house also (*custodia*) was often added, in which the person lived who looked after the monument, and provided the requisites for the annual festivals, and for his support the gardens, vineyards, &c., were set apart as a perpetual endowment.

Plan of Catacombs shows the mode and limits of the excavations.

The Catacombs themselves not only illustrate these remarks, by showing the care that was taken lest the subterranean excavations should transgress the limits assigned above ground to the *area* of the sepulchre; but also show how a comparatively small *area* might be made available for the burial of a great number of bodies. The crypt of St Lucina, for example, which now forms part of the Catacomb of St Callixtus, and in which St Cornelius was buried in the middle of the third century, was originally confined within an *area* the dimensions of which can be exactly determined—100 feet *in fronte*, 180 *in agro*;

* Gruter, Inscript. p. cccxcix. 1.

and there was a building of some kind above it, which in the beginning of the fourth century, (prior to the conversion of Constantine,) if not at a much earlier period, was certainly in the possession of the Christians. Now in this crypt M. de Rossi has counted upwards of 700 *loculi*, and considers that, allowing for galleries destroyed, and others not yet thoroughly explored, 2000 would be a very moderate figure at which to estimate the number of persons buried within this area, which forms a very small and by no means crowded part of the cemetery of St Callixtus.

Hitherto we have considered the facilities afforded by the Roman laws relating to private mausoleums, under cover of which individual Christians, possessing property, might, by observing the requisite formalities, secure to themselves and to their poorer brethren an inalienable resting-place for their dead. But though the charity of the more wealthy Christians was in the early ages proverbial, and we may be sure that they took heed to the burial of the poor, and even of the slaves, whose bodies were laid side by side with their masters in the Christian cemeteries,* yet as, from apostolic example, we find that the Church, in its corporate capacity, provided for the maintenance of those Christians who were unable to maintain themselves,† it is worth while to inquire whether there were any provisions under the Roman laws whereby a society of men might hold a place of burial in the name and for the use of the members of that society. Now, a multitude of testimonies have come down to us of the existence, both in republican and imperial Rome, of a number of *collegia*, as they were called,—corporations, confraternities, guilds or clubs, as we should rather call them,—whose members were associated with a view to the due performance of the funeral-rites. In-

_{Funeral confraternities in Rome.}

---

* "Apud nos inter pauperes et divites, servos et dominos interest nihil."
—*Lactant. Div. Inst.* v. 14, 15.
† Acts ii. 44, 45 ; iv. 34–37 ; vi. 1 ; 1 Tim. v. 16.

scriptions, which are still extant, testify to nearly eighty of these *collegia*, each consisting of the members of a different trade or profession. There are the masons and carpenters, soldiers and sailors, bakers and cooks, corn-merchants and wine-merchants, hunters and fishermen, goldsmiths and blacksmiths, dealers in drugs and carders of wool, boatmen and divers, doctors and bankers, scribes and musicians; in a word, it would be hard to say what trade or employment had not its *collegium*. Nor was this the only bond of fellowship upon which such confraternities were built. Sometimes (generally, indeed) the members were united in the worship of some deity. They were *cultores Jovis*, or *Herculis*, or *Apollinis et Dianæ*. Sometimes they merely took the title of some deceased benefactor whose memory they desired to honour, *e.g., cultores statuarum et clipeorum L. Abulli Dextri;* and sometimes the only bond of union appears to have been service in the same house or family.* A long and curious inscription, belonging to a *collegium* which consisted mainly of slaves, and was erected "in honour of Diana and Antinous, *and for the burial of the dead*," in the year A.D. 133, reveals a number of most interesting particulars as to its internal organisation, which it will not be altogether beside our purpose to repeat. A certain fixed sum was to be paid on entrance, with a keg of good wine besides, and then so much a month afterwards. For every member who had regularly paid up his contribution, so much was to be allowed for his funeral, a certain proportion of which was to be distributed amongst those who assisted. If a member died at a distance of more than twenty miles from Rome, three of the confraternity were to be sent to fetch the body, and so much was to be

Description of a funeral confraternity.

* One *collegium* was "*convictorum qui una epulo vesci solent.*" Can this vague and ambiguous phraseology have been adopted by some congregation of Christians for the purpose of concealment? See *Bullettino*, 1864, 62. A *collegium quod est in domo Sergiæ Paulinæ*, reminds us of "the Church which is in their house," (Rom. xvi. 5.) It is also worthy of notice that the ancient privileges of these *collegia* were confirmed by an edict of Septimius Severus about A D. 200.

Roman Laws and Customs affecting Burial. 51

allowed them for travelling expenses. If the master of the slave would not give up the body, the deceased member was nevertheless to receive all the funeral-rites. He was to be buried in effigy. If any of the members, being a slave, received his freedom, he owed the *collegium* an *amphora* of good wine. The newly-elected president (*magister*) must inaugurate his accession to office by giving a supper to all the members. Six times a year the members dine together in honour of Diana, Antinous, and the patron of the *collegium;* and the allowance of bread and wine on these occasions was specified,—so much to every mess of four. No complaints or disputed questions might be mooted at these festivals, "to the end that our feasts may be merry and glad." Finally, whoever wished to enter this confraternity, was requested to study all the rules before he entered, that he might not grumble afterwards, or leave a dispute as a legacy to his heir. *

In connection with these *collegia*, it is to be remarked that, though the ordinary assemblies of the Christians were forbidden by the edicts of Trajan against clubs (*hetæriæ*), as appears from Pliny's letter, yet an exception was expressly made in favour of associations which consisted of "poorer members of society, who met together every month to make a small contribution towards the expenses of their funerals." † To understand how Christians might shelter their funeral-rites under this exception, we have only to recall the words in which Tertullian describes to a heathen ruler the habits of Christians at the end of the second century: "Every one makes a small contribution, *on a certain day in the month*, or when he chooses, provided he is only willing and able; for no one is compelled, all is voluntary. The amount is, as it were, a common fund of piety; since it is expended, not in feasting

Christians might avail themselves of the legal sanction of these societies,

---

* "Les Antonins," par le Cte. de Champagny, tom. iii., Append. 399.
† "Permittitur tenuioribus *stipem menstruam* conferre, dum tamen semel in mense coeant."—*Digest.* xlvii. 22, 1.

or in drinking, or in indecent excesses, but in feeding and *burying the poor*," &c.*

and even of other practices in connection with funeral-rites.

This subject has lately received still further important illustrations from a Pagan will, which had once been engraved in marble on a Roman sepulchre in Langres; was copied thence by some disciple of the school of Alcuin in the eighth or ninth century; and now two pages of his copy have been discovered in the binding of a MS. of the tenth century in the library at Basle. This curious document begins by ordering the completion of the *cella memoriæ* which the testator had already commenced. It was to be finished in exact accordance with the plan he should leave behind him; in it were to be set up two statues of himself of a certain size—the one in bronze, the other in marble—and in front of it, an altar of the finest Carrara marble, in which his bones should be laid. Provision was to be made for the easy opening and shutting of this *cella*; couches and benches also were to be provided for those days on which it was to be opened, and even garments for the guests.† Orchards and other property were assigned for the maintenance of the sepulchre, which was left in charge of two freedmen, who are named, and certain fines imposed upon the heirs if they should allow this duty to be neglected. Finally, all the testator's freedmen were to make a yearly contribution,

---

* "Modicam unusquisque *stipem menstrua die*, vel quum velit, et si modo velit, et si modo possit, apponit . . . . Nam inde non epulis . . . . sed egenis alendis *humandisque*," &c.—*Tert. Apol.* 39.

† This reminds us of the history of the man in the gospel who "had not on a wedding-garment." In the legal inventory of the goods which were confiscated under Diocletian in Cista, "in the house where the Christians used to meet," besides two chalices of gold, and six of silver, and six cruets, and seven candlesticks, all of the same metal, small brazen candlesticks and lamps with their chains, there were found also eighty-two garments for women, sixteen for men, thirteen pairs of men's shoes, forty-seven of women's, &c.—*Acta Purgat: Cœcil: post Optati Opera*, ed. Dupin, 168. Nor is this the only feature in this description whereby the reader will be reminded of the *agapæ*, or Christian love-feasts, which, before they had degenerated into the scenes of excess and superstition so feelingly deplored and condemned by the Fathers of the fifth century, were held at the tombs of the martyrs and others of the faithful.

out of which a feast was to be provided on a certain day, and duly consumed by them on the spot.

The constitution of the *collegium*, of which we have already said so much, gives a long *ordo cænarum*, or list of days on which convivial entertainments were to be celebrated; and in this *ordo* there are such entries as the following :—*viii Idus Martias natali Cæsenni patris . . . xiii k. Sept. natali Cæsenni Silvani fratris . . . xix Jan. natali Cæsenni Rufi patroni municipi.* Even the anniversary of the dedication, or first opening of the monument itself, seems sometimes to have been celebrated : *Natalis monumenti v. Id. Maias* was lately found on a pagan inscription. The eye-witnesses of St Ignatius' martyrdom testify to the Christian practice of observing the *natalitia* of the martyrs, for they make known " the day and the time, that being assembled together at the season of his martyrdom, we may communicate with the combatant and noble martyr of Christ ;"* and it must be obvious to all what an admirable cover for this and other pious practices of Christianity was provided by the existence of such institutions as we have described. That they were actually so used by Christians seems almost certain when we compare with the foregoing inscriptions the following Christian monument, discovered recently in the ruins of Cæsarea, one of the Roman towns in Africa :—

e.g., Ordo cœnarum.

Anniversaries, &c.

Instance of their doing so.

AREAM AT [AD] SEPVLCHRA CVLTOR VERBI CONTVLIT
ET CELLAM STRVXIT SVIS CVNCTIS SVMPTIBVS
ECCLESIÆ SANCTÆ HANC RELIQVIT MEMORIAM
SALVETE FRATRES PVRO CORDE ET SIMPLICI
EVELPIVS VOS SATOS SANCTO SPIRITV
ECCLESIA FRATRVM HVNC RESTITVIT TITVLVM. MA. I. SEVERIANI. C. V
EX ING . ASTERI.†

" Euelpius, a worshipper of the Word, has given this *area* for sepulchres,

---

* Mart. S. Ignat., 9, A.D. 107.
† *Ex ingenio Asteri* denotes that Asterius was the poet who composed this epitaph. Cf. Tertull. Apol., c. 39.

and has built a *cella* entirely at his own cost. He left this *memoria* to the Holy Church. Hail, brethren! Euelpius with a pure and simple heart salutes you, born of the Holy Spirit."

The identity of the expressions *cultor verbi, aream, cellam, memoriam*, with the corresponding terms used by the *collegia*, can hardly be the result of accident. It is true that this inscription, as we now have it, is not the original stone; it is expressly added at the foot of the tablet, that *Ecclesia fratrum** has restored this *titulus*, at a period subsequent to the persecution, during which the original had been destroyed; but both the sense and the words forbid us to suppose that any change had been made in the language of the epitaph, to which we cannot assign a date later than the middle of the third century. It may have been destroyed either in the persecution of A.D. 257 or of 304.

<small>First express edict against Christian cemeteries, A.D. 257.</small>

From all that we have said, then, it appears certain that in the earliest ages there was no special interference with Christians in their burial of the dead, and therefore no special necessity for secresy and concealment. In fact, the assemblies of the Christians would be less liable to interruption at the buildings erected over the burial-places than anywhere else. And it seems that the fact of these assemblies being frequently held there was the cause of the invasion of the sanctity of Christian graves by popular violence and express legal enactments. The first historical notice of such an invasion which has come down to us, belongs to Africa in the year A.D. 203. We are then told by Tertullian, that at Carthage there was a popular outcry raised *de areis sepulturarum nostrarum*, and a demand for their destruction.† These, however, were not subterranean cemeteries, and probably differed externally in little or nothing from the burial-places of the heathen which surrounded them; still they were known to belong to the Christians as their exclusive property. The first general edict

---

* This very term, unknown to theology, savours of being adopted for sake of concealment and its similarity to *collegium convictorum*, &c.

† "Areæ non sint!"—*Tertull. ad Scapulam*, c. 3.

Roman Laws and Customs affecting Burial. 55

by which the Roman Catacombs were affected was published by the Emperor Valerian, A D. 257, and was aimed rather at their use as places of worship, or at least of secret assembly, than as mere places of burial. After this, they enter expressly into most, if not all, of the imperial edicts concerning the Christians, so that the relations between the Roman laws and the Christian cemeteries will henceforward be most conveniently considered in our direct chronological account of the Catacombs themselves.

FIG. 8.—*Sepulchral Stone found in a cemetery on the Via Latina.*

CHAPTER IV.

BEGINNING OF THE CATACOMBS.

Roman burial-places, extramural.

IT has been shown that there was nothing, either in the social or religious position of the first Christians in Rome to interfere with their freedom of action in the mode of disposing of their dead. The law left them entire liberty, and there were not wanting to them either the means or the will to discharge this duty in the most becoming way. There was indeed one limit set to their liberty, viz., as to the choice of place; but this attached to all Roman sepulchres alike,* and was not peculiar to the Christians. It was strictly forbidden by the ancient laws to bury within the walls of the city; and, excepting in one or two instances where the pressure of persecution forced them for a while to unusual secrecy, the Christians seem never to have disregarded this prohibition. The law was really restricted in its application to the old walls of Servius Tullius; but with the exception of the burial of Saints John and Paul in their own house on the Cælian, and the bodies secretly buried by St Pudentiana, we do not find any trace of a Christian cemetery within the circuit of the walls of Aurelian and Honorius. Beyond these limits they were free to consult their own convenience, laws, or tastes, in this matter; and being a mixed company of Greeks, Romans, and Jews, they had the examples of various nations from which to choose. Among the Greeks, the corpse was either buried or burnt; both practices appear to have been always used

* Even the few privileged families who had a legal right of burial within the walls did not avail themselves of it.—*Cic. de Leg.* ii. 23.

to a greater or less extent at different periods. In Rome, the ordinary custom, at least from the later times of the Republic, was not to bury, but to burn, the bodies of the dead, and to enclose the ashes in an urn. The urn was then placed in a recess in the family sepulchre, which, from its containing a number of these little niches, like so many pigeon-holes, was called a *columbarium* or dove-cot. This, however general, and latterly almost universal, was not the primitive custom.* Warriors, lying at full length in their armour, have been found in Etruscan tombs, and outside the ancient Porta Capena (though within the present walls of Rome) may still be seen the sepulchre of the Scipios, with its full-sized sarcophagi, showing that that great family followed the ancient practice. Fabretti gives another example, which he saw four miles out of Rome, on the Via Flaminia, on which road are also the sepulchres of the Nasones, described by Bartoli. These latter, and some others that might be named, resemble the plan which was adopted by the Christians more closely than do the tombs of the Scipios, inasmuch as they have chambers cut in the *tufa*, with horizontal niches for bodies; whereas the tombs of the Scipios are both irregular in form, as though the place had been a deserted quarry, and have no graves cut in the wall, but only recesses for sarcophagi, which are half-buried, as it were, in the living rock.† The principal marks which distinguish these Pagan sepulchres from the Christian cemeteries are—their comparatively small size; their exclusiveness in containing only the remains of a single family, as contrasted with the all-embracing catholicity of the Christian cemetery; and that the *loculi* of the Pagan sepulchre were often left open, because it was their custom to close the chamber for ever when it had once received its destined occupants, while the Christian *loculi* were always hermetically sealed, since the chambers in which they were situated were frequently visited by the faithful.

margin: Pagan *columbaria*, and other tombs,

margin: contrasted with Christian cemeteries.

* Plin. Hist. Nat. vii. 55.
† Opere di Ennio Visconti, i. 10, Milano.

These particulars, however, are not of the essence of this mode of burial; and the examples referred to are abundantly sufficient for the purpose for which they have been alleged, viz., to show that the practice of burying in sepulchres hewn out of the rock was not altogether unknown even to the Pagans of Rome. To the Jews it had always been familiar, and numerous examples are to be found in every part of the world, wherever they have settled themselves and the nature of the soil permitted it—in Palestine, in Southern Italy,* and in Rome itself. One was discovered not long since on the opposite side of the Via Appia from the Church of St Sebastian, and somewhat nearer to Rome, in the Vigna Randanini. Here the galleries resemble those of the Christian cemeteries very closely, except that they are not quite so regular. The *loculi* are closed with stone and terra-cotta, like those in the Catacombs; but the lowest range are sunk beneath the floor, and the stone closing these leans against the wall in a slanting, instead of an upright position. There are no *cubicula*, properly so called, but sometimes an opening leads to a small recess where two or three graves are sunk behind the ordinary range of *loculi*. The inscriptions are in Greek, with unmistakeable Jewish expressions and symbols, amongst which the seven-branched candlestick holds the first place. From the variety of names, and the absence of the usual exclusive occupation of the tombs by one family which characterises most Jewish sepulchres of a similar kind, it has been conjectured that here the Jews rather imitated than set an example to the Christians.†

Bosio,‡ however, describes a Jewish Catacomb which he saw on Monte Verde, outside the Porta Portese, which was far more ancient, and seems certainly to have been of an earlier date than the Christian cemetery of San Ponziano on the same hill. However, it is not worth while to discuss minutely the chronology

---

* See Murray's Handbook for Southern Italy, 361.
† Cimitero degli Antichi Ebrei, &c., per P. Garrucci, Roma, 1862.
‡ Bosio, Rom. Sott. 142.

Beginning of the Catacombs. 59

of the specimens of Jewish Catacombs to be seen in Rome. We need only refer to the language of the prophets when speaking of places of burial in the Old Testament,* or quote the instance of the Father of the Faithful himself, whose only possession in the land of promise was "the field wherein was the double cave, which Abraham bought for a possession of a burying-place."† It is, of course, still more to the purpose to name the new sepulchre hewn out in a rock in which Joseph of Arimathea laid the Body of our Lord—an example which was not likely to be without effect on His earliest disciples.

A modern writer, indeed, has ventured to say of the first Christians in Rome, that as they continued to dwell in the midst of their unconverted countrymen, so they continued also their ordinary usages of daily social life; in particular, "that they burnt their dead after the Roman fashion, gathered their ashes into the sepulchres of their patrons, and inscribed over them the customary dedication to the *Divine Spirits*." ‡ The only authority given for this statement is "the frequent occurrence of the letters D. M. on the tombs of the early Christians," which is certainly quite inadequate to support the weight of so new and startling a theory. We do not for a moment doubt that wherever these letters were used, they were intended to stand for *Dis Manibus*, and not (as Boldetti, Fabretti, and others have tried to maintain) for *Deo Maximo*. But it is one of the discoveries for which we are indebted to the skill and diligence of De Rossi, in attempting a chronological arrangement of the Christian inscriptions of Rome, that we are able to fix the date of the Christian epitaphs on which these letters have been found—and they are extremely rare,§ not frequent—to the end of the third century, by which time they may perhaps have been almost accounted a characteristic of mortuary inscriptions, and so have been used thoughtlessly, without any

<small>Christians did not burn, but buried, their dead.</small>

---

* Isaias xxii. 16.   † Gen. xxiii. 17-20.   ‡ Merivale, vi. 444.
§ "Quam *rarissime*, partim oscitantia, partim aliis de causis, Christianis adhibitam epitaphiis fuisse satis constat," says De Rossi.—*Spic. Solesm.* iii. 551.

advertence to their real meaning,* *e.g.*, they are found, in one instance, coupled with the sacred monogram itself, D. M. ☧ S. Or the tombstone may have been bought with the letters already inscribed; the surviving relatives who put it up may have been ill-instructed in the faith; or many other explanations might be given, any one of which seems to us more easily admissible than that suggested by Mr Merivale. For whilst, on the one hand, it is not pretended that among the innumerable cinerary urns of the Roman *columbaria*,† a single specimen has yet been found with Christian emblems or inscriptions, we have very distinct testimony, on the other hand, that the Christians condemned the destruction of dead bodies by fire, and insisted on restoring them to the earth, whence they came.‡

We conclude, then, that there was nothing strange or unnatural in the mode of burial adopted by the early Christians of Rome, although the spirit of Christianity soon made itself felt in the characteristics which distinguish its cemeteries from the sepulchres both of Jews and of Pagans, just as the Christian Church itself grew up, men knew not how, in the midst of

* They only came into use among the heathen themselves under the first Cæsars.

† Mr Merivale, indeed, in another place, refers to the inscriptions in the *columbaria* of Claudius, recently discovered, as containing several of the same names as occur in the salutations of St Paul to his fellow-countrymen in Rome, and he considers that one at least, Sentia Renata, bespeaks a Christian baptism. The whole of the inscription referred to stands thus—

Sentiæ Renatæ
q. v. Ann. iiii. m. xi. d. viii.
Sentius Felicissimus
Et Amabilis Filiæ
Dulcissimæ.

We do not know of any Christian inscription in which the title *amabilis* is assumed by the survivor; it is, of course, often given to the deceased. The instances of identity of name are only seven or eight out of 250, and seem to prove nothing but that such names were not uncommon in Rome. —*Di due Sepolcri Romani del Secolo di Augusto, &c., da Gio. Pietro Campana*, ed. 2da, *Roma*, 1852.

‡ Execrantur rogos et damnant ignium sepulturas.—*Minuc Felix. Octav.* c. ii. 451, ed. 1838. Veterum et meliorum consuetudinem humandi frequentamus.—Ib., c. x. 468.

Beginning of the Catacombs.

Judaism and Paganism, claimed as its own all that was good and true in the religions around it, and, at the same time, preserved intact its own identity as a "holy nation," the kingdom of God which shall stand for ever. But in the beginning of the Christian Catacombs, there was absolutely nothing extraordinary or requiring explanation; the faithful did but use their liberty in the way that suited them best, burying their dead according to a fashion to which many of them had been long accustomed, and which enabled them at the same time to follow in death the example of Him who was also their model in life. Accordingly, they began cemeteries here and there on different sides of the city, as occasion required and opportunity served, not at all foreseeing the enormous proportions which their work would ultimately attain, nor the manifold uses it would serve. It is quite possible that some of these cemeteries may always have remained the burial-place of single families, as in point of fact Christian subterranean sepulchres have really been found in the neighbourhood of Rome, consisting each of a single chamber only. Others again, begun with the same intent, may have been afterwards indefinitely enlarged, and particular portions only appropriated to private use by means of inscriptions, such as that recently discovered in the Catacomb of St Nicomedes, in the garden of the Villa Patrizi, just outside the Porta Pia;* First catacombs, small and private. Examples.

```
MONVMENTVM · VALERI · M
ERCVRI · ET · JVLITTES · JVLIAN
I · ET · QVINTILIES · VERECVNDES
LIBERTIS-LIBERTABVSQUE-POSTE
RISQUE · EORVM · AT · RELIGIONE
M · PERTINENTES · MEA · M · HOC · A
MPLIVS · IN · CIRCVITVM · CIRCA ·
MONVMENTVM · LATI · LONGI ·
PER · PEDES · BINOS · QUOD · PERTIN
ET · AT · IPSVM · MONVMENT ·
```

* It is stated in his Acts that he was buried "in the garden of Justus,

or this other, which may yet be seen in a most ancient part of the Catacomb of Sts Nereus and Achilles, at no great distance from the sepulchre of those saints.

```
M   · ANTONI
VS  · RESTVTV
S · FECIT · YPO
GEV · SIBI · ET ·
SVIS · FIDENTI
BVS · IN · DOMINO.
```

Both of these monuments are very ancient. Neither of them seems to have contemplated the existence of penal laws, proscribing the free exercise of the Christian religion, or interfering with the privacy and sacredness of their graves. They merely announce with simplicity and candour, as an inscription on a pagan monument might have done, for whose benefit that place of burial had been provided. Each desires to include those only who belong to his own religion, and it is attempted to secure the fulfilment of this desire, in the one case by limiting the use of the *hypogeum* to those relatives " who believe in the Lord," in the other, by declaring that the monument is for the use only of those of my dependents " who belong to my religion." No precedent can be found for such a phrase as this amid the tens of thousands of pagan epitaphs which are still extant. It is doubtful whether it would have conveyed any meaning at all to a pagan mind; it could have been used by a Jew or a Christian, but by no one else, and even a Christian could not have used it in public when once his *religion* had been condemned and declared unlawful by the state. It might have been used, therefore, before persecution was begun by Nero, or, again, between his death and the accession of Domitian, or under Nerva and in the earlier part of the reign of Trajan, and it is very possible that to one of these periods this inscription really belongs.

near the city walls." The author quoted by William of Malmesbury also places his tomb very near this gate of the city.

BOOK II.

HISTORY OF THE CATACOMBS.

CHAPTER I.

THE CATACOMBS IN THE FIRST AGES.

WE now enter upon a most interesting portion of our subject; on which, however, little reliable information could be obtained until the archæological genius of De Rossi succeeded in reducing to order the fragments of tradition scattered through the writings of antiquity, so laboriously collected by Bosio and others, and verifying these by the monuments found in the Catacombs themselves. By these means we have at length the outlines at least of a chronological history of *Roma Sotterranea*, which we may hope that future discoveries will correct and enlarge. Our readers will not expect us to produce the testimony of cotemporaneous, or nearly cotemporaneous authors, for the history of the Catacombs during the first ages. So terrible was the tenth and last persecution under Diocletian, that hardly any of the ancient records of the Roman Church escaped destruction. We have already enumerated the principal documents from which the early history of that Church is to be reconstructed ; and all that can now be done is briefly to collect the informa-

Apostolic origin of some of the Catacombs.

tion we derive from those sources, and then to examine the Catacombs themselves for whatever confirmation of it they may be able to give.

It has been said or implied that the history of the Catacombs probably dates from the burial of the first Roman Christian. Are there, then, to be found in any of the existing Catacombs traces of apostolical antiquity? De Rossi replies :—" Precisely in those cemeteries to which history or tradition assigns apostolic origin, I see, in the light of the most searching archæological criticism, the cradle of Christian art and of Christian inscriptions; there I find memorials of persons who appear to belong to the times of the Flavii and of Trajan; and finally, I discover precise dates of those times."* This is a bold statement, and we purpose in the present chapter to bring together some at least of the proofs upon which it is based.

Papal crypt on the Vatican. Among the cemeteries ascribed by tradition to apostolic times, the crypts of the Vatican would have the first claim on our attention, had they not been almost destroyed by the foundations of the vast basilica which guards the tomb of St Peter. We cannot, however, pass them by altogether, especially as the most ancient notice of them that we have confirms in some degree what has been said as to the perfect liberty of the first Christians in the burial even of their martyrs. The *Liber Pontificalis* states that Anacletus, the successor of Clement in the Apostolic See, "*built* and adorned the sepulchral monument (*construxit memoriam*) of blessed Peter, since he had been ordained priest by St Peter, and other burial-places where the bishops might be laid." It is added that he himself was buried there; and the same is recorded of Linus and Cletus, and of Evaristus, Sixtus I., Telesphorus, Hyginus, Pius I., Eleutherius, and Victor, the last of whom was buried A.D. 203 ; and, after St Victor, no other Pontiff is recorded to

* R. S. i. 185.

The Catacombs in the First Ages. 65

have been buried at the Vatican until St Leo the Great was laid in St Peter's, A.D. 461. The idea conveyed by the words *construxit memoriam* is that of a monument above ground according to the usual Roman custom; and we have seen that such a monument, even though it covered the tombs of Christian bishops, would not be likely to be disturbed at any time during the first or second century. For the reason we have already stated, it is impossible to confront these ancient notices with any existing monuments. It is worth mentioning, however, that De Rossi believes that the sepulchre of St Linus was discovered in this very place early in the seventeenth century, bearing simply the name of LINUS.*

From St Peter's on the Vatican the mind passes naturally to the resting-place of the apostle of the Gentiles on the other side of the river and of Rome. But here, too, the hill has been cut away to make room for the Basilica of St Paul *extra muros;* and hence the greater part of the Catacomb of St Lucina, or of St Commodilla, as it is sometimes called in ancient records, has been destroyed, and what galleries yet remain are so choked with earth and ruins of various kinds as to be almost impassable. Nevertheless, it must not be forgotten that Boldetti read within this Catacomb the most ancient inscription with a consular date that has come down to us.† It was scratched on the mortar of one of the *loculi*, and the consulate of *Sura et Senecio* marks the year A.D. 107. A second was also found in the same place, in marble, recording the names of *Piso et Bolano*, consuls A.D. 110. The same explorer discovered here also yet a third inscrip-

St Paul's on the Via Ostiensis.

---

* *Bullettino*, 1864, p. 50.
† There is, indeed, a more ancient dated Christian inscription of the third year of Vespasian, *i.e.*, A.D. 72; but, unfortunately, it is no longer possible to ascertain to what cemetery this inscription belonged. It must be remembered that a very small proportion of the inscriptions have the date of the year upon them. The day of the month was sufficient to mark the anniversary; the particular year was regarded as of less importance.

E

tion, which De Rossi considers one of the most ancient in Rome:—

> DORMITIONI
> T. FLA. EVTY
> CHIO. QVI. VI
> XIT. ANN. XVIIII
> MES. XI. D. III
> HVNC. LOCVM
> DONABIT. M
> ORBIVS HELI
> VS. AMICVS
> KARISSIMVS
> KARE BALE

"As a resting-place for Titus Flavius Eutychius, who lived nineteen years, eleven months, three days. His dearest friend, Marcus Orbius, gave this spot. Farewell, beloved."

The place where it was found, and certain symbols rudely carved at the bottom (apparently intended to represent loaves and fishes), show this inscription to be Christian; while the style, the ancient nomenclature differing from the usual Christian epitaphs, and the prænomen, T. Flavius, point to the age of the Flavian emperors, *i.e.*, the end of the first century. It can hardly be a mere accident that these rare and cotemporaneous dates should have been discovered in the same place, and precisely in the cemetery where less than forty years before had been deposited the body of the apostle Paul. They may be taken as certain proofs that a Catacomb was begun here not long after his martyrdom.

St Priscilla on the Via Salaria. The cemetery of St Priscilla, on the Via Salaria Nova, is said to have been dug in the property of the family of Pudens, converted by the apostles; and a particular chapel in it, known, from the language of its inscriptions, as the *Cappella Greca*, is supposed to have been the burial-place of St Pudentiana, St. Praxedes, and other members of the family. The classical style of the frescoes, the scenes depicted in most of them differing widely from the usual well-known subjects which in after-times repeat themselves so frequently, when Christian symbolism had assumed a more fixed and stereotyped character; the beautiful ornaments in stucco, like those in the baths of Titus; a special family of inscriptions traced in vermilion on the tiles, and unlike later Christian epigraphs in their language (being sometimes bare names, sometimes the apostolic salutation PAX TECVM, very often the symbol of the anchor); the classic forms of the characters of the inscriptions on marble; the name TITO FLAVIO FELICISSIMO; the construction of the principal crypt, which is not excavated in the *tufa*, but regularly built, and, without any *loculus* in the walls, was evidently intended for the reception of sarcophagi; —all these variations from the uniformity of Christian subterranean cemeteries, such as we find them in the third century, point to a date anterior to any such systematic arrangement, and confirm in a remarkable manner the high antiquity assigned to this cemetery by tradition.

In certain acts of Pope Liberius mention is made of the cemetery of Ostrianus as being "not far from the cemetery of Novella, which was on the third mile of the Via Salaria." When Panvinius compiled his catalogue of the cemeteries,* he set down this as having been the oldest of all, "because it was in use when St Peter preached the faith to the Romans." Bosio, however, and all other antiquarians have failed in any attempt to identify it; whilst De Rossi's more scientific mode of procedure seems to have been more successful. He observed that the Abbot John, in the papyrus MS.† at Monza, in which he gives a list of oils from the lamps before the celebrated shrines of Rome which he visited, after "the oil of St Agnes and many others" on the Via Nomentana and before "the oil of St Vitalis, St Alexander, and others on the Via Salaria," mentions "oil from the chair where Peter the apostle was first enthroned (*prius sedit*)," as though this were situated somewhere between the roads that have been named. In like manner, in the index of the cemeteries in the *Liber Mirabilium*, between that of St Agnes and that of St Priscilla, that is, be-

Cemetery of Ostrianus or Fons Petri.

* See page 32.   † See page 23.

tween the same two roads, is placed the cemetery of the font of St Peter (*fontis S. Petri*—in other copies *Ad Nymphas S. Petri*), near the basilica of St Emerentiana. Now, this situation exactly corresponds with that of the cemetery upon which Father Marchi bestowed all his labours, and which has therefore become so familiar to all Roman visitors under the name of the Catacomb of St Agnes; but the galleries and chambers which are at present accessible there do not bear marks of greater antiquity than the third century. Bosio, however, tells us that he went down by a square hole (which is at present undiscovered), and found a crypt, also unknown to us, evidently of an historical character, from the frequency of the *luminaria* and the beauty of the ornamentation. Near one of these light-holes, which he found still open, "without the light of a candle," he writes, "one sees a large niche like a tribune, with leaves in stucco-work, and within the niche are seen some red letters, which, being almost all obliterated, are illegible, but some few which remain are beautifully formed; under that niche must anciently have been the altar, the place being sufficiently spacious."* De Rossi observes that it is now well ascertained that the ancient custom was to place in the tribune, not the altar, but the pontifical chair; and this passage from Bosio seems to him to read like an account of the crypt where was formerly venerated on the 18th of January, "the chair in which Peter was first enthroned"—*sedes ubi prius sedit*—and which was also known in the martyrologies of Ado and Bede as the *Cœmeterium ad Nymphas ubi Petrus baptizabat.*† The extreme antiquity of some cemetery in this neighbourhood is still further confirmed by the inscriptions which have been found here; their classical and laconic style, form, and nomenclature, all betoken a most ancient date. In nearly a hundred instances the names are of Claudii, Flavii, Ulpii, Aurelii, and others of the same class; once the deceased is stated to have been the freedwoman (*liberta*) of Lucius Clo-

* Roma Sott. 438. † See Note C in Appendix.

dius Crescens; often nothing whatever is added to the names, or only the relationship between the deceased and the person setting up the tablet, with perhaps the epithet of affection, *dulcissimo* or *dulcissimæ*. In fact, these epitaphs vary so little from the old classical type, that had they not been seen by Marini and other competent witnesses in their original position, and some of them been marked with the Christian symbol of the anchor, we might have hesitated whether they ought not rather to be classed among pagan monuments.

The Cemetery of St Domitilla, or of her chamberlains, Saints Nereus and Achilles, on the Via Ardeatina, claims to be of the same age, and its claim deserves a more detailed examination, as it is connected with what has been already mentioned as one of the most remarkable facts in the annals of the early Church, the profession of the Christian faith by some of the Imperial family. For this Domitilla was the same of whom we have spoken in a former chapter as having been banished* to the island of Ponza. St Jerome† tells us that in his days this island was frequented by pious Christian pilgrims, "who delighted to visit with devotion the cells in which Flavia Domitilla had suffered a life-long martyrdom." Whether she really shed her blood at the last for the faith is uncertain, the acts of Saints Nereus and Achilles being of doubtful authenticity. They state, however, that she and two of her female companions were buried in a sarcophagus at Terracina, but that her chamberlains suffered death by the sword, and were buried in a cemetery about a mile and a half out of Rome, on the Via Ardeatina, in a farm belonging to their mistress. The farm, now known by the name of Tor Marancia, is situated just at this distance from Rome, and on the road named; and inscriptions which have been found there show clearly that it once belonged to this very person, Flavia Domitilla. One of them gives the measurements of a sepulchral area of 35 feet in front and 40 into the field, whether for a pagan or a Chris-

marginal note: St Domitilla at Tor Marancia.

* See page 39.   † Ep. ad Eustoch. 86.

tian monument we cannot say; but at all events the ground had been granted *ex indulgentiâ Flaviæ Domitillæ, neptis Vespasiani;* another is *ex beneficio* of the same, and the others also are equally unequivocal. Moreover, within the cemetery which underlies this farm, or at least in its immediate neighbourhood, two or three other inscriptions have been found of a Bruttia Crispina and others of the Gens Bruttia, from which we may infer that there was some sort of connexion between the two families, and that this was the reason which induced Bruttius the historian to make special mention of the exile of Domitilla in his narrative of the public events of his day.* Although, therefore, no historical monuments have been found within the cemetery itself, which like those in the cemetery of St Callixtus, declare its identity beyond all power of reclamation, yet nobody now doubts but that at Tor Marancia we have certainly recovered that cemetery which, in ancient times, was sometimes called by the name of St Domitilla, and sometimes of Saints Nereus and Achilles.

One of the chapels, in the second story, at the left-hand side after you have descended a very handsome flight of steps from the open air, is pointed out as the probable scene of the burial of the two saints. This, however, does not now concern us; a recent discovery on the outer surface of the hill, and at no great distance from this part of the cemetery, claims all our attention. De Rossi unhesitatingly introduces it to us as a monument of some member or special friend of the Flavian family, who lived and died in the days of Domitian. It is certainly one of the most ancient and remarkable Christian monuments yet discovered. Its position, close to the highway; its front of fine brickwork, with a cornice of terra-cotta, with the usual space for an inscription (which has now, alas! perished); the spaciousness of its gallery, with only four or five separate

* See page 39.

niches prepared for as many sarcophagi; the fine stucco on the wall; the eminently classical character of its decorations; all these things make it perfectly clear that it was the monument of a Christian family of distinction, excavated at great cost, and without the slightest attempt at concealment. On each side of the entrance there was a small chamber; the one on the right (*c*) was probably for the *schola*, as it was called, or place of meeting for those of the *gens* or *religio*, whose duty it was to assemble here on the anniversaries, to do honour to the deceased; that on the left (*b*) bears evident tokens of having

FIG. 9.—*Entrance to a most ancient Christian Sepulchre at Tor Marancia.*

been a place of residence, probably for the guardian of the monument, just as we find attached to so many pagan monuments of the same period.

After descending two steps from the portico, the pathway slopes gradually for a short distance, leaving, as we have said, only a few recesses, capable of receiving each a large sarcophagus, all of which however have long since been removed. One of these recesses was enlarged at a subsequent period, and a tomb in the form of an *arcosolium* made in it; and the whole *hypogæum* was ultimately united by additional galleries to the adjacent catacomb. Before this was done, however, the vestibule had been filled with sarcophagi of various sizes, of which numerous fragments may still be seen lying about; we find them also (of terra-cotta) buried underneath the ground; and the date even of the last of these seems not to come below the middle of the second century.

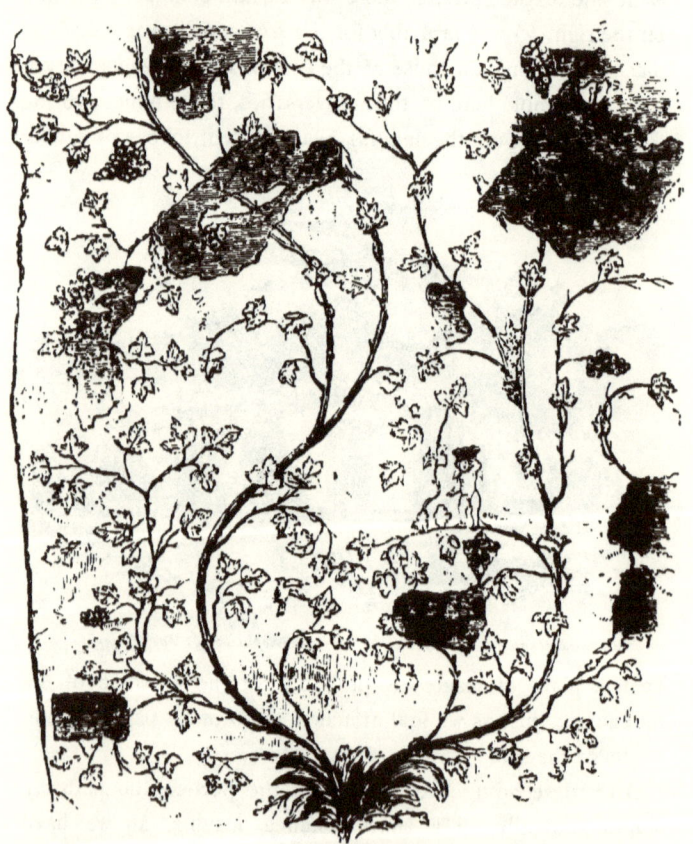

Fig. 10.—*Painting on roof of most ancient part of Cemetery of St Domitilla.*

In passing from the vestibule into the catacomb, we recognise the transition from the use of the sarcophagus to that of the common *loculus;* for the first two or three graves on either side, though really mere shelves in the wall, are so disguised

The Catacombs in the First Ages. 73

by painting on the outside as to present to passers-by the complete outward appearance of a sarcophagus. Some few of these graves are marked with the names of the dead, written in black on the largest tiles—just like those which we have seen in the most ancient part of the Catacomb of St Priscilla; and the inscriptions on the other graves are all of the simplest and oldest form. Lastly, the whole of the vaulted

FIG. 11.—*Fragment of Daniel in the Lions' Den, from most ancient part of Cemetery of St Domitilla.*

roof is covered with the most exquisitely graceful designs, of branches of the vine (with birds and winged genii among them) trailing with all the freedom of nature over the whole walls, not fearing any interruption by graves, nor confined by any of those lines of geometrical symmetry which characterise similar productions in the next century. Traces also of landscapes may be seen here and there, which are of rare occurrence anywhere in the Catacombs, though another specimen may be seen in the chamber assigned by De Rossi to Sts Nereus and Achilles. The Good Shepherd, an *Agape*, or the heavenly feast, a man fishing, and Daniel in the lions' den,* are the chief historical or allegorical representations of Christian mysteries which were painted here. Unfortunately they have been almost destroyed by persons attempting to detach them from the wall; a process which, while it effectually ruined them for those who should come after, can never have yielded anything but a handful of mortar and broken *tufa* to the plunderers themselves. Would that we could have seen this chamber or vestibule in its original condition! Perhaps we should have found, as De Rossi conjectures, that it was the very *memoria* of Flavius Clemens himself, the martyred consul, whose remains were afterwards translated to the Basilica of St Clement within the walls. At any rate we are quite sure that we have been here brought face to face with one of the earliest specimens of Christian subterranean burial in Rome.

We have now visited the principal Catacombs for which a claim is made to apostolic antiquity; and it will be well for us to take a brief review of the results that may be gathered from our visits. They may be stated thus:—

General conclusions from an examination of these cemeteries.

The local traditions of ancient Christian Rome have come down to us, partly embodied in the Acts of the Martyrs; partly in the stories that were told to foreigners visiting the city in the seventh and eighth centuries, and by them committed to writing in itineraries; partly in the "Books of Indulgences" and in the "Book of the Wonders of Rome," compiled both for the use of strangers and of citizens; partly also, but more sparingly, in the scattered notices of a few mediæval writers. From a diligent comparison of all these various authorities, it is

* The fragment which remains of this picture, and which is given on the preceding page, small as it is, displays a much higher skill in execution than any other representation of the same subject that we have seen throughout the Catacombs.

gathered that some five or six of the subterranean cemeteries of Rome were believed to have had their origin in apostolic times; and in every one of these instances, so far as we have an opportunity of examining them, something peculiar has been either noted by our predecessors, or seen by ourselves, which gives countenance to the tradition. When these peculiarities are brought together, they are found to be in perfect harmony, not only with one another, but also with what we should have been led to expect from a careful consideration of the period to which they are supposed to belong. The peculiarities are such as these:—paintings in the most classical style, and scarcely inferior in execution to the best specimens of cotemporary pagan art; a system of ornamentation in fine stucco such as has not yet been found in any Christian subterranean work later than the second century; crypts of considerable dimensions, not hewn out of the bare rock, but carefully, and even elegantly, built with pilasters and cornices of bricks or terra-cotta; no narrow galleries with shelf-like graves thickly pierced in their walls, but spacious *ambulacra*, with painted walls, and recesses provided only for the reception of sarcophagi; whole families of inscriptions, with classical names, and without any distinctly Christian forms of speech; and lastly, actual dates of the first or second century. It is impossible that such a marvellous uniformity of phenomena, collected with most patient accuracy from different and distant cemeteries on all sides of the city, and from authors writing at so many different periods, should be the result of accident or of preconceived opinion. There never was any opinion preconceived on the subject; or rather, the opinion that was in general vogue a few years ago was diametrically opposed to this. But the opinion which has now been enunciated by De Rossi, and is gaining universal acceptance among those who have an opportunity of examining the monuments for themselves, has been the result of careful observation; it is the fruit of the phenomena, not their cause. Whereas then former writers have always taken it for granted that the first beginnings of *Roma Sotterranea* must have been poor and mean and insignificant, and that any appearance of subterranean works on a large scale, or richly decorated, must necessarily belong to a later and more peaceful age, it is now certain that this statement cannot be reconciled with the monuments and facts that modern discovery has brought to light. All who have any knowledge of the history of the fine arts are agreed that the decorations of the many remarkable crypts lately discovered are much more ancient than those which form the great bulk of the paintings in the catacombs with which we were familiar before, and which have been always justly regarded as the work of the third century. Nor can any thoughtful and impartial judge fail to recognise in the social and political condition of the first Roman Christians, and in the laws and usages of Roman burial, an adequate cause for all that is thus thrown back on the first and second centuries. On the subject of Christian art we shall have to speak more fully hereafter, and the architectural analysis which we propose to give of a part of the cemetery of St Callixtus will furnish a convenient occasion for distinguishing the various features which characterise the work of successive periods in the construction of subterranean Rome.

Our present chapter will be fittingly concluded by some account of another cemetery, which, though we have no authentic record of the precise date of its commencement, was certainly in use in the middle or before the end of the second century; that is to say, it was made whilst yet there had been no legal interference, and (so far as we know) no outbreak of popular violence against the liberty of Christian burials. We have a right, therefore, to look for some, at least, of the same characteristics which we have already seen in the first and most ancient of the cemeteries, nor will this expectation be disappointed.

The Catacomb to which we refer is that of St Prætextatus, on

The Catacombs in the First Ages. 77

the Via Appia, nearly opposite to the Catacomb of St Callixtus. It has only lately been recovered. An accidental opening into it was effected in 1848, and as a painting of St Sixtus (identified by the legend SVSTVS) was found on one of the sepulchres, it was conjectured that this must be the cemetery of that martyr. In 1850 another crypt in it was brought to light, ornamented with some of the oldest and most classical paintings that had yet been seen; and in 1852, De Rossi read a paper to the *Pontificia Academia di Archeologia*, in which he argued, solely on topographical grounds—*i.e.*, on arguments derived from the position of the cemetery, as compared with other cemeteries, and with the descriptions given in the old itineraries—that this must certainly have been a part of the cemetery anciently known by the name of St Prætextatus, and which was famous as the scene of St Sixtus's martyrdom, and as the place of burial of St Januarius, the eldest of the seven sons of St Felicitas, who laid down their lives for Christ on July 10, A.D. 162; also of St Felicissimus and Agapitus, deacons of St Sixtus, and many others. At the same time, he insisted upon identifying the ruins of two buildings, the one round, the other rectangular, which still remain in the vineyard above ground, as having once been the *basilicæ* dedicated to Saints Tiburtius, Valerian, and Maximus, companions of the martyrdom of St Cecilia, and to St Zeno. Later discoveries completely established the truth of his reasoning. In 1857 the labourers employed in the Catacombs came here to seek for stones, tiles, or other materials for repairs which were being executed in St Callixtus', and in the course of their quest they opened a way to the ruins of a very large and beautiful crypt. As soon as De Rossi had scrambled through the opening, he looked about for the usual *arcosolium*; but of this there was no sign. Nevertheless, it was clear that the absence of this ordinary feature of a chapel in the Catacombs in no way detracted from its value, nor indicated that this was a chamber without a history. On the

St Prætextatus, on the Via Appia.

Its architecture and decoration of second century.

contrary, further and more careful examination revealed the fact that this crypt was not hewn out of the living rock, but that, though underground, it had been all built with solid masonry, and that its three sides had been originally intended only for three sarcophagi. It had once been lined throughout with Greek marble, and its internal face (towards the cemetery) was a piece of excellent yellow brickwork, ornamented with pilasters of the same material in red, and cornices of terra-cotta. The workmanship points clearly to an early date, and specimens of pagan architecture in the same neighbourhood enable us to fix the middle of the latter half of the second century (A.D. 175) as a very probable date for its erection. The Acts of the Saints explain to us why it was built with bricks, and not hewn out of the rock—viz., because the Christian who made it (St Marmenia) had caused it to be excavated immediately below her own house; and now that we see it, we understand the precise meaning of the words used by the itineraries describing it—viz., "a large square cavern, most firmly built" (*ingens antrum quadratum, et firmissimæ fabricæ*). The vault of the chapel is most elaborately painted, in a style by no means inferior to the best classical productions of the age. It is divided into four bands of wreaths, one of roses, another of corn-sheaves, a third of vine-leaves and grapes (and in all these, birds are introduced visiting their young in nests), and the last or highest, of leaves of laurel or the bay-tree. Of course these represent severally the seasons of spring, summer, autumn, and winter. The last is a well-known figure or symbol of death; and probably the laurel, as the token of victory, was intended to represent the new and Christian idea of the ever-lasting reward of a blessed immortality. Below these bands is another border, more indistinct, in which reapers are gathering in the corn; and at the back of the arch is a rural scene, of which the central figure is the Good Shepherd carrying a sheep upon his shoulders. This, however, has been destroyed by graves pierced through the wall and the rock behind it, from that eager desire, of which we shall have occasion to speak elsewhere, to bury the dead of a later generation as near as possible to the tombs of the martyrs. As De Rossi proceeded to examine these graves in detail, he could hardly

St Januarius, A.D. 162.

FIG. 12.—*Painting on Vault of an Arcosolium in Cemetery of St Prætextatus.*

believe his eyes when he read around the edge of one of them these words and fragments of words:—. . . *mi Refrigeri Januarius Agatopus Felicissim martyres*—" Januarius, Agapetus, Felicissimus, martyrs, refresh the soul of . . ." The words had been scratched upon the mortar whilst yet it was fresh, fifteen centuries ago, as the prayer of some bereaved relative for the soul of him whom he was burying here, and now they revealed to the antiquarian of the nineteenth century the secret he was in quest of—viz., the place of burial of the saints whose aid is here invoked; for the numerous examples to be seen in other cemeteries warrant us in concluding that the bodies of the saints, to whose intercession the soul of the deceased is here recommended, were at the time of his burial lying at no great distance, and the reader will have observed that they are three of the very martyrs whose relics once rendered famous the cemetery of St Prætextatus. De Rossi, therefore, really needed no further evidence in corroboration of the topographical outline which he had sketched five years before to the Roman archæologists; yet further evidence was in store for him, though it did not come to light until six years later, when the commission of Sacred Archæology were persuaded to take this cemetery as the special scene of their labours. Then, amid the soil which encumbered the entrance to this crypt, three or four fragments were discovered of a large marble slab, marked by a few letters of most certain Damasine form, but of unusual size. More fragments * have been discovered since, so that we are able to say with certainty that the whole inscription once stood thus :—

Damasine inscription.

St Quirinus, A.D. 130.

The excavations of the commission revealed the existence of another crypt on the opposite side of the gallery, which is still older than that of St Januarius; so that, whereas the martyrdom of St Januarius belongs to the year A.D. 162, De

* Only those letters, or parts of letters, which are in darker tints, have been found; but in inscriptions executed with such mathematical precision as these, they are quite enough to enable us to restore the whole.

Rossi does not fear to designate this second crypt as the probable burial-place of St Quirinus, somewhere about A.D. 130. We have no detailed account as yet of its contents or even its principal characteristics ; nor has it been possible, for want of funds, to continue the work of excavation in this cemetery. Most heartily do we repeat the wish, so modestly expressed by De Rossi,* that some generous souls could be found who would do for the advancement of Christian archæology in Rome what so many—and some of our own country, as the Duchess of Devonshire—have done there at various times in the interests of Pagan antiquity, viz., place funds at the disposal of the proper authorities to enable them to resume their suspended labours both here and elsewhere, and to begin them *de novo* in those many other places which our present improved knowledge, both of books and of the locality, enable us to point out as promising a plentiful harvest.

There is yet another catacomb belonging to the second century which deserves to be mentioned, though the particular portion of it which was of that date has undergone so much alteration since that time as to be no longer capable of recognition. It is recorded in the *Liber Pontificalis* that St Alexander, Bishop of Rome, who suffered martyrdom A.D. 132, was buried on the Via Nomentana, where he was beheaded, not far from the seventh milestone ; and there, accordingly, an ancient Christian cemetery was discovered some twelve or fourteen years since ; and amid its ruins a portion of an epitaph, or rather of an inscription set up in honour of St Alexander, in very ancient times, in a basilica which was then built over his grave, and has lately been restored. In the small subterranean galleries round this basilica, many of the *loculi* have remained undisturbed to the present day; but these scarcely belong to the oldest part of the cemetery. Moreover, this whole cemetery lay beyond the limit we have assigned to the Roman Catacombs proper ; and therefore we

St Alexander's, on Via Nomentana.

* *Bullettino*, 1865, 99.

do not at present care to examine it. We only mention it at all as an additional instance of the trustworthiness of the ancient documents whose guidance we have been following. We have seen how, in six several instances, an examination of the actual condition of a Catacomb most singularly confirms what the language of these old authorities taught us. There yet remain two or three others which are attributed by the same writers to the apostolic, or immediately post-apostolic times, but as these have not yet been identified, there is no occasion to enumerate them.

FIG. 12.—*Tombstone from the very ancient Crypt of St Lucina, now united with the Catacomb of St Callixtus.*

CHAPTER II.

HISTORY OF THE CATACOMBS FROM THE BEGINNING OF THE THIRD CENTURY TO CONSTANTINE'S EDICT OF PEACE, A.D. 312.

WE have now brought our history of the Catacombs down to the period when, as we said before, they first come under the express notice of the Roman law. The popular violence against the Christian burial-grounds in Africa, at the beginning of the third century,* reveals the fact of the Christians there possessing a common burial-place; and it is impossible to suppose that so great a Church as that of Rome should not also by this time have possessed some common cemetery. The *memoria* of St Peter must have been known to be the common burial-place of his successors; and, in fact, Caius, a priest of this same period, disputing with a heretic, Proclus, says, "I can show the *trophies* of the Apostles. For if you go to the Vatican, or to the Via Ostiensis, you will find the *trophies* of those who have laid the foundation of this Church." † It is a remarkable coincidence that the date of Tertullian's mention of the popular outbreak against the African Christian cemeteries, A.D. 202, should synchronise so exactly with the death of St Victor, the last Pope who was buried in the public *memoria* on the Vatican. Victor's successor, Zephyrinus, as we are informed by the author of the *Philosophumena*, "intrusted Callixtus with the government of the clergy, and set him over *the cemetery.*" ‡ These words naturally excite our curiosity, and require comment. What

Public Christian cemeteries.

Cemetery of St Callixtus, A.D. 200.

* See page 54.   † Euseb. Hist. Eccl. ii. 25.   ‡ Philosoph. ix. 11.

was *the* cemetery of Rome? Rome had already many cemeteries on all sides—of St Priscilla on the Via Salaria, of St Lucina on the Via Ostiensis, of St Prætextatus on the Via Appia, of St Domitilla on the Via Ardeatina, and several others. What was the distinction between them? and what was there so special and singular about any that it should have been put under the charge of one of the highest ecclesiastical authorities after the Pope, the same as was entrusted also with "the government of the clergy"? We shall have no difficulty in solving these questions, if we call to mind what was said in a former chapter* about the burial-confraternities in Rome, and the solemn renewal, or at least renewed publication of their rights and privileges, precisely at this time, by Septimius Severus. Let us set side by side with this fact the words of Tertullian, also written about the same time, in which he describes the Christian society as it might have appeared, and as he wished to make it appear, to their heathen neighbours and rulers. "There preside over us," he says, "certain approved elders, who have attained that honour, not by purchase, but by the good testimony of others. . . . And if there be any kind of treasury (*arcæ*) among us, it is made up, not of fees paid by these presidents or others on their appointment,† as if religion were bought and sold among us, but each person contributes a small sum once a month, or whenever he likes, and *if* he likes, and has the means. . . . All these contributions are, as it were, pious deposits; for they are spent, not on feasting, but on feeding the hungry, on burying the poor, on orphans, old men confined to their houses, and shipwrecked persons, and if any are condemned to the mines, or exiled, or in prison, provided only that it be on account of God's sect, these also become the foster-children of their confession," *i.e.*,

* See page 49.

† This has now been clearly ascertained from ancient inscriptions found in Africa and elsewhere, to be the true meaning of Tertullian's words, *de honoraria summa*, which have been the cause of so much perplexity to earlier commentators.—*Bullett.*, 1866, 11.

provided they suffer these punishments for the profession of Christianity, they are supported by the Church. *

It is clear from this passage, and from all that has been said elsewhere, that it would have been easy for the Roman Christians of the third century, under cover of a mere burial-confraternity, to make collections for other charitable purposes, and even to meet together for purposes of religious worship; and we can hardly doubt that they did so. Moreover, we know, from the history of St Laurence and many other sources, that the care of the poor and distribution of alms was the special province of one of the deacons. Indeed, the very office of deacon had been originally instituted for this purpose. But not the poor only, the clergy also received what was necessary for their sustenance out of this common chest, and the deacon kept the register (*matricula*) of their numbers and offices. By and by, in obedience to that law whereby the moral and the material life of any society are so intimately linked together, that he who provides for the one is sure to gain a powerful influence over the other, the first deacon grew into an archdeacon; that is to say, he became, in some sense, the guardian and judge of the other clergy, and his authority was inferior to none, save only the bishops. Hence it came to be almost a law in Rome, that on the death of the Pope, not a priest, but the first deacon, succeeded to the vacant see; and to promote this deacon to the priesthood was sometimes resented, because it seemed to shut the door against his attainment of the highest rank in the hierarchy.

These considerations will enable us to appreciate more justly the import of the words we have quoted from the author of the *Philosophumena*, viz., that St Zephyrinus " intrusted Callixtus with the government of the clergy, and set him over the cemetery." The Christian community in Rome was entering at this time upon a new phase of its existence; it availed itself of the protection which the laws afforded to

* Apol., c. 39.

certain corporate bodies, and, as those laws required,* one of its members was appointed as the agent, or syndic, in whose name the common property should be held, and by whom its business should be transacted. The cemetery, therefore, entrusted to Callixtus was one common to the Christians as a body; and it was "the cemetery on the Via Appia," which the *Liber Pontificalis* states that Callixtus "made, where many priests and martyrs repose, and which is called, even to the present day, the *cœmeterium Callixti.*" This also explains to us why henceforward the Popes were buried here, and no longer at the Vatican; out of the eighteen, from Zephyrinus to Sylvester, thirteen having certainly been laid in this cemetery, according to the testimony of the same *Liber Pontificalis.* And it is a striking confirmation of De Rossi's conjecture that this was the first common cemetery given to the Pope by some noble family for the whole Christian community, when we find that St Fabian, A.D. 238, "divided the regions among the Deacons, ... and ordered numerous buildings (*fabricas*) to be constructed in the *cemeteries.*"† It seems to imply that other wealthy Christians soon followed the example of those who had given the cemetery of Callixtus to the Church; and these *fabricæ* were probably little oratories constructed above the cemeteries, either for purposes of worship, or the celebration of the *agapæ*, or of mere guardianship of the tombs, according to the common practice of the Romans, of which we have probably seen an instance in the more ancient *fabricæ* attached to the Catacomb of St Domitilla. ‡ The long peace from the

Popes buried there.

Other cemeteries for common use of the Church.

---

* "Quibus permissum est *corpus* habere *collegii*, societatis *sive cujusque alterius eorum nomine*, proprium est ... habere res communes, arcam communem, et actorem sive syndicum, per quem, quod communiter agi fierique oporteat, agatur, fiat."—*Digest.* iii. 4, 1, § 1. Compare with this the words of the letter of Licinius and Constantine, (*apud* Lactant., De Mort. Persec., § 48, and Euseb., Hist. Eccl., x. 5) :—"Quoniam Christiani non ea loca tantum, ad quæ convenire consueverunt, sed alia etiam habuisse noscuntur, *ad jus corporis eorum, id est, Ecclesiarum, non hominum singulorum pertinentia,*" &c. Also the words, used in the case of Paul of Samosata, "τοῦ τῆς ἐκκλησίας οἴκου."—*Euseb. Hist. Eccl.* vii. 30.

† Lib. Pont., *Fabianus*.   ‡ See fig. 8, at page 71.

reign of Caracalla to that of Decius might well have encouraged the Christians to erect such buildings, and allowed them to make frequent use of them, notwithstanding occasional disturbances from popular violence, the short persecution of Maximin, and other similar interruptions.

In January A.D. 250, St. Fabian fell a victim to the persecution of Decius; but it does not appear either from the edicts of that Emperor, from ecclesiastical history, or from the Acts of the Martyrs, that Decius made any special decree against the cemeteries. Not so, however, in the persecution of Valerian, which broke out in A.D. 257. Although the edict itself has not come down to us, yet, from words spoken by Emilianus, Prefect of Alexandria,* and by Aspasius Paternus, Pro-consul of Africa, we learn that it forbade the sacred assemblies, and all visits to the sepulchres in the cemeteries. In fact, Pope Sixtus II. was, with his deacons and sacred ministers, (St Laurence was the chief of them, and we have seen the tombs of two others,†) hunted out, surprised, and beheaded in the cemetery of Prætextatus,‡ "because he had set at nought the commands of Valerian." §

A.D. 250. Persecution of Decius.

A.D. 257. Edict of Valerian forbidding visits to cemeteries;

In A.D. 260, Gallienus revoked the edicts of persecution, and sent throughout the empire a rescript by virtue of which the possessors of *loca religiosa* belonging to the Christians and confiscated by Valerian, were to make restitution to the bishops of each church. By *loca religiosa* seem to have been meant all churches or places of assembly; for besides this general order, he directed rescripts to particular bishops by which they might recover the free use of "what they call their *cemeteries*."|| And both the one and the other enter into the account which has reached us of the acts of Dionysius, the successor of Sixtus II.,

---

* "Neither you nor any others shall in anywise be permitted either to hold assemblies or to enter *what you call your cemeteries*." (These expressions prove the exclusively Christian origin of the word "cemetery.")— *Letter of St Dionysius of Alexandria in Euseb. Hist. Eccl.* vii. c. 11.
† See page 80.   ‡ St Cypr. Ep. 82.
§ Lib. Pont. || Euseb. Hist. Eccl., vii. c. 13.

of whom it is recorded,* that "he divided the churches and cemeteries among the priests, and constituted parishes and dioceses."

Hence came necessity of concealment. It was, however, only too evident to the Christians that henceforward they could not reckon upon the inviolability of their graves; and it is from this period that we must date those studious efforts to conceal the entrance to the cemeteries which are visible even now in the staircases leading from the *arenariæ*, and in other ways. Even at a much earlier period, Tertullian testifies to the occasional interruption of Christian worship by a sudden invasion of the heathen. "We are daily besieged," he says, "and betrayed and caught unawares in our very assemblies and congregations;"† and again, in another place, still addressing the heathen,‡ he says, "You know the days of our meetings; hence we are besieged, entrapped, and often detained in our most secret congregations." But it is specially to the latter half of the third century that those accounts belong which have come down to us of Christians being pursued and overtaken and sometimes martyred in the *arenariæ*. Thus, in an account preserved by St Gregory of Tours, we are told that, under Numerianus, the martyrs Chrysanthus and Daria were put to death in an *arenaria*, and that a great number of the faithful having been seen entering the subterranean crypt on the Via Salaria to visit their tombs, the heathen Emperor ordered the entrance to be hastily built up, and a vast mound of sand and stones to be heaped in front of it, so that they might be all buried alive, even as the martyrs whom they had come to venerate. St Gregory adds, that when the tombs of these martyrs were re-discovered, after the ages of persecution had ceased, there were found with them, not only the relics of those worshippers who had been thus cruelly put to death, skeletons of men, women, and children lying on the floor, but also the silver cruets (*urcei argentei*) which they had taken down with them for the celebration of the sacred mys-

Christians attacked in cemeteries.

Martyrdom in cemetery, A.D. 284.

* Lib. Pont., *Dionysius*. † Apol., vii. ‡ Ad Nationes, i. 7.

teries.* St Damasus was unwilling to destroy so touching a memorial of past ages. He abstained from making any of those changes by which he usually decorated the martyrs' tombs, but contented himself with setting up one of his invaluable historical inscriptions, and opening a window in the adjacent wall or rock, that all might see, without disturbing, this monument so unique in its kind—this Christian Pompeii in miniature. These things might still be seen in St Gregory's time, in the sixth century; and De Rossi holds out hopes that some traces of them may be restored even to our own generation,† some fragments of the inscription perhaps, or even the window itself through which our ancestors once saw so moving a spectacle, assisting, as it were, at a mass celebrated in the third century. Instances like these explain the common reproach of the Pagans at this time, that the Christians were "a skulking, darkness-loving race;"‡ and the numerous traditions of the same period, even though the authenticity of many of them may be doubtful, of Christians and even Popes§ taking refuge in the crypts, testify the importance attached by the faithful to their cemeteries, and the jealousy with which they were now regarded by their enemies.

<small>Catacombs used as hiding-places.</small>

The edicts of Aurelian, a little before his death, against the Church which he had legally recognised, even to the length of ordering the buildings occupied by Paul of Samosata at Antioch "to be given up into the hands of those in communion with Christian bishops of Italy and Rome,"|| show how precarious a security for the cemeteries was even that legal recognition; still we find the Christians taking courage, at the commencement of the reign of Diocletian, to pull down the

<small>From Aurelian to Diocletian.</small>

---

* St Greg., Turon., De Gloria Mart., i. c. 28.

† "Cette esperance est fondée; j'oserais presque dire, elle sera remplie," are De Rossi's words in " Rome dans sa Grandeur," part 2me, p. 6, Charpentier, Nantes.

‡ " Latebrosa et lucifugax natio."—*Minuc. Felix.*

§ "Caius . . . fugiens persecutionem Diocletiani in cryptis habitando, martyrio coronatur." *Lib. Pont.*

|| Euseb. Hist. Eccl., vii. c. 30.

old churches and to build new ones, and we shall presently see the deacon Severus about the same time constructing a large double sepulchral chamber, with its open light-hole, in the cemetery of St Callixtus.

Cemeteries confiscated, A.D. 303.

The storm of the tenth persecution, under Diocletian, burst upon the Church with frightful violence in A.D. 303. The churches erected during the peace were burned and demolished, the farms or gardens under which the cemeteries lay were confiscated; and though the acts of confiscation in Rome have perished, yet a significant trace of them is left in the fact that Pope Marcellinus, and his successor Marcellus, were neither of them buried in the Papal crypt of St Callixtus, but the former reposed in "a *cubiculum* which he himself had prepared in the cemetery of Priscilla:" and the latter "requested leave from a matron named Priscilla, and made a *cœmeterium* on the Via Salaria." And a vast region of the deepest level of that cemetery, of a lineal regularity hitherto unique in *Roma Sotterranea*, bears witness to the efforts of the Pope, while persecution was raging, to provide for the necessities of the faithful in some other place than that which had been discovered and forfeited to the Government, on the Via Appia.

Restored to Church, A.D. 311. Testimony of St Augustine.

At the close of A.D. 306, Maxentius put a stop to the persecution, but the property of the Church was not restored until the Pontificate of Melchiades, A.D. 311. St Augustine tells us that the Donatists "recited the Acts in which it was read how Melchiades sent deacons with the letters of the Emperor Maxentius and the letters of the Præfect of the prætorium to the Præfect of the city, that they might receive the property which the aforesaid Emperor had commanded to be restored to the Christians, as having been taken from them in time of persecution. . . . The Donatists said that the deacon Strato, whom Melchiades had sent with the rest to receive the *loca ecclesiastica*, was declared in the above acts to be a *traditor* and . . . the Donatists also calumniated Melchiades on account of Cassian, because this name is found also among the deacons whom Melchiades sent to the Præfect," &c.* In fact, this Pontiff having recovered the cemetery of St Callixtus through his deacons, two of whom were named Strato and Cassian, buried there the body of his predecessor Eusebius, who had died in exile in Sicily, and placed him in one of the largest crypts in the Catacomb. But even while the persecution was raging, Marcellus had provided, as best he could, for the re-organisation of the parishes and their cemeteries; for we read† that "he constituted the twenty-five *tituli* in the city of Rome as parishes (*diœceses*) for the reception by baptism and penance of the multitudes who were converted from among the Pagans, and for the burial-places of the martyrs."

Titles were, of course, of much older date than the time of Marcellus, though their number might have varied according to the increase in the number of the faithful. Thus, it is recorded in the *Liber Pontificalis*, that Evaristus, the sixth from St Peter, divided the *titles* in the city of Rome among the priests, and appointed seven deacons. St Fabian, nearly a century and a half later, is said by the same authority to have divided the fourteen regions of Rome among the deacons; and now Marcellus constitutes (or more probably restores) twenty five, which is the number most frequently met with in all the most ancient notices on the subject.‡ The objects which are contemplated in this arrangement are stated to be the administration of the sacraments and the burial of the dead; and this is not the only occasion on which we learn from authentic records that the care of the cemeteries entered into the details of ecclesiastical management. It seems probable that, at least from the time of St Fabian, each *title* within the city had its corresponding cemetery or cemeteries, outside the walls, and the priest or priests of the title had jurisdiction over the cemetery also. In the time of St Damasus, each church had

Titles, or parish churches,

had each its own cemetery.

---

* St Aug. Brev. Coll. cum Donat., iii. 34-36.   † Lib. Pont.
‡ Blanchinii, Anast. Vit. Pont., ii. 37.

two priests,* and even in the days of St Cyprian† we find two priests attached to the same church, one as a subordinate to the other. If we might suppose the number of *titles* in the time of St Cornelius to have been twenty-three, (or, if more, that some of them were vacant,) this would account for the number of Roman priests, which he sets down at forty-six,‡ two for each *title*, one of whom might well have ministered at the *cella* or oratory (in later times *basilica* §) above the cemetery, whilst the other ministered in the city. It is not difficult to understand, after what has been said upon the Roman law respecting burials and burial-confraternities, how this system of administration might, under ordinary circumstances, have been carried on without any interference from the Government, even during the ages of persecution. And perhaps the following inscription on a grave-stone, in the cemetery of St Domitilla, may be quoted in illustration and confirmation of the theory that is here suggested, *jussu* being the official expression in use among the heathen magistrates of that time for a command or permission given by one having jurisdiction, and Archelaus and Dulcitus being the two priests of the *title* to which that cemetery belonged.

ALEXIVS ET CAPRIOLA FECERVNT SE VIVI
IVSSV ARCHELAI ET DVLCITI PRESBB

Moreover, if we suppose, as we very reasonably may, that the

---

* " Nunc autem septem diaconos esse oportet et aliquantos presbyteros, ut bini sint per Ecclesias."—*Ambros.* [Hilar.], in 1 Tim. iii.

† Ep. xviii., "Felix qui presbyterium subministrabat sub Decimo."

‡ "There were forty-six priests, seven deacons, seven sub-deacons, forty-two acolytes, exorcists, lectors, and ostiarii, in all fifty-two ; widows, with the afflicted and needy, more than 1500, all of which the goodness and love of God doth nourish."—Cornelius to Fabius of Antioch, *apud* Euseb.. H. E., vi. 43. See also the "*quadraginta et quod excurrit basilicas*," mentioned by Optatus, c. Don. ii. 4.

§ This name seems to have been in occasional use from the days of Diocletian.—*R. S.* i. 205.

Popes who succeeded Zephyrinus continued to retain the cemetery of St Callixtus under their own immediate jurisdiction, administered by their chief deacon (or archdeacon, as he was afterwards called), we have another illustration of the same system in the following inscription, belonging to the time of Marcellinus, which records that Severus, his deacon, made, *by the permission of his Pope,* (*jussu papæ sui,*) a double chamber, with arched tombs and light-hole, for himself and his relations :— *Cemetery of St Callixtus under the direct care of the Pope.*

> CVBICVLVM DVPLEX CVM ARCISOLIIS ET LVMINARE
> IVSSV PP SVI MARCELLINI DIACONVS ISTE
> SEVERVS FECIT MANSIONEM IN PACE QVIETAM
> SIBI SVISQVE. . . .

It would be easy to show, from a multitude of testimonies belonging to the fifth and sixth centuries, that each suburban cemetery was at that time dependent on some particular parish within the walls. But about this there can be no dispute. It is only when we seek to penetrate the thick darkness which envelopes the history of the earlier ages, that it is difficult to find clear and abundant proofs; and the precise province of an archæologist is to supply these deficiencies, not out of his own imagination, but by acute and cautious induction, based on a most careful examination of every fragment that remains. If we set before a skilful professor of comparative anatomy a few bones dug out of the bowels of the earth, he will reconstruct the whole form of the animal to which they belonged; and it often happens that these theoretical constructions are singularly justified by later discoveries. The work of an archæologist is much of the same kind. An historian only rearranges, transcribes, or interprets annals already composed and faithfully transmitted by his predecessors. He may have to gather his materials from various sources; must be able to distinguish the true from the false, and give form, consistency, and life to the whole; but, for the most part at least, he has little to supply that is new from his own resources. An archæologist, on the contrary, if he be really a man of learning and *Reflections on this portion of the history of the Catacombs.*

science, and not a mere collector of old curiosities, aims at discovering and restoring annals that are lost, by means of a careful and intelligent use of every fragment, often of heterogeneous materials, that the most unwearied diligence has been able to bring together.

This remark seems not uncalled for, at the end of a chapter in which we have professed to set before our readers a continuous history of the subterranean cemeteries of Rome during the ages of persecution, and even to unfold the system of their ecclesiastical administration. Such a history has never been written before, and some readers may be disposed to think that even now the materials for it are too scanty. De Rossi frankly acknowledges that each fact that he has been able to collect, if taken alone, throws but a faint and uncertain light upon the obscurity of the subject; but he justly argues that the wonderful harmony which he has been able to establish between facts and documents, so unlike one another, and separated so far asunder, both in point of time and place, are a very strong presumption of truth. The "Lives of the Popes," compiled in the seventh or eighth century; the *Philosophumena*, written in a spirit of bitter personal hatred against a Pope of the third century, and only brought to light in the nineteenth; sepulchral inscriptions also, of the third century, in like manner unknown before our own time; ecclesiastical historians and learned commentators of different times and countries; each of these has been made by De Rossi to contribute its quota to this chapter of history as it stands in his own voluminous work; and even in this imperfect abridgment of it, the readers will have been struck with the number and variety of fragments out of which so complete a skeleton, if we ought not rather to say so full and life-like a body, has been composed.

CHAPTER III.

FROM THE EDICT OF MILAN, A.D. 312, TO THE SACK OF ROME BY THE GOTHS, A.D. 410.

WITH the conversion of Constantine and the Edict of Milan a new era opens in the history of the Catacombs. Melchiades, the first Pope who sat in the Lateran, was the last who was buried in the subterranean cemetery of St Callixtus—*in cœmeterio Callixti in crypta*. Sylvester, his successor, had his sepulchre *in cœmeterio Priscillæ*, not, however, *in crypta*, but in a basilica, which, having always preserved his name, had probably been built by him. The next Pontiff, Mark, was in like manner buried *in cœmeterio Balbinæ*, explained by the *Liber Pontificalis* to be a *basilica quam cœmeterium constituit;* that is to say, he probably built a small basilica or *cella memoriæ*, near the entrance of a subterranean cemetery already existing, to which he now assigned its own priest and guardian, as the other principal cemeteries had already had. Other instances might be given to show that the cemeteries in which succeeding Pontiffs are said to have been buried were really basilicas above ground; and though subterranean burial continued to be practised, yet the example set by the Pontiffs was not long in being followed, and graves within and around the basilicas gradually superseded the *loculi* of the Catacombs. The inscriptions with consular dates probably furnish us with a sufficiently accurate guide to the relative proportions of the two modes of burial. From A.D. 338 to A.D. 360 two out of three burials appear to have taken place in the subterranean portion of the cemeteries, while from A.D. 364 to A.D. 369 the proportions are equal. During the next two years hardly any

Gradual disuse of subterranean cemeteries after peace was given to the Church.

notices of burials *above* ground appear, but after that the subterranean crypts fall rapidly into disuse. This marked and sudden change demands an explanation, and history at once supplies it.

Basilicas erected over tombs of martyrs,

The first care of the Christians, when peace and liberty had been secured to the Church by the conversion of Constantine, was to honour those illustrious martyrs whose bodies lay concealed in the recesses of the various Catacombs. Basilicas more or less sumptuous began to be erected over their sepulchres, and as the faithful shrank from disturbing their original resting-places, it became the ordinary custom to cut away the surface of the ground on the side of the hill in which the galleries had been excavated, and thus gain access to the martyr's tomb.

caused much damage to Catacombs.

The Vatican hill behind St Peter's, the hill opposite to St Paul's outside the walls, the galleries and chambers still visible in the hill cut away for the site of San Lorenzo in Agro Verano, are witnesses to this practice. Sometimes, as in St Agnese *fuori le mura*, it was necessary to go down to a great depth; for the martyrs had perhaps been buried in the second floor of the Catacomb; and hence the long flight of steps by which we descend to that church at the present day. Such a wholesale sacrificing of hundreds of graves for the sake of one illustrious sepulchre must have been displeasing to many; and St Damasus in particular, ardently as he laboured in the search for the bodies and the furthering of the devotion to the remains of the martyrs, yet found means to encourage that devotion without destroying the character of the subterranean cemeteries. When the cemeteries had been taken from the Christians, and made over to other hands by Diocletian, there is evidence to show that the Church provided for the inviolability of the tombs of her more venerated heroes by blocking up the galleries which led to them; and it was a labour of love in after-years to re-discover[*] these tombs,

Devotion of St Damasus to Catacombs;

---

[*] "Quæritur, inventus colitur" is the language of St Damasus' inscriptions.

The Catacombs in the Fourth Century. 97

the precise situation of which was only known by tradition. St Damasus then removed the earth, widened the passages so as to make them more serviceable for the crowd of pilgrims, constructed flights of stairs leading to the more illustrious shrines, and adorned the chambers with marbles, opening shafts to admit air and light where practicable, and supporting the friable *tufa* walls and galleries, wherever it was necessary, with arches of brick and stone work. Almost all the catacombs bear traces of his labours, and modern discovery is continually bringing to light fragments of the inscriptions which he composed in honour of the martyrs, and caused to be engraved on marble slabs, in a peculiarly beautiful character, by a very able artist, Furius Dionysius Filocalus. It is a singular fact that no original inscription of Pope Damasus has ever yet been found executed by any other hand, nor have any inscriptions been found, excepting those of Damasus, in precisely the same form of letters. Hence the type is well known to students of Christian epigraphy as the Damasine characters.* [his labours and inscriptions.]

Now, the sudden return to the subterranean mode of burial in the years A.D. 370, 371, exactly corresponds with the time of the labours of St Damasus, and it is obvious to conjecture, that the faithful who visited the tombs of the martyrs, came away with a desire to lay their own bones beside theirs. Some, as the priest St Barbazianus, even made little cells underground, and led the lives of hermits in their immediate neighbourhood, and all were assiduous in visiting them. St Jerome gives a vivid description of a devout Roman youth's feelings on such a visit; but his words seem more immediately applicable to the ordinary condition of the common galleries, than to any that had been specially decorated by the Pope. "When I was a boy," he writes, "being educated at Rome, I used every Sunday, in company with other boys of my own age and tastes, to visit the tombs of the apostles and martyrs, [Catacombs as places of pilgrimage. St Jerome, A.D. 354.]

* Specimens may be seen in Plates I. and III. at the end of the volume.

and to go into the crypts excavated there in the bowels of the earth. The walls on either side as you enter are full of the bodies of the dead, and the whole place is so dark, that one seems almost to see the fulfilment of those words of the prophet, 'Let them go down alive into Hades.' Here and there a little light, admitted from above, suffices to give a momentary relief to the horror of the darkness; but as you go forwards, and find yourself again immersed in the utter blackness of night, the words of the poet come spontaneously to your mind: 'The very silence fills the soul with dread.'"* On the contrary, the words of the poet Prudentius, written about the same time, clearly commemorate the results of some such labours as we have been describing those of St Damasus to have been. He is writing of the tomb of St Hippolytus, and his description runs thus:—

Prudentius on cemetery of St Hippolytus.

"Not far from the city walls, among the well-trimmed orchards, there lies a crypt buried in darksome pits. Into its secret recesses a steep path with winding stairs directs one, even though the turnings shut out the light. The light of day, indeed, comes in through the doorway, as far as the surface of the opening, and illuminates the threshold of the portico; and when, as you advance further, the darkness as of night seems to get more and more obscure throughout the mazes of the cavern, there occur at intervals apertures cut in the roof which convey the bright rays of the sun upon the cave. Although the recesses, twisting at random this way and that, form narrow chambers with darksome galleries, yet a considerable quantity of light finds its way through the pierced vaulting down into the hollow bowels of the mountain. And thus throughout the subterranean crypt it is possible to perceive the brightness and enjoy the light of the absent sun. To such secret places is the body of Hippolytus conveyed, near to the spot where now stands the altar dedicated to God. That same altar-slab (*mensa*) gives the

* St Hieron. in Ezech. c. lx.

sacrament, and is the faithful guardian of its martyr's bones, which it keeps laid up there in expectation of the eternal Judge, while it feeds the dwellers of the Tiber with holy food. Wondrous is the sanctity of the place! the altar is at hand for those who pray, and it assists the hopes of men by mercifully granting what they need. Here have I, when sick with ills both of soul and body, oftentimes prostrated myself in prayer and found relief. Yes, O glorious priest! I will tell with what joy I return to enjoy the privilege of embracing thee, and that I know that I owe all this to Hippolytus, to whom Christ, our God, has granted power to obtain whatever any one asks of him. That little chapel (*ædicula*) which contains the cast-off garments of his soul [his relics] is bright with solid silver. Wealthy hands have put up tablets glistening with a smooth surface [of silver], bright as a concave mirror; and, not content with overlaying the entrance with Parian marble, they have lavished large sums of money on the ornamentation of the work." He goes on to describe the pilgrimages to the shrine, and with somewhat of poetic licence continues: "Early in the morning they come to salute [the saint]: all the youth of the place worship there: they come and go until the setting of the sun. Love of religion collects together into one dense crowd both Latins and foreigners; they imprint their kisses on the shining silver; they pour out their sweet balsams; they bedew their faces with tears." His description of the scene on the *festa* of the martyr, his *dies natalis*, reminds one forcibly of the way in which the modern Romans stream out to San Lorenzo, or to San Paolo *fuori le mura*, or to any other of the old churches, when a festival or a station is held there. "The imperial city vomits forth her stream of Romans, and the plebeian crowd, animated by one and the same desire, jostle on equal terms their patrician neighbours, faith hurrying them forward to the shrine. Albano's gates, too, send forth their white-robed host in a long-drawn line. The noise on the various roads on all sides waxes loud: the native of the Abruzzi and the Etruscan

[marginal notes:] Shrine richly decorated, and devoutly visited.

Scene on the *festa* of the saint.

100   *Roma Sotterranea.*

peasant come, the fierce Samnite, the countryman of lofty Capua and of Nola, is there; each with his wife and children delights to hasten on his road. The broad fields scarcely suffice to contain the joyful people, and even where the space is wide, the crowd is so great as to cause delay. No doubt, then, that that cavern, wide though its mouth be stretched, is too narrow for such crowds; but hard by is another church (*templum*), enriched with royal magnificence, which this great gathering may visit;"* and then follows the description of a basilica, supposed by many to be the basilica of San Lorenzo in Agro Verano.

Damage done to Catacombs by indiscreet devotion. This devotion to the cemeteries, which, as we have seen, caused them to be used again as burial-places so frequently in the time of St Damasus, was not always regulated by prudence. In the anxiety of Christians to be buried as near as possible to the saints, they excavated *loculi* at the back of the *arcosolia*, not sparing even the most beautiful paintings with which their forefathers had adorned them. They destroyed the symmetry of the chapels with new monuments and sarcophagi, and often endangered the safety of the constructions by indiscreet excavations. One ancient inscription speaks of "a new crypt behind the saints," in which two ladies bought a *bisomum* for themselves during their lifetime from two *fossores*.

Examples.

      IN CRYPTA NOBA RETRO SAN
      CTVS EMERVM SE VIVAS BALER
      RA ET SABINA MERVM LOC
      V BISOM AB APRONE ET A
      BIATORE

Here is another inscription which testifies to a similar purchase "from Quintus the *fossor*," of a single grave near St Cornelius.

      SEREPENTIV
      S EMIT LOC
      M A QUINTO
      FOSSORE AD
      SANTVM C
      RNELIVM

---

* Prudent. Peristeph. xi. ll. 153, &c.

A third records the purchase of a grave for a father and mother and one daughter, "above the *arcosolium*," at the very tomb of St Hippolytus, of which we have heard so much from Prudentius (*at Ippolytv svper arcosoliv*).

A fourth inscription of the year 381 (during the Pontificate of Damasus) tells us of one who obtained the privilege of burial "within the thresholds of the saints, a thing which many desire and few obtain" (*intra limina sanctorum, quod multi cupiunt et rari accipiunt*). *

It appears that, at this time, the work of excavation was no longer continued at the public expense under the special care of the parish priests, but that it was left as a matter of private bargain between the deceased's friends and the *fossores*. No vestige of contracts of this kind with *fossors* has been found earlier than the last years of the fourth century, and no record of the existence of this body of men has come to light later than the first quarter of the fifth century. But the monuments are very numerous during this short period which testify to their having had in their own hands the disposal of new graves in the Catacombs. It is no longer *jussu* of the Pope or of the priests that such and such a tomb has been made, but the names of both buyers and sellers are recorded on the tombstone, together with the witnesses to the contract, and even the price that was paid; and the sellers are always *fossors*. It is generally supposed that the *fossors* were themselves clerics, the lowest order in the hierarchy. But even though it should be considered that there is not sufficient ground for this opinion, yet, at least, it is obvious, that, in the earlier ages, they must have been on very intimate relations with the clergy, and, no doubt, were supported by the Church, whose most devoted and laborious servants they were. It is not difficult, therefore, to understand how, under the altered circumstances of the times, the whole matter had been allowed to fall more entirely under their management. Nevertheless, we must be

They are under the management of the fossors, not of the priests.

* Inscr. Christ. i. 142.

allowed to regret that they should not have used a more wholesome severity in withstanding the pious but indiscreet desires of the faithful. How common those desires were is sufficiently attested, not only by these and other similar inscriptions, but still more by the fact that it forms the subject of a long letter, or short treatise, by the great St Augustine, written at the request of his friend, St Paulinus of Nola, in which he explains and justifies them.* Nevertheless we may easily imagine the displeasure with which so ardent a lover of the cemeteries as St Damasus would regard a system which tended to their destruction. His own example spoke more eloquently than any words could do. No one had a greater right to be buried there than he, and yet he was content to build himself a tomb *above* the cemetery of St Callixtus, and to write upon a tablet in the papal crypt the reason for his not being buried within it :—

HIC FATEOR DAMASVS VOLVI MEA CONDERE MEMBRA,
SED TIMVI SANCTOS CINERES VEXARE PIORVM.

"Here I, Damasus, wished to bury my limbs, but I was afraid of disturbing the holy ashes of the saints." †

The archdeacon Sabinus, in his epitaph lately found at San Lorenzo, tells the faithful plainly, that the only way to obtain a place near the saints is to imitate their lives :—

NIL JVVAT IMMO GRAVAT TVMVLIS HÆRERE PIORVM
SANCTORVM MERITIS OPTIMA VITA PROPE EST.
CORPORE NON OPVS EST, ANIMA TENDAMVS AD ILLOS
QVÆ BENE SALVA POTEST CORPORIS ESSE SALVS.

"It nothing helps, but rather hinders, [merely] to stick close to the tombs of the saints; a good life is the best approach to the saints' merits. Not with the body, but with the soul, we must make our way to them; when that is well saved, it may prove the salvation of the body also." ‡

Rapid disuse of Catacombs for burial. Whether in consequence of any direct prohibition, or merely from difficulties being put in the way, whatever cause may have produced the result, the evidence of the dated inscriptions makes

* See Note D. in Appendix. † Rom. Sott. i. 214.
‡ *Bullettino*, 1864, 33.

The Catacombs in the Fourth Century. 103

it clear, that after the brief *furore* for subterranean interment during the years 370 and 371 there was a rapid disuse of that mode of burial. Between A.D. 373 and 400, the subterranean epitaphs are only one out of three. From A.D. 400 to 409, the decrease is still more rapid, until, after A.D. 410, scarcely a single certain example is to be found.* In that fatal year, to use the language of St Jerome, "The brightest light of all the world was extinguished; the Roman empire lost its head; and, to speak more truly, in one city the whole world perished."† Rome was taken by Alaric; the citizens were reduced, many by slaughter, some by captivity, all by loss of wealth, and there was neither time nor means to adorn the sepulchres or even to pay the customary honours to the departed.

Rome taken by Alaric, A.D. 410.

* Inscr. Christ. i. 117, &c.
† Hieron. Proleg. in lib. i. Ezech. v. 16, ed. Migne.

FIG. 14.—*Fresco in one of the oldest Cubicula of the Crypts of St Lucina.*

CHAPTER IV.

FROM THE YEAR A.D. 410 UNTIL THEIR FINAL ABANDONMENT.

A.D. 410. Catacombs abandoned as burial-places.

SERIOUS as was the ruin and damage done to the Eternal City by the Goths in A.D. 410, yet neither then nor at their second sack of Rome, in A.D. 457, do we find any record of their having destroyed either the cemeteries or the basilicas of the martyrs. Still the use of the subterranean cemeteries as places of burial was never after this resumed, and the inscriptions and notices which seem to refer to them will, on closer examination, be found to relate to basilicas and cemeteries above ground. The *fossors'* occupation was gone, and after A.D. 426 their name ceases to be mentioned. The liturgical books of the fifth century refer constantly, in the prayers for the dead and benediction of graves, to burials in and around the basilicas, never to the subterranean cemeteries.

Still frequented as shrines.

The Catacombs, however, though they ceased to be used for burial, yet continued to be frequented as shrines and places of pilgrimage. Occasionally, in times of popular tumult, they seem to have been used also as places of refuge. Thus Boniface I. was concealed for a time in the Cemetery of St Felicitas, which he afterwards ornamented.* Pope Symmachus, towards the end of the fifth century, is said, in one copy of the *Liber Pontificalis*, to have restored and beautified the cemeteries of

A.D. 537. Profaned by Goths under Vitiges.

the martyrs. The irruption of the Goths under Vitiges, in A.D. 537, carried havoc even into the peaceful sanctuaries of the saints.† As soon, however, as the storm passed over, Pope

* Lib. Pont.
† "Ecclesiæ et corpora Martyrum exterminata sunt a Gothis."—*Lib. Pont.*

Vigilius repaired the damage which, we are told, saddened him to see, and replaced some of the broken epitaphs of St Damasus by copies, often very imperfect, some of which still remain.* About this time, when necessity had compelled the citizens to relax the strictness of the ancient laws against burying within the walls, cemeteries began to be formed on the Esquiline and on the site of the old Prætorian camp. It was becoming dangerous to venture far outside the walls.

The Pontiffs, however, continued their care for the ancient cemeteries. John III., about A.D. 568, "restored the cemeteries of the holy martyrs, and ordered that oblations, cruets, and candles [for the holy sacrifice] should be supplied from the Lateran Palace throughout the cemeteries every Sunday."† This was after the desolation of Rome by Totila. But the return to the old custom of the priests of the city-title serving the extra-mural cemetery every Sunday did not last long. It is recorded in the seventh century, to the special praise of Sergius I., that, "during the time of his priesthood, he used diligently to celebrate the solemnities of mass through different cemeteries." ‡ As *titular* of St Susanna, he would, according to the ancient practice, have been confined to the cemetery belonging to that title. Sixty years later, about A.D. 735, Gregory III., a zealous restorer and builder of churches, "instituted a body of priests to celebrate masses every week, and arranged that in

Repaired by the care of Popes. Mass said there.

---

* *e.g.*, The inscription in honour of Eusebius in the cemetery of San Callisto, presently to be seen. A copy of some verses of Pope Vigilius, referring to this practice, may be seen in the third column of the collection in the gallery at the Lateran. It runs thus :—

" Dum peritura Getæ posuissent castra sub urbem,
　Moverunt Sanctis bella nefanda prius.
　Totaque sacrilego verterunt corde sepulcra,
　Martyribus quondam rite sacrata piis.
　Quos monstrante Deo Damasus sibi Papa probatos
　Affixo monuit *carmine* jure coli.
　Sed *periit titulus confracto marmore sanctus*,
　Nec tamen his iterum posse latere fuit.
　Diruta Vigilius nam posthæc Papa gemiscens,
　Hostibus expulsis *omne novavit opus*."

† Lib. Pont.　　　　　　　　‡ Ib.

the cemeteries situated all round Rome, the lights for keeping the vigils on the days of their *natalitia*, and the oblation for the celebration of the masses, should be carried down from the palace by the *oblationarius*, through whom the Pontiff would name the priest who should officiate on the occasion."*

<small>A.D. 756. First translation of bodies of saints from Catacombs,</small>

There is ground for supposing that some few bodies of saints had been in Rome, as we know they were in other cities,† removed from their original resting-places to churches prepared for their reception, even as early as the fifth century. ‡ One of the itineraries, which describes the martyrs' shrines, distinctly mentions the bodies of some saints being in basilicas above ground, whom we know to have been originally buried in the subterranean cemeteries. It was, however, with great reluctance, and not until after the devastations and sacrileges committed by the Lombards under Astolphus, A.D. 756, that

<small>by Paul I.</small>

Paul I., elected in the following year, resolved upon translating on a large scale the relics of the saints, in order to save them from profanation.

In a constitution, dated June 2, 761, he complains that, whereas, even before the siege of Rome by Astolphus, some of these subterranean cemeteries had been neglected and ruined, yet by the impious Lombards this ruin had now been made more complete; for they had broken open the graves and carried off some bodies of the saints. " From that time forward," he says, "people have been very slothful and negligent in paying due honour to the cemeteries; animals have been allowed to have access to them; even folds have been purposely set up in them, so that they have been defiled with all

---

* Lib. Pont.

† *e.g.*, Milan in the time of St Ambrose.

‡ Rom. Sott. i. 219. In the "Sacramentary of St Leo," in the Preface for Saints John and Paul, it is said, "Of Thy merciful providence Thou hast vouchsafed to crown not only the circuit of the city with the glorious passions of the martyrs, but also to hide in the very heart of the city itself the victorious limbs of Saints John and Paul." This looks as if these martyrs were then the only saints whose bodies rested within the walls; and *they* had never been anywhere else.

sorts of corruption. Seeing, then, and deeply lamenting this careless indifference to such holy places, I have thought it good, with God's help, to remove the bodies of the martyrs and confessors and virgins of Christ, and with hymns and spiritual songs I have brought them into this city of Rome, and I have placed them in the church which I have lately built, in honour of St Stephen and St Sylvester, on the site of the house in which I was born and bred, which has now descended to me by inheritance from my father." Lists of the saints, whose relics were thus translated, have come down to us,* and there must have been more than a hundred in all.

The example set by Paul was not followed by either of his immediate successors, Stephen III. or Adrian I.; in fact, the latter strained every nerve to bring back the ancient honour and magnificence of the cemeteries. Nearly all of them bore witness to his zeal; and his restorations were continued by his successor, Leo III.† Notwithstanding all the efforts of these Popes to revive the interest in these sacred crypts, Paschal I. was constrained to imitate the example of Paul, because the crypts of the martyrs were being destroyed and abandoned. The inscription in Sta Prassede still attests how he translated thither two thousand three hundred bodies on July 20, 817. Sergius II. and Leo IV. continued the same work, for the greater dignity of the churches which they had either built or restored, viz., SS. Silvestro and Martino, and Santi Quattro Coronati; they also re-translated to these churches relics which had already been removed from the Catacombs and deposited elsewhere in Rome. To these times also doubtless belongs the account of many cart-loads of relics of martyrs being carried to the Pantheon; a record which has been confounded with that of the *reliquiæ* placed there by Boniface IV. long before the tombs in the subterranean cemeteries were touched.

^{margin:} Paschal I. and others.

* Mai. Script. Vet. v. 56.
† See the long enumeration of their works in Lib. Pont. xcvii. xcviii.

Final abandonment of Catacombs.

All the documents which mention these translations assign the cause of them to the abandonment and ruin of the cemeteries; and, of course, the translations, in their turn, still further hurried forward and completed the work of ruin and abandonment. The sacred treasures which had caused them to be regarded with so much love and veneration having been removed, there was no longer the same motive for protecting or ornamenting them; and thus the first half of the ninth century may be said to have ended the history of the Catacombs as shrines or places of pilgrimage, just as the beginning of the fifth had ended their history as cemeteries. Pope Nicholas I., A.D. 860, is said to have visited them, and to have restored in some of them the celebration of mass (*quod multos per temporum cursus ab eo discesserit*); and in the eleventh and twelfth centuries we still read of visits to the cemeteries, and of lamps kept burning in some of them which were near to monasteries. But these insignificant exceptions to the general oblivion into which they fell are the last and only records which remain to us of any attempt to keep up the ancient glories of the Catacombs of Rome. Henceforward only those in the vicinity of some church or monastery were visited out of curiosity by occasional travellers, as we find the cemetery of St Valentine, on the Via Flaminia, noticed by a pilgrim of the eleventh, and again by a writer of the twelfth century. Like the cemetery of St Agnes, it lay under property belonging to the Augustinian Order, and hence was not utterly lost sight of. In a statistical account of the Roman churches and clergy, written in the fourteenth century, only three of the suburban churches attached to the cemeteries are mentioned, viz., those of St Hermes, St Valentine, and St Saturninus. When we come to the fifteeenth century even these disappear, and only one subterranean cemetery remained always open and frequented by pilgrims, the same which may still be seen beneath the Church of St Sebastian, and which was called in all ancient documents, *cœmeterium ad catacumbas*.

The Catacombs Rifled and Abandoned. 109

This is an important fact to be noticed, because it accounts both for the use of this word, *Catacomb*, as applied to the Roman cemeteries, and also for the very grave topographical error respecting the cemetery of St Callixtus, which has perplexed and misled all Roman archæologists until the present day. The earliest document now extant in which the word *catacumbas* is used as descriptive of the locality of St Sebastian's belongs to the sixth century, where we read in a list of the Roman cemeteries *cimeterium catecumbas ad St Sebastianum Via Appia*. But it was used before this, apparently, as the name of that part of the campagna in which St Sebastian's is situated, for the Roman circus built by Maxentius, and whose ruins in this neighbourhood are so well known, was anciently called the *circus ad catacumbas*. When, then, the locality of the other Roman cemeteries was forgotten, and this alone remained known, (because it was still open, and always retained its place in the *Libri Indulgentiarum*, composed at various times and in different languages for the use of pilgrims,) the names of all the other cemeteries, occurring so frequently in the Martyrologies and Lives of the Popes, appear to have been ignorantly confused with this particular spot; a visit to the cemeteries became synonymous with a visit *ad catacumbas*, and the term Catacomb gradually came to be regarded as the specific name for all subterranean excavations for purposes of burial, not only in the neighbourhood of Rome, but also in Naples, Malta, Paris, Sicily, and wherever else similar excavations have been discovered.

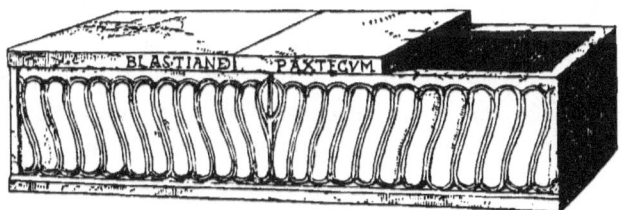

FIG. 15.—*Very ancient Sarcophagus, found in Crypt of St Lucina.*

Origin of the name "Catacomb."

BOOK III.

CATACOMB OF ST CALLIXTUS.

CHAPTER I.

ITS DISCOVERY AND IDENTIFICATION.

Pre-eminence of the Via Appia, both in Pagan and Christian Rome. "IN the history of Pagan Rome," says Father Marchi,* "the Via Appia bears the proud title of Queen of Roman roads; and it makes this boast with good reason, both because of the grander scale on which it was constructed, the greater magnificence of the buildings and sepulchres which adorned it, the greater variety of conquered nations who used it, and the number and celebrity of the events connected with it. The history of Christian Rome gives to this same road titles of glory incomparably more solid, just, and indisputable. We are forced to acknowledge it as the Queen of Christian roads, by reason of the greater number and extent of its cemeteries, and still more for the greater number and celebrity of its martyrs." And in another place † he speaks of one of the cemeteries upon this road as standing to other cemeteries much in the same relation as St Peter's to other churches; he says it is "the colossal region of *Roma Sotterranea*, all the others are only small or middling provinces." Unfortunately

* Monum. Art Crist. Prim. 73. † P. 172.

the plan of his own work was complete, and most of it already executed, before he effected an entrance into the cemeteries which so strongly impressed his imagination; and the wonders we have now to narrate have been the discovery of De Rossi. Indeed this has been the especial field of his labours, and the two volumes of his great work already published have not exhausted his narration of them. We shall not be doing justice either to the subject or to our author, unless we enter into the details of the cemeteries on the Via Appia at some length; and first, we will hear what our ancient guides of the seventh and eighth centuries have to tell us upon the subject, for so we shall be better able to follow the course of De Rossi's investigations, and to appreciate both their ingenuity and importance.

One of these guides, then, the most ancient and accurate of all, describing what he himself saw and visited at some time between the years 625 and 638, writes as follows:—"After- *Testimonies of ancient authors.* wards, you arrive by the Via Appia at St Sebastian, martyr, whose body lies in a very low spot; and there are the sepulchres of the Apostles Peter and Paul, in which they rested forty years; and you go down by steps on the western side of the church, where St Cyrinus, Pope and martyr, rests. And on the north side of the same road you come to the holy martyrs, Tiburtius, Valerian, and Maximus. There you will enter into a great cave, and you will find there St Urban, bishop and confessor; and in another place, Felicissimus and Agapitus, martyrs, and deacons of Sixtus; and in a third place, Cyrinus, martyr; and in a fourth, Januarius, martyr; and in a third church again, St Zeno, martyr, rests. On the same road, at St Cecilia's, there is an innumerable multitude of martyrs: first, Sixtus, Pope and martyr; Dionysius, Pope and martyr; Julian, Pope and martyr; Flavianus, martyr; St Cecilia, virgin and martyr. Eighty martyrs rest there below [in the subterranean cemetery]; Zephyrinus, Pope and confessor, rests [in a church] above. Eusebius, Pope and martyr, rests in a cave some way off. Cornelius, Pope and martyr, lies in another cave some way off. After this, you come to the holy virgin and martyr, Soteris, whose body lies towards the north side; and then you leave the Via Appia, and arrive," &c.

The route described by the next witness[*] proceeds in the opposite direction. He has just described what was to be seen on the Via Ardeatina, and then he continues:—" Near the Via Appia, on the eastern side of the city, is the Church of St Soteris, martyr, where she lies with many other martyrs; and near the same road is the Church of St Sixtus, Pope, where he sleeps; there also St Cecilia, virgin, rests; and there St Tharsicius and St Zephyrinus lie, in one tomb; and there St Eusebius, and St Calocerus and St Parthenius lie, each apart; and 800 martyrs rest there. Not far from thence, in the cemetery of St Callixtus, Cornelius and Cyprian sleeps [sic] in a church. There is also near the same road a church of many martyrs, i.e., of Januarius, who was the eldest of the seven sons of Felicitas; of Urban, of Agapitus, Felicissimus, Cyrinus, Zeno, the brother of Valentine; Tiburtius and Valerian, and many martyrs rest there. And near the same road is the Church of St Sebastian, martyr, where he himself sleeps; where are also the burial-places of the Apostles, in which they rested forty years. There also the martyr Cyrinus is buried. By the same road also you go to the city of Albano," &c.

Division of subject.

Without entering into the minute details of any apparent discrepancies between these two accounts, their substantial agreement is abundantly manifest. Nobody can read them attentively without observing that they describe four distinct groups, or centres, of martyrs' tombs on the Appian road. One, the most distant from Rome, as you go towards Albano, is the Church of St Sebastian, with the cemetery belonging to it. Another, on the north side of the road, contained the graves of St Cecilia's husband and brother-in-law, Valerian and Tiburtius; of Felicissimus and Agapitus, two of St Sixtus's

---

[*] These are the two itineraries mentioned in pp. 22, 23.

deacons; of Januarius, the eldest of the seven sons of St Felicitas; and of many other martyrs. The third is described in still more glowing terms, as containing an "innumerable multitude of martyrs;" amongst whom are specified several Popes, St Cecilia, St Tharsycius, and others. Lastly, there is the church and cemetery of the holy virgin and martyr, St Soteris, before you leave this road and cross over to the Via Ardeatina. It is only with the third of these groups that we are more immediately concerned; nevertheless, it will be necessary that we should begin by saying a few words about the first.*

The basilica of St Sebastian, built by Constantine over the tomb where the body of this martyr still rests, is well known to every visitor of Rome. It stands on the Appian road, between two and three miles out of the city; and a friar from the adjoining monastery being always ready to act as guide and descend into the extensive subterranean cemetery, this has been more visited perhaps than any other portion of the Roman Catacombs. He cannot, indeed, show you "the steps on the western side of the church, whereby we descend to the grave of St Cyrinus, Pope and martyr," though De Rossi is of opinion that these also might now be found without much difficulty; but we can still read the inscription with which Pope Damasus adorned his tomb. We can also go round to the back of the high altar and examine the semi-subterranean building in which, according to a very ancient and authentic tradition, the bodies of St Peter and St Paul once found a temporary resting-place. The form of this building is so irregular that it would never have been selected by any architect for its own sake, but seems manifestly designed to inclose some particular point or points of interest, without interfering more than was absolutely necessary with what lay around it.

St Sebastian's.

Temporary resting-place of the relics of Saints Peter and Paul.

---

* The second has been already spoken of, under the name of St Prætextatus, in page 77; and the fourth will be described, as far as our present knowledge of it extends, in the next chapter, page 128.

We cannot therefore assent to the theory which would recognise in it some ancient heathen temple; but think it more probable that it was erected merely for the sake of commemorating a spot endeared to the Church by associations connected with her days of persecution. It seems probable that it was begun by Pope Liberius; it is certain that Damasus provided a marble pavement for its floor, and otherwise adorned it, at the same time setting up one of his usual metrical and historical inscriptions, which may still be seen there.* A low step, or seat of stone, runs round the interior, destined (Father Marchi conjectures) for the use of those who recited here in choir the psalms and public offices of the Church. In the middle of the area is a small square aperture, widening at the depth of about two feet into a large pit or double grave, measuring between six and seven feet both in length, breadth, and depth. This pit is divided into two equal compartments by a slab of marble; its sides are also cased with marble to the height of three feet, and its vaulted roof is covered with paintings of our Lord and His apostles. This, then, is the spot where, according to the testimony of both our ancient witnesses, "the bodies of St Peter and St Paul rested for a period of forty years."

Their first resting here.

There is some difficulty in unravelling the true history of this temporary translation of the bodies of the apostles. We have seen that they were originally buried, each near the scene of

> * " Hic habitasse prius Sanctos cognoscere debes,
> Nomina quisque Petri pariter Paulique requiris.
> Discipulos Oriens misit, quod sponte fatemur,
> Sanguinis ob meritum Christumque per astra secuuti,
> Aetherios petiere sinus et regna piorum.
> Roma suos potius meruit defendere cives.
> Hæc Damasus vestras referat nova sidera laudes."

"Here, you must know, that saints once dwelt. If you ask their names, they were Peter and Paul. The East sent disciples, as we willingly acknowledge. The saints themselves had, by the merit of their bloodshedding, followed Christ to the stars, and sought the home of heaven and the kingdoms of the blest. Rome, however, obtained to defend her own citizens. May Damasus be allowed to record these things for your praise, O new stars [of the heavenly host]."

his own martyrdom, the one on the Vatican Hill, the other on the Ostian Way. But we learn from other equally authentic sources, that as soon as the Oriental Christians had heard of their death, they sent some of the brethren to remove the bodies and bring them back to the East, where they claimed them as their fellow-citizens and countrymen. These messengers so far prospered in their mission as to gain a momentary possession of the sacred relics, which they carried off along the Appian Way, as far as this spot which we have been just now examining, adjoining the basilica of St Sebastian. This was probably their appointed place of rendezvous before starting on their homeward journey by way of Brundusium; for just at this point a cross-road, coming directly from St Paul's, joins the Appian and Ostian Ways, by which ways the bodies of St Peter and St Paul respectively must have been brought. What happened to them whilst they rested here we cannot exactly tell. The language of Pope Damasus, which we have given above, while it hints at the claim of the Orientals and the successful opposition of the Romans, bears evident tokens of reserve, and we can easily understand his unwillingness to perpetuate on a public monument, which would be seen by pilgrims from all parts of the world, a history that might hereafter become a subject of angry and jealous recrimination between the Eastern and Western Christians. But St Gregory the Great, writing two centuries later, and only in a private letter, had no such motive for reticence. A chapel having been built in the Imperial Palace at Constantinople, to be dedicated to St Paul, the Empress Constantina wished to enrich the altar with some considerable relic, and begged from the Sovereign Pontiff nothing less than the head of the great apostle. St Gregory, in justification of his refusal to comply with her request, relates the story of the attempt of the Oriental Christians to carry off his relics soon after his martyrdom, and says,—" It is well known that at the time when they suffered, Christians from the East came to recover their bodies as [the relics] of their fellow-citizens, and having carried them as far as the second milestone from the city, laid them in the place which is called *ad catacumbas;* but when the whole mass of them assembled together and attempted to take them up from hence, a storm of thunder and lightning so greatly terrified them and dispersed them, that after that they durst not make any more attempts. The Romans, however, then went out and took up their bodies, having been counted worthy to do this by the goodness of the Lord, and laid them in the places where they are now buried."* These last words of St Gregory do not seem to be quite accurate. There is no doubt that the Romans first buried them where they recovered them, in or near the cemetery *ad catacumbas,* and there was an old tradition, embodied in one of the lessons formerly used on St Peter's Feast in the French Church, which said that they were restored to their original places of sepulture after the lapse of a year and seven months; nor is there any reason to suppose that the body of St Paul was ever again removed. Of the relics of St Peter there are faint traces of a second translation, which is assigned by some writers to the first half of the third century. They are too indistinct, however, to be depended upon, and we must be content to acknowledge our ignorance as to the authority on which it was believed by the writers of the itineraries in the seventh and eighth centuries, that the bodies of the apostles had lain near the basilica of St Sebastian's for a period of forty years.

Second translation of St Peter's relics.

We have now seen all that the writers of those itineraries thought worthy of being mentioned in connexion with the basilica of St Sebastian. A guide, however, of the present day would certainly press us to descend also into the subterranean cemetery which lies around and underneath the church, and if we are persuaded to accept his invitation, we shall see there inscriptions professing to point out to us other and yet higher objects of interest. An inscription set up by one William,

Erroneous inscriptions of fifteenth century.

* Opp. St Greg., tom. ii., Ep. 30.

Archbishop of Bourges, in the year 1409, bids us venerate here the tomb of St Cecilia; other inscriptions also, of the same or a later date, speak of the tombs of nearly half a hundred Popes, and of several thousands of martyrs. Whence is this? A glance at the ancient documents which we have quoted is sufficient to arouse our suspicions as to the truthfulness of these inscriptions, since the two authorities are manifestly at variance with one another, and we can scarcely hesitate in making our choice between them, when we remember that the one was written whilst yet the bodies of the martyrs lay each in its own sepulchre, and that the other belongs precisely to that very age during which the Catacombs were buried in the most profound darkness and oblivion. We have already explained how it came to pass that whilst the other ancient cemeteries were inaccessible and unknown, this one still remained partially open; and we can easily understand the religious feeling which prompted the good Archbishop to make an appeal to the devotion of the faithful not to lose the memory of those glorious martyrs who had once been buried in places like this, and even somewhere in this neighbourhood. But whilst we admire his piety, we cannot accept his testimony upon a topographical question, which he had no means of deciding, and in respect to which recent discoveries, as well as a more critical examination of ancient documents, have proved to a demonstration that he was certainly wrong.

It was in the year 1849 that De Rossi found in the cellar of a vineyard on the Via Appia, but much nearer to Rome than St Sebastian's is, a large fragment of a marble slab, having on it the upper part of the letter R, followed by the complete letters NELIUS . MARTYR. He immediately divined that this fragment was part of the tombstone of St Cornelius, Pope in the middle of the third century. He persuaded Pope Pius IX. to purchase both this and the adjacent vineyard; and three years afterwards, during the excavations of 1852, the other half of the same marble slab came to light

<small>Reasons why this cannot be the cemetery of Callixtus.

Epitaph of St Cornelius.</small>

in the depths of the subterranean cemetery which underlay this vineyard. It was found at the foot of the grave, for which it had evidently been made at the first. It contained the other half of the letter R, preceded by CO, with the letters EP on a lower line, so that De Rossi's happy conjecture was

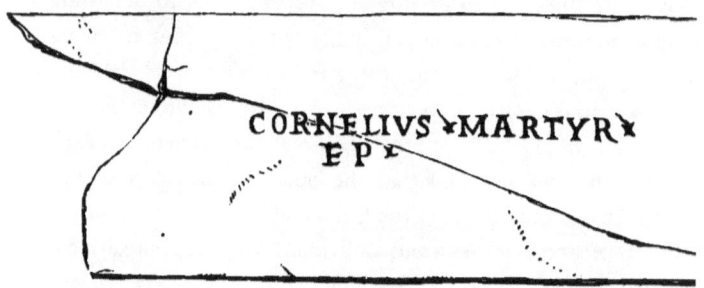

thus crowned with the seal of absolute certainty. Moreover, he had satisfied himself by a diligent study of all ancient documents within his reach, that the tomb of St Cornelius was very near, though not absolutely within the limits of, the famous cemetery of St Callixtus, and that in this cemetery there was a single chapel more famous than the rest, in which had once been laid the bodies of many Popes of the third and fourth centuries, and in another chapel adjoining it, St Cecilia. Excavations having been made in accordance with his suggestions, a fragment of marble was at length discovered, bearing on it three letters, or rather the same letter (H) repeated three times, one over the other, as the beginning of three successive lines.* His keen eye recognising the well-known beauty of the Damasine characters, immediately fastened upon this as "a confirmation strong as text of Holy Writ," that this was the Papal vault in which Damasus had set up one of his most celebrated inscriptions. As the work of excavation proceeded, a hundred and twenty other fragments of the same inscription were re-

Damasine inscription in the Papal crypt.

* See Plate I. at end of volume. The fragment was the beginning of lines 4-6.

covered. These all have been put together, and the few missing portions having been supplied in letters of a different colour, the whole may now again be read, just where our forefathers in the faith first read it fifteen hundred years ago. We shall have occasion to examine it more closely by and by, when we meet with it in its own place in the interior of the cemetery. We appeal to it now as a decisive proof, from which it is impossible to escape, that the cemetery of St Callixtus has been re-discovered, and that the mediæval inscriptions underneath the church of St Sebastian were set up in ignorance, and now only help to perpetuate the memory of an error. They confound the first and third of the cemeteries so carefully distinguished in the itineraries, and which we ourselves also are now happily able to distinguish again.

FIG. 16.—A fresco representing the Baptism of our Lord in one of the cubicula in the crypt of St Lucina.

CHAPTER II.

DISTINCTION OF ITS SEVERAL PARTS.

Distinct areæ in each Catacomb.

ON the same side of the Appian Way as the church of St Sebastian's, but about a quarter of a mile nearer to Rome, a doorway, with the words *Cœmeterium S. Callixti* carved above it, leads us to the vineyard beneath which lies this celebrated cemetery. We call it indeed by this name for convenience sake, and because the cemetery which Callixtus made is really the centre and most important part of the vast subterranean city on which we are about to enter. In truth, however, it is made up of several distinct groups of excavations, each having its own history, and still capable of being distinguished, at least in outline, from one another, though now, and for many centuries past, actually united. They may be distinguished not only by their contents, certain peculiarities of form, or different families of inscriptions, or other similar tokens, but much more by the disposition of the main galleries, which was determined by the size and shape of the area the *fossors* were at liberty to occupy, and the situation of the roads or buildings which may have been in its immediate neighbourhood above ground.

Defects of former maps.

This is almost a new branch of study in the subject of *Roma Sotterranea*, for which, as for so much else, we are indebted to De Rossi. Indeed it was scarcely possible for earlier writers to gain any clear notion of the manner in which these cemeteries had been constructed, since their knowledge of the plan of any one of them was very incomplete; and of most they never had an opportunity of seeing any plan at all. Bosio himself had not lived to prepare that part of his work; and of the half-dozen maps which Cardinal Barberini procured at so much labour and expense for the illustration of Bosio's book, not one was really complete. For the main object in their construction had been rather to show the sites of particular monuments than to exhibit the interior arrangement of the whole cemetery, either as designed by its originators or as subsequently modified in execution. The four additional maps supplied by Aringhi are mere fragments, and the only one which is of any size is strangely inexact. To these, D'Agincourt added another, but this also was too small to be of much service in a scientific point of view. Finally, Father Marchi produced a very valuable map of what he believed to be about the eighth part of the Catacomb of St Agnes; and the only portion of his book which he completed was intended to illustrate this particular branch of the subject, the architecture of the first Christians in Rome. He never pretended, however, to observe any chronological order, but pursued a simply eclectic principle in his choice of specimens. The whole of the Catacombs were for him a monument of primitive antiquity, and his sphere of observation was too limited to allow of his drawing any general conclusions from nice distinctions that might be observed between one part and another of the excavations. Since his time a complete revolution has been effected in this respect, by means of a most ingenious instrument, invented by Michele De Rossi, brother of the archæologist, which renders the process of surveying and mapping these subterranean crypts far easier, as well as more accurate, than it was before. Under his auspices, we may hope by and by to see the maps of the streets of subterranean Rome as complete as those of any modern city above ground. Already we have entered into some fruits of his labours, and the value of the light which they throw on the history of the Catacombs can hardly be exaggerated. With his map of the Catacomb

Important discoveries from Michele De Rossi's new method of mapping subterranean galleries.

of St Callixtus, for example, lying open before us, we are able to trace with certainty several features in its growth and development which before it was impossible to detect. We distinguish the boundaries of certain *areæ*, originally quite independent of one another, but united at a later period by paths of more or less irregularity. We see the first galleries, following the form and respecting the limits of these *areæ* with mathematical precision; we mark others, after proceeding for a considerable distance in one direction, turn abruptly into another, or break off altogether; and a glance at the condition of the external soil at once explains the cause of the digression. There are traces of some building, or the building itself is still there, at that precise spot, which clearly must have existed before the subterranean excavation, and which the Christians dared not undermine; or there was some chamber or gallery in this or an adjoining Christian cemetery, or some Pagan *hypogæum*, which stayed their further progress. In a future book we will set before our readers as minute an analysis as our space will allow of one at least of the more remarkable groups of galleries in the cemetery of St Callixtus, which will enable them to appreciate the importance of M. De Rossi's invention. At present we will only enumerate and distinguish those groups, as far as we can, not so much by reference to their construction, as by their inscriptions and other contents.

Crypt of St Lucina.

The most ancient area included in the Catacomb we are now examining is that which was once called "the crypt of Lucina, *near to* the cemetery of Callixtus." The original limits of this area can be determined with the greatest precision, in consequence of its having a small Pagan sepulchre on either side of it. Like the tombs of the Scipios, of Cecilia Metella, and other renowned sepulchres on the Via Appia, it occupied a frontage of 100 Roman feet, and it extended 230 feet *in agro*. Of these 230 feet, the first fifty appear to have been originally left free, thus forming an area in front of 100 feet by 50, in the centre of which stood the monument* whose vast ruins still form a striking object from the road. Behind this area extended another (*area adjecta monumento*), and it was beneath this that the earliest Christian excavations were made. The property belonged to some members of the Gens Cæcilia. We know from Cicero that this was one of the families who had their burial-places on this road; and about the beginning of this century, *columbaria* and inscriptions belonging to other Pagan monuments of the Cæcilii, were found at no great distance from this precise spot. It cannot, then, be considered a fortuitous circumstance that in the chambers and galleries of this part of the Catacomb there have come to light epitaphs and other memorials of several Cæcilii and Cæciliani, and these not mere freedmen who had adopted the name of the *gens*, but real members of the family, as is distinctly marked by the official adjuncts to their names, *vir clarissimus*, *clarissima fœmina* or *puella*, *honesta femina*, &c. Moreover, we note among the "illustrious dead" who lie in this aristocratic cemetery certain descendants of the Antonines, who were clearly connected with Annia Faustina, the granddaughter of Marcus Aurelius, and the wife of Pomponius Bassus, and afterwards of Heliogabalus. Now, it is known that these Pomponii Bassi, towards the end of the first century, lived on the Quirinal; and it can be *almost* proved that they inherited the house of the celebrated Atticus, the friend and correspondent of Cicero, of whom every classical scholar knows that he certainly lived on the Quirinal, and that he passed from the Gens Pomponia to the Gens Cæcilia, when he was adopted by his maternal uncle, Q. Cæcilius. Hence it is easy to account for the number of Christian epitaphs which have been found here, exhibiting these names mixed in various ways, *e.g.*, more than one Cæcilius Faustus, a Faustinus Atti-

Originally belonged to the Gens Cæcilia.

---

* De Rossi considers it probable that even this was originally a Christian monument (R. S. ii. 367), and quotes Tertullian (De Resurrect. Carnis., c. 27) as a witness that Christians had *monumenta et mausolea* from the first (R. S. i. 210).

cus, an Atticianus, a Pompeia Attica, an Attica Cæciliana, &c. We have the gravestones also of some heathen members of the same family, sawn in two or otherwise defaced, and used to close some of the Christian graves. One of these was of a Pomponius Bassus, who had lived in the third century, and had filled some of the highest offices of the state, been twice consul, prefect of Rome, &c., and another of L. Pomponius, proconsul of Gallia Narbonensis.

From the union of all these names on the same spot, and under these circumstances, De Rossi ventured to conjecture that the Cæcilii, to whom this property belonged and who were certainly Christian, must have been intimately connected with the Pomponii, Attici, and Bassi; and that *possibly* the Lucina, in whose property the ecclesiastical records state this catacomb to have been excavated, may have been the very Pomponia Græcina of whose conversion to Christianity, in the year 58, we have already spoken.* We need not say how frequently this name of Lucina occurs in ancient ecclesiastical history; it crops up in the history of every persecution, from the apostolic age to the days of Constantine, and has been the occasion of no slight confusion, and the subject of many learned discussions, among students of hagiography. De Rossi suggests that the name was a Christian *sobriquet* (alluding to the illumination of baptism, &c.) rather than a real family name, and that it may have been borne by many Roman matrons in succession without any real connexion of relationship between them, these ladies being of course known in society and among their heathen kinsfolk by their proper family names. When first he threw out the idea of Pomponia Græcina and the first Lucina having been possibly one and the same person, he spoke with extreme caution and reserve. "It is a mere guess," he said; † "I don't wish to claim for it any value as an argument; perhaps it hardly even deserves the name of a conjecture. But attempts of this kind, violent

St Lucina probably the Pomponia Græcina of A.D. 58.

* Page 39.   † R. S. i. 319.

efforts of the mind, which arouses itself at the faintest glimmer of light amid the thick darkness of antiquity, and seeks to rush forward to the acquisition of new truth, may at least serve to awaken attention, and to keep it keenly on the alert for every scrap of additional information which future discoveries may bring to light, and out of which prudent study may extract the full knowledge of historical facts, now only guessed at and offered *in confuso*." De Rossi wrote thus in his first volume, in 1864. In the middle of the second volume, written early in 1867, he says, with reference to the same subject, that "although his guess has been very favourably received by the learned, yet it must not be taken for more than it is worth, until new and more important monumental discoveries shall place it on a more solid foundation." At the end of the volume, however, he is able to explain what was the monumental evidence he desired, and to announce that he had found it. He had no positive evidence either of the relationship between the Pomponii Bassi and the Pomponii Græcini, or that the profession of Christianity had prevailed in either family. He now publishes inscriptions, or at least sufficient fragments of inscriptions, found in this cemetery, and belonging to the end of the second century, two of which testify to the Christian burial here of Pomponii Bassi, and one of a Pomponius Græcinus; and although even now the argument has not the force of demonstration, yet it is impossible to deny that it has a great deal of probability in its favour, and impossible not to admire the modesty, learning, and ingenuity by which it has been supported.

We shall have occasion to return to these genealogical particulars in a future chapter, as illustrating the fact of Pope Cornelius having been buried here, apart from the other Popes, his immediate predecessors and successors, in the middle of the third century. But before the making of his sepulchre, which involved considerable alterations in its immediate neighbourhood, two floors of galleries had been already excavated and filled. The upper of these floors is not one sixth of the extent of the lower; indeed, it is unusually limited, from the necessity of the case. It had been dug at a depth of not more than twenty feet below the surface; and as the hill slopes rapidly, the galleries would have run out into the open air, had they continued far upon the same level. The general characteristics of this primitive area of the cemetery are a certain marked uniformity of plan in the form and decoration of the roof, the unusual height of the galleries, and the frequent recurrence of square, narrow chambers, not opposite one another on different sides of the gallery, but opening one out of the other. Most of these chambers are adorned with paintings of a very early style. Only two instances of *arcosolia* occur, and both of these are in portions of evidently late construction.

Characteristics of this area.

About the time of Marcus Aurelius, in the second half of the second century, another plot of ground, at no great distance from the crypt of St Lucina, was given (apparently by the same family) for the same purpose. It bordered on a road which joined the Via Appia and Via Ardeatina, and its measurement was 250 feet by 100. We shall not enter now upon any detailed description either of this or of the next area, as their construction and development will form the subject of the more minute analysis already promised, and several of their chapels are of sufficient importance to claim each one a chapter to itself. It will be sufficient to mention here, that in the first area, as in the crypts of St Lucina, there are no *cubicula* opposite to one another, but five or six in a row, opening out of the same side of a broad spacious *ambulacrum*, like so many bedrooms out of the passage of a private house; and most of them very richly ornamented with symbolical paintings of the highest antiquity and importance. This was the first area of the cemetery of St Callixtus, properly so called, the crypts of St Lucina having, as we have seen, once formed a cemetery by themselves. It contains many tombs of a very peculiar form, such as are to be seen only in one other part of the whole

Cemetery of St Callixtus begun before A. D. 200.

cemetery;—graves having no more than the ordinary opening on the outer side, yet so excavated interiorly, at the cost of infinite labour, as to be capable of containing many bodies. In a second area, measuring 150 feet *in fronte* by 125 *in agro*, and made not long after the first, we find large crypts on opposite sides of the pathway, lit by the same *luminare*. *Arcosolia* are here very abundant, both in the crypts and galleries. There is not much painting in the chambers, but in some of them we find for the first time traces of their having been faced with slabs of marble. A third area, of the same dimensions as the last, seems to have belonged to the days of Diocletian, or perhaps a few years earlier. If we may conjecture from the family names which occur in this third area of St Callixtus', we should be disposed to suspect that it had been given to the church by Anatolia, the wealthy daughter of the Consul Æmilianus. It is certain that he had property in this neighbourhood, and we find here epitaphs of an Æmilius Partenius, an Æmilianus, an Æmil . . . a Tulinus, and a Petronia, which names also belonged to the consul. Moreover, Calocerus and Parthenius, whom Æmilianus had apppointed to be his daughter's guardians, were buried here; and a painting here, which seems to represent two martyrs or confessors standing before the tribunal of the heathen magistrate, probably has reference to their history. One of the peculiarities of this area, which we do not find in either of those we have described before, is a great variety of representations of the cross, all more or less disguised, yet still to the eyes of the initiated sufficiently significant; but that which was afterwards adopted as the monogram of Christ's name and the cross combined (the well-known Chi and Rho—the Labarum of Constantine) is not amongst them. This also seems exactly to correspond with the age we have attributed to it; indeed, the question of chronology is clearly settled by the dates of epitaphs found here,* belonging to the end of the third and

Enlarged about A.D. 300.

---

* The inscription of the Deacon Severus, p. 93, belongs to this area.

beginning of the fourth century. Once or twice we find here three chambers united instead of two, all receiving light and ventilation from the same *luminare;* clearly, for the sake of assemblies, not of burials; and although we do not see any traces of the seats for the presbytery, or the episcopal chair, hewn out of the rock, as in the somewhat analogous chambers in the so-called cemetery of St Agnes, this is probably because they were made of more costly materials, and moveable from place to place.

Cemeteries of Sta. Soteris,

To the same date belongs also the adjoining cemetery of Sta. Soteris, a virgin of the family to which St Ambrose belonged in a later generation. She had been buried in her own cemetery (*cœmeterio suo*) A.D. 304; and we have already seen that the itineraries spoke of a separate church erected to her honour somewhere in the neighbourhood of St Callixtus', yet distinct from it. The two cemeteries really adjoined one another; not perhaps in their first beginnings, but in course of time, as each attained its full development, a communication was established between them.*

and of Sta. Balbina,

The same is to be said also of another cemetery in this neighbourhood, that of Sta. Balbina, which is placed by some of the old itineraries on the Via Appia, by others on the Ardeatina, and really lies between the two. Bosio and Boldetti erroneously fixed its locality as having been where we have now found the Catacomb of St Callixtus. De Rossi, following his usual guides, determined its situation long since,† but was unable to recover it. His brother fixed his eye on the ruins of an ancient building and some suspicious-looking fissures in the soil, in the precise spot indicated by the archæologist; but though he managed to effect an entrance, he found nothing to reward his search. At last, not long since,

---

* The several areas of the cemetery of Sta. Soteris have not yet been sufficiently explored to allow of their being described. De Rossi has only mentioned that in the first area everything is on an exceptional scale of grandeur, with double, treble, and even quadruple *cubicula*.

† R. S. i. 265.

some unusually heavy rains revealed a new opening for him into the bowels of the earth, and this time he was able to wander about for an hour and more in the newly-discovered Catacomb. The Commission of Sacred Archæology are too much crippled by want of means to be able to pursue the investigation far. Enough, however, has been seen to enable De Rossi to say that the size of the necropolis between the Appian and Ardeatine roads is nearly doubled by the discovery; that the proportions of this subterranean labyrinth surpass all his imaginations founded on previous experience, and fill him with amazement. It is not only of immense extent, but it is excavated on several different levels, has many large crypts, and is illuminated by shafts of grander proportions and more highly-developed architectural forms than any he has found before. In particular, he specifies one *luminare*, not square, but hexagonal or nearly so, which opens on the subterranean excavations with not less than eight rays of light. Two serve to illuminate as many large rectangular chambers, each ending in a circular apse; two others, the adjacent galleries, which here cross one another at right angles; and the other four descend upon four long and narrow openings at the corners, which are not yet explored, but which he believes will be found to end in an equal number of *cubicula*. Should his anticipation be realised, this will be the largest and most regular group of subterranean crypts that has ever yet been seen. We must remember, however, that this cemetery was considerably enlarged by St Mark, who was Pope A.D. 336, and built a basilica here, in which he was himself buried.*

---

* Constantine endowed it with a *fundus rosarius*, and an adjoining field. The *Rosatio*, or strewing with roses, was a rite observed at some pagan tombs on the anniversaries of deaths, and funds were specially set apart for celebrating this *dies rosationis vel violationis*, as it was called. This particular *fundus rosarius* must have been for some reason confiscated to the imperial *fiscus*, after which Constantine again devoted it to sepulchral purposes, but in a Christian way.

CHAPTER III.

THE PAPAL CRYPT.

Entrance of the papal crypt.

ON entering the vineyard, over whose doorway we read the words *Cœmeterium S. Callixti*, we come first to the crypts of St Lucina. It will be more convenient, however, to pass them by for the present, and to go forward to the more modest building which stands before us in the interior of the vineyard. Even of this, however, we do not intend to discuss the history; we will only remind our readers that whereas it was supposed by Marangoni to have been the basilica which St Damasus provided for the burial of himself, his mother, and sister, and Father Marchi took it to be the Church of St Mark and St Marcellinus (both of which are mentioned in the Itineraries), De Rossi, as we have already had occasion to notice, identifies it as the *cella memoriæ*, sometimes called of St Sixtus, sometimes of St Cecilia (because built immediately over the tombs of those celebrated martyrs), by St Fabian in the third century.*

Graffiti on the walls.

As we descend into the interior, by means of an ancient staircase restored, we are struck, at the bottom of the stairs, and still more at the entrance of the first chapel we come to, by the number of *graffiti*, as they are called, which cover the walls. It is comparatively a new thing to pay any attention to these rude scribblings of ancient visitors on the walls of places of public resort, and to take pains to decipher them. But of late years many valuable discoveries have been made by means of them, and they have proved to be a most interesting subject

* See page 86.

of study, whether found on the tombs of Egyptian kings in Thebes, on the walls of the barracks and theatres in Pompeii, in the prisons and cellars of Pagan Rome, or, lastly, in the Christian Catacombs. Here especially they have proved to be of immense importance, being, as De Rossi justly calls them, "the faithful echo of history and infallible guides through the labyrinth of subterranean galleries." Those with which we are at present concerned may be divided into three classes. Of three kinds, They are either the mere names of persons, with the occasional adjunct of their titles; or they are good wishes, prayers, salutations, or acclamations, on behalf of friends and relatives, living or dead; or, lastly, they are invocations of the martyrs on whose tombs they are inscribed. Numerous specimens of all of these may be easily read on the spot of which we are now speaking.

Of the names we find two classes; one, the most ancient 1. Names. and most numerous, scribbled in the most convenient and accessible parts of the wall, are names of the old classical type, such as Rufina, Felix, Eustathius, Polyneices, Leo, Maximus, Probinianus, and the like; the other, belonging manifestly to a somewhat later period, because written high above the first, and in more inaccessible places, are such as Lupo, Ildebrand, Bonizo, Joannes Presb., &c. &c.

Prayers or acclamations for absent or departed friends are 2. Prayers, or mixed among the most ancient names, and generally run in acclamations. the same form as the earliest and most simple Christian epitaphs, *e.g.*, VIVAS, VIVAS IN DEO CRISTO, VIVAS IN ETERNO, ZHC EN ΘΕΩ, BIBAC IN ΘΕΩ, TE IN PACE, &c. "Mayest thou live in God Christ, for ever, Thee in peace," * &c. The feeling which prompted the pilgrims who visited these shrines thus to inscribe in sacred places the names of those they loved and would fain benefit, is natural to the human heart: instances of it may be found even among the heathen themselves.

* These simple forms have never yet been found on any epitaphs which can be shown to be later than the days of Constantine. On rings and articles of domestic furniture they are sometimes found, even as late as the end of the fourth century.

Thus, one Sarapion, son of Aristomachus, having visited the island of Phyle in Egypt, writes there, that "having come to the great Isis, Goddess of Phyle, he makes a remembrance there of his parents, for their good." Just so, the Christian pilgrims of the third and fourth centuries visiting all the holy places in this Catacomb of St Callixtus, wrote the names of some dear friend or relative, with some pious ejaculation, "for their good."

Example. One of these it is specially interesting to track, after an interval probably of fifteen hundred years, along the precise path of his pilgrimage. He had come with his heart full of the most affectionate memory of one Sofronia—whether wife, or mother, or sister, does not appear. Before entering on the vestibule of the principal sanctuary, he wrote, *Sofronia, vibas cum tuis;* then, at the entrance itself, *Sofronia, vivas in Domino;* by and by, in larger characters, and almost in the form of a regular epitaph, he scratched on the principal altar-tomb of another chapel, *Sofronia dulcis, semper vives Deo;* and yet once more he repeats in the same place, *Sofronia, vives,** where we can hardly doubt but that the change of mood and tense reflected, almost unconsciously perhaps, a corresponding change of inward feeling; the language of fervent love and hope, fed by earnest prayer at the shrines of the saints, had been exchanged at last for the bolder tones of firm, unhesitating confidence.

3. Invocation of martyrs. But besides mere names and short acclamations, there are also in the same place, and manifestly belonging to the same age, prayers and invocations of the martyrs who lay buried in these chapels. Sometimes the holy souls of all the martyrs are addressed collectively, and petitioned to hold such or such an one in remembrance, and sometimes this prayer is addressed to one individually; generally to St Sixtus II., whose name always enjoyed a special pre-eminence in this Catacomb, *e.g.,*

---

* Sophronia, mayest thou live with thine own. Sophronia, mayest thou live in the Lord. Sweet Sophronia, thou shalt ever live in God. Sophronia, thou shalt live.

The Papal Crypt.

MARCIANUM SUCCESSUM SEVERUM SPIRITA SANCTA * IN MENTE HAVETE, ET OMNES FRATRES NOSTROS. PETITE SPIRITA SANCTA UT VERECUNDUS CUM SUIS BENE NAVIGET. † OTIA PETITE ET PRO PARENTE ET PRO FRATRIBUS EJUS; VIBANT CUM BONO. SANTE SUSTE, IN MENTE HABEAS IN HORATIONES AURELIU REPENTINU. ΔΙΟΝΥΣΙΝ ΕΙΣ ΜΝΙΑΝ ΕΧΕΤΑΙ (for EXETE.) "Holy souls, have in remembrance Marcianus Successus Severus and all our brethren. Holy souls, ask that Verecundus and his friends may have a prosperous voyage. Ask for rest both for my parent and his brethren; may they live with good. Holy Sixtus, have in remembrance in your prayers Aurelius Repentinus. Have ye in remembrance Dionysius."

There is a simplicity and a warmth of affection about these brief petitions, which savours of the earliest ages; they are very different from the dry and verbose epitaphs of the fourth or fifth centuries; indeed, there is something almost classical about the third, reminding us, says De Rossi, of Horace's *Otium Divos rogat in patenti prensus Ægæo*; ‡ and the phrase, which is so frequently repeated in them, *in mente habere*, points to the same antiquity. It is found on an inscription in Pompeii, on two Christian epitaphs of the third and fourth centuries, and is used by St Cyprian in one of his letters: "have in mind," he says, "our brothers and sisters in your prayers;" *fratres nostros ac sorores in mente habeatis in orationibus vestris*. These nameless pilgrims made the same petition to the saints in heaven that St Cyprian made to the saints on earth, and perhaps about the same time, or not much later. For it is to be observed that many of these *graffiti* have been spoilt, cut off in the middle, or rendered otherwise illegible, by the enlargement of the doorway, the renewal of the stucco, and other changes which were made in this chapel by St Fabian, perhaps about the year 245, or St Damasus in 370.

Their antiquity.

---
* In epitaphs of the third century *spiritum*, instead of *spiritus*, is often used for the soul or spirit of a man.—*Insc. Christ.*, I. cxii.

† *Optat sibi ut bene naviget* is one of the *graffiti* at Pompeii, published by P. Garrucci, S. J.   ‡ Od. ii. 16.

One of those that has been thus mutilated is undoubtedly the most ancient of all, for it was written whilst yet the plaster was wet, and it is an apostrophe to one Pontianus, whom De Rossi believes to have been the Pope of this name, brought back from Sardinia, where he had died in exile, and buried in this very chapel by St Fabian.

There is yet one other inscription on the entrance of the first chapel, of a somewhat different kind, but too remarkable to be passed over. Unhappily the writer never finished it; but what he did write is easily legible, and abundantly sufficient to show the enthusiastic devotion with which his heart was warmed towards the sanctuary on whose threshold he stood. It runs thus, *Gerusale civitas et ornamentum Martyrum Domini, cujus* . . . The idea present to the writer's mind was evidently the same as we find both in Holy Scripture and in some of the earliest uninspired Christian writers, who not unfrequently speak of the glory of the Church triumphant under the title of the Holy City, the New Jerusalem.* He looked upon the chapel he was about to enter as a type or figure of the future Jerusalem. It was adorned and made venerable by the remains of many martyrs of the Lord, which should one day arise to receive new life and rejoice in His presence for ever.

Examination of papal crypt.
The inspection of these *graffiti*, then, is enough to warn us that we are on the threshold of a very special sanctuary of the ancient Church, and to excite our deepest interest in all that we may find it to contain. Our first impression on entering will probably be one of disappointment. We were led to expect that we were about to visit a Christian burial-place and place of worship of the third or fourth century, but the greater part of the masonry we see around us is manifestly of quite recent construction. The truth is, that when this chamber

---

* See Psalm cxxi., Apoc. xxi. 2., Tertullian de Spectac., c. xxx. This same writer speaks also of the world as *expressus in ornamentum majestatis Dei.—Apolog.*, c. xvii.

was rediscovered in 1854, it was in a complete state of ruin; access was gained to it only through the *luminare*, which, as usual, had served for many centuries as a channel for pouring into it all the adjacent soil, fragments of grave-stones, decaying brickwork, and every kind of rubbish. When this was removed, the vault of the chamber, deprived of its usual support, soon gave way; so that, if any portion of it was to be preserved and put in a condition to be visited with safety, it was absolutely necessary to build fresh walls, and otherwise strengthen it. This has been done with the utmost care, and so as still to preserve, wherever it was possible, abundant tokens of the more ancient condition of the chapel and of its decoration in succeeding ages. Thus we are able to trace very clearly three stages or conditions of ornamentation by means of three different coatings of plaster, each retaining some remnant of its original painting. We can trace also the remains of the marble slabs with which, at a later period, the whole chapel was faced; and even this *later* period takes us back to the earlier half of the fifth century, when, as the *Liber Pontificalis* tells us, St Sixtus III. *platoniam fecit in Cœmeterio Sti Callixti.* The fragments of marble columns and other ornamental work, which lie scattered about on the pavement, belong probably to the work of St Leo III., the last pontiff of whom we read that he made restorations here before the translation of the relics by Pope Paschal I. Again, the raised step or dais of marble, which we see directly opposite to us at the further end of the chapel, having four holes or sockets in it, suggests at once the presence here of an altar in former times, supported on four pillars; but in the wall behind this platform we can still detect the existence of an older and more simple kind of altar—a sepulchre hewn out of the rock, the flat covering of which was once the *mensa* whereon the holy mysteries were celebrated. It was not a real *arcosolium*, however, but what we have called a table-tomb; moreover, the front of the sepulchre itself was not a mere wall of the rock, so left in the original process of

Successive periods of decoration.

Ancient altar.

excavation, but is an excellent piece of brickwork, precisely such as we find in the crypt of St Januarius in the cemetery of St Prætextatus, and to which we cannot assign a later date than the earliest part of the third century—indeed, it might not improbably have belonged to the end of the second. The presence of these two altars seems to tell a tale, which is corroborated by other indications also, too minute to be appreciated without a personal inspection of the locality—viz., of some alteration in this or the adjoining chapel made at a very early period, which necessitated the translation of the martyr originally buried in this principal tomb of the *cubiculum;* and De Rossi's conjecture is certainly most ingenious, that this martyr was no other than St Zephyrinus himself, the original designer of the whole cemetery, for whom, therefore, the chief place in the first vault might very naturally have been reserved; and that the body of this pope was translated at some early date, before the practice had become common, is proved by what we have already read in one of the old Itineraries, that his body lay *in a church above ground*, and (as we learn from another source) St Tharsycius in the same tomb with him.

Original epitaphs of popes of third century.

Thus, spite of the ruin and the neglect of ages, and spite of the work of restoration which has been thereby made necessary in our own time, many clear traces still remain both of its original condition and of the reverent care with which successive generations of the ancient Church did their best to adorn this chamber. The cause of this extraordinary and long-continued veneration is revealed to us by a few grave-stones which have been recovered from amid the rubbish, and which are now restored, if not to the precise spots they originally occupied (which we cannot tell), yet certainly to the *walls* in which they were first placed. An exact copy of them is given on the opposite page.

ΑΝΤΕΡΩΣ ΕΠΙ

ΦΑΒΙΑΝΟΣ ΕΠΙ

ΛΟΥΚΙΣ

We have every reason to believe that these are the original tombstones of St Anteros and St Fabian, who sat in the chair of Peter from A.D. 235 to 250; of St Lucius, who reigned in 252; and of St Eutychianus, who died nearly thirty years later. De Rossi says so most unhesitatingly, and his special familiarity with ancient Christian epigraphy renders his verdict almost conclusive. The objection that has been urged against them, from their extreme brevity and simplicity, is itself a strong proof of their great antiquity; nor do we know a single argument of any weight whatever that has been adduced against the claim which De Rossi makes for them. At any rate, whether originals or later copies, they are the epitaphs of four Bishops of Rome in the third century.

Rarity of epitaphs of bishops.

It is a remarkable fact, the full significance of which has only lately been appreciated, that neither Bosio, Fabretti, Boldetti, nor any other of the ancient explorers of subterranean Rome, ever found an inscription bearing the title of Bishop. It is true, indeed, that in the first age this title had not acquired that determinate ecclesiastical sense which it subsequently received. The word had been in use among the Pagans in a wider and more general signification. Among the Greeks, for example, it was used for the president of the athletic sports and public games, and this may have been a sufficient reason, perhaps, for omitting the title on the grave-stones of the first bishops.* By the middle of the third century, however, its ecclesiastical sense was well defined, and accordingly we find it here on three out of these four grave-stones of the Popes. The tombstones of St Cornelius, also, and of St Eusebius, popes and martyrs, which we shall presently see in this cemetery, are similarly marked; and in the cemetery of St Alexander, discovered fifteen or twenty years ago on the Via Nomentana, at least three epitaphs display the same title.

The fact that so many have been found in the same place, whereas they have not been found elsewhere, might suggest to

* See page 65 on the tombstone of Linus.

an intelligent student of archæology that perhaps it was the practice in the ancient Church to reserve some special place of burial for those who had filled the highest rank in her hierarchy. And this conjecture receives strong confirmation from the fact, which we learn from various sources, that the earliest successors of St Peter (with a very few exceptions, which can generally be accounted for) lay buried each in his own sepulchre, " near the body of blessed Peter in the Vatican,"* just as the bishops of Alexandria were buried near the body of St Mark. Moreover, it was an object of great jealousy to the several Churches that their bishops should be buried in the midst of them; their tombs were appealed to as a testimony to the apostolic tradition and doctrine having come to them through a legitimate succession of bishops. Thus Polycrates, Bishop of Ephesus, writing to St Victor, carefully enumerates the burial-places in different cities of Asia of the several bishops, " great pillars of the Church " as he calls them, whom he alleges as witnesses in his behalf.† Caius, in like manner, disputing against the Cataphrygians at the end of the second century, appeals to the tombs of Saints Peter and Paul; so also Optatus in his controversy with the Donatists. ‡ Hence, if a bishop happened to die at a distance from his own see, his body was ordinarily brought home, even at considerable inconvenience; *e.g.*, the body of St Eusebius from Sicily; of St Cornelius from Civita Vecchia; and of St Pontianus from the island of Sardinia. The bodies of all these Popes were brought back to Rome, though two of them at least had died in exile; for the law distinctly allowed the bodies of exiles to be brought home for interment, provided the Emperor's leave had been first obtained, and in the instances here alleged, the translation was

Care in their burial.

Their bodies often brought home from a distance.

* See the *Liber Pontificalis* at the end of each pope's life; also the testimony of the Itinerary, which, after mentioning St Peter's tomb, immediately adds, " Et Pontificalis ordo, excepto numero pauco, *in eodem loco* in tumbis propriis requiescit."—R. S. i. 141.
† Euseb. H. E. v. 24.
‡ Euseb. H. E. ii. 25 ; Opt. lib. ii. c. 5.

not made until a change in the imperial policy towards the Church made it possible to obtain such leave. Nor was this translation an honour peculiar to the bodies of deceased Roman Pontiffs. On the contrary, the relics of St Ignatius were restored to Antioch; the body of Dionysius, Bishop of Milan, was recovered by St Ambrose, and that of St Felix, Bishop of Tiburtium, martyred at Venosa, was returned to Africa. Perhaps, also, this practice furnishes the best explanation which can be given of the attempt made by the Christians of the East to recover the bodies of Saints Peter and Paul.

Many foreign Bishops buried in Rome. There would be always, of course, some exceptions to the practical observance of such a custom as this, and Rome was likely to be the most frequent witness of these exceptions, for bishops were constantly flowing thither from the earliest times, *propter potiorem principalitatem*, as St Irenæus says, and proofs are not wanting that this was far more common, even in the ages of persecution, than we should have been prepared to expect. Thus we learn from St Cyprian that sixteen bishops from other sees were present in Rome at the election of St Cornelius in the year 251, of whom two at least were from Africa, and two others arrived from the same country not long afterwards; and St Cornelius was able to call together no fewer than sixty to take counsel about the system of discipline to be observed in reconciling apostates. That some foreign bishops, then, should have been overtaken by death during their sojourn in Rome was nothing improbable; and if their dioceses were unwilling or unable to recover their remains, we may be sure that the Roman Pontiffs would have made honourable provision for their interment.* Hence we are not surprised at finding some traces of bishops, who certainly were not bishops of Rome, even in this very chamber, which we be-

---

* It was a decree of the Council of Arles, A.D. 314, that foreign bishops visiting Rome should have a church assigned them for the celebration of the holy sacrifice.—*Conc. Arel.*, can. xix., *apud* Collect. Reg. Max., i. 266. See also Euseb. H. E. v. 24, *in fin.*, on the respect shown to St Polycarp in Rome by St Anicetus.

lieve to have been specially prepared as a place of burial for the popes from the date of its first commencement at the beginning of the third century. Bosio, indeed, and some others, following some editions of the *Liber Pontificalis* would place the burials of St Anicetus and St Soter, popes of the middle of the second century, in this Catacomb. But this is certainly an error. In all the older recensions of that book they are placed in the Vatican, where at that time all the popes were buried. The mistake, with reference to St Soter, originated very probably from some confusion of the name with that of St Soteris, virgin and martyr, whose cemetery has been already mentioned as being in this neighbourhood.

The first pope of whom it is distinctly recorded that he was buried in the cemetery of St Callixtus was St Zephyrinus, its chief author. His successor, St Callixtus, who so long presided over it, was not buried here, but this was owing to the peculiar circumstances of his death. He did not suffer martyrdom after a judicial sentence and under the penal laws of the government, but privately, and as the result of a popular tumult. He was thrown out of the window of his house in Trastevere, and his body cast into a well, whence it was secretly removed to the nearest cemetery, that of St Calepodius, on the Via Aurelia, which has therefore been sometimes called another cemetery of St Callixtus. Callixtus was succeeded by St Urban, and a broken tombstone was found in this very chamber, which had never belonged to a mere ordinary grave in the wall, but had served as the *mensa* of an altar-tomb, and bore the letters OVPBANOC E . . .; and although it is commonly stated that St Urban was buried in the cemetery of St Prætextatus, on the other side of the road, De Rossi believes, as Tillemont, Sollier, and many other men of learning, have believed before him, that there has been a confusion in the old martyrologies, from a very early date, between two bishops of the name of Urban—the one a martyr, who was buried in St Prætextatus, the other pope and confessor, buried

[margin: Popes buried in this cemetery.]
[margin: Zephyrinus.]
[margin: Urban I.]

Pontianus.

Anteros.

Fabian.

in St Callixtus. The next in order of succession was St Pontianus, who, having been banished to Sardinia, there resigned his pontifical dignity,* and was succeeded by St Antherus or Anteros, whose monument we just now saw. He filled the chair of Peter only for a few weeks, and because he diligently sought out the acts of the martyrs in the official records of the Prætor Urbanus, he suffered martyrdom before the death of his predecessor. His successor, St Fabian, brought the body of St Pontianus back to Rome, and buried it in this chapel, where its position, *after* that of St Anteros, caused some of the early chroniclers to invert the true order of these two popes, and so to introduce an element of endless confusion into the history of those times. The inscription on St Fabian's tomb, besides his name and title, exhibits a monogram, clearly

intended to denote the fact of his martyrdom. It will be observed that this monogram is not cut nearly so deep as the earlier part of the inscription, and it would seem as though it had been added after the stone was fixed in its place. This suppression of the title of martyr could hardly have been necessary as an act of prudence, since neither the tombstone of St Cornelius in this cemetery, nor that of St Hyacinth in the cemetery of St Hermes, observed the same reticence. De Rossi conjectures that perhaps already it was not lawful to publish this claim on the veneration of the faithful without the sanction of the highest authority, which, in the present instance, was delayed for eighteen months, in consequence of the Holy See remaining vacant during that period; in other words, though actually a martyr, St Fabian was not

* *Discinctus* is the word used used in the *Liber Pontificalis*.

at once a martyr *vindicatus*.* Between St Fabian and St Lucius. Lucius intervened St Cornelius, of whose burial we shall have to speak in another chapter. Of St Lucius we have seen the grave-stone, where, however, his name is written ΛΟΥΚΙC, omitting the O. This elliptic form of termination of a Roman name was one which belonged rather to private than public use; yet it is found on a few Pagan monuments of about this date, on many graves in the Jewish cemetery, and is quite universal in the Catacombs. Another example of it may be seen on a monument, still lying in its place in the pavement of this very chapel, where ΔΗΜΕΤΡΙC stands for Demetrius.

The next pope of whom the tombstone has been discovered among the *débris* of this chapel is St Eutychianus; nevertheless it is recorded of the four who intervened between St Lucius and himself that they also were buried here, and there is no reason to question the truth of the record. Indeed, of one of them, St Sixtus, we have seen numerous and authentic memorials in the *graffiti* already examined. He was, *par excellence*, the martyr of this Catacomb, and of the Catacombs generally; for we have the cotemporary evidence of St Cyprian† that he received the crown of martyrdom in one of them on the 6th of August A.D. 258. Valerian and Gallienus had issued a decree in the preceding year forbidding the Christians to assemble in the cemeteries. In defiance of this prohibition, St Sixtus was celebrating mass in the Catacomb of St Prætextatus—probably because it was less known and less narrowly watched than the Papal Chapel (so to call it) in St Callixtus'—when he was discovered and seized by the heathen soldiery, led into the city, and after judgment, brought back again for execution to the scene of his offence, where he was beheaded in his episcopal chair, or at least so near it that it was besprinkled with his blood. Many memorials of his martyrdom may be recognised

Eutychianus.

Sixtus II.

His martyrdom in the Catacombs

---

* Optat. de Sch. Don. i. 16.

† "Xistum *in cimiterio* animadversum sciatis octavo Iduum Augustarum die et cum eo diaconos quatuor."—*S. Cyp.* Ep. lxxx., *ad Successum.*, ed. Leipsic, 1858.

in the monuments of the Catacomb of St Prætextatus—as, for instance, the figure of one sitting in a chair, with a deacon standing by his side, holding a book in his hand, or elsewhere of the chair only; paintings also of St Sixtus, with his name appended. Moreover, a small basilica was built there to mark the spot of his execution. Two of the deacons who suffered with him, Felicissimus and Agapitus, were buried in this cemetery; but St Sixtus himself and others of his companions were buried in St Callixtus', where St Damasus afterwards celebrated his memory by the following inscription:—

> "Tempore quo gladius secuit pia viscera Matris
> Hic positus rector cælestia jussa docebam;
> Adveniunt subito, rapiunt qui forte sedentem;
> Militibus missis, populi tunc colla dedere.
> Mox sibi cognovit senior quis tollere vellet
> Palmam seque suumque caput prior obtulit ipse,
> Impatiens feritas posset ne l*æde*re quemquam.
> Ostendit Christus reddit qu*i præmi*a vitæ
> Pastoris meritum, numerum g*regi*s ipse tuetur."

"At the time when the sword [of persecution] pierced the tender heart of Mother [Church], I, the Pope buried here, was teaching the laws of heaven. On a sudden came [the enemy], seized me seated as I happened to be in my chair; the soldiers were sent in; then did the people give their necks [to the slaughter]. Presently the old man saw who wished to bear away the palm from him, and he was the first to offer himself and his own head, that the hasty cruelty [of the Pagans] might injure no one else. Christ, who renders [to the just] the rewards of life [eternal], manifests the merit of the pastor: He Himself defends the mass of the flock."

Probably confounded with that of St Stephen.

This inscription alludes to circumstances of the incident it records, which were doubtless familiar to those for whom he wrote, but the memory of which has now unhappily perished. It does not even mention the name of the Pope whose martyrdom it celebrates, and hence, the whole history has been transferred in some of the spurious Acts of the Martyrs—for what reason we cannot now determine—from St Sixtus to his predecessor, St Stephen. We cannot doubt, however, that De Rossi is right in reclaiming it for St Sixtus, partly on the strength of the cotemporary testimony of St Cyprian already quoted, partly on that of the *graffiti* at the doorway and else-

The Papal Crypt. 145

where in the neighbourhood of this subterranean sanctuary, showing the marked pre-eminence in which the memory of St Sixtus was held in reverence here from the very earliest times, and still more, perhaps, after following him through a critical examination of all the notices on the subject which have come down to us in the martyrologies, itineraries, and other ancient *monumenta* of Church history. These, however, are too minute to be handled in this place. Nor is their testimony really needed; what has been already alleged, coupled with the fact that this inscription of Pope Damasus was set up in this very chapel, scarcely leaves room for doubt; and that it *was* so set up, two small fragments of the stone itself have survived to tell us. It is true that they scarcely contain ten perfect letters out of the three or four hundred which formed the whole inscription—they are the few which we have printed in italics—nevertheless, being of the peculiar Damasine type, it is impossible to question their identity.

Next to St Eutychianus came St Caius in the list of Popes; St Caius. and though we have no monument to produce of his burial in this cemetery, the ancient authorities have recorded it. That St Marcellinus had especial charge over this same cemetery, and directed excavations that were made in it, we have already seen very interesting proof;* nevertheless, neither he nor his successor, St Marcellus, was buried in it; they were both buried in the cemetery of St Priscilla, on the Via Salara. The cause of this change is at once explained by reference to the history of the times. Diocletian had now confiscated all the cemeteries that were known, and the *fiscus* had taken possession of them; access, therefore, to the most public and notorious of all the Catacombs was no longer possible. Not only would the Christians cease to assemble and to bury there, but it is probable also that precautions would be taken to protect so precious a sanctuary as the sepulchre of the Popes from falling into the hands of the heathen. It would have been

* See page 93.

K

Traces of the Diocletian persecution.

easy to do this either by blocking up the approaches by means of earth taken from the adjacent galleries, or in some other way; and it is at least a curious coincidence, if it be not rather an almost convincing proof of the accuracy of this conjecture, that Michele De Rossi has been persuaded—merely by an examination of the monuments of the place, from an architectural point of view—that all the galleries in the immediate neighbourhood of this *sanctum sanctorum* were actually blocked up in this way, during some time or other in the ages of persecution. He can even point to the staircase in the tufa, whose lower steps were all cut off, thereby rendering the whole inaccessible. Moreover, if we accept this theory, it is at once accounted for why the next two Popes, St Eusebius and St Melchiades, though buried in the cemetery of St Callixtus after its restoration to the Christians, yet did not occupy graves in the Papal vault, but lay each in his own *cubiculum* apart. Maxentius did not indeed restore the *loca ecclesiastica* until after the death of Eusebius; but that Pontiff died an exile in Sicily, and his body was only brought back to Rome some years afterwards by his successor, just as Pontian's had been by Fabian. It was then buried in a very fine crypt, especially prepared for it, of which we shall have to speak presently.

Melchiades the last Pope buried in the Catacomb.

Melchiades, too, we are told by some of the ancient authorities, was buried in another separate crypt; and although we cannot now with any certainty identify it, it seems extremely probable that it is the one pointed out by De Rossi, and that the top or cover of the sarcophagus in which he lay is that which may still be seen on the floor of one of the crypts not far from the Papal vault.

With St Melchiades, the long succession of martyred Popes comes to a close; and a new era opens in the history of Christianity from St Sylvester. New customs are now of necessity introduced, or old ones are at least considerably modified. Christian sepulchres are made freely above ground; small basilicas or mausoleums are erected for the purpose; and we have already seen that St Sylvester himself, St Mark, St Julius, and even St Damasus, were all buried in oratories of this kind, placed near the entrance of the Catacombs, but not within them. Our history, therefore, of the Papal Crypt, as a place of burial, is now complete, and we shall not attempt to draw out any history of the changes it underwent, either in its form or its decorations, to fit it for its use as a sanctuary.

De Rossi has given his readers a beautiful sketch of the chapel, as he believes it to have been after its completion (Plate XV.); reminding them, at the same time, that this "restoration" is no mere product of his own fancy, void of all authority. On the contrary, it has been suggested in nearly all its details—in some it is even required—by what may still be recognised amid the wreck of its former splendour, *e. g.*, the bases of the pillars and the monuments at the sides remain in their original places, portions of the columns and of the marble lattice-work were found lying upon the ground, &c. &c. But for these and many other particulars we must refer to De Rossi's own work, which here, as often elsewhere, refuses to be abridged.

We must not, however, take our leave of this most interesting chapel without making a few remarks on *one* part of the restoration at least, which is unquestionably correct—the Damasine inscription. We shall find ourselves much better able to appreciate its meaning now than when first we saw it on our entrance into the *cubiculum*.

Inscription of Pope Damasus in this crypt.

> Hic congesta jacet quæris si turba Piorum,
> Corpora Sanctorum retinent veneranda sepulchra,
> Sublimes animas rapuit sibi Regia Cœli :
> Hic comites Xysti portant qui ex hoste tropæa ;
> Hic numerus procerum servat qui altaria Christi ;
> Hic positus longâ vixit qui in pace Sacerdos ;
> Hic Confessores sancti quos Græcia misit ;
> Hic juvenes, puerique, senes castique nepotes,
> Quis mage virgineum placuit retinere pudorem.
> Hic fateor Damasus volui mea condere membra,
> Sed cineres timui sanctos vexare Piorum.

> " Here, if you would know, lie heaped together a whole crowd of holy
> ones.
> These honoured sepulchres inclose the bodies of the saints,
> Their noble souls the palace of Heaven has taken to itself.
> Here lie the companions of Xystus, who bear away the trophies
> from the enemy;
> Here a number of elders, who guard the altars of Christ;
> Here is buried the Priest, who long lived in peace;
> Here the holy Confessors whom Greece sent us;
> Here lie youths and boys, old men, and their chaste offspring,
> Who chose, as the better part, to keep their virgin chastity.
> Here I, Damasus, confess I wished to lay my bones,
> But I feared to disturb the holy ashes of the saints."

Vast number of martyrs not improbable. In the first lines, the poet seems to allude to a number of martyrs laid together in one large tomb, such as we know, from Prudentius,* were to be seen in some parts of the Roman Catacombs; and it is a singular fact that whereas both of the old itineraries which we quoted in the beginning of this book speak, the one of 80, the other of 800, martyrs in immediate connection with this part of the cemetery, a pit of extraordinary depth is still to be seen in the corner of this very chapel, before we pass on to St Cecilia's. Such a number of concurrent testimonies make it worth while to pause and consider the subject somewhat more attentively. It is common, indeed, with a certain class of writers, to set these statements on one side as manifest and absurd exaggerations; and yet the language of Prudentius is precise, and an accurate knowledge of the laws and customs of Pagan Rome predisposes us to accept it as a literal statement of the truth. Prudentius supposes his friend to have asked him the names of those who had shed their blood for the faith in Rome, and the epitaphs (*tituli*) inscribed on their tombs. He replies that it would be very difficult to do this, for that the relics of the saints in Rome are innumerable; that so long as the city continued to worship their Pagan gods, their wicked rage slew vast multitudes of the just. On many tombs, indeed, he says, you may read the name of the martyr, and some short inscription, but there are

* Peristeph. xi. 1-17.

also many others which are silent as to the name, and only
express the number. "You can ascertain the number which
lie heaped up together" (*congestis corpora acervis*), but nothing
more; and he specifies in particular one grave, in which he
learnt that the relics of sixty men had been laid, whose names
were known only to Christ as being His special friends. Let
us put side by side with this a narrative from the Annals of
Tacitus,* and we shall be satisfied that such wholesale butchery
of those whom the law condemned was by no means improbable. It appears that it had been provided by the ancient
law of Rome that, if a master was ever murdered by his slave,
all his fellow-slaves were to suffer death together with the
culprit. Such a murder happened in the year A.D. 62, of one
Pedanius Secundus, who had lately been the Prefect of the
city, and who was the master of four hundred slaves. The
innocence of the great majority of these slaves was notorious,
and this, coupled with the unusual number of the victims,
created a considerable excitement among the people. The
matter was discussed in the Senate, and some of its members
ventured to express compassion, and to deprecate the rigorous
execution of the law. It was decided, however, apparently by
a very large majority, that the law should take its course
(*nihil mutandum*), and when the people threatened violence,
the troops were called out, the whole line of road was guarded
by them, and the unhappy four hundred were put to death at
once. Tacitus has recorded the speech of one of those who
took the chief part in the debate, and his language and arguments are precisely those which we can imagine to have been
used again and again in the second and third centuries by
orators persuading a general persecution of the Christians.
"Now that we have nations amongst us," said Cassius, "who
have different rites and ceremonies, a foreign religion, or perhaps no religion at all, it is impossible to keep such a rabble
(*conluviem istam*) under restraint in any other way than by

* Tac. An., xiv. 43–45.

fear. True, indeed, some innocent persons will perish with the guilty. But, wherever it is necessary to make some striking example of severity for the public good, there will be always incidental injustice to certain individuals." Nor is this the only testimony that could be alleged upon this point. We will only add, however, that of Lactantius, or the author of *De Mortibus Persecutorum*, who was at least a cotemporary witness of what he describes, and who tells us that when the number of Christians condemned was very great, they were not executed singly, but surrounded by fire on all sides, and thus burnt together (*gregatim amburebantur*).*
This explains to us how it was possible for the relics of so many to have been buried in one grave. On the whole, therefore, we conclude that there seems to be no solid reason for calling in question the truth of what ancient authorities generally have told us on this subject, however difficult it may be, in this or that particular instance, to verify the number recorded.

Of the companions of St Sixtus, and of the many Popes who had been buried in this chapel, and whom the inscription of Damasus next commemorates, we have already given a full account, nor will our readers have any difficulty in recognising St Melchiades in the priest, or bishop (*Sacerdos*), " who had enjoyed a long life of peace," after the persecutions had ceased. " The confessors sent from Greece," are to be found in the various martyrologies, and the names of some are enumerated by De Rossi as Hippolytus, Adrias, Maria, Neo, and Paulina. Of the remainder, their names are " in the Book of Life," but no distinct memorial of them remains on earth.

* C. xv.

CHAPTER IV.

CRYPT OF ST CECILIA.

A NARROW doorway, cut somewhat irregularly through the rock in the corner of the Papal Crypt, introduces us at once into another chamber. As we pass through this doorway we observe that the sides were once covered with slabs of marble, and the arch over our heads adorned with mosaics. The first impression we receive from this chamber is one of strong contrast with what we have just left behind us. The room is much larger: it is nearly 20 feet square (the other had been only 14 by 11); it is irregular in shape, and has a wide *luminare* over it, completely flooding it with light; yet we see no altar-tomb, no cotemporary epitaphs of popes or martyrs, nor indeed anything else which at once engages our attention and promises to give us any valuable information. Perhaps a more careful examination may detect objects of interest still remaining on the walls; but if we would understand and enjoy them when they are found, it is necessary that our minds should first be stored with some knowledge of the history of St Cecilia, before whose tomb we are. This confident statement may perhaps provoke a smile in some of our readers, who know that the sceptical criticism of the last century endeavoured to throw a doubt upon the existence of such a martyr; or would insist, at least, on transferring the scene of her history from Rome to Sicily. Moreover, we have just now seen the announcement of a French archbishop in the fifteenth century, bidding us venerate the grave of St Cecilia in the cemetery at St Sebastian's, more than a quarter of a mile

Chapel of St Cecilia.

off. What fresh knowledge, then, has been gained since that time, which enables us not only to detect his error, but also to insist with confidence upon the correctness of our own assertion in its stead? And is there no danger of later critics rising up to set aside our judgment as peremptorily as we are setting aside those of our predecessors? We hope thoroughly to satisfy our readers on these questions before we leave this chapel; but first we must set before them, as we have said, some sketch of the legend of St Cecilia.

History of St Cecilia.

The Acts of her Martyrdom, as they have come down to us, cannot lay claim to any higher antiquity than the fifth century; and yet, though their corruption and interpolation be freely admitted, recent discoveries have proved that they are unquestionably true in all their chief features, and in many even of their minutest details. We shall, therefore, first give as much of the legend as is necessary for our purpose, in its popular form, and then point out the few but important particulars in which sound criticism obliges us to correct them.

St Cecilia, then, was a maiden of noble blood, born of parents of senatorial rank; the language of the Acts is most precise upon this point, using the exact technical words which distinguished her rank—*Ingenua, nobilis, clarissima*. She had been brought up a Christian from her earliest infancy, having probably a Christian mother. Her father, however, must have been a pagan, for the saint was given in marriage to a young patrician of very amiable and excellent dispositions, but a pagan, named Valerian. St Cecilia had already consecrated herself by secret vow to the service of her Lord in the state of virginity; and on the day of her marriage she persuaded her husband to visit Pope Urban, lying hid in a cemetery on the Appian Way, by whom he was instructed and baptized. So also was his brother, Tiburtius. These two were presently martyred for refusing to offer sacrifice to the gods, and Maximus, the officer who presided at their execution, was so moved by their constancy, that he too was brought to the faith,

Crypt of St Cecilia. 153

and received the crown of martyrdom with them. These all were buried in the Catacomb of St Prætextatus, where, as we have seen, the ancient pilgrims thought them worthy of special mention. Cecilia still lived, and as Almachius thought it best that her punishment should be as secret as possible, he ordered that she should be shut up in the *Caldarium*, or room of the warm bath in her own palace, and that the pipes with which the walls on all sides were perforated, should be heated to such a degree as to cause suffocation. Instances of this kind of secret execution are very common in Roman history, whenever it was thought desirable, for any reason, to avoid publicity. Cecilia entered the room appointed her; the furnace was heated "seven times more than it was wont to be heated ;" she remained there for a whole day and night, yet at the end of the time it was found that, as with the Three Children in the fiery furnace, so now with this virgin, " the fire had no power over her body, nor was a hair of her head singed, neither were her garments changed, nor the smell of fire had passed on her." No sweat stood upon her brow, no lassitude oppressed her limbs, but she was sound and whole as at the beginning. When this unlooked-for intelligence was conveyed to the prefect, he sent one of the lictors with orders to strike off her head. He found her in the very room of her victory, and proceeded at once to accomplish his errand. Three times did the axe fall upon her tender neck, inflicting deep and mortal wounds, but, whether it was that the sight of so young and noble a victim unnerved the heart of the executioner, or whether his hand was supernaturally stayed by the hand of God, certain it is that his work was not complete, and as the law did not allow more than three strokes to be given, he went away, leaving her yet alive, though bathed in her own blood. The manner of death having been thus changed, it was no longer necessary that the door of the chamber in which she lay should be kept closed ; and as soon, therefore, as the executioner had withdrawn, the faithful of her house and neighbourhood flocked in to receive the last breath of the dying martyr. They found her stretched upon the marble pavement, calmly awaiting the moment of her release, and as they crowded round her, dipping their handkerchiefs or any other piece of linen they could find in her sacred blood, that they might reverently collect it all as blood that had been spilt for the love of Jesus, and was therefore precious in His sight, she spoke to all according to their several needs. For two days and nights she continued in this state, hovering, as it were, between life and death; and on the third morning the venerable Pope Urban—it is necessary again to remind our readers that we are only repeating what is written in the Acts—came to bid farewell to his beloved daughter. "I have prayed," she said, "that I might not die during these three days, until I had first had an opportunity of recommending to your Blessedness"—the title by which the popes were then addressed, just as we now address them as "your Holiness"—"the poor, whom I have always nourished, and of giving you this house, to the intent that it may be made a church for ever." The bishop had no sooner signified his assent to her dying requests, and given her his blessing, than, turning her face towards the ground, and letting her arms and hands fall gently together upon her right side, she breathed forth her pure spirit, and passed into the presence of her God. That same evening her body was placed in a rough coffin of cypress-wood,* just in the attitude in which she had died; and Urban and his deacons bore it out of the city into the cemetery of St Callixtus, where he buried her in a chamber "near his own colleagues, the bishops and martyrs."

Body of St Cecilia translated by Paschal I., A.D. 821.

Such is the legend of St Cecilia's martyrdom. The history of her relics is still more remarkable and equally important to our narrative. Pope Paschal I. succeeded to the see of Peter

---

* The use of a coffin was very unusual among the early Christians, at least among those who were buried in the Catacombs; nevertheless, there are arguments which oblige us to believe that one was used on this occasion.

Crypt of St Cecilia. 155

in January A.D. 817, and in the following July he translated into different churches in the city the relics of 2300 martyrs, collected from the various suburban cemeteries, which at that time were lying in a deplorable state of ruin. Amongst the relics thus removed were those of the popes from the Papal Crypt we have just described. He had wished to remove at the same time the relics of St Cecilia, but he could not discover her tomb; so at length he reluctantly acquiesced in the report that her body had been carried off by Astulfus, the Lombard king, by whom Rome had been besieged and these cemeteries plundered.* Some four years afterwards, however, St Cecilia appeared to him in a dream or vision—it is Paschal himself who tells us the story,† as well as his cotemporary biographer, the continuator of the *Liber Pontificalis* —and told him that when he was translating the bodies of the popes, she was so close to him that they might have conversed together. In consequence of this vision he returned to the search, and found the body where he had been told. It was fresh and perfect as when it was first laid in the tomb, and clad in rich garments mixed with gold, with linen cloths stained with blood rolled up at her feet, lying in a cypress coffin.

Paschal himself tells us that he lined the coffin with fringed silk, spread over the body a covering of silk gauze, and then, placing it within a sarcophagus of white marble, deposited it under the high altar of the Church of Sta. Cecilia in Trastevere.

Nearly eight hundred years afterwards, Cardinal Sfondrati, of the title of St Cecilia, made considerable alterations in the church, and in course of his excavations in the sanctuary, he came upon a wide vault beneath the altar. Two marble sarcophagi met his eyes. Trustworthy witnesses had been already summoned, and in their presence one of these sarcophagi was opened. It was found to contain a coffin of cypress-wood. The

Found incorrupt A.D. 1599.

---

* See page 106.
† This vision forms the subject of an old fresco, some fragments of which may still be seen at the end of the Church of Sta. Cecilia in Trastevere.

cardinal himself drew back the coffin-lid. First appeared the precious lining and silk gauze with which Paschal had covered the body nearly eight centuries before. Its colour had faded, but the fabric was still entire, and through its transparent folds could be seen the shining gold of the robes in which the martyr herself was clothed. After pausing a few moments, the cardinal gently removed this silken covering, and the virgin form of St Cecilia appeared in the very same attitude in which she had breathed her last on the pavement of the house in which the spectators were then standing, and which neither Urban nor Paschal had ventured to disturb. She lay clothed in her robes of golden tissue, on which were still visible the glorious stains of her blood, and at her feet were the linen cloths mentioned by Pope Paschal and his biographer. Lying on her right side, with her arms extended in front of her body, she looked like one in a deep sleep. Her head, in a singularly touching manner, was turned round towards the bottom of the coffin; her knees were slightly bent, and drawn together. The body was perfectly incorrupt, and by a special miracle retained, after more than thirteen hundred years, all its grace and modesty, and recalled with the most truthful exactness Cecilia breathing forth her soul on the pavement of her bath.*

A more signal vindication of the Church's traditions; a more consoling spectacle for a devout Catholic, mourning over the schisms and heresies of those miserable times; a more striking commentary on the Divine promise, "The Lord keepeth all the bones of His servants; He will not lose one of them!"† it would be difficult to conceive. One is not surprised at the profound sensation which the intelligence of this discovery created in the Eternal City.

Pope Clement VIII., at that time sick at Frascati, deputed Cardinal Baronius to make a careful examination of the pre-

---

* De Rossi has himself assisted at the translation of a body from the Catacombs to a church two miles distant, lying on the marble slab on which it was found, without the least displacement of a single bone.— *R. S.* ii. 127. † Psalm xxxiii. 21.

cious remains, and both he and Bosio have left accounts of what they witnessed. All Rome came to satisfy its curiosity and devotion for the space of four or five weeks, during which the virgin martyr lay exposed for veneration; and when the tomb was again closed, on St Cecilia's day, the Pope himself sang the Mass. Cardinal Sfondrati erected the beautiful high-altar which now stands over the saint's tomb, and beneath it he placed a statue by Maderna, who had frequently seen the body, as the inscription intimates.

"EN TIBI SANCTISSIMÆ VIRGINIS CÆCILIÆ IMAGINEM QUAM IPSE INTEGRAM IN SEPULCHRO JACENTEM VIDI, EAMDEM TIBI PRORSUS EODEM CORPORIS SITU HOC MARMORE EXPRESSI."

"Behold the image of the most holy Virgin Cecilia, whom I myself saw lying incorrupt in her tomb. I have in this marble expressed for thee the same Saint in the very same posture of body."

FIG. 17.—*Maderna's Statue of St Cecilia.*

An engraving also was published at the same time—a few copies of which may yet be found in foreign libraries, (*e.g.*, at Carpentras, among the MSS. of Peiresc, a cotemporary)—with the inscription, *Hoc habitu inventa est.*

It has no special bearing upon our subject, yet we cannot help adding that in the other sarcophagus which we mentioned as having been found by Sfondrati, and which, according to the tradition, ought to have contained the bodies of Saints Tiburtius, Valerian, and Maximus (translated from St Prætextatus'), the remains of three bodies were seen, two of which, apparently of the same age and size, had manifestly been beheaded, whilst the skull of the third was broken, and the abundant hair upon it was thickly matted with blood, as though the martyr had been beaten to death by those *plumbatæ* or leaded scourges of which Prudentius and others tell us, and of which a specimen has been found in the Catacombs even in our own times,* and which the Acts of St Cecilia's martyrdom distinctly state to have been the instrument of the death of St Maximus.

<small>Critical examination of the crypt.</small>

And now we must confront the whole of this marvellous narrative with the actual monuments of the cemetery, so far as they still exist, and can be made to throw any light upon it. We have seen that the Acts assert that Pope Urban had buried the Virgin Martyr near to his own colleagues. Both the itineraries which we quoted at the beginning † mention her grave, immediately before, or immediately after, those of the Popes. Pope Paschal says that he found her body quite close to the place whence he had withdrawn the bodies of his saintly predecessors. Are all these topographical notices true or false? This is the question which must have agitated the mind of De Rossi when he discovered that there was a second chamber immediately contiguous to that in which the Popes had been buried, and we may easily imagine the eagerness with which he longed to penetrate it. But this could not be done at once. The chapel was full of earth, even to the very top of the *luminare*, and all this soil must first be removed through the *luminare* itself. As the work of excavation proceeded, there came to light, first, on the wall of the *luminare*, the figure of a woman in the usual attitude of prayer, but of this both the outlines and colour were too indistinct to enable him to identify it. Below this there appeared a Latin cross between two sheep. These also were much faded. Still lower down the wall—the wall, that is, of the *luminare*, not of the chamber itself—he came upon the figures of three saints, executed apparently in the fourth, or perhaps even the fifth

<small>Its discovery and excavation by De Rossi.</small>

<small>Paintings in the *luminare*,</small>

---

* R. S. ii. 164. † See pages 111, 113.

century; but they were all of men, and their names inscribed at the side showed no trace of any connection with the history of St Cecilia. They were Policamus, whose martyrdom was proclaimed by a palm-branch springing up by his side, Sabastianus, and Curinus, this last having his head tonsured with the *corona* usually found on episcopal portraits of that period. De Rossi had never had any reason to expect a representation of either of these saints near the tomb of St Cecilia. It will save us from some embarrassment, therefore, if we postpone what we have to say about them for the present, and proceed with our work of clearance of the whole chamber.

As we come nearer to the floor, we find upon the wall, *close* to the entrance from the burial-place of the popes, a painting which may be attributed, perhaps, to the seventh century, of a woman, richly attired, and ornamented with bracelets and necklaces, such as might be looked for in a high-born and wealthy Roman bride, and might well be intended to represent St Cecilia. Still further down, upon the same wall, we come to a niche such as is found in some other parts of the Catacombs to receive the large shallow vessel of oil, or precious unguents, which, in ancient times, were used to feed the lamps burning before special shrines. At the back of this niche is a large head of our Lord, represented according to the Byzantine type, and with rays of glory behind it in the form of a Greek cross. Side by side with this, but on the flat surface of the wall, is a figure of St Urban, in full pontifical dress, with his name inscribed.

and on the wall of the crypt.

Examination of these paintings shows that they were not the original ornaments of this place. The painting of St Cecilia was executed on the surface of ruined mosaic work, portions of which may still be easily detected. The niche in which our Lord's head is painted bears evident traces of having once been encased with marble, and both it and the figure of St Urban can hardly have been executed before the tenth or eleventh century. The continued renewal of ornamentation

Signs of more ancient decorations.

in any part of the Catacombs, especially if prolonged beyond the eighth and ninth centuries, is a sure mark of high religious and historical interest attaching to that particular spot; and when we add that immediately by the side of these paintings is a deep recess in the wall, capable of receiving a large sarcophagus, and that between the back of this recess, and the back of one of the papal graves in the adjoining chamber, there is scarcely an inch of rock, we think the most sceptical of critics will confess that we have here certainly recovered a lost thread of tradition, and may claim to have discovered the original resting-place of one of the most ancient and famous of Rome's virgin saints.

Here was the original tomb of St Cecilia.

It will be asked, however, if this is really the place where St Cecilia was buried, and if Paschal really visited the adjoining chapel, how is it possible that he could have had any difficulty in finding her tomb? To this we may reply by reminding our readers of the condition in which the Catacombs were at that time. These translations of relics were being made, because the cemeteries in which they lay were utterly ruined. Moreover, it is possible that the doorway, or the recess, or both, may have been walled up or otherwise concealed, for the express purpose of baffling the search of the sacrilegious Lombards. Nor is this mere conjecture. Among the *débris* of this spot De Rossi has found several fragments of a wall, too thin ever to have been used as a means of support, but manifestly serviceable as a curtain of concealment; and, although, with that perfect candour and truthfulness which so enhances all his other merits, he adds that these fragments seem to him to bear tokens of a later date, this does not show that there had not been another wall of the same kind at an earlier period, and he is also able to quote from his own experience the instance of an *arcosolium* in the Catacomb of St Prætextatus thus carefully concealed by the erection of a wall.

Evidence of this from inscriptions.

However, be the true explanation of this difficulty what it may, our ignorance on this subject cannot be allowed to

Crypt of St Cecilia.

outweigh the explicit testimony of Paschal, and the abundant corroborations which it receives both from ancient and modern sources. Not the least important among these is the number of epitaphs that have been found here belonging to the Cæcilii and other noble families connected with them by ties of blood or marriage. These are so numerous that we cannot doubt that this cemetery was originally the private property of that *gens*, and that the Saint herself belonged to it. There is a gravestone even now lying in the pavement of this chamber, which seems to offer some testimony on the subject. It is to the memory of one Septimus Pretextatus Cæcilianus, a " servant of God, who had lived worthy [of his vocation] for three and thirty years," and exclaims at the end of them, "If I have served Thee, I shall not repent of it, and I will bless Thy name." The names on this monument are very suggestive. The Itineraries tell us that the husband and brother-in-law of St Cecilia were buried in the Catacomb of St Prætextatus ; and here we find a Prætextatus Cæcilianus privileged to have his place of burial close to that of the Virgin Martyr herself. Does not this denote some connection between the families? so that, whereas St Cecilia was privy to the movements of Urban, lying hid in the cemetery under her own property on one side of the road, she could also obtain burial for her husband and others in the cemetery of St Prætextatus on the other side.

Again, De Rossi is of opinion that we have distinct—we had almost said authentic and documentary—evidence of the translation on the walls of the chapel itself. If we examine closely the picture of St Cecilia, we shall find it covered with a number of *graffiti*, which are easily divided into two classes ; the one class quite irregular both as to place and style of writing, consisting only of the names of pilgrims who had visited the shrine, and several of these, either by name or express title, confess themselves to be strangers. Thus, one is named Ildebrandus, another is a Bishop Ethelred, and two

From the chapel itself.

L

others write themselves down Spaniards. The other class of *graffiti* is quite regular, arranged in four lines, and containing almost exclusively the names of priests; the only exceptions to this rule being that one woman appears amongst them, but it is added that she is the mother of the priest who signed before her, and that the last signature of all was of a *scriniarius*, or secretary. There is something about this arrangement of names which suggests the idea of an official act; neither can it be attributed to chance that several of the same names appear on the painting of St Cornelius, presently to be visited, in this same Catacomb, whence his body was translated about the same time as St Cecilia's. Some of them appear also on a painting lately discovered in the subterranean San Clemente; and others again in the subscriptions to the decrees of a Roman Council, held A.D. 826. Of course some of the names are very common, such as Leo, Benedictus, or Joannes, and the mere repetition of these would not suffice to raise a suspicion of identity; but when such names as George and Mercury appear, and are signed in both instances with the same peculiarity of writing, some letters having been made square, others written in a running hand, it cannot be rejected as an improbable conjecture that these men were among the leading parochial clergy of Rome, who attended the Pope in some official capacity, attesting the translation of relics in one instance, or signing the decrees of a Council in another. No *graffiti* of this kind appear on the picture of St Urbanus, which, as we have already seen, is of a much later date than that of St Cecilia, and was, in fact, only added as an ornament to her sepulchre,—DECORI SEPVLCRI S. CÆCILIÆ MARTYRIS, says a half obliterated scroll or tablet still remaining by its side,—after her body had been removed; for the crosses which appear on the shoulders of the *pallium* were not in use before the tenth or eleventh century.

Verification and correction of the Acts of St Cecilia. It yet remains to say a few words about the history of St Cecilia's martyrdom, with which we began. We have already acknowledged that the Acts are not genuine, and yet we have seen that in substance their accuracy has been marvellously confirmed by all that has since been discovered. The truth is, that the monuments discovered in the Catacombs almost enable us to restore the Acts to their primitive form, by recalling the probable occasion of some of their present errors. For the chief difficulty that has always been urged against them concerns chronology. The Acts imply, or indeed directly assert, that a furious persecution was raging at the time of St Cecilia's death, and they speak of the edicts of the reigning *princes* as though there were more than one; yet the mention of Pope Urban fixes the date to a time when Alexander Severus ruled the empire alone, and the Christians enjoyed tranquillity. The martyrology of Ado, however, whilst still retaining the name of Urban, adds, with apparently unconscious inconsistency, that the saint suffered in the times of Aurelius and Commodus, *i.e.*, nearly fifty years before that pope. Whence did Ado obtain this particular item of his information, that the martyrdom of St Cecilia belonged to the year 177 or thereabouts? This is what we cannot now tell, but we may be very certain that he derived it from some ancient authority which he trusted, and if *we* trust it also, the difficulties it will solve are manifold. The language of the Acts now becomes consistent with the known facts of history. Not only were two princes reigning, who hated and persecuted the Church, but the words of the judge as he pronounces sentence upon the martyrs are precisely equivalent to, are in fact a mere translation of, the very words in which Eusebius* has reported the edict of those Emperors, viz., that as many as should refuse to deny that they were Christians, should be punished, but that if they denied the charge they should be at once dismissed. *First, in change of date.*

The chronological difficulty is now shifted from the emperors to the pope. If St Cecilia suffered A.D. 177, our readers will ask how she could have had anything to do with St Urban. *Secondly, in change of Bishop.*

* H. E. v. 1.

But they can also answer this question at once, by calling to mind what has been already alluded to, the existence of two bishops of the same name at various times; the one, Bishop of Rome, the other, bishop of some unknown see; the one, pope and confessor, buried in St Callixtus', the other, a martyr, buried in St Prætextatus'. We need only suppose that the earlier of these two bishops was resident in Rome during the episcopacy of St Eleutherius, and occasionally acted for him, as we know that the Bishops Caldonius and Ercolanus acted at one time in Carthage for St Cyprian.

<small>And other exaggerations.</small> The corruptions of ancient Acts are ordinarily in the way of exaggeration. As every magistrate becomes the chief magistrate or prefect, so it was only natural that Urbanus, a bishop, should become Urbanus, the Pope; and since the interpolations were made whilst yet the bodies, both of the pope and the virgin martyr, lay each in their original tomb, and could be seen in immediate proximity to one another, the connection between them must have seemed obvious and certain, and the copyist who transcribed or compiled the acts, had only to use the license, common to all historians, of assigning the motives or causes of effects which he had to record. St Cecilia and St Urban were buried in adjoining chambers, and a bishop of the name of Urban had been a friend of hers during life; therefore they were one and the same Urban, and the Pope had given this honourable place of burial to the saint, because of his affection for her, and admiration of her distinguished merit.

So argued the scribe of the fifth or sixth century, conscientiously doing his best to chronicle the glories of the Church, and to repair the injuries which she had suffered from the wholesale destruction of her ancient records; whereas we of the nineteenth century, though removed to a greater distance from the time of action, yet having a larger field of observation, and exercising a sound criticism upon the multitude of contradictory notices that have come down to us, venture to propose another mode of reconstructing the history.

Crypt of St Cecilia.

We feel more disposed to believe that St Cecilia was buried here, because the cemetery was her own property; that her whole family, or at least several important branches of it, embraced the Christian faith before the close of the second century (so numerous are the Christian epitaphs of that period belonging to them), and that they then transferred this cemetery, and a considerable portion of the adjacent ground, for the general use of the Church, to Pope Zephyrinus, who forthwith appointed his deacon, Callixtus, to take charge of it, and it became in time the most extensive and important of all the subterranean cemeteries; that St Cecilia's vault was originally a very small and dark chamber,* but that Damasus opened a new entrance into it by the staircase and vestibule which now exist, and enlarged the chamber at considerable labour and expense, as the large brick arches and walls abundantly prove; and that this was done for the better accommodation of the many pilgrims who flocked to visit it. Finally, we believe that at a somewhat later period—probably in the pontificate of Sixtus III.—the *luminare* was opened over it, and those figures of Polycamus, Sabastianus, and Optatus, painted upon its sides.

We know of no other Sebastian that can be meant here but the famous martyr, whose basilica is not far off. Cyrinus or Quirinus was a martyr and Bishop of Siscia in Illyria, who, in the days of Prudentius,† lay in his own city, but when Illyria was invaded by the barbarians, his body was brought to Rome and buried in the basilica of St Sebastian about the year 420. Of Polycamus the history is altogether lost; neither the martyrologies nor ecclesiastical historians have left us any record of his life. Only this we know, on the authority of two ancient witnesses, that among the relics translated to the churches of

_{The saints on the *luminare* accounted for.}

---

* De Rossi suggests, as a solution of the difficulties which his brother's architectural analysis throws in the way of this modification of St Cecilia's history, that her body was probably placed in this chamber after the Papal Crypt had been set apart for the burial of the Popes. This would account for the coffin having been used in this instance, contrary to the usual custom. See page 154, *note*. † Peristeph. vii.

Sta. Prassede and of San Silvestro in Capite, in Rome, in the ninth century, were those of Polycamus and Optatus, and that the tomb of Polycamus had been very near St Cecilia's. Whether Rome had been the scene of his martyrdom, and this Catacomb the original place of his burial, we cannot tell. We think it more probable that it was not. Perhaps his relics were brought from abroad, like those of St Quirinus, and about the same time, and their figures may have been painted in the interior of this *luminare* merely by way of ornament, and because their names were just then in men's mouths. This seems also to be the only account that can be given of the appearance on this wall of the third figure, Optatus. We can only conjecture that he was the Bishop of Vesceter, in Numidia, of whom we read that he was put to death by the Vandals, and that his body was brought to Rome about A.D. 430.

VLPIO FLORENTIO
BENEMERENTI QVI
VIXIT ANNOS LXXVII
DIES XI QVIESCIT IN
PACE III KAL IVNIAS

FIG. 18. *On the mensa of an Arcosolium in Cemetery of St Soteris.*

CHAPTER V.

THE EPITAPH OF ST EUSEBIUS.

THE Itineraries, after mentioning St Cecilia and the popes, and "the innumerable multitude of martyrs" that rest near them, go on to say that Eusebius, pope and martyr, rests in a cave some way off; and St Cornelius, pope and martyr, in another cave still farther off. That we may complete our review of the historical monuments of the cemetery of St Callixtus, it is necessary that we should visit both of these *caves* or subterranean chambers; and we will take that of St Eusebius first, as being the nearest. It lies, in fact, just where our guides would have led us to expect, viz., between St Cornelius and the other popes; not much more than a hundred paces from the latter. *Crypt of St Eusebius.*

It was whilst searching for the popes' chapel, in the year 1852, that De Rossi came upon half a dozen bits of marble, with letters in a character somewhat like the Damasine in form, yet very inferior in execution. The only perfect words were SCINDITUR and SEDITIO, and the fragments were EUS, EXEMPL, and INTEG. Immediately he remembered the inscription about a certain Eusebius, which, having been found in old MSS., without any indication of the place whence it had been copied, had furnished a subject of much discussion to Baronius, Tillemont, and others, as to its sense and authorship. Some, like Tillemont and the Bollandists, had almost taken it for granted that the Eusebius spoken of had been the pope of that name, and had attributed the verses, therefore, to Pope Damasus; whilst others thought it incredible that history *Fragments found of a Damasine inscription.*

should have been so absolutely silent about incidents of such magnitude to the Church of Rome, and chose rather to refer them to some priest or bishop holding a less exalted position.

We need not say towards which side leaned the opinion of De Rossi, after finding these fragments just where he had reason to believe Pope Eusebius had been buried; and he took the earliest opportunity of publishing the discovery in a lecture before one of the learned societies in Rome. He had yet to wait nearly five years before the work of excavation enabled him to penetrate fully into the interior of the cemetery at this place, and to set the question finally at rest. The labours of the Commission of Sacred Archæology had been employed during the interval in disinterring those chapels of the popes and St Cecilia which have been just described. But in 1856 they returned to this spot, and as they removed the soil which here, as elsewhere throughout all the crypts of historical interest, had been poured in for centuries through an open *luminare*, De Rossi discovered forty other fragments of the same inscription.

Importance of this crypt.

When the excavation was completed, it was easy to see the importance which had once attached to the chapels that were now recovered. Not only was there a staircase descending to them from the upper air, but walls had been built in the subterranean itself, to prevent those who entered it from going astray, and losing themselves in the labyrinth of surrounding galleries. They were guided of necessity to two chapels, opposite to one another, on different sides of the path. One was about 9 feet by 12, the other considerably larger, 16 by 13. The smaller one had once been highly decorated with paintings, mosaics, and slabs of marble. All is now sadly ruined, but it is still possible to distinguish among the mosaic work one of the most common Christian symbols, a double-handed vessel, with a bird on either side of it; and among the paintings, the representations of the seasons (apparently) and other accessories of ornament; but the main figures and general design have perished. The walls of the opposite chamber were never cased with marble, so that the pilgrims were able to leave here the same tokens of their presence as they left at St Sixtus'. The *graffiti* are of the same general character, only of a somewhat later date; the old forms of prayer, *in mente habete*, &c., have disappeared; the inscriptions are mostly in Latin, and among the few that are Greek, there are symptoms of Byzantine peculiarities. On the whole, we may say with confidence, that they belong to the fifth century rather than to the third.

The interest of these chambers, however, is centred in the inscription, which now occupies the middle of the smaller room. Of course, this was not its original position; but it has been so placed, in order that we may see both sides of the stone without difficulty. On the one side is an imperial inscription belonging to pagan times; on the other, a Damasine, in honour of Eusebius. We call it Damasine, because it had been published in the later editions of his works, even before its discovery in this place; and also because it lays claim to that title itself. But everybody can see at a glance* that it was never executed by the same hand to which we are indebted for so many other beautiful productions of that pope. Whilst De Rossi had only recovered three or four fragments, he was disposed to think that it might have been one of the earliest efforts of the artist who subsequently attained such perfection; but as the number of specimens increased, he became more and more convinced that it was a copy made in a later age—a *restoration*, as we should now say, and partaking of the characteristics of many other modern restorations, which are not improvements. In his lecture to the Roman antiquaries in the summer of 1856, he proclaimed his firm persuasion that the stone, which he was then partially recovering, was not the original on which the epitaph of St Damasus had been first engraved; but that it had been set up by Pope

Inscription to St Eusebius, a restoration of the sixth or seventh century.

* See Plate II., at end of volume.

Symmachus, or Vigilius, or John III. (A.D. 498-574), of all of whom we know that they did their best to repair the damage which had been done in the Catacombs by the Lombards and others. We have already quoted * an inscription of Pope Vigilius, in which he expressly mentions that he had restored some of the *tituli* of Damasus, which had perished, or at least the marble tablets on which they were engraved had been broken; and De Rossi thought it very probable that this might be one of them. He had also, on another occasion, publicly hazarded a conjecture that the artist who had engraved all the Damasine inscriptions was Furius Dionysius Filocalus, the same who had illustrated the civil and ecclesiastical calendar, of which we have spoken elsewhere as being one of our most valuable ancient Christian documents.† In course of time, both of these conjectures of De Rossi have been established by most incontrovertible evidence. When all the fragments that could be found were put together, there appeared at the top and bottom of the tablet the following title—

DAMASUS EPISCOPUS FECIT EUSEBIO EPISCOPO ET MARTYRI.

"Damasus, Bishop, set up this to Eusebius, Bishop and Martyr."

and on either side of the verses, a single file of letters reveals to us

FURIUS DIONYSIUS FILOCALUS SCRIBSIT DAMASIS PAPPÆ
CULTOR ATQUE AMATOT.

"Furius Dionysius Filocalus, a worshipper ‡ and lover of Pope Damasus, wrote this."

The inscription itself ran thus :—

"Heraclius forbad the lapsed to grieve for their sins. Eusebius taught those unhappy ones to weep for their crimes. The people were rent into parties, and with increasing fury began sedition, slaughter, fighting, discord, and strife. Straightway both [the pope and the heretic] were banished by the cruelty of the tyrant, although the pope was preserving

---

* See page 105. † See page 19.

‡ Used, of course, in the old sense of worship, *i.e.* honour. De Rossi reads *Damasi sui Papa*, which is confirmed by other inscriptions.

The Epitaph of St Eusebius. 171

the bonds of peace inviolate. He bore his exile with joy, looking to the Lord as his Judge, and on the shore of Sicily gave up the world and his life." *

Moreover, a diligent search among the minute fragments of stone and marble lying amid the rubbish of the chamber brought to light several bits of the original Damasine inscription, executed with the same faultlessness as all the other specimens of its class; and amongst these bits were one or two which had escaped the search of the man who attempted to copy the whole in the sixth or seventh century; as, for instance, the word IN, which the copyist entirely omitted from the third line. He seems to have been an ignorant man, only able to transcribe the letters which were before him, and even leaving, occasionally, a vacant space where he was conscious that a letter was wanting, which, however, he could not supply. *Fragments of the original still to be seen.*

Our readers have an opportunity of comparing the original inscription with its restoration in Plates II. and III., at the end of the volume; and although the task of correcting the errors and supplying the omissions of the copyist may now seem very easy to any scholar, we must remember that it was much more difficult for those who saw it only on the stone itself, where there is no separation of the letters of one word from those of another. It is curious, therefore, to observe in the MSS. which have come down to us (the writers of which never saw the original stone) the fresh blunders introduced by the ineffectual attempts at correction made in earlier ages. The substitution of *sua* for *sum* in the second line, and the insertion of *in* in the third, were too obvious to be overlooked; but *seditiocaede* of the fourth line was dissolved into *sed et loca ede* in the MS. first adopted by Gruter; whilst the word *omino*, in the penultimate, is changed, in one MS., into *homine*, and into *omnino* in another. *Former editions of this inscription.*

It is not without reason that De Rossi rejoices in the recovery of this stone as one of the happiest fruits of his *Importance of this inscription.*

* The original can be seen in Plate III.

labours in this cemetery. It is, in fact, the recovery of a lost chapter in the history of the Church. The scholars of Alcuin's days, who had transcribed it, omitted its title or dedication; nor did they give any information as to where they had seen it. Baronius, therefore, as we have said, refused to accept it as belonging to Pope Eusebius. He could not believe that the memory of so important an incident in the history of the Roman Church, and the life of one of its chief pastors, could have so entirely perished, as never to have come to the knowledge of Eusebius the historian, for example, nor have left a trace behind it in any other cotemporary records. Now, however, that the identity of the person spoken of is put beyond question, we are able to see how admirably it fits into the circumstances of the times it belongs to; and our readers will be interested in studying this page of ancient history just rescued from the devouring jaws of time.

Its interpretation.

Every student is familiar with one phase, at least, of the disputes of the second and third centuries, as to the proper discipline to be observed towards those unhappy Christians who had denied the faith and relapsed into the outward profession of paganism, under the pressure of persecution. The schism of Novatian has impressed upon us the existence in those days of a hard, proud, self-satisfied temper in many members of the Christian flock, like that of the elder brother in the parable of the prodigal son, which would fain close the door of reconciliation against these miserable apostates. It has brought out in bold relief to this hateful severity the

Mercy of the Church towards apostates,

tender and merciful conduct of our true mother the Church, ever ready to follow the teaching and example of her Divine Head, to pour oil and wine into the wounds of bleeding souls, and to welcome the penitent returning to his home. But we had not been so conscious perhaps of another difficulty which the Church had to encounter, about this same time, on the other side. We had not watched so keenly her prudent firmness in imposing conditions upon her grant of forgiveness,

and exacting wholesome penance from those who would
obtain it. Nevertheless, there is not wanting in cotemporary *tempered by severity.*
records very distinct testimony to her exercise of a divinely-
inspired wisdom in this particular; and the pontificates, both
of Eusebius and of his predecessor Marcellus, illustrate in a
most striking way this part of her character. The letters of
the Roman clergy to St Cyprian, written at a time when the
see of Peter was vacant, speak quite clearly as to the tradition
and practice of the Church. They show us the *lapsi*, armed
with letters of recommendation, which they had obtained from
martyrs or confessors of the faith, pressing for immediate
reconciliation; and the priests and deacons insisting upon a
middle course, between too great severity and sternness, and
too easy an acquiescence with their demand (*pronam nostram
facilitatem et nostram quasi duram crudelitatem*). They say
that the remedy must not be less than the wound, and that if
the remedy be applied too hastily, a new and more fatal wound
will be created: "Let the groans of the penitents be heard,
not once only, but again and again; let them shed abundant
tears, that so those eyes, which have wickedly looked upon
idols, may blot out before God, by sufficient tears, the unlawful deeds they have committed:" and they repeat maxims of
this kind again and again. St Cyprian, too, in his own letters, *Consequent disturbances*
speaks of riots and disturbances having been caused in some
towns of Africa by the overweening presumption and violence
of apostates, who would fain extort from the rulers of the
Church an immediate restoration to her peace and communion. After this date, we do not read of any more disturbances arising from this cause, until the persecution of
Diocletian. That persecution had been preceded by a long
term of peace, during which men's minds had somewhat
relaxed from their primitive strength and fervour. Many,
therefore, fell away; but when the persecution ceased, they
would fain return. Marcellus was firm in upholding the *under Marcellus*
Church's discipline. He was resisted with violence, especially

by one who, least of all, had any right to plead for a mitigation of it, as he had denied the faith even in time of peace. Angry passions were roused, and the public tranquillity was disturbed by the violence of the contending factions, to such an extent that Maxentius, who had no love for Christianity, and whose edict of toleration was dictated by the merest political motives, determined on sending the Pope into exile. This history is contained in the epitaph with which St Damasus adorned his tomb—

> VERIDICUS RECTOR, LAPSOS QUIA CRIMINA FLERE
> PRÆDIXIT, MISERIS FUIT OMNIBUS HOSTIS AMARUS.
> HINC FUROR, HINC ODIUM SEQUITUR, DISCORDIA, LITES,
> SEDITIO, CÆDES, SOLVUNTUR FŒDERA PACIS.
> CRIMEN OB ALTERIUS CHRISTUM QUI IN PACE NEGAVIT,
> FINIBUS EXPULSUS PATRIÆ EST FERITATE TYRANNI.
> HÆC BREVITER DAMASUS VOLUIT COMPERTA REFERRE,
> MARCELLI UT POPULUS MERITUM COGNOSCERE POSSET.

"The truth-speaking Pope, because he preached that the lapsed should weep for their crimes, was bitterly hated by all those unhappy ones. Hence followed fury, hatred, discord, contentions, sedition, and slaughter, and the bonds of peace were ruptured. For the crime of another, who in [a time of] peace had denied Christ, [the Pontiff] was expelled the shores of his country by the cruelty of the tyrant. These things Damasus having learnt, was desirous to relate briefly, that people might recognise the merit of Marcellus."

and Eusebius. If we compare this epitaph on Marcellus with the recently-discovered one on Eusebius, it is easy to recognise a continuation of the same history. Perhaps the Heraclius, named in the later inscription as the leader of the heretical faction, was the very man whose apostacy during a time of peace is commemorated in the former. Anyhow, the nature of the strife in which Eusebius was engaged is clear; and we learn with much surprise that a strife of this nature was capable of attracting the attention and drawing down one of the heaviest punishments of the civil power, not out of any professed hatred of the Christian name, but merely in the interests of public peace.

CHAPTER VI.

THE SEPULCHRE OF ST CORNELIUS.

AS we leave the *cubiculum* of St Eusebius we observe how the ruined walls around us must once have shut off every gallery from the visiting of pilgrims, save only that to the left, where we soon come upon another double chamber, half being on either side of the gallery. At the entrance of one of these is a *graffito* of insignificant appearance, yet really of considerable historical importance. The words are these, *tertio Idus Fefrua Parteni Martiri Caloceri Martiri.* The reader who remembers the testimony of our ancient pilgrims, will not need to be told that he has here a probable, if not a certain, indication of the burial-place of the two martyrs, Parthenius and Calocerus,* who are coupled by them with St Eusebius. If he knows anything, however, of the old Church calendars, he may wonder at the date assigned, since the *Passio* of these martyrs was always celebrated on the 19th of May. The inscription which records the translation of their relics to San Silvestro in Capite, in the eighth century, names the same date as is here written in the Catacombs, the 11th of February, for their *natale.* So does the martyrology of Bede, and others also yet earlier. This date, then, did not mark the day of their martyrdom, for the calendars gave another, nor yet of the translation of their relics from the Catacombs to the Roman Churches, for it belonged to them before that translation was made. Can the Bollandists be right in conjecturing

Inscription to Saints Parthenius and Calocerus.

---

* See page 102.

that it refers to some earlier translation of their relics from one place to another, within the Catacombs themselves, for purposes of greater security under some special danger?* A comparison of the statements by various ancient authors seems to require it. Recent discoveries in the Catacombs give it considerable countenance, and De Rossi does not hesitate to adopt it. He places their martyrdom in the middle of the third century, and believes this first translation to have been made in the earliest years of the fourth, when all the *loca Ecclesiastica* were confiscated by the persecution of Diocletian. The evidence in support of this theory is certainly very strong, but its details are too minute for insertion in this place. We must be content to have noticed it, and then pass on rapidly in search of the tomb of St Cornelius.

<small>Labyrinth connecting the crypts of St Lucina with those of St Callixtus.</small>

We need not tarry by the way, for indeed there is nothing to attract our attention. We are traversing that vast network of galleries which intervenes between the cemetery of St Callixtus and that of St Lucina. These galleries are of later date than either cemetery. They are generally very narrow, crossing one another in all directions, and impossible to be reduced to any regular plan. They observe, for the most part, the horizontal level in each of the two stories in which they have been made; but as they come in contact with portions of different *areæ*, their height is very variable. Each *flat* of this labyrinth has its staircase, and the higher system of galleries spreads over the whole Catacomb without any regard to the ancient limits of the different *areæ*. The lower flat is chiefly remarkable for the entire absence of every kind of ornament. No painting nor slabs of marble, no *cubiculum*, nor even an *arcosolium*, relieves the monotony of its long straight passages, which we may therefore safely conclude belong to an age posterior to the regular construction of both the *hypogæa*. The union of the different groups of independent cemeteries into

---

* This conjecture is not found in the Acta of the Bollandists; but Sollier gives it on the authority of Papebroch in his notes on Usuard's Martyrology.

The Sepulchre of St Cornelius.

one vast necropolis was not effected without difficulty, owing to the very different levels at which their principal galleries had been excavated. The attentive observer who traverses this portion of the labyrinth which lies between the Papal Crypt and the tomb of St Cornelius, will not fail to recognise the point of junction, and will have many opportunities of appreciating the ingenuity with which the *fossors* accomplished their task. He will, not improbably, also be set on thinking whence it came to pass that St Cornelius should have been buried at so great a distance from the other occupants of the Holy See; and if he happens to know that learned men have long since fancied that they could discover grounds for suspecting some relationship between Cornelius and the *Gens Cornelia*, he will note this separate place of burial as a circumstance seeming to corroborate that suspicion. *Family of St Cornelius;*

At first, perhaps, it may have been suggested by the fact that this is the only Pope, down to the days of St Sylvester, who bore the name of any noble Roman family, and it is certainly a remarkable fact that this relationship, supposing it to have existed, would have connected him with the owners of the very cemetery in which, by a singular exception, he was buried, many very ancient epitaphs having been found here of the *Cornelii*, as well as of the *Maximi Cæcilii*. Nor can it be considered as altogether an unimportant circumstance that the epitaph of St Cornelius should have been in Latin, whilst all the *official* epitaphs, so to call them, of those who were buried in the papal vault, were in Greek. It is now an acknowledged fact that the earliest language of the Church was Greek. St Paul, a Roman citizen, writes in Greek to the Christians of Rome. So does St James "to the twelve tribes which are scattered abroad." The Apostolic Fathers, the apologists and historians of the early Church, and her greatest theologians, wrote and spoke Greek. The proceedings of the first seven Councils were carried on in the same language. Nor did Western Christendom lay it aside, even in her ritual and liturgy, as *his epitaph in Latin, while Greek was the official language of the Church.*

M

soon as it ceased to be a generally-spoken tongue. Roman sacramentaries, even of the seventh century, will be found in which the responses are made first in Greek, and then repeated in a Latin translation; and to this day this ancient use of the Greek language has left a deep impress on our own, in all ecclesiastical terms, such as hymn, psalm, liturgy, homily, catechism, baptism, eucharist, priest, bishop, and pope.*

Sepulchre of St Cornelius. The Latin inscription, therefore, on the grave of St Cornelius was certainly a departure from the ordinary practice of that age; quite as much so as the fact of his burial in a place apart from the rest of his order. And when we come to examine the grave itself, we find this, too, was not of the usual kind, nor was its position such as we should have expected for the grave of a martyr pope. It was neither one of the common *loculi* with which the galleries or the walls of the *cubicula* are pierced, and which, as we have seen, served for the tombs of most of the other popes, nor is it precisely an *arcosolium* or altar-tomb of a chapel. Indeed, there is no regular chapel here at all, but only a gallery of unusual width, in a corner of which a large grave has been excavated, of dimensions sufficient to receive three or four bodies, and in shape not unlike the grave of an *arcosolium*, but with the difference that has been pointed out before as a token of greater antiquity, viz., that the space above the *grave* is rectangular, not circular. There is no trace of any slab having been let into the wall to lie flat on the surface of the grave. We may conclude, then, that the body of the pope was buried in a sarcophagus which once occupied this empty space, and that its top served as the *mensa* or altar. A close examination, both of the architecture and the inscriptions in the neighbourhood of this tomb, will satisfy us that it was made on a lower level than that of the surrounding galleries, and at a somewhat later period. Some of the older tombs are partially blocked up by the pilasters which flank the tomb of the pope, yet these pilasters are of

* History of Classical Education, p. 3.

very great antiquity, probably of the same date as the tomb itself. They are covered with the finest stucco, the same as once covered the inner sides also of the excavation in which we suppose the sarcophagus to have been placed; much finer, and much older, therefore, than that which appears above, upon the arches made by Damasus to support the *luminare*.

Both above and below the opening of the tomb are fragments of large slabs of marble, still adhering to the wall, and containing a few letters of what were once important inscriptions. The upper one was unquestionably the work of Damasus. The letters of the lower, though strongly resembling the Damasine type, yet present a few points of difference, sufficient to warrant the conjecture of De Rossi that they were executed by the same hand, designedly introducing slight variations, to mark that it did not belong to the numerous class of monuments set up by the devotion of that pontiff. Of the upper inscription, eight or ten fragments remain, enabling us to read with certainty the latter halves of seven hexameter lines. Of the lower one, which was written in much larger type, two fragments only remain, containing the first letter of the first line, and the first two letters of the last two lines, together with the bottoms of the six last letters of all. Of the second line we have recovered nothing. *Fragments of inscriptions in crypt of St Cornelius.*

At first sight it might seem madness to attempt the complete restoration of these two inscriptions—certainly of the latter—on the strength of such slender data as these; yet the attempt has been made by De Rossi, and the result is such as to commend itself with very great force to all who have given due consideration to the subject. We must not detain our readers by repeating De Rossi's most interesting account of his many and laborious efforts, which for so long a time proved utterly fruitless, and of the happy inspiration which at length cleared away all his difficulties, and furnished him with a clue delivering him from the labyrinth in which he was entangled. But we cannot resist the occasion of transcribing the epitaphs as *Attempt to complete them.*

he supposes them to have been originally written. The difference of type will distinguish the conjectured restorations from the parts that are certain, and, in estimating their degree of probability, the reader must remember two things; *first*, that inscriptions of this kind were engraved with such exquisite mathematical precision that no emendations can be admitted which would materially increase or diminish the number of letters in each line: and, *secondly*, that Damasus was in the habit of repeating himself very frequently in his epitaphs, and that several of De Rossi's restorations reproduce some of his favourite expressions and forms of speech. Had the following epitaph been found in some ancient MS., we are confident that no critic would have seen any reason to question its genuineness—

```
"ASPICE, DESCENSU EXSTRUCTO TENEBRISQUE FUGATIS
CORNELI MONUMENTA VIDES TUMULUMQUE SACRATUM
HOC OPUS ÆGROTI DAMASI PRÆSTANTIA FECIT,
ESSET UT ACCESSUS MELIOR, POPULISQUE PARATUM
AUXILIUM SANCTI, ET VALEAS SI FUNDERE PURO
CORDE PRECES, DAMASUS MELIOR CONSURGERE POSSET,
QUEM NON LUCIS AMOR, TENUIT MAGE CURA LABORIS."
```

"Behold! a way down has been constructed, and the darkness dispelled; you see the monuments of Cornelius, and his sacred tomb. This work the zeal of Damasus has accomplished, sick as he is, in order that the approach might be better, and the aid of the saint might be made convenient for the people; and that, if you will pour forth your prayers from a pure heart, Damasus may rise up in better health, though it has not been love of life, but care for work, that has kept him [here below]."

If this reading be correct, it would follow that Damasus made his usual additions of a *luminare*, and a more commodious staircase perhaps to this tomb of St Cornelius, at a time when he was suffering from severe illness, so that his life was considered in danger, and this harmonises exactly with what De Rossi would suggest as a probable restoration of the second epitaph, viz. :—

```
"SIRICIUS PERFECIT OPUS
CONCLUSIT ET ARCAM
MARMORE CORNELI QUONIAM
PIA MEMBRA RETENTAT."
```

"Siricius completed the work, and enclosed the shrine with marble, for it contains the sacred remains of Cornelius."

Of course, this restoration is much more purely conjectural than the preceding one; nevertheless, those who know De Rossi best, will be the least inclined to pass over slightingly even his very lightest conjecture. He is so modest in making them, and so careful not to over-estimate them when made, whilst yet subsequent discoveries have, in so many instances, confirmed them to the utmost, that we feel almost the same confidence in his hints and guesses at truth, as we do in the most positive assurances of some other writers on similar subjects.

This same tomb of St Cornelius will supply us with an example of his power of happy conjecture, confirmed with certainty by subsequent discoveries. He had often publicly expressed his confident expectation of finding at the tomb of St Cornelius some memorial of his cotemporary and correspondent, St Cyprian. These two saints were martyred on the same day, though in different years; and their feasts were, therefore, always celebrated together, just as they are now, on the 16th of September, all the liturgical prayers for the day belonging equally to both; and the celebration was held at this spot in the cemetery of St Callixtus, as the most ancient calendars and missals assure us—*e.g.*, in the Bucherian calendar, so often quoted, we read *xviii. Kal: Oct: Cypriani, Africæ; Romæ celebratur in Callisti*, and in an old codex of the Roman liturgy, on the same day, *Natale SS. Cornelii et Cypriani, viâ Appiâ in Callisti*.* Now De Rossi had found in one of his old guides,to which he had been so much indebted, an extraordinary misstatement, viz., that the bodies both of St Cyprian and St Cornelius rested in the same cemetery (of St Callixtus), though even this was told in such a way as almost to betray the truth that the name of St Cyprian had

Frescoes of St Cornelius and St Cyprian.

---

* See also S. Leo. M. Op. ed. Ballerini II. p. 96.

been added by a later copyist.* He was satisfied that this blunder had not been made without a cause, but that the pilgrim or copyist had been led into error by something he had seen at the tomb of St Cornelius. And here, on the re-discovery of the tomb, the cause stands at once revealed. Immediately on the right hand side of the grave are two large figures of bishops,† painted on the wall in the Byzantine style, with a legend by the side of each, declaring them to be St Cornelius and St Cyprian. Of course this had not been the first ornamentation which this wall received. It is still possible to detect traces of more ancient painting, and even of *graffiti* upon it, underlying this later work. When the later work was executed, it is hard to determine with certainty. Each of the bishops carries the book of the Gospels in his hands, and is habited in pontifical vestments, even including the *pallium*, which had not yet been confined as a mark of distinction to metropolitans. If we compare it, however, with the other specimen of a *pallium* which we saw at the grave of St Cecilia on the figure of St Urban, we shall observe a difference, which is of value as a note of chronology. Here there is but one cross marked upon the *pallium*, and that on the lower extremity in front. On St Urban there are crosses also on the shoulders, which are nowhere found on paintings or mosaics earlier than the tenth century. Nor is this the only note of higher antiquity which may be recognised on these paintings at the tomb of St Cornelius; the whole style of art is manifestly superior to that at the tomb of St Cecilia. Indeed, the force and dignity expressed in the head of St Cyprian would lead us to assign to it a much earlier date, did not other indications seem to point with some degree of certainty to the beginning of the ninth century. These indications are chiefly to be noted in the painting on the other side of the tomb, on the wall at the end of the gallery. Here, too, are the figures of two other bishops, executed in the same style, each having

---

* See page 112. "Cornelius et Cyprianus *dormit.*" † Plate V.

been originally designated by his own proper name and title, though only one can now be deciphered. That one stands plainly SCS XVSTVS PP ROM; the name of the other began with O. It is extremely probable that this was St Optatus, a saint whom we have had occasion to mention before; whom we know from other sources to have been buried in the same cemetery with St Sixtus; who was venerated in the Western Church, on the 27th November, down to the ninth century or later; whose name may still be seen on the tablet recording the translation of relics in the basilica of Sta Prassede, but of whose real history nearly all traces have now been lost. The SCS XVSTVS is, of course, the second pontiff of that name, whose connexion with this cemetery has been already explained; and the title PP ROM is the same that we find given to other popes down to the middle of the ninth century or later, the name *Papa* not having been yet confined to the bishops of Rome.* It is found, for example, in one of the pictures lately discovered in the subterranean of San Clemente, as the title of Leo IV., A.D. 847; and in the presbytery of Sta Sabina, of Eugenius II., A.D. 824. ˙ It is to Leo III., A.D. 795–815, that we would attribute the paintings we are now examining. It is expressly recorded of him in the *Liber Pontificalis* that "he renewed the cemetery of Sts Xystus and Cornelius on the Appian Way;" and the legend which runs round these portraits has a singular significance, if we consider it as the work of this pontiff. There is some difficulty in deciphering the latter part of the legend; but the earlier portion is clearly taken from the 17th verse of the 58th Psalm, and runs thus— "*Ego autem cantabo virtutem* † *Tuam et exaltabo misericordiam Tuam quia factus es et susceptor meus.*" . . . . "I will sing Thy strength, and will extol Thy mercy, for Thou art become my support;" and these words of thanksgiving would have been

---

* See Ducange, Gloss. in Verb.
† The Vulgate has here *fortitudinem*, but the version used in the Roman Church in older times had *virtutem*. See Tomasi Opp. t. ii. p. 108.

specially appropriate in the mouth of one who had suffered such extraordinary contradictions, calumnies, and misfortunes as Leo had, and had then been almost miraculously delivered out of the hands of his enemies, through the instrumentality of the Emperor Charlemagne. We can hardly doubt, then, that we have here some of that work of "renovation of the cemetery of St Xystus and St Cornelius," which his biographer attributes to him.

<small>Pillar in crypt of St Cornelius.</small>

The low round block or pillar which stands by the side of Cornelius' tomb, and immediately before his picture, was much older than the time of Leo III., though we cannot say with certainty that it was made cotemporaneously with the tomb itself, as we can of similar pillars in some other parts of the Catacombs. For this is not made out of the natural rock, as *they* are, but is a construction of masonry, covered with a somewhat coarse cement. De Rossi conjectures that it may at one time have supported the *mensa*, or altar, necessary for the celebration of the holy mysteries, which (we gather from Prudentius)* was not always directly over the body of the martyr, but only somewhere in the immediate neighbourhood. Ordinarily, however, no doubt, there was placed here, as elsewhere at the martyrs' shrines, one of those large shallow vases, full of oil and precious unguents, with which the floating wicks of papyrus were always fed in these holy places, and from which the faithful were wont to carry off some few drops as a precious relic of the saint. Among the relics collected by John the Deacon, for the Lombard Queen Theodelinda, one *ex oleo S. Cornelii* must have come from this very place ; and, in fact, many fragments of a vase, saturated with some unctuous substance, have been collected from among the rubbish accumulated at this spot.

<small>Graffiti.</small>

Of the *graffiti* upon the painting of St Cornelius we have nothing special to commemorate. They are not old and affectionate prayers, but the mere record of ecclesiastical

---

* In Hippolyt. 171-175. See Note E in Appendix.

The Sepulchre of St Cornelius. 185

names and titles, of men who either came here to offer the holy sacrifice, or to assist those who did ; or, perhaps, once for all, to take part in the translation of the sacred relics. They are such as these, " *Leo prb.*, *Petrus prb.*, *Theodorus prb.*, *Kiprianus Diaconus*," &c. &c. Another and far more ancient *graffito* under the neighbouring archway runs in this wise, " S̄c̄tus *Cerealis et Sallustia cum xxi.;*" and although we know absolutely nothing of their history, yet it is interesting to have recovered even this scanty notice of the existence of these martyrs, thereby corroborating the statement of one of the ancient guide-books, which placed their subterranean shrines somewhere near to St Cornelius. This *graffito* is certainly of great antiquity, though it is impossible to fix its precise date ; were it not for the contracted prefix of *Sctus*, De Rossi would have been almost tempted to look upon it as an original and cotemporary memorial of the martyrdom.

FIG. 19 —*Fresco on wall of ancient crypt in Cemetery of St Lucina.*

BOOK IV.

CHRISTIAN ART.

CHAPTER I.

THE ANTIQUITY AND ORIGINAL TYPES OF CHRISTIAN ART.

The antiquity of Christian paintings.

THE subject of early Christian art has been unhappily the battle-field of such violent religious disputes, that it is hard to gain an impartial hearing for any history that may be given of the ancient decorations of the Roman Catacombs. And this difficulty has increased rather than diminished in the last few years; because the paintings that have been lately discovered have obliged Catholic writers to claim still more strongly than before the voice of antiquity as bearing unequivocal testimony to their own teaching and practice upon this important point.

Opinions of D'Agincourt, Raoul Rochette, De Rossi, and others.

Up to the end of the last century, it had been generally supposed that Christianity in the first ages had looked upon painting with a very jealous eye, because of its prostitution in pagan hands to purposes of idolatry and licentiousness. And when D'Agincourt, writing about the year 1825, ventured to assign a few of the paintings he had seen in the Catacombs to a very early date, they were considered rather as exceptions than examples of the general rule. Twenty years later, Raoul Rochette spoke more confidently. He averred that the lan-

Types of Christian Art. 187

guage of Tertullian, always a violent and somewhat exaggerated writer, had been misunderstood; that, whereas he was only censuring a particular abuse of the art which deserved censure, he was generally quoted as having altogether proscribed it; and he concluded by saying, that "the question whether it entered into the views and principles of the primitive Church to authorise the execution of such paintings has been long since decided,—for the Christian by the authority of the Church, and for the antiquarian by the study of monuments." * Within the last few years, however, the standard of knowledge respecting art and its history has been much changed, and we may now claim with confidence almost apostolic antiquity for some of the existing specimens of Christian painting.

It was said by Niebuhr that ancient art had ceased before Christianity began; and it has been the fashion with most writers upon the subject, to cry down the paintings of the Catacombs as "poor productions, in which the meagreness of invention is only equalled by the feebleness of execution." † But Niebuhr's *dictum* was certainly an exaggeration, and these writers have generally shown that they are not very intimately acquainted with what they so confidently condemn. Thus Lord Lindsay himself, in the very passage from which we have quoted, speaks of the Catacombs as "for the most part closed up and inaccessible," and "the frescoes, obliterated by time and destroyed." But this is by no means true of the Catacombs as they now are; and since the recent discoveries in them, later writers have taken a higher and truer estimate both of the antiquity and of the value of the specimens of art they contain. Kugler, in the later editions of his "Handbook of Painting," complains that the engravings taken of the Catacomb pictures in former days give no adequate conception of their style. He says that "as regards the distribution

---

* Tableau des Catacombes Romaines, 162, 176, &c., ed. Bruxelles, 1837.
† Lord Lindsay's Sketches of the History of Christian Art, i. 39.

of the spaces and mode of decoration, they approach very near to the wall-paintings of the best period of the empire ; that the light arabesques remind us of the paintings at Pompeii, and in the Baths of Titus," &c. * De Rossi, fully conscious of the delicate nature of the subject he is handling, yet does not hesitate to claim the first century, or the earliest part of the second, as the true date of some paintings in the crypts of St Lucina, in the cemetery of St Domitilla, and elsewhere ; others again, he attributes to the middle and end of the second century, or beginning of the third ; and he sets aside the objections of Protestants or others, as being sufficiently disposed of by the facts of the case. " It may be asked," he says, " whether it is credible that the faithful, in the age of the apostles or of their disciples, when the Church, fresh from the bosom of the image-hating synagogue, was in deadly conflict with idolatry, should have so promptly and so generally adopted and (so to speak) baptized the fine arts ?" And he answers, that so grave a question deserves to be discussed in a special treatise ; but that, for the present, he " will only say that the universality of the pictures in the subterranean cemeteries, and the richness, the variety, the freedom of the more ancient types, when contrasted with the cycle of pictures which I clearly see becoming more stiff in manner and poor in conception towards the end of the third century,—these things prove the impossibility of accepting the hypothesis of those who affirm the use of pictures to have been introduced, little by little, on the sly, as it were, and in opposition to the practice of the primitive Church."† And again, " The flourishing condition of the fine arts in the days of the Flavii, of Trajan, of Hadrian, and of the Antonines, and the great number of their professors in the metropolis of the empire, the conversion to the faith of powerful personages, and even of members of imperial families, such as Domitilla and Flavius Clemens, certainly very much favoured the introduction and develop-

* Page 14, ed. Sir C. Eastlake, 1851.   † Roma Sott., i. 196, 197.

ment of Christian pictorial art. And, on the contrary, the decline of those same fine arts in the third and fourth centuries; the increasing cost of the handiwork of the painter and the sculptor, as their numbers diminished every day; the gradual but continuous impoverishment of public and private fortunes, which induced even the senate and the emperors to make their new monuments at the expense of others more ancient, all this could not much facilitate the multiplication of new works of Christian art during that period; so that, even if the faithful had gained in proselytes, in power, and in liberty, they lost quite as much, if I may say so, in the conditions required for the flourishing of Christian art."

Le Normant, Welcker, De Witte, and other French and German critics, confirm this judgment in the strongest manner;* and even the most bitter anti-Catholic writers of our own country have been obliged to yield to the weight of evidence which can now be adduced in its support, though, of course, they have their own way of accounting for it. "The early Christians ornamented their subterranean cemeteries," writes one of these,† "not because it was congenial to the mind of Christianity so to illustrate the faith, but because it was the heathen custom so to honour the dead;" that is to say, the Pagans had been wont to ornament with painting their vaults or sepulchral chambers, and the Christians did the same, seeing no reason why they should not. The fact that these sepulchral chambers were used *also* for purposes of religious worship presented no difficulty to their minds. At first, they even used many of the same devices for mural decoration as the Pagans had used, always excepting anything that was immoral or idolatrous; introducing, however, here and there, as the ideas occurred to them, something more significant of

Protestant testimony to the same effect.

---

* Le Normant considered some of the paintings in St Domitilla's cemetery to be of the same style with those in the well-known pyramidical tomb of Caius Sextius, B.C. 32. Welcker attributed the paintings in the crypts of St Lucina to the first century.—R. S. i. 321 ; *Bullett.* 1863, p. 3.

† Letters from Rome, by Rev. W. Burgon, p. 250.

their own creed, until by and by the whole was exclusively Christian. Hence it is hardly an exaggeration to say, with the same Protestant writer, that in some of the most ancient chapels of the Catacombs "you are not certain for a few moments whether you are looking on a Pagan or a Christian work." There is the same geometrical division of the roof, the same general arrangement of the subjects, "the same fabulous animals, the same graceful curves, the same foliage, fruit, and flowers, and birds in both;" presently you detect a figure of the Good Shepherd occupying the centre compartment of the composition, or the figure of a woman in prayer, or of Daniel in the lions' den, (see Plate VI.) or some other well-known Christian symbol, and you are at once satisfied as to the religion of the art you are studying.

The birth and growth of Christian art natural.

It is a remark of Raoul Rochette, that "*un art ne s'improvise pas*," and that it was no more in the power of the early Christians to invent a new imitative language in painting than it was to produce at once a new idiom of Greek or Latin. No doubt this is quite true; but just as new ideas require new words to express them,—and in this way Christianity has made most important changes in the language of every country where it has gained a footing,—so they require new forms in art, or at least modifications of old forms; and these would naturally go on increasing day by day until at length a whole cycle of Christian subjects would be created, departing more and more widely from those which were familiar to the heathen, and finally, perhaps, excluding them altogether. This seems to be the natural and necessary order of things; and it at once illustrates and explains an observation which has been sometimes made, as though it were something strange, that we do not recognise in the history of Christian art the first efforts of imitation common to the nations of antiquity,—beginning in rude and formless essays, the result of indistinct notions, and advancing step by step towards excellence; but rather, on the contrary, find the earliest specimens of the art to be the best, if not always in conception, yet certainly in execution. For the Christians were not a new and distinct nation, either geographically or politically; they were indeed "a holy nation, a purchased people,"* knit together by the closest bonds of a supernatural charity, but they were made up of persons gathered out "of all nations and tribes and peoples and tongues;"† and they nowhere refused to avail themselves of anything that was good, useful, or beautiful, among the gifts or occupations of those amongst whom they lived. Whereas, then, "the creatures of God had heretofore"—(by painting as well as by other means)—"been turned to an abomination to the souls of men, and a snare to the feet of the unwise," ‡ He, "who had now become visible expressly that through Him we might be led to the love of things invisible," § did not forbid His Church to avail herself of the pictorial art as a means of rendering spiritual things sensible, and thereby moving and instructing the minds of men.

It is not necessary that we should suppose the action of the Church in this matter to have been at first conscious and deliberate. Rather, the birth and earliest growth of Christian art was wholly spontaneous, the natural fruit of the circumstances in which the Christians of those days found themselves; and it was only after the lapse of two or three centuries, that the violent invasion of her sanctuaries, by pagan persecutors, obliged the Church to interfere by legislation with the natural progress and development of the art. Then it was that the famous canon of the Council of Elvira was passed, which forbad ‖ "pictures to be placed in a church, or that which is worshipped and adored to be painted on the walls." This disciplinary enactment was, as Raoul Rochette happily

Its progress checked by the persecutions.

Canon of Council of Elvira, A.D. 303, explained.

---

* 1 Pet. ii. 9.   † Apoc. vii. 9.
‡ Wisdom xiv. 11.   § Præf. Missæ in Nativ. Dom.
‖ "Placuit picturas in ecclesia esse non debere, nec quod colitur et adoratur in parietibus depingatur."—*Conc. Illib.* can. 36. Count de Broglie interprets this canon as forbidding any but symbolical paintings.

expresses it, "*toute accidentelle, toute de circonstance.*" Not only had the churches above ground been often violently entered, and some of them destroyed by order of the emperors before the time when this decree was made, but the heathen soldiery had penetrated even the most hidden sanctuaries of the faithful in the depths of the earth; and there was only too much reason to fear that the sacred subjects painted on the walls, often under almost unintelligible symbols, would be turned into ridicule, after the fashion of the blasphemous caricature of the crucifixion, lately found on the walls of Cæsar's palace.

This explanation of the decree is naturally suggested by the circumstances of the time when it was passed. It is also supported in the most striking way by all the facts which recent excavations in the Catacombs have brought to our knowledge. Even thirty years ago, the same author from whom we have just quoted could say with truth, "*Le fait vient ici a l'appui du raisonnement;*" but he had not at his command a tenth part of the evidence of this statement by which it can be now confirmed. With our present increased knowledge as to the chronological succession of the several parts of the Catacombs, we are able to say with confidence, that whereas those Christian paintings, which critics in art have agreed in considering the most ancient, have always hitherto been found in the most ancient parts of the excavations, those chambers (on the contrary) which belong to the latest period of their history exhibit but few and poor specimens of decoration, or often have no vestiges of painting about them at all.

Means of distinguishing the dates of paintings.

In the course of the following pages, we shall often have occasion to speak of the date of this or that painting; and this is a consideration of the utmost importance in determining the value of its testimony in matters of doctrine. It is manifest, however, that this is a chronological question which cannot often be brought within very precise boundaries. Nevertheless, some paintings carry evidence of their chronology on their faces, or at least testify to their not having

Types of Christian Art.

been executed previously to such or such a date; as, for instance, all those which exhibit the *nimbus*, or circular aureole of glory, round the heads of Christ or of His saints.

This ornament had been used by Pagan artists for the decoration of their false deities; but with what meaning does not clearly appear. It is said to have been first invented among the Egyptians; thence it passed to the Greeks and Romans, who, in the days of the empire, placed it even on the heads of their emperors, in that spirit of fulsome adulation which characterised both the art and literature of the period. Thus it may be seen round the head of Trajan in the triumphal arch of Constantine, and on a medal of Antoninus Pius. Afterwards its use became yet more frequent and common, so that, finally, it ceased to be looked upon as a token of divinity, and was considered simply as an artistic ornament, proper to royalty or other pre-eminence. Hence, in the Christian mosaics of the fifth century, it was placed not only on the heads of Our Lord, His Holy Mother, and the angels, but (at Ravenna) on those of Justinian and his wife Theodora, and at St Mary Major's in Rome (A.D. 433) even on that of Herod. It is scarcely possible to define with accuracy the period at which Christians first began to use it. In the glass cups or plates found in the Catacombs, of which we shall have to speak later, it is very rarely to be seen; and it is generally allowed that most of these glasses range from the middle of the third to the middle of the fourth century. In many of them, crowns may be seen by the side of the saints, being offered to them by birds, or held in their own hands, but not placed upon their heads; in some also Our Lord is represented in the act of crowning Saints Peter and Paul, or others; but the *nimbus* itself will scarcely be found on a dozen of them altogether. In the mosaics, on the other hand, which belong to the later age, it is far otherwise. In those of the church (or mausoleum, whichever it should be rightly called) of Sta. Costanza, belonging to the age of Constantine, Our Lord has the *nimbus*, the apostles

[margin: The use of the nimbus introduced and gradually extended.]

have not. A similar distinction is to be noted in the mosaics of St Agatha in Ravenna, of the year 400; but here Our Lord has it in its more modern form, enclosing a cross, and on the head of the angels it is unornamented. The same decorated form of the *nimbus* is used on the head of Christ in the mosaics of Sta. Sabina (A.D. 424) and of St Paul's (A.D. 441), both in Rome; where the apostles, evangelists, and others either have it plain, or none at all. It would seem, then, that it was first used to distinguish the head of our Lord, then His Holy Mother and the angels,* next, the apostles and evangelists (as also the symbolical animals which represented them), and lastly, the saints in general. Padre Garrucci, S.J., concludes that in the fifth century Christian artists either used or omitted it indifferently, but after that time its use became universal. Martigny,† a more recent and cautious authority, distinguishes with greater accuracy when he says that it was used for Our Blessed Lord occasionally before the days of Constantine, and constantly afterwards; for the angels, from the beginning of the fifth century, and universally before the end of the sixth; but that it was not till towards the end of the seventh that it became the rule for all saints indifferently.

Whenever, therefore, we meet with any paintings in the Catacombs which represent a bishop or martyr with a *nimbus* round his head, we know with certainty that they belong to a period later than the ages of persecution, and, in many instances, perhaps to a period considerably later; for as the Church delighted in venerating the heroes of her past age of struggle, it was only natural that she should continue to adorn their tombs as long, at least, as their bodies still reposed in them. After their translation, such ornamentation would probably not, under ordinary circumstances, be renewed. We

---

* De Rossi says it began to be given to the Blessed Virgin and Saints Peter and Paul in the fourth century. In the cemetery of St Domitilla, it is only found on the heads of Christ and St Peter.—*Bullett.* 1867, p. 44; Marangani, Acta St Victorini, pp. 39, 40.

† Dictionnaire des Antiquités Chrétiennes, p. 436, in verb. Nimbus.

have already seen some examples of these later paintings at the tombs of St Cornelius and St Cecilia; and these may suffice for specimens of their class.

Another chronological note of easy application, and of some use in determining the age of the paintings in the Catacombs, is the appearance of the letter ⊥, or of some other letter, or some form of the cross, on the border of the garments of the principal figures. In older paintings, the vestments are either quite plain, or with a few light purple stripes upon them; and the practice of ornamenting with these letters does not seem to have become general until the beginning of the fourth century, or at least the end of the third.* Letters on garments, the monogram, &c.

In other instances, the presence of the monogram ☧, in one or other of its manifold varieties, may suffice to assure us of the comparatively recent date of a painting. For although we do not believe that the invention of this *tessera* took its origin from the famous vision of Constantine, yet no certain example of its use in paintings has yet been discovered before that time.

It is not often, however, that there is need of such palpable tokens as these to determine the period to which any particular specimen of ancient Christian art is to be referred. In most cases, its own internal evidence, whether of subject or of style, is almost or quite sufficient to enable us to distinguish—if not a work of the age of Trajan, for example, from one of the days of Hadrian, yet certainly—a work of the first or second century from one of the third or fourth. For the same differences which characterise the works of art produced by Pagan hands during those periods are reflected also, in their degree, in the paintings of the Catacombs; and there are not wanting cotemporary examples which may be compared with one another. The skill of the Christian artist always bears a certain proportion to the general skill of his cotemporaries; only the darkness of the place and other unfavourable circumstances would naturally lead us to expect that the execution of his work Internal evidence from style, choice of subject, &c.

---

* Garrucci, Vetri, &c., p. 112, 113.

would be generally somewhat inferior to that of his fellow-craftsmen, decorating under imperial patronage the palaces or temples of the city; and this expectation is usually, though not always, justified by a careful examination of the two classes of paintings.

We cannot, therefore, always trust to the mere internal evidence of style and the degree of merit in the execution. We must also take into account the place where the paintings are found, and the epitaphs or other indications of time in the neighbourhood. And it is in this respect that the researches of De Rossi on the history and topography of the Catacombs have thrown so much new light on the history of ancient Christian art. Following his guidance, we are able to trace a certain order and gradual development of Christian painting.

<small>Sketch of the early history of Christian art.</small>

In its first beginnings, it was intent only on creating or selecting certain necessary types or figures that might stand for the religious truths it desired to represent. It did not concern itself to make a complete provision of appropriate accessory ornaments of its own, but borrowed these without scruple from the works of the Pagan school, from the midst of which it was springing forth. The principal figure in the composition, some biblical or, at least, symbolical subject, gave the religious and Christian character to the whole. The *entourage* was then completed by an abundance of merely decorative figures, freely imitated from the types of classical Roman art, such as birds, garlands, vases of fruits or flowers, fantastic heads, winged genii, personifications of the seasons, &c., and this is the leading characteristic of the first age of Christian painting. By and by the cycle of symbolical types grew more rich and complicated by the addition of the mystical interpretation of biblical stories, and was used with great skill and freedom under the direction, it would appear, of learned theological guides. By the end of the third century, this cycle had received a fixed traditional form, and was constantly reiterated. It had become, as it were, consecrated, and Christian art was almost hieratic in its character, as in ancient Egypt or modern Greece, so fixed and immovable were its types, "always like one another, and always unlike nature." But the biblical histories had now almost superseded the use of symbols. These had already begun to decline from the middle of the third century, when the formularies of Christian epigraphy were gradually developing; and in the next century, one might almost say that they disappeared altogether. Towards the end of the fourth or beginning of the fifth century, the radical revolution which the conversion of Constantine had effected in the social and political position of Christians had set an equally distinct mark upon Christian art. The age of symbolism has passed away. Scenes from real life are now introduced. Even the details of bloody martyrdoms are painted on the tombs or the walls of churches; and the liberty and publicity of Christian worship in the basilicas finds a pleasure in the contrast, suggested by these harrowing representations.

Our sketch of the history of Christian art will not embrace this development at all; we confine ourselves to that more mysterious and interesting form of it which more especially belongs to *Roma Sotterranea*, and which the progress of discovery enables us day by day more clearly to trace back to the highest antiquity—almost, if not quite, to apostolic times. De Rossi speaks of the painting of Our Blessed Lady with the prophet Isaias in the Catacomb of Sta Priscilla (Plate X.), and again of the vine on the roof of the entrance to St Domitilla,* as being probably works of the first century; the more regular lines which mark the roof of St Januarius'† chapel in St Prætextatus, he attributes to the second, as well as certain symbolical paintings of the fish carrying a basket,‡ and lambs or sheep on either side of a milk-pail§ placed on an altar, which appear on the walls of a cubiculum in the crypt of St

In apostolic times.

* Fig. 9 in p. 72. † Fig. 11 in p. 79.
‡ See Plate XIV. § Fig. 13 in p. 103.

Lucina, while the great bulk of the biblical paintings throughout the Catacombs are generally allowed to belong to the third.

Refutation of theory as to the Pagan models of early Christian art.

Before examining these first efforts of Christian art in detail, a few words must be said as to the models upon which they were formed. We have already quoted Raoul Rochette's words, that no school of art can be created of a sudden, springing into existence fully formed, like Minerva from the brain of Jupiter. This writer, however, carried his theory too far when he insisted that there had been always a direct positive imitation by the Christians of pagan models, and that this imitation could be clearly seen, not only in the general distribution of the whole, but also in all the details of each composition. He even imagined that they had been guided in their selection of subjects for painting by the fact that, of one there were Pagan models that might be copied, of the other there were none. The peculiarities of costume, and all the minor accessories of the painting were, according to him, determined by the same cause. Nay, further still, he maintained that the Christian artists were so servile in their imitation of these Pagan models, that it even led them astray from the teaching of their Divine Master, and caused them to introduce false and unseemly details into their representations of the most solemn subjects. Thus, they dared to paint a goat receiving the caresses of the Good Shepherd; and as this animal had no place in the sacred parable, but, on the contrary, was in another parable identified with the wicked, its presence here could only be accounted for on the supposition that the artist was imitating, consciously or unconsciously, some Pagan composition. Again, they often put into the hands of the same figure the shepherd's reed or pipe, and this, too, could only be the effect of some reminiscence, at least, either of the statue of Pan, or of some pagan shepherd.

The ability and pertinacity with which this author insisted upon his theory, had gained for it a certain measure of accept-

Types of Christian Art. 199

ance. Nevertheless, the principal arguments by which it was supposed to be confirmed being now destroyed, it has of late years fallen rapidly into disrepute. Raoul Rochette had been misled in part by certain paintings of a semi-Pagan character, published by Bottari, and by him attributed to a Christian Catacomb. It is now ascertained that this cemetery was the work of one of the Gnostic sects, and we are no longer surprised at the mixture of Paganism and Christianity which it exhibits; *e.g.*, Pluto and Proserpine, under the names of Dispater and Abracura; the Divine Fates, and Mercury as the messenger of the gods, carrying off the soul of the deceased in a chariot drawn by four horses, and descending with it into some abyss in the middle of the earth. In the genuine paintings of the Christian Catacombs, nothing whatever of this kind has ever been found. The only mythical personage who appears there in paintings is the Thracian Orpheus,* charming the wild beasts by his lyre, a figure which was very popular in the first centuries of the Christian era, being often repeated on medals of Antoninus Pius, and Marcus Aurelius, which were struck at Alexandria. Moreover, we are told that Alexander Severus placed in his *Lararium* statues or pictures of Apollonius of Thyane, and of Christ, of Abraham, and of Orpheus. There was nothing far-fetched, then, in the resemblance which some of the Fathers delighted to trace between Christ and the Thracian bard. His taming of the wild beasts was taken as a faint shadow of our Lord's softening the hard hearts of men by the persuasive sweetness of His preaching.

It was precisely for the same reason that the *syrinx*, or pipe, was placed in the hands of Christ as the Good Shepherd. It was no thoughtless or profane adaptation of one of the *insignia* of Pan. In fact, it very rarely appears in the most ancient paintings, when such imitation, according to the theory we are combating, was most to have been expected, but, being an ordinary adjunct of all shepherds, it had a special significance,

[margin: That theory founded on frescoes in Gnostic cemetery.]

[margin: Christ as Orpheus, or with the shepherd's pipe of reeds.]

* See Plate XI.

a certain dogmatic value, when applied to the chief "Shepherd and Bishop of souls."* The pastoral staff itself was even named by St Gregory Nazianzen ἡ ποιμενίη σύριγξ; and another early Christian writer has said, "I know that shepherds who are skilled in their art seldom use their crook or staff, but lead their sheep by the pipe." † It was, in fact, only another way of setting forth the same truth as our Lord expressed when He said that "the sheep follow their shepherd because they know his voice."‡ So far, then, from the presence of the pipe in the hands of Christ being an anomaly, due to some Pagan artist or model, and so requiring explanation, it denoted an essential feature of the pastoral character, so that Christians could hardly have failed to introduce it in process of time, even if it had never been painted before. We need not pursue this subject any further now, though it may be necessary to recur to it again hereafter. At present we will only express our conviction that it would not be difficult to find similarly simple, yet complete, explanations of every particular by which M. Raoul Rochette seeks to confirm his theory. And, at any rate, it is quite certain that, however closely Christianity may have imitated the traditions and examples of the Greco-Roman school in which their first education had been received, their fidelity to those traditions was united with a most scrupulous and enlightened wisdom, for they never failed to eliminate from their imitations everything which was really inconsistent either with the doctrines or the *convenances* of the Christian religion. All figures or scenes of a really polytheistic signification remained, throughout the whole of the first three centuries, carefully proscribed from all their monuments.

Division of Christian painting into six classes.

The Christian paintings of that period have been divided into six classes; and although these classes are of very unequal extent and importance, and it will be found practically impossible to keep them quite distinct in treatment, yet the division is worth remembering, and may serve to impress upon our minds

* 1 Peter ii. 25.   † See Garrucci, Vetri, &c., p. 63.   ‡ St John x. 4.

the main characteristics of the subject. The first and largest class of paintings, then, may be called symbolical, as merely expressing, under pictorial emblems, religious thoughts or ideas. The second we will call allegorical; they represent, more or less accurately, some of the parables of the Gospel. The third is of biblical histories, either from the Old or New Testaments. Fourthly, we will speak of sacred pictures of Our Divine Lord, of His Holy Mother and the saints; then of scenes from the lives of the saints, or the history of the Church ; and lastly, of scenes from the Liturgy.

Such is De Rossi's division of this part of our subject, in which, however, it must be remembered that we shall not have the advantage of his direct and immediate guidance so entirely as we have hitherto had. The main object of his work is to give a topographical, historical, and chronological edition of all the monuments of each Catacomb. It is not a treatise on Christian epigraphy, nor art, nor symbolism, yet, incidentally, it gives abundant valuable information on all these subjects, and we shall seldom have occasion to quote any other authority than his as to the teaching of *Roma Sotterranea* upon any of them.

FIG. 20.—*The Good Shepherd in the centre of the ceiling of one of the most ancient cubicula in the Crypts of St Lucina.*

CHAPTER II.

SYMBOLICAL PAINTINGS.

Symbolism explained.

BY symbolical paintings we mean those in which the object set before the eye is not depicted for its own sake, but in order to convey to the mind some further idea beyond itself, yet connected with it either naturally or by convention. The interpretation, therefore, of symbolical paintings is a work of care and delicacy. It requires both learning, prudence, and integrity; and it has been so often abused and made a field for the unlimited indulgence of the imagination, that many persons, not unreasonably, are inclined to listen with profound mistrust to any specimen of it that may come before them. It has even been wittily described as a system in which "anything or nothing may be made to mean everything."

Nevertheless, it is quite certain that symbolism has always held a very prominent place in the history of art, and not least at the very period with which we are most concerned. Kugler, in speaking of Roman art at this time, says, that "instead of directly denoting the object represented, the forms of art had now become the mere exponents of an abstract idea; in other words, symbols of a more comprehensive character. Instead of influencing the feelings, they now engaged the thought;" and although we do not see any authority for his statement that "it was the dread of idolatry which introduced and consecrated in Christian art a system of merely typical representation," yet he is certainly right in assigning this typical and symbolical character as the leading feature of the earliest productions of that art. The question then arises, What are the laws by which we must be guided in our interpretation of ancient Christian symbols?

Obviously the truest key to their meaning is to be found in anything that will give us certain knowledge of the thoughts and ideas of the artists themselves, or of those amongst whom they lived, and for whom they worked. A single text from a Father of the Church, writing about the same time that the symbols were being painted, or not long afterwards, is infinitely more valuable and trustworthy as a guide than a whole volume of hypothetical suggestions, however ingeniously invented, and speciously supported by the arguments of some modern commentator. And in proportion to the number and clearness of the texts that can be quoted, or the position and weight of their author, will be the certainty of the interpretation which they support. For instance, an apparent agreement between some passage in an obscure ecclesiastical author of the ninth century, and some Christian painting of the second or third, would not suffice to assure us of any real identity of meaning between them; the agreement might be merely fortuitous. But if, on the contrary, a witness or witnesses can be produced, cotemporary with the artists, or with their predecessors perhaps, who had helped to form that school and atmosphere of thought in which the artists lived; if it can be shown that certain ideas and modes of thought and expression were dominant in the Christian world at such a time, and formed a part of the common intellectual property (so to speak) of the faithful, we cannot hope to find a surer guide in the interpretation of the works of art of the same period.' *Rules for interpretation.*

Thus, when an Anglican controversialist appeals to the picture of a dove or doves drinking out of a vase, as an argument from primitive antiquity against " withholding the cup from the laity" in the administration of the Holy Eucharist, intelligent and careful readers must feel at once that he is doing violence *Instance of abuse in interpretation.*

to the monuments he is professing to interpret; he is guilty of a flagrant anachronism, carrying back to the early ages a controversy which had not then been dreamt of. Contrariwise, if a writer, interpreting the numerous paintings of the Good Shepherd, should insist upon certain details in its execution, such as the frequent introduction of a goat instead of a sheep, as having been intended to denote the infinite mercy of Christ in receiving even sinners to repentance, his explanation receives immense support from the well-known language of Tertullian and others of the Fathers, and from the general testimony of history as to the earliest subjects of dispute in the Christian Church.

The sense, then, of the various symbols used in the decoration of the graves and chambers of the Roman Catacombs must be determined, not by the shrewd conjectures of the learned, nor by the distorted reasonings of the controversialist, but by the strictest rules of argument and testimony; by a comparison of the various ornaments, first with one another, and then with inscriptions written only in words; by appeals also to Holy Scripture, and to the writings of the early Fathers. Where these fail us, or seem to be inconsistent and therefore inconclusive, we must be content to hold our judgment in suspense, and to await the discovery of further monuments which may throw fresh light on our obscurity. In the meanwhile, there are at least some symbols on which we may speak without fear of contradiction.

Anchor, symbol of hope;

Thus, St Paul's Epistle to the Hebrews,* and the instruction of St Clement of Alexandria,† are sufficient to show us that the anchor, a symbol almost more frequently used in the most ancient parts of the Catacombs than any other, is a token expressive of hope, as old as Christianity itself; and it confirms us in our belief that the early Christians used it with this intention, when we observe how commonly it is found on the gravestones of persons bearing the name of

* Heb. vi. 19. † Pedagog. iii. 106.

Hope, either in its Greek or Latin form, such as SPES, ELPIS, ELPIDIUS, ELPISUSA, &c., &c. Sometimes the anchor is so formed, evidently by design, as to suggest to the Christian eye the idea of the cross,* the very foundation of all Christian hope; and this suggestion is still more apparent, where the trident is substituted, as it sometimes is, for the anchor.

It cannot be necessary to appeal to any authority beyond the discourses of our blessed Lord himself, to justify us in saying that a lamb or sheep represented one of Christ's fold. A sheep and dove, of living and deceased Christians. dove also was often used to denote a Christian soul; but the bird seems more especially to have denoted the soul after it had been released from its earthly tabernacle and had entered into its rest; the sheep, a soul which still "goes in and out finding pasture" in this life. Of course, the dove was primarily a type of the Holy Ghost, and we have already seen it so used in a painting of Our Lord's Baptism.† But this did not in any way militate against its use in the secondary sense we have assigned to it. On the contrary, we find not only the same symbols, but even the same words, used in these two senses. The Holy Ghost is *Spiritus Sanctus*, and the same title appears as the designation of the departed souls of the just man, and in the plural number, of the saints generally.‡ The Holy Ghost is also called by the Fathers§ a dove without gall, *Palumbus sine felle;* and again and again we find on the gravestones of the Catacombs the very same words applied to the souls of the deceased; especially, in a diminutive form, *palumbulus sine felle*, to the souls of young children. Sometimes the dove itself is engraved side by side with this title, or with others which resemble it, *Anima innocens, anima simplex*, "Innocent soul, simple soul," &c.; and in one epitaph belonging to a *bisomum*, the names of the two deceased are written over the

---

* See, for example, fig. 12 in p. 82. † See fig. 15 in p. 119.
‡ Inscr. Christ. ex.
§ St Cyprian de Unit. Eccl. ix.; Tertull. De Baptismo, viii.

heads of two doves, BENERIA and SABBATIA.* We must not however, conclude too hastily, that every bird, either painted on the walls or carved on the gravestones of these cemeteries, was meant to represent a dove. Some birds seem to have been introduced merely as ornaments in the corners of the vaulted roofs of the chapels, just as they were used by cotemporary Pagan artists; others again, especially those bearing a palm-branch in their mouths, seem not improbably to have been intended for the phœnix or "palm-bird," † the well-known emblem of immortality. The phœnix, however, was never in such common use in Christian art, especially of the second and third centuries, as the dove. Sometimes the dove is drinking out of a vase. or pecking at grapes, as though to denote the soul's enjoyment of the fruits and refreshing draughts ‡ of eternal happiness; still more frequently it bears an olive-branch in its mouth, and then, as Tertullian says, it is a symbol of peace, even older than Christianity itself, "the herald of the peace of God from the very beginning." § Sometimes also the word itself *Pax* is added, thereby marking the sense beyond all possibility of dispute; viz., that it is meant to assert of the soul of the deceased, that it has departed in the peace of God and of His Church.

The dove joined with other symbols.

Sometimes two or more symbols are found united on one monument, as for instance in fig. 12,|| where the union of the cross-shaped anchor, the sheep and the dove on the tombstone of Faustinianus, seem to proclaim a Christian redeemed by the cross of Christ, and placing all his hope in it, now released from the chains of this earthly coil, and in possession

---

* Inscr. Christ. i. 421; *Bullett.*, 1864, p. 11.

† The Greek name for this bird and the palm-tree is the same.

‡ See St Aug. Conf. ix. 3. Speaking of his deceased friend Nebridius, he says, "Jam ponit spirituale os ad fontem Tuum Domine, et bibit quantum potest," &c. ΠΙΕ ΕΝ ΘΕΩ, *Drink in God*, is found in some epitaphs, and on drinking-glasses.

§ Adv. Valent. ii., *in fin.*; and De Baptismo, c. viii.

|| See page 52.

Symbolical Paintings. 207

of the hoped-for peace. Sometimes the symbol was engraved even after the tombstone was in its place, as in the annexed figure—

FIG. 21.—*Epitaph from very ancient part of Catacomb of St Priscilla.*

where perhaps the dove was added by way of correcting, in some respect, the blunder of the fossor, who had fixed the stone with its written name upside down.

The use of the dove as a symbol still remained in the mosaics of the fourth, fifth, and sixth centuries, with the same mystical meaning, as we learn both from the letters of Paulinus,* and from some of the monuments themselves which survive, and in which we see twelve doves sitting in or around the cross, to represent the twelve Apostles. At a much later period, in a Spanish MS. of the twelfth century, in the British Museum, birds flying under the blue vault of heaven have the legend, *Animæ interfectorum*,† "the souls of them that were slain." Indeed, we may venture to say that this fragment of the alphabet of Christian symbolism has never been wholly forgotten or fallen into disuse. *This symbol never dropped.*

This cannot be said of the fish, which is the next sacred symbol we would mention; the most important perhaps of all, and certainly as ancient as any, but whose use grew gradually less frequent, even as early as in the first half of the third century, and may almost be said to have ceased altogether as soon as the ages of persecution had ended, and the *disciplina arcani* was relaxed. This question of the period during which the symbol was used being of some importance, we will *The fish: when used as a symbol?*

---

* S. Paulin. Ep. xii. ad Severum, p. 152, ed. 1622.
† Apoc. vi. 9.

say a few more words about it in this place before we go on to inquire into the mystical meaning of the fish. It appears, then, that there is no instance of a single fish being used with any theological sense on a Christian monument later than the fifth century. Fishes, indeed, may be found carved at the bottom of fonts, or on the *ambones* of Ravenna, in the sixth century. They also form a part of the mosaic pavement of a Baptistery at Pesaro, of the age of Justinian, where both the artistic representation and the legend accompanying it * clearly attest an allusion to the sacrament of Baptism. But in these and any similar instances that might be adduced, they seem to be used chiefly for ornament's sake, and are placed among other Christian emblems which are quite clear, and not symbolical at all. But in the older Christian epitaphs and paintings, the fish stands alone as a manifest token of the Christian faith; and we find it so used much more frequently in the second and third than in the fourth and fifth centuries. Of all the epitaphs from the Catacombs having dates, it is found on one only after the date of Constantine, and on one before it,† A.D. 400 and A.D. 234. But it is found on nearly a hundred other epitaphs which, from various indications, we can refer with confidence to the first three centuries; so that, on the whole, De Rossi considers it quite proved that, whereas we cannot say how early the mystical use of this emblem began, we are sure that it had almost, if not altogether, ceased by the beginning of the fifth century. It had become extremely rare by the latter end of the fourth, so that, whereas nearly two thousand inscriptions subsequent to Constantine are ornamented with palms, crowns, birds, sheep, crosses, and monograms, not one is to be found amongst them bearing the symbol of a fish.

* " Est homo non totus, medius sed piscis ab imo."
† In estimating this statement, we must remember that we have not more than thirty dated epitaphs prior to Constantine, and more than thirteen hundred after him. In the inscription of 234, the fish and the anchor are found together.

Symbolical Paintings. 209

It follows next to inquire in what sense the symbol was used. The thoughts of most of our readers would naturally recur to the parable in which our Lord compares the kingdom of heaven to a net cast into the sea, and gathering together of all kinds of fishes; or again, to the words with which He called Simon and Andrew to the apostolate, saying "Come ye after me, and I will make you to be fishers of men." The idea, however, suggested by these passages, though not unknown either to the Christian liturgies or to Christian art,* was certainly not the leading idea which directed the use of this symbol in the early Church. The fish entered into the cycle of Christian thought and art in primitive times chiefly for two reasons: first, because Christians owed their new and spiritual birth to the element of water; and secondly, because Christ Himself was commonly spoken of and represented as a fish. *A symbol both of Christ and of a Christian.*

The precise origin of this latter representation may admit of some doubt, but the universality of its use is unquestionable. It can be established by a catena of Fathers, beginning from St Clement of Alexandria, Origen, and Tertullian, in the second century, down to St Peter Damian, in the eleventh. It is even believed that it was in use in apostolic times, and suggested that famous acrostic quoted by Eusebius † and St Augustine ‡ from the so-called Sibylline verses, which gives us, by taking the initial letters of so many successive lines, the Greek words ΙΗΣΟΥΣ ΧΡΕΙΣΤΟΣ ΘΕΟΥ ΥΙΟΣ ΣΩΤΗΡ, "Jesus Christ, Son of God, Saviour;" § and then the initials of *Origin of its use as symbol of Christ.*

---

* Nearly all the hymns provided in the Greek Liturgy for the various feasts of the apostles make some allusion to their vocation as fishers of men; they speak of the *rod* of the cross, the *hook* of preaching, the *bait* of charity, of nations *caught like fish,* &c., &c.: and some mediæval artists have even represented a hook and line proceeding from the very Body of our Lord as He hung upon the cross.—*Cahier, Mélanges d'Archeol.* iv. p. 118.

† Oratio Constant. ad Cœt. Sanct. § 18.

‡ De Civ. Dei, xviii. 23. We know from the testimony of Cicero (De Divin. ii. c. 54) that acrostics were a characteristic of the Sibylline verses.

§ In the original, the initials of the next lines give the word ΣΤΑΥΡΟΣ, viz., "Cross." In olden times it was customary in the Church of France to

these several words taken together make up the word ΙΧΘΥ, or "fish." We have already said that St Clement of Alexandria is the earliest witness to the use of this symbol; and it is by no means improbable that the schools of Alexandria were really the first to originate it. The Church of that city was composed largely of converts from Judaism; and we know that nothing was more familiar to the Jews than the habit of coining names for their leaders or other great men, by means of a combination of the initial letters of some other names, or legend, or motto, closely connected with them. The name of Macchabees, for instance, is said to be made up of the initial letters of the motto which Judas Macchabeus is supposed to have ever had upon his lips or on his banners, "Who is like to Thee among the strong, O Lord?"*

Instances of its use by the Fathers in this sense;

Whether, however, the Sibylline verses received their inspiration from Alexandrine Christians, or whether these verses themselves first originated the idea, at any rate we cannot wonder that when once a mystical meaning had been suggested for the word fish, it gained general acceptance in the Church. It became a sacred *tessera*, embodying, with wonderful brevity and distinctness, a complete abridgment of the Creed—a profession of faith, as it were, both in the two natures, and unity of Person, and in the redemptorial office of Our Blessed Lord. "It contains in one name, by means of its single letters," says Optatus,† "a whole multitude (*turbam*) of holy names." Hence St Clement names the fish as one of several figures that might very properly be used on Christian seals. Origen speaks simply and without explanation of our Lord as "figuratively called the fish;" and in every story of

---

sing these Sibylline verses in church at Christmas with all the solemnity they could.—*Martene, De Ant. Eccl. Rit.*, lib. iv. c. xii. 13.

* Exodus xv. 11. See Grotius, Critic. Sac. t. iii. c. 2695. The interpretation given in the epistle of Barnabas of the number 318, the servants born to Abraham in his house (Genesis xiv. 14), is only another example of the same kind. See a very interesting paper by P. Cahier in his *Mélanges d'Archeol.* i. 192. † Adv. Parmen. lib. iii.

sacred writ connected with a fish, the early Church recognised some Christian figure or allusion. "We little fishes," says Tertullian,* "are born in water after the example of *Jesus Christ our fish.*" "He descends," says Optatus,† "in baptism, in answer to our prayers, into the baptismal font, so that what before was water is now called from the fish *piscina* (*a pisce*)." "The fish which is first taken," says St Jerome, "in whose mouth was the coin which was paid as the tribute-money to those who demanded it, was Christ, the second Adam, at the cost of whose blood both the first Adam and Peter, that is, all other sinners, were redeemed." "By that fish whereof we read, which was caught in the river Tigris, whose gall and liver Tobias took for the protection of his wife Sarah and the enlightenment of the blind Tobias, we understand Christ." "By the interior remedies of that fish," says St Prosper of Aquitania,‡ "we are daily enlightened and fed;" —words which contain a manifest allusion to the two Sacraments of Baptism and the Holy Eucharist.

It would be easy still further to multiply quotations from the Fathers, showing how familiar to them was this identification of the fish, wherever it might be found, with Our Blessed Lord. But such an accumulation of proof is unnecessary. The important thing to observe is already sufficiently clear, viz., that all these hidden meanings of Holy Scripture were derived from the simple fact tacitly assumed by them all, viz., that the fish was the recognised conventional sign for Christ. Hence we find a multitude of little fishes, in crystal, ivory, and in monu-mother of pearl, enamel, and precious stones, in the graves of ments of art. the Catacombs;§ some of them with holes drilled through the head, to be worn round the neck; one with the word ΣΩCAIC ("Mayest Thou save us") engraved upon its back; once, also, we find a tombstone with a Pagan inscription on either side, but

* De Baptismo. † Lib. iii. Adv. Parmen.
‡ Or the author of the book *De Promiss. et Prædic. Dei*, which goes by his name, ii. 39. § *Bullett.* 1863, p. 38.

now used to close a Christian tomb, and, besides chipping and cancelling the Pagan epitaph, a fish was roughly cut upon the stone, as sufficient to claim for it a Christian sense.

<small>The fish seldom used alone.</small>

Hence, also, we can interpret with certainty a number of various complications of artistic symbols into which the fish enters. And this is an important test of the truth of our interpretation. For it is comparatively easy to assign a meaning to a single symbol standing alone, since any isolated fact will often lend itself to several different interpretations. But if this symbol be found united with others of a similar character, springing from the same source, but taking a different form, and if this same meaning suffices to explain them all, it receives and communicates a light and force quite irresistible, wresting conviction even from the most unwilling mind. The differences of the symbols thus brought together mutually illustrate and perfect one another, and prove as fruitful of instruction as their resemblances. Together they fix and establish with certainty, what each, taken separately, may have left only undetermined and probable. It is in this way that innumerable questions have been decided in the interpretation of profane antiquities, and the process is as legitimate and as successful when applied to Christian antiquities.

Moreover, this test is the more easy of application here, because it happens that the fish is rarely found quite alone (either the word or the symbol) in the monuments of the Roman cemeteries. In more than two-thirds of the numerous instances in which it is repeated, it is found in union with other symbols, and so intimately united with them as manifestly to have been intended as a part of one whole. Thus, it is sometimes found in connexion with a ship. In three or four

<small>Used together with a ship, a dove, or an anchor.</small>

instances the fish is bearing a ship on its back; and this combination naturally suggests to us Christ upholding His Church. Much more frequently,—in more than twenty epitaphs, for example, to say nothing of gems, in which these two symbols are almost inseparable,—it is found in conjunction with the anchor; and we understand at once, as plainly as if it had been written in ordinary letters of the alphabet (as indeed it often was), SPES IN CHRISTO, SPES IN DEO, SPES IN DEO CHRISTO, "Hope in Christ," &c. Another combination of the symbol of the fish is with the dove. This we meet with in nearly

FIG. 22.—*Gravestone from most ancient part of St Priscilla.*

twenty instances; and as we have already seen that this bird with its olive branch, when found on a Christian gravestone, is only another mode of expressing the most common of all ancient epitaphs, SPIRITUS [TUUS] IN PACE, "Thy spirit [be, *or* is] in peace," so, when the fish is added, we recognise the same inscription in its longer and fuller form, as we sometimes find it written also, IN PACE ET IN CHRISTO. On some ancient rings or seals, a lamb or a dove may be seen standing on a fish, representing a Christian soul supported by Christ through the waves and storms of this world. The fish is found also, either in figure or in word, with the name of Jesus, or Christ, or the monogram, or with the Good Shepherd.* These all speak for themselves and require no comment.

There is another combination, however, of the fish with bread, which is the most interesting and important of all Christian symbols, and it deserves the most careful study. Probably it will at once occur to the reader to connect these representations with the miracles of multiplying the loaves and fishes, and sometimes, indeed, there is certain evidence that the artist intended to allude to those incidents. Even then, however, he nearly always violated the literal truth of the Gospel

Fish and bread.

* *e.g.*, Fig. 7 in page 55.

story, for the express purpose (as it would seem) of showing his intention to go beyond the letter, and to penetrate to the hidden meaning of the text; to idealise the history, as it were, and raise it to the height of a symbol. Were it otherwise, we should have no right to speak of it in this place, but ought rather to reserve the whole subject till we come to speak of the paintings which represent biblical histories. But what biblical history can suffice to explain such paintings as these?—a fish swimming and carrying on its back a basket of bread?—a three-legged table with a large fish and two or three loaves lying upon it?—or the same again, with a man standing before the table, apparently in the act of blessing what is upon it, whilst a woman stands opposite, with her hands expanded in prayer?* If these are not mere caprices of the artist, it is clear that they must have been intended to render sensible some doctrine rather than to represent any fact, since there is no history to which they correspond; they were signs of religious ideas and truths, rather than faithful imitations of facts; in a word, they were symbolical, or as Raoul Rochette calls them, ideographical paintings, not historical; and therefore they find their most fitting place in this division of our subject. Nevertheless, it will be necessary, for their full and complete elucidation, that we should first speak of a painting which is of frequent recurrence in the Catacombs, and which may be said to be partly historical and partly symbolical. Its interpretation is provided by the Fathers themselves.

A particular instance of these symbols united (St John xxi.)

On the walls of several subterranean chapels there is a painting in which seven men are represented seated at a table, with bread and fish before them;† and there is a history in the last chapter of the Gospel according to St John, of which it might be taken as a literal representation. Jesus was manifesting Himself to His disciples for the third time after His resurrection, and the evangelist has recorded the circumstances of

---

* See Plate XIV. 1, 2, 3. † See Plate XIII.

the manifestation with great minuteness. Of ourselves we might not perhaps have noted anything very special in these circumstances, of such a character as to lay a singular claim upon the Christian artist above all other manifestations; nevertheless we find, that as a matter of fact it did claim their attention and occupy their pencil in a pre-eminent degree, and even to the exclusion of every other history of the same class. The details of the incident, which it is important for us to observe, are these. Seven of the disciples had spent the night in fishing, but had caught nothing. But when the morning was come, Jesus stood on the shore, and bade them cast the net on the right side of the ship. They cast therefore, and were rewarded by a miraculous draught of fishes. And as soon as they came to land, they saw hot coals lying, and a fish laid thereon, and bread. And Jesus bade them bring also of the fishes which they had themselves caught. And when they had done so, He invited them to come and dine, and "Jesus cometh and taketh bread and giveth them, and fish in like manner.*

All thoughtful students of Holy Scripture can hardly fail to recognise in this miraculous draught of fishes a prophetic type of the success which should attend the labours of the Apostles, when engaged as fishers of men. Most of them also will probably suspect some connexion between the giving of bread by Christ to His apostles (not on this occasion only, but on others also, of His manifestation after His resurrection) with the taking of bread and giving it them in the institution of the Holy Eucharist; more especially, since on one of these occasions it is expressly mentioned that "He was made known to them in the breaking of bread."† The following commentary, then, of St Augustine on the narrative of St John, ought not to appear strange or fanciful to any one, even though, in some of its details, it may chance to be new to many of our readers. He says that "in the dinner which the Lord made for those *Explained of the Holy Eucharist; by St Augustine;*

* St John xxi. 13.   † St Luke xxiv 35.

seven disciples, of the fish which they had seen laid upon the coals, to which He added of the fish they themselves had caught, and of bread, Christ who suffered was really the fish that was broiled (*Piscis assus, Christus passus*); He is also the bread, 'the bread which came down from heaven.' The Church is the fish caught by the Apostles, which must be incorporated into Christ, for the participation of everlasting happiness; we ourselves, and all true believers to the end of time, are represented by those seven disciples" (the number seven being often used in Holy Scripture for completeness or universality), "that so we may understand that we too have a share in so great a sacrament, and are associated in the same happiness." And he concludes—"This is the dinner of our Lord with His disciples, with which St John finishes his Gospel, though he had many other things to say about Christ, *magna ut existimo et rerum magnarum contemplatione;*"* as though he would say, This history forms a suitable conclusion to the whole Gospel, because it "exhibits a kind of link or transition from Christ's earthly to His heavenly kingdom;"† inasmuch as it sets forth under a veil, or in a mystical manner, the union of all Christian souls with Christ their Head, first, by means of the bread from heaven, the Holy Eucharist, in this world, and then in that yet more intimate enjoyment of Him in the next world, whereof the sacrament of the altar is at once a pledge and a foretaste.‡

and the rest of the Fathers.

We have said that no thoughtful student of Scripture can justly object to this interpretation of St John's words by the great Doctor of the West, as though it were the mere fruit of his own imagination, since it rests upon principles which are even now universally acknowledged; but this is far short of what might have been said. For the truth is, that in the early ages of the Church no other interpretation of the narrative was

---

* In Joann. Ev. Tract. 123, sec. 2, tom. iii. p. 2460, ed. Gaume.
† Keble on Eucharistical Adoration, c. ii.
‡ "In captura piscium commendavit Ecclesiæ Sacramentum, qualis futura est ultima resurrectione mortuorum."—*St Aug. ubi supra.*

Symbolical Paintings. 217

ever dreamt of. So unanimous is the *consensus* of the Fathers in seeing here a mystical representation of the Holy Eucharist, that Cardinal Pitra can only find a single ancient writer (the pseudo-Athanasius) who does not so interpret it. We shall content ourselves with quoting but one testimony. Prosper Africanus, commenting upon this same part of the Gospels, speaks of our blessed Lord as "that great Fish who satisfied from Himself (*ex Se Ipso*) the disciples on the shore, and offered Himself as a fish (ΙΧΘΥΝ) to the whole world." *

And we must remember that this is not the only passage of Holy Writ in which the Fathers recognised the Blessed Sacrament of the altar under the same symbol. We have already quoted one who speaks of Christ as "that fish from whose interior remedies we are both enlightened and fed;" referring, of course, to the history of Tobias on the one hand, and to the two sacraments of Baptism and the Holy Eucharist on the other. St Augustine † also, speaking of the authority given to man at the creation over the fishes of the sea, is immediately reminded of these same sacraments, which he describes as "that solemnity of sacraments whereby those whom God's mercy seeks out amid many waters are first initiated, or that other solemnity wherein that fish is manifested, which, when it has been drawn forth from the deep, pious mortals eat." These words would be absolutely unintelligible, unless we suppose that to the writer himself, as well as to his readers, the idea of the fish as a symbol of the Holy Eucharist were perfectly familiar.

This familiarity is still further remarkably attested by two most ancient epitaphs; one, of St Abercius, Bishop of Hierapolis, in Phrygia, towards the end of the second century; the other, of one Pectorius (as it would appear), who was buried in the cemetery of St Pierre d'Estrier, near Autun, probably during some part of the third century. The first of these epitaphs has been long known, but was only imperfectly under-

This interpretation confirmed by the epitaph of St Abercius,

* De Promiss. ii. 39.   † Confess. xiii. 23.

stood, until recent discoveries of Christian monuments had thrown fresh light upon its mystical language.* The only part of it which concerns our present subject is contained in a few lines towards its conclusion. Abercius has been describing his many and distant travels through Syria and to Rome, and he says—

Πίστις δὲ προσῆγε,
Καὶ παρέθηκε τροφὴν Ἰχθὺν τε μιῆς ἀπὸ πηγῆς
παμμεγέθη, καθαρὸν, ὃν ἐδράξατο παρθένος ἁγνή·
καὶ τοῦτον παρέδωκε φίλοις ἔσθειν διὰ παντός,
οἶνον χρηστὸν ἔχουσα, κέρασμα διδοῦσα μετ' ἄρτου·
. . . .
ταῦθ' ὁ νοῶν εὔξαιτο ὑπὲρ μου πᾶς ὁ συνῳδός.

"Faith led me on the road, and set before me for food fish from the one fountain, the great and spotless fish which the pure Virgin embraced; and this fish she gave to friends to eat everywhere, having good wine, giving wine mixed with water, and bread. May he who understands these things pray for me." The allusion contained in the words, "the one fountain," will be better explained at a future time,† when we come to speak of the representations of Moses striking the rock, and the fountain flowing forth; but all the rest is easily understood when once we recognise that the fish was used as a symbol of Christ and of the Holy Eucharist; then bread and wine and the fish come naturally together as the visible and invisible parts of one great mystery.

<small>and another epitaph found at Autun;</small> The second epitaph we have spoken of was only discovered about thirty years ago in the place already mentioned; and its chronology has been made the subject of much critical discussion, some placing it as early as the time of the Antonines in the second century, others as late as the middle of the fourth. Cardinal Pitra, P. Secchi, P. Garrucci, and other

---

* Spicil. Solesm. iii. 533; Acta SS. Bolland. Oct. tom. ix. p. 491.
† Chapter VII. of this Book. The bread and the fountain are also brought together in a line of the Sibylline verses, vi. 15. ἐκ δὲ μιῆς πηγῆς ἄρτου κόρος ἔσσεται ἀνδρῶν. And bread and the blessed Virgin in i. 359. Pitra quotes an ancient title of our blessed Lady, *fons Bethlemicus*; and Bethlehem means the House of Bread.

learned authorities, assign it with more probability to the earlier part of the third.* There is a flavour of antiquity about it which cannot be mistaken, so that even those who think it may have been put together in its present form in the fourth century, do not hesitate to say that the particular part of it which has reference to the fish, may have been as old as the days of St Irenæus. In it Christians are called "the divine children of the Heavenly Fish," and after an allusion to their new and immortal life, received in the sacred waters which enrich the soul with wisdom, it goes on to bid them "receive the sweet food of the Saviour of the saints;" "Eat and drink," it says, "receiving and holding the fish in your hands."

Ἰχθύος οὐρανίου θεῖον γένος,
. . . . .
Σωτῆρος δ' ἁγίων μελιηδέα λάμβανε βρῶσιν·
Ἔσθιε, πῖνε, δυσὶν Ἰχθὺν ἔχων παλάμαις.

No one can doubt what is here alluded to, and no one, we think, can call in question our right to attribute to the early Christian artists the same thoughts on this subject as were so manifestly familiar to Christian writers. Nevertheless, that we may satisfy the most sceptical of readers, we will add yet other particulars, taken from the monuments of Christian art themselves, which, even if they stood alone, would in our opinion abundantly justify the interpretation we have put upon this ancient and popular symbol of the fish, when found together with bread. These particulars are twofold; first, there is the fact that in all, or nearly all, the paintings of this dinner of our Lord to seven of His disciples, there is added some representation, either of the miraculous multiplication of the loaves and fishes, or the changing of water into wine at Cana in Galilee, events which had absolutely no connexion with it, or with each other, historically, though mystically they are all most intimately united. It can hardly be necessary to make many citations *and by monuments of art. Miracles of the multiplication of the loaves and fishes, and of the changing water into wine.*

* See Cahier, Mel. d'Arch. iii. 156, iv. 118; Spic. Solesm. i. 560.

from the Fathers, to prove that they saw in both these miracles foreshadowings of the great mystery of the Holy Eucharist; and when they are brought together in the monuments of art, the allusion to the two species in the Blessed Sacrament is too transparent to be denied. We are all familiar with the argument urged by St Cyril of Alexandria, that since our Lord once turned water into wine, which is something akin to blood, it ought not to be counted an incredible thing that He should also have turned wine into blood; and St Ambrose, commenting on the other miracle as recorded by St Luke,* says distinctly, "In the ministry of the Apostles on this occasion, the future distribution of the Body and Blood of the Lord is foreshadowed;" and in another place he brings the two miracles together, and makes the same application of them both; or rather, he quotes Pope Liberius as having done so in a homily delivered on Christmas Day in St Peter's.†

The Christian artists could not have been ignorant of this spiritual interpretation of our Lord's miracles, and for this reason they united in one scene events that were really very distinct in time and place. Thus, a number of baskets of bread always forms the foreground of the picture we have described of the feast of the seven disciples. Moreover, because they desired that the minds of those who saw their paintings should not rest in the outward semblance of the scene, but be carried forward to its hidden and mystical meaning, they always departed, more or less, from its literal truth; *e.g.*, we never find seven or twelve baskets of bread, but eight; nor six water-pots of wine, but seven. It was the symbolism of a religious idea they aimed at, and not the representation of a real history.

Similar paintings in a Catacomb at Alexandria.
The second item of artistic evidence is still more conclusive. An ancient Christian cemetery has lately been discovered in Alexandria, subterranean, and in other respects also bearing

* Comment. in S. Luc. c. ix. lib. vi. 84.   † De Virginibus, iii. 1.

Symbolical Paintings.

a certain resemblance to the Roman Catacombs. In one of the chapels, and precisely over the altar where the sacred mysteries would have been celebrated, there are the remains of a painting, belonging (De Rossi believes) to the fourth century, in which all these various scenes are brought together, and their interpretation given in writing. That is to say—In the middle is our blessed Lord, with Peter on His right hand and Andrew on His left, holding a plate with two fish, whilst several baskets of loaves lie on the ground before Him. Further to the right is the miracle at Cana, our blessed Lady and the servants having legends over their heads,—Η ΑΓΙΑ ΜΑΡΙΑ — ΤΑ ΠΑΙΔΙΑ — "Holy Mary" and "The Servants;" and in the corresponding compartment on the other side are a certain number of persons seated at a feast, with a legend over their heads, ΤΑΣ ΕΥΛΟΓΙΑΣ ΤΟΥ Χ͞Υ ΕΣΘΙΟΝΤΕΣ,—"Eating the benedictions of Christ." Now, this same word, which we have here translated *benedictions*, is the word used by St Paul* when speaking of the communion of the Body and Blood of Christ. The verb belonging to it is used by the Evangelists indifferently with the

Fig. 23.—*Painting from the Catacomb of Alexandria.*

* 1 Cor. x. 16.

corresponding verb of the Eucharist, both in their account of the miracles of multiplication, and also of the institution of the Blessed Sacrament.* Lastly, it is the very word always used by St Cyril of Alexandria (in whose city this painting is found) to denote the consecrated bread and wine; and when the devotion of the faithful waxed less fervent, and communions became more rare, the same word was naturally retained, and has ever since remained, to denote the blest bread which was now received, instead of It. Here, then, we have the evidence of the Christian artist himself, that the two miracles we have referred to were understood and used as "a kind of sacramental anticipation" (to use the words of St Maximus) "of the chalice of the New Testament."

Summary of evidence, and importance of the conclusion.

We fear this discussion may have appeared somewhat long and tedious, perhaps, to some of our readers, or at any rate out of place, yet it was not possible to avoid it if we desired to show that we are building on solid foundations. For we have been accused of wishing to force upon the paintings of the Catacombs a meaning they will not bear, whereas we most sincerely desire to ascertain what their meaning really is; and we have thought the best means of doing this is to compare them with the literary and biographical details which have come down to us with reference to the thoughts and feelings of those who executed them, or for whom they were executed. We have been accused of "attempting to connect the fish with the doctrine of Transubstantiation." What we have really done is to prove by abundant testimonies that when fish and bread were represented together on ancient Christian monuments, there was meant a secret reference to the Holy Eucharist, of which the bread denotes the outward and visible form, the fish the inward and hidden reality, viz., Christ Jesus Our Lord.

Before the recent discoveries, this was only a conjecture of

* St Matt. xiv. 19; xv. 36; xxvi. 26, 27. St Mark, vi. 41; xiv. 22. St Luke ix. 16; xxii. 19. St John vi. 11.

acute and learned antiquarians, but the pictures discovered in the cemetery of St Callixtus set before us most plain and unquestionable representations of the Eucharistic table, side by side with pictures recording the Gospel histories of the repasts on bread and fish, and the baskets of multiplied loaves, and thus they put in the strongest light the symbolical link which united those repasts and miracles with the Holy Eucharist. The secret of this connecting link was no less illustrated and confirmed by the celebrated epitaph of Autun, where the hieroglyphic of the fish is openly applied to the bread of the Holy Table. From the first moment of the discovery of that venerable monument, Cardinal Pitra—then a professor in a neighbouring seminary—invited the attention of the learned to the light which it threw on this instance of ancient Christian symbolism; and the monuments of various kinds which have since been brought to light, together with many others which had been known indeed long before, but not fully understood, provide so complete a demonstration of that secret symbol, and of its gradual development in the hands of Christian artists, that it is no longer possible for any reasonable man to refuse his assent to the interpretation, or to make a demand for more abundant evidence. It is quite certain that these figures, however unmeaning they might have been to strangers, were as perfectly intelligible to cotemporary Christians as the hieroglyphics of ancient Egypt to those who used them, or the letters of the English alphabet to ourselves.

When, then, we see on a Christian tombstone, as on a very *Examples.*

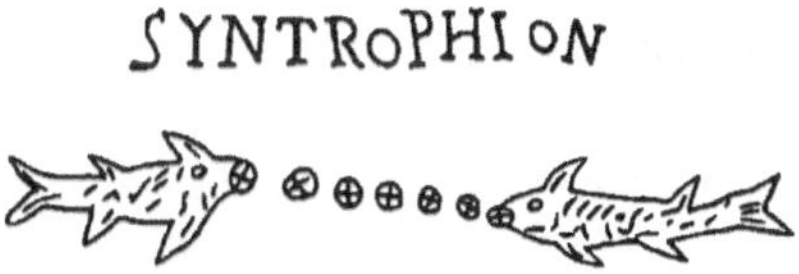

ΣΥΝΤΡΟΦΙΟΝ

FIG. 24.—*Tombstone from an ancient Christian Cemetery at Modena.*

ancient one found at Modena, and represented in this figure, a couple of fish, each holding a loaf of bread in its mouth, and five other loaves between them, we feel certain that the survivors of Serapion, whose tombstone it is, intended a symbolical representation of the Holy Eucharist, that blessed sacrament which had, doubtless, been his strength in life, and now gave the sure hope of his resurrection to everlasting life.* In like manner we have no difficulty in giving a Christian meaning to that strange-looking ornament which is twice repeated in one of the most ancient *cubicula* in the crypts of St Lucina, and of which the reader will find an accurate copy in Plate XIV. A fish, apparently alive and swimming, bears upon its back a basket of bread. This bread is not of the ordinary kind, but of a gray ashen colour, such as was used by the people of the East, and especially by the Jews, as a sacred offering of the first fruits to the priests, and was known to the Romans by the barbarous name of *mamphala*. The bread lies on the top of the basket, but in the middle of it, in both pictures, may be clearly distinguished a something red, a something that seems best to represent a glass containing red wine; and De Rossi produces a text from St Jerome, of which he says he was irresistibly reminded as soon as he saw this painting. St Jerome is speaking of Exuperius, Bishop of Toulouse, who had spent all his substance for the relief of the poor, and he goes on to remark that "nothing, however, can be richer than one who carries the Body of Christ in a basket made of twigs, and the Blood of Christ in a chalice of glass."† In the painting before us the basket is precisely of this kind, and it was already known from other sources that baskets of wickerwork were used in the sacrificial rites both of the Jews and Gentiles, and that the Christians also had continued the use of vessels of the same material for carrying the Blessed Sacrament, where gold or silver could not be had.‡ We cannot doubt, therefore, that this singular painting—at once the most

Fish carrying a basket of bread.

---

* St John, vi. 55.
† Ep. 125, *alias* 4, ad. Rusticum. tom. i. 1085, ed. Migne.
‡ See Marini, Fratr. Arvali, 396, 423.

Symbolical Paintings.

ancient and the most simple that we know, of the fish united with bread—was intended to refer to the mystery of the Holy Eucharist.

Probably the painting also on the opposite wall of the same *cubiculum* is another symbol of the Holy Eucharist, though this is less obvious and certain. A milk-pail rests on a kind of altar between two sheep,* and the same instrument may be seen in the next chamber, on the right-hand side of the Good Shepherd. Elsewhere it appears also in his hands. In these latter instances, it might not unreasonably be taken as merely one of the ornamental accessories of pastoral life, inserted without any religious signification, but its position in the present example seems to indicate something more important. So also when we find it, as in some most ancient pictures in the cemetery of St Domitilla, suspended from the pastoral staff and by the side of the lamb; or, as in a later painting in the

Lamb carrying milk-pail;

Fig. 25.—*Lamb carrying the milk-pail from Catacomb of SS. Peter and Marcellinus.*

Fig. 26.—*Milk-pail and shepherd's crook by side of lamb from Catacomb of St Domitilla.*

cemetery of SS. Peter and Marcellinus, resting on the back of the lamb itself, we are reminded of the undoubted fact that

* See fig. 14, page 103.

milk was often used as a symbol of the Holy Eucharist.* Indeed, the lamb carrying the milk-pail on its own back seems exactly analogous to the picture we have just been studying of the fish carrying the bread.

interpreted by the Acts of St Perpetua,
The Acts of St Perpetua—generally acknowledged as a genuine document of the beginning of the third century—describe, as a part of the vision by which that saint was consoled and strengthened in prison, the Good Shepherd appearing to her, milking His flock, and giving her to eat some of the curds of the milk which He had drawn. "She received them with hands crossed upon one another, and all the people answered, Amen,"—just the word and the action then used in partaking of the Holy Eucharist, of which it was here evidently intended to be a symbol. Something of the same kind also occurs in other ancient Acts; and some of the old commentators point out that the good things of the Gospel are sometimes prophesied and foretold under the figure of flesh, sometimes of mixed wine, sometimes of milk. It may not be out of place also to call to mind the primitive practice of giving milk and honey to infants after baptism,—a practice borne witness to by Tertullian and St Jerome as one of those things which were handed on by tradition to the Church, and which was continued, at least on Holy Saturday, as late as the ninth or tenth century.†

and by the language of St Augustine,
It is still more to our purpose to quote the language of St Augustine in his commentary on one of the Psalms; ‡ and the whole sermon in which it occurs is so remarkable, and bears so directly upon the question of symbolism with which we are engaged, that we are sure our readers will need no apology if we quote from it at some length. The Doctor is commenting on the title of the 33d Psalm, which refers to an incident in

---

* Buonarroti, Vetri, 32; Garrucci, Vetri. 62, 63, ed. 2da.
† Tertullian, De Cor. Militis, c. 3; Hieron. Dial. adv. Lucif. See Martene, De Ant. Eccl. Rit. lib. i. c. i. xv. 16.
‡ Enarr. 1ma in Ps. xxxiii. tom. iv. p. 301, ed. Gaume.

the life of David, not exactly as it is recorded in the historical books: that is to say, in the Book of Kings the incident is told of one person, and in the title of the Psalm it seems to be attributed to another. And the Saint argues that this change of name has not been made without a reason. He inquires, therefore, into the mystical meaning of the whole incident, which he maintains it certainly *must* have, whether we can discover it or not; because every other part of the history of the Jewish people has such a meaning; and he appeals to his hearers as knowing this fact as well as he does. He specifies amongst other details of Jewish story, which foreshadowed mysteries of the Christian Church, the manna, the passage through the Red Sea, and the striking of the rock. He then speaks of David slaying the giant Goliath, as a type of Christ killing Satan :—" But what is Christ who slew Satan? It is humility slaying pride. When then I speak to you, my brethren, of Christ, it is humility that is specially commended to you. For He made a way to us by humility. . . . God was made humble, that so the pride of the human race might not disdain to follow the footsteps of God." And he continues immediately as follows :—" But there was, as you know, in former times a sacrifice of the Jews according to the order of Aaron, with victims of cattle; and this, too, was in a mystery, because, as yet, there was not the sacrifice of the Body and Blood of the Lord, which the faithful know and those who have read the Gospels; which sacrifice is now spread (*diffusum*) throughout the whole world. Put then before your eyes those two sacrifices; the former one according to Aaron, and this one according to Melchisedec. For it is written, 'The Lord swore, and will not repent; Thou art a priest for ever according to the order of Melchisedec.' Of whom is this said, ' Thou art a priest for ever according to the order of Melchisedec?' Of our Lord Jesus Christ. But who was Melchisedec?" Then, after giving the history of Melchisedec, and calling particular attention to his priesthood, to the blessing which he gave to Abraham, and to his having brought forth bread and wine, he continues, "The sacrifice of Aaron, then, is taken away, and the sacrifice according to the order of Melchisedec has begun to be. . . . Our Lord Jesus Christ has willed our salvation to be in His Body and Blood. But whence has He commended to us His Body and Blood? From His humility; for except he were humble, He would not be eaten and drunk. Consider His greatness: 'In the beginning was the Word, and the Word was with God, and the Word was God.' Behold this everlasting food; but food for Angels. Angels eat of it, and the powers above, and heavenly spirits; and eating, they are filled and satisfied; yet, that which satisfies and gladdens them still remains whole. But what mortal could approach that food? Whence could he have a heart suitable for such food? It was necessary that that food should be made milk (*mensa illa lactesceret*), and so come to little ones. But how does meat become milk? How is meat changed into milk, unless it first be passed through flesh? And this is done by the mother. What the mother eats, the same is also eaten by the infant; but because the infant is not fit to eat bread, the mother changes the bread into her flesh (*ipsum panem mater incarnat*), and so feeds the infant on that very bread, through the lowliness of the breast and the juice of milk. How then has the Wisdom of God fed us on bread? 'Because the Word was made flesh, and dwelt in us' (*in nobis*). Behold then His humility; for man has eaten the bread of Angels, as it is written, 'He gave them the bread of heaven; man ate the bread of Angels;'* that is, man has eaten of that Word whereon the Angels feed, and which is equal to the Father; for, 'being in the form of God, He thought it not robbery to be equal with God.' The Angels feed on him, but 'He debased Himself,' that man might eat the bread of Angels, 'taking the form of a servant, being made in the likeness of men and in habit found as a man, He

---

* Ps. lxxvii. 24.

humbled Himself, becoming obedient unto death, even the death of the cross,'* in order that from the Cross might be commended to us the new sacrifice, the flesh and blood of Christ."

Manifestly, then, it is by no means improbable that the milk-pails to which we have called attention in early Christian monuments may have had a religious symbolical meaning, though we do not by any means pretend to put it on the same level with the symbol of the bread and the fish. The examples of the one symbol are comparatively rare, and its interpretation is borrowed from the language of a few; the other was incessantly repeated in every variety of combination, and is attested by a great multitude of authorities.

Some of our readers may be surprised that nothing should have been yet said about the cross or the monogram, which by some writers are stated to have been the earliest and most common of all Christian symbols. This statement is not, however, borne out by archæological facts. We have already spoken of the anchor being, in some instances, so formed in Christian epitaphs as naturally to suggest the thought of the cross; and we need not quote the well-known passages of Tertullian and others, which show the love of the early Christians for this sign of salvation, and their frequent use of it. Christians were *crucis religiosi*;† the cross was the *signum Christi*, τὸ κυριακὸν σημεῖον.‡ Nevertheless, there were obvious reasons why this sign should not be freely exposed to public gaze; the famous caricature of the Crucifixion, found on the Palatine, is a sufficient proof of this. In the most ancient part of the lowest *piano* of the crypt of St Lucina, we meet with a *loculus* with the inscription

ΡΟΥΦΙΝΑ
ΕΙΡΗΝΗ

Different forms of the cross.

with a simple Greek cross beneath the latter name. But

---

* Philip. ii. 6-8.   † Tertull. Apol. 16.
‡ St Clem. Alex. Strom. vi. 11.

most of the earliest forms of it that we can discover are more or less disguised. It is contained, for instance, in the monogram (Fig. 26, *b*), which occurs on an inscription of the

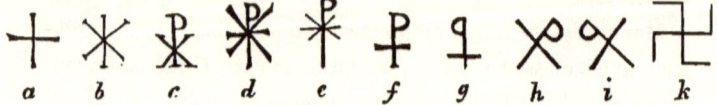

Fig. 27.—*Different forms of the Cross and Monogram.*

year 268 or 279, as well as upon others not bearing certain dates. It seems to have been intended to combine the first letters of IHCOYC XPICTOC, and may be considered rather a compendious form of writing than a symbol properly so called. Tertullian quotes Ezech. ix. 4. *Signa Tau super frontes*, &c., and says: "Now the Greek letter Tau and our own T is the very form of the Cross, which he predicted would be the sign on our foreheads in the true Catholic Jerusalem."* The number 300 being expressed in Greek by this letter Tau, came itself, even in apostolic times, to be regarded as equivalent to the cross.† We see examples of this in the inscription IRETNE, lately discovered in a part of the Catacomb of San Callisto, belonging to the third century;‡ and also in the monogram of TYRANIO (Fig. 27, p. 232), in both of which the T is made prominent, evidently with a symbolical meaning. We even find the letter itself inscribed alone, or in combination with the letter P, on a tombstone. §

and of the monogram.

The Constantinian monogram, as it is called (Fig. 26, *c*), is formed of the first two letters of the Greek word for Christ, the X with the P. It is not easy to fix its date with any certainty, but it was known to the Christians long before the triumph of Constantine, although the few dated inscriptions

---

* Contr. Marc. iii. 22.
† See Barnab. Ep. Cath., c. 9, ed. Hefele., p. 22.
‡ *Bullet.*, 1863, 35.
§ Rom. Sott., tom. 2, xxxix. 28.

before that event do not supply us with any specimen of it. It has been found scratched on the plaster, side by side with the earlier forms (*a* and *b*), both in San Callisto and the Catacomb of St Agnes, in galleries which bear every sign of being prior to the time of Constantine. This monogram, and also the simple Greek cross, appear on the coins of that emperor, and shortly after his time we meet with the modifications of it (*d* and *e*). The tail of the P is sometimes prolonged, as in *f*; in other cases the same letter is reversed as in *g*, or the whole is placed obliquely as in *h* and *i*. A form of the Cross, *k*, is sometimes found on the garments of some of the figures painted in the Catacombs during the fourth century, which is composed of a fourfold repetition of the Greek Γ; and because the symbol thus formed was in use among the Buddhists and in other Oriental superstitions, some French writers have attempted to establish an historical connexion between them and the Christian religion. It has been demonstrated, however, by De Rossi, that this *crux gammata*, as it was called, was of comparatively late introduction into the Christian Church. It was no spontaneous invention of the early Christians, no fruit of early tradition; but rather was borrowed by the Christians from some other source, and adopted for a while for concealment's sake.

It may be remarked that the form ⳨ is an extremely slight modification of a mode of writing the Greek P, with a transverse line across it, not unfrequently met with in ancient Greek inscriptions, and to be seen on some of the coins of Herod the Great. This also, like the *crux gammata*, was afterwards studiously adopted by the Christians and supplanted the original Constantinian monogram which that emperor commanded his soldiers to inscribe on their shields.* The plain Latin cross seems to have been used much earlier in Africa

* " Fecit et jussus est, ut transversa × littera, summo capite circumflexo, Christum in scutis notat."—Lactant de mort. persec. c. 44. See P. Garrucci, *Vetri Ornati*, &c., where he describes and discusses all the coins of Constantine.

than in Italy;* indeed, it was used more frequently in that country than any form of the monogram. In Italy it began about the beginning of the fifth century, and by the end of the sixth century was very common everywhere. Once or twice also we find on tombs in the Catacombs a monogram formed from the union of ⳨ and the letter N, being intended, apparently, for the initials of the words XPICTOC NIKA, *Christ conquers*, and belonging, of course, to post-Constantinian times.

* De Rossi de Titul. Carthag. apud Spic. Solesm. iv.

Fig. 28.—*Sarcophagus found in Crypt of St Lucina, representing Ulysses and the Siren.*

CHAPTER III.

ALLEGORICAL PAINTINGS.

THE second class of paintings in the Catacombs of which we promised to speak, is of those which were *suggested* at least by some of our Lord's parables, though they can hardly be said really to reproduce them, and therefore we have called them allegorical. In truth, they are but a particular application and a further development of the same principle which has been already described under the name of symbolism. They proceed from hieroglyphic writing to artistic composition. Instead of a single symbol, or combination of symbols, they are whole scenes, inspired or suggested, as we have said, by our Lord's parables, and themselves suggesting the truths which He thereby designed to teach. We do not, however, wish to be understood as saying that the first Christians composed these scenes as a careful statement of doctrine, and painted them on the walls of their cemeteries or chapels with a distinct dogmatic purpose, *for the sake of* teaching. Rather, we believe, that their minds and souls being full of certain ideas, they naturally gave expression to those ideas in corresponding artistic forms, which forms again, when seen by others, necessarily revived and strengthened the impression of the truths they typified. The teaching was real, but unconscious.
Parables not accurately reproduced in ancient art.

Among the parables or parabolical instructions of our Lord, that of the vine and grapes was certainly adopted by His disciples during the first century;* and the illustration we
The vine.

* Pitra, Spicil. Solesm. ii. 449-458.

have given in page 72, from the most ancient part of the Catacomb of St Domitilla, is probably an example of it. The presence of little winged *putti* amongst the branches does not militate in any way against its Christian sense, though we cannot agree with those who consider that those little figures were intended to represent either men or angels. It seems more probable that they were used as mere ornaments, pretty but senseless accessories, according to the custom of the classical school of art, from which the Christian school had sprung and necessarily drawn some of its first inspirations.

The wise and foolish virgins.

The parable of the wise and foolish virgins appears occasionally in some of the *cubicula;* at least the wise virgins are to be seen, not the foolish;* and even these have not lamps in their hands, but burning torches, according to the Roman fashion with which the artists were more familiar. On a gravestone, a man is represented in the act of sowing seed; but it is impossible to say with certainty that any allusion was here intended to the parable. The scene may have had reference to the occupation of the deceased, or to something else which we cannot now discover.

The Good Shepherd an essentially Christian subject,

The parable, however, of the Good Shepherd is one which cannot be mistaken. Raoul Rochette, indeed, has made such a display of the old heathen representations of Mercury carrying a ram, of the Fauns, of shepherds and other young men carrying a lamb, a sheep, or a goat on their backs, that it would almost seem as if he doubted whether the Good Shepherd were a certain sign of Christianity, or, at any rate, that he supposed the first Christians had taken the idea of their Shepherd from the traditions of Pagan art rather than the Gospel. Yet, in truth, these naked young men in the tomb of the Nasones and elsewhere have very little in common with what we see on Christian monuments. Sometimes, but

---

* The foolish virgins have been lately found painted in a *cubiculum* in the Catacomb of St Cyriaca; but the painting is of a later date; it belongs to the time of the first *Christian* emperors.—*Bullett.*, 1863, p. 77.

Allegorical Paintings.

very rarely, we find in Pagan tombs a shepherd dancing with a lamb or goat on his neck. The only one we know which could at all be compared * with those in the Catacombs, is represented quite naked, among a lot of other figures, manifestly alluding to the seasons, and is essentially different from the grave picture of the Good Shepherd, which occupies the principal place in the roof or on the walls of so many Christian chapels. Once, in St Domitilla's cemetery, both the Good Shepherd and the dancer are to be found in the same chapel; but no one could pretend that there was no difference between them, or that one could be mistaken for the other. Of course it is not unlikely that, amid so frequent a repetition of pastoral scenes both by Pagan and Christian artists, there should be an occasional resemblance, possibly even a direct imitation, of some ancient and classical type; but if so, Christian artists have at least departed from the Pagan type in a thousand different ways.

It seems to have been quite their favourite subject. We of very frequent use, cannot go through any part of the Catacombs, or turn over the pages of any collection of ancient Christian monuments, without coming across it again and again. We know from Tertullian that it was often designed upon chalices. We find it ourselves painted in fresco upon the roofs and walls of the sepulchral chambers; rudely scratched upon grave-stones, or more carefully sculptured on sarcophagi; traced in gold upon glass, moulded on lamps, engraved on rings; and, in a word, represented on every species of Christian monument that has come down to us. Of course, amid such a multitude of examples, there is considerable variety of treatment. We cannot, however, appreciate the suggestion of Kügler, that this frequent repetition of the subject is probably to be attributed to the capabilities which it possessed in an artistic point of view. Rather, it was selected because it expressed the whole sum and substance of the Christian dispensation. In the

* Bellori, p. 58; Picturæ Ant. Crypt. Rom., ed. Bottari, p. 58.

language even of the Old Testament, the action of Divine Providence upon the world is frequently expressed by images and allegories borrowed from pastoral life; God is the Shepherd, and men are His sheep. But in a still more special way our Divine Redeemer offers Himself to our regards as the Good Shepherd. He came down from His eternal throne in heaven into the wilderness of this world to seek the lost sheep of the whole human race, and having brought them together into one fold upon earth, thence to transport them into the ever-verdant pastures of paradise. Moreover, in this work He vouchsafes to receive some of His own creatures as coadjutors. His gospel was committed to the ministration, not of angels, but of men, and the commission was given to the Prince of the Apostles, and in him to all His ministers, to "feed His sheep." Hence He is sometimes represented alone with His flock; at other times accompanied by His apostles, each attended by one or more sheep. Sometimes He stands amidst many sheep; sometimes He caresses one only; but most commonly—*so* commonly as almost to form a rule to which other scenes might be considered the exceptions—He bears a lost sheep, or even a goat, upon His shoulders; and we cannot doubt that He was painted in these various attitudes, not for artistic effect, but for their spiritual sense.

and variously represented.

Reasonably so. Of course, since Jesus Himself had vouchsafed to assume this name and title of a Shepherd, it was natural and lawful for Christian artists to represent Him in all the attitudes, and with all the instruments, of the pastoral profession, such as the crook, the pipe of reeds, the milk-pail, &c.; but even these, as we have seen, are each capable of receiving a very apposite Christian interpretation. And although it may please some writers to turn into ridicule any attempt to affix a Christian sense to every detail of an ancient fresco, it is hard to see upon what principle such objectors rely, which would not absolutely debar us from attempting to interpret the "motive" of any painting whatever, of which the artist did not happen to have

Allegorical Paintings. 237

left his own explanation in writing. If it be attempted to put a sense upon a painting, which it cannot be proved was ever known to the age in which the artist lived, the attempt is likely both to provoke and to deserve contempt; but where it is certain, on the contrary, that the sense suggested must have been quite familiar to the artist, either from its being contained in the broadest outlines and leading features of his religion, or from its having been pressed upon his notice by the controversies of his age, it seems reasonable to conclude that such sense was intended; as, for instance, that the Good Shepherd leading or caressing a goat was intended to be a protest against the hateful severity of the Novatians and other heretics refusing reconciliation to penitent sinners. So again, when we find on either side of the Good Shepherd, other men busying themselves about other sheep, and those sheep all disposed in various attitudes, it is natural and legitimate to conclude, first, that those men are the apostles and ministers of God's word and sacraments, whose duty it is to carry on the work of the Good Shepherd; and, secondly, that the various attitudes of the sheep denote the various dispositions of those to whom they are sent. And this is precisely what we see in Plate XVI., which represents a painting over an *arcosolium* in the Catacomb of St Callixtus, that was afterwards cut through in very ancient times for the sake of making a grave— a sure sign of the high antiquity of the painting thus damaged. On either side of the Good Shepherd, who occupies the centre, we see two men, probably SS. Peter and Paul, "representing the whole Apostolate from the beginning to the end, hastening away from Christ, as sent by Him to the world. On either side, before each of the two, there rises a rock, which is Christ himself, the true Rock* of the desert, pouring down streams of living waters.† These waters include all the sacraments and graces of Christianity. The apostles are seen joining their hands to catch this water, in order to turn it afterwards on

Explanation of Plate XVI.

---

* 1 Cor. x. 4.   † St John iv. 10, 13, &c.

our heads, *i.e.*, in order to communicate it to the world. The world to which they are sent is represented by two sheep standing before each of them. On one side, one of the sheep is listening attentively, not quite understanding as yet, but meditating and seeking to understand; the other turns his tail; it is an unwelcome subject, and he will have nothing to do with it. On the other side, one of the two sheep is drinking in all he hears with simplicity and affection; the other is eating grass; he has something else to do; he is occupied with the cares and pleasures and riches of this world."* Moreover, the artist has so distributed the streams of water as they flow forth from the rock, that they fall in exact accordance with the spiritual condition we have supposed the artist to have intended by the various positions into which he has placed his sheep; for, whereas a perfect torrent is falling on the head of the animal that stands with outstretched neck and head lifted towards the apostle, the other, which has turned its back, is left without any water at all.

* Palmer's Early Christian Symbolism, p. 3.

FIG. 29.—*Inscription from the Crypts of St Lucina. See p. 206.*

CHAPTER IV.

BIBLICAL PAINTINGS.

WE have found it impossible, as we anticipated, to keep inviolate that distinction between the several classes of paintings in the Catacombs with which we set out. The classification itself is just, but there is such an intimate relation between the several members of it, and they are so frequently intermixed, even in the same composition, that in treating of some, it became necessary to anticipate our explanation of others, if we did not wish to leave our whole commentary incomplete and unsupported by its legitimate proofs. We are forcibly reminded of this, now that we come to treat of the paintings which represent histories from the Bible. *Even the biblical paintings symbolical.*

This class is far more rich and varied than that of the parables; yet, when compared with the abundance of the source from which they are taken, even these seem poor and limited. If we had been told that the early Christians were in the habit of decorating their burial-places and places of assembly with paintings of subjects taken from the Bible, and had been invited to speculate on the probable subjects of their choice, we should certainly not have confined the range of Christian art within those narrow limits which we find from an examination of its existing monuments that it really observed. Nor is it easy, at this distance of time, to discover the causes which led to so great a restriction of the artists' liberty. The fact, however, is plain and undeniable. Out of the infinite variety of histories in the Old and New Testaments, which *Their limited number,* seemed to offer both fitting subjects for the pencil and useful lessons of instruction or consolation to the faithful, only a few were taken; nor did either painter or sculptor often venture to transgress the boundaries assigned to them. "The incidents that exemplified the leading dogmas of faith were chosen in preference to others," says Kügler, "and thus the arts become the index of the tenets that were prominent at different periods."

and fixed character.

Not only were the artists limited within a narrow cycle of subjects; even in their mode of treating these, they were not left wholly to themselves. They did not treat them either accurately as facts of history, nor freely as subjects of the imagination, but strictly with a view to their spiritual meaning; and since this is always the same, religious dogma imparted something of its own fixedness of character to the art which it vouchsafed to employ. We may apply almost literally to the state of Christian art as exhibited in the Catacombs, the same language that was used so many centuries afterwards during the Iconoclast controversy :—*Non est imaginum structura pictorum inventio, sed ecclesiæ Catholicæ probata legislatio et traditio.*[*] The details only of the execution belonged to the artist; the choice of subjects, the general design and plan of the whole was more or less under the control of authority. And this or that story was selected, not at all for its own sake, but for the sake of what was associated with it in the mind of the Church; in other words, even the historical paintings were essentially symbolical.

"'The symbolical system of this hieratic cycle," says De Rossi, "is established beyond all dispute, not only by the choice and arrangement of subjects, but also by the mode of representing them, and, in a few instances, even by inscriptions accompanying them." Take the history of Noe, for example : of what an endless variety of compositions is not this subject capable, and how variously has it not been treated in all the schools

Noe in the ark typical of baptism,

* Conc. Nic. III. Actio vi. Collect. Labbe, tom. vii. fol. 831, 832.

Biblical Paintings. 241

of modern art? Yet throughout the whole range of the Roman Catacombs we find but one type of it, and that removed as far as possible from historical truth. Instead of a huge ark riding upon the waves, and containing eight persons, together with a vast multitude of living animals, we have a single individual almost filling the small box in which he stands, whilst a dove, bearing an olive-branch, flies towards him.* Some persons have supposed that this scene was a direct but imperfect imitation of the famous coins of Apamea, belonging to the reign of Septimius Severus, on which a man and his wife stand in a similar box, with a raven perched behind them, and a dove flying towards them: and however difficult it may be to account for this representation on a heathen coin struck in Phrygia in the beginning of the third century, the letters NΩ or NΩE, which appear on the front of the box, leave us no choice as to referring it to the history of the patriarch. Nevertheless, De Rossi claims for some paintings of the same subject in the Catacombs, particularly for those in the entrance to the Catacomb of St Domitilla, referred to in a former chapter,† an undoubted priority in point of time. Moreover, as he justly remarks, there is no proof of any community of idea between the Christian and the Pagan artist, except as to the form of the ark, and this was in a manner forced upon them both, by the conditions of space within which they worked; in all other parts of the composition there are many differences. In the Christian paintings, the raven never appears, nor is there any legend identifying the person as Noe. On the contrary, it is often not a man but a woman; and once her name is added,—the name of the deceased on whose grave it was painted, Juliana. We have not far to seek for an explanation of this painting. St Peter, in one of his Epistles,‡ had spoken of a certain figurative resemblance between those eight souls who were "saved by water in the

marginal note: not copied from coins of Apamea.

---

* See Plate VIII. 2.   † See page 73; and *Bullett.* 1865, p. 43.
‡ 1 Peter iii. 20, 21.

days of Noe, when the ark was a-building," and those Christians who are now "saved by baptism, being of the like form;" and some of the most ancient commentators on Holy Scripture draw out the resemblance in all its details. As the waters of the deluge cleansed the earth from all its iniquities, so the waters of baptism cleanse the soul; as those only were saved who took refuge in the ark, so now also the Lord "adds daily to the Church such as should be saved;"* and these are taken from among "all nations, and tribes, and peoples, and tongues," even as the ark also contained "of every living creature of all flesh, wherein was the breath of life." We must confine ourselves to a single witness, Tertullian, who has expressed this doctrine with his usual terseness in the following words :†—" As after the waters of the deluge, in which the old iniquity was purged away, as after that *baptism* (so to call it) of the old world, a dove sent out of the ark and returning with an olive-branch, was the herald to announce to the earth peace and the cessation of the wrath of heaven, so by a similar disposition with reference to matters spiritual, the dove of the Holy Spirit, sent forth from heaven, flies to the earth, *i.e.*, to our flesh, as it comes out of the bath of regeneration after its old sins, and brings to us the peace of God; where the Church is clearly prefigured by the ark." When, therefore, we find this scene of a man inclosed in an ark, and receiving the olive-branch from the mouth of a dove, painted upon the walls of a chapel in the Catacombs, we cannot doubt that it was intended to express the same general doctrine, viz., that the faithful, having obtained the remission of their sins through baptism, have received from the Holy Spirit the gift of Divine peace, and are saved in the mystical ark of the Church from the destruction which awaits the world. And if the same picture be rudely scratched on a single tomb, it denotes the sure faith and hope of the survivors that the deceased, being a faithful

---

* Acts ii. 47. † Lib. de Baptismo, vii.

member of the Church, had died in the peace of God, and had now entered into his rest.

This picture of Noe and the ark is not unfrequently placed very near to the history of Jonas; indeed, in one instance,* the dove which belongs to Noe is represented on the poop of the vessel which is carrying off the prophet. The history of Jonas having been put forward so emphatically by our Lord Himself,† as a type both of His own and of the general resurrection, it is not to be wondered at that it should have held the first place among all the subjects from the Old Testament represented in the Catacombs. It was continually repeated in every kind of monument connected with the ancient Christian cemeteries; in the frescoes on the walls, on the bas-reliefs of the sarcophagi, on lamps and medals, and glasses, and even on the ordinary grave-stones. Christian artists, however, by no means confined themselves to that one scene in the life of the prophet in which he foreshadowed the resurrection, viz., his three days' burial in the belly of the fish, and his deliverance from it, as it were from the jaws of the grave. The other incident of his life was painted quite as commonly, viz., his lying "under the shadow of the booth covered with ivy on the east side of the city" for refreshment and rest; or again, his misery and discontent, as he lay in the same place, when the sun was beating upon his head and the ivy had withered away.

Jonas and the fish a type of the resurrection.

We speak of the *ivy*, because it is so called in the Vulgate; but all scholars are familiar with the dispute between St Jerome and St Austin as to the right translation of the Hebrew word used in this place; and although the language of Ruffinus in his invectives against St Jerome for his new translation of the Scriptures‡ would seem to imply that the learned Saint had appealed to the pictures in the Catacombs in defence of his own rendering of the word, their authority certainly

The ivy or the gourd.

---

* Bottari, Tav. cxxxi.   † St Matt. xii. 39.
‡ Op. S. Hieron., vol. ii., p. 663, ed. Vallas, 1735.

appears to us to be all in favour of St Austin and the gourd. However, this is unimportant; the real point of present interest to us, in this matter, is that the paintings in the cemeteries should have been appealed to at all in the course of a religious controversy before the close of the fourth century, and appealed to as already an *ancient* witness (*in veterum sepulchris*), by one whom we know* to have been a frequent visitor to them in the days of his youth. No direct Patristic testimony is at hand, showing the particular intent with which this part of the history of Jonas was so frequently set before the eyes of the faithful: it is not difficult, however, to see how salutary a lesson of patience and encouragement it could be made to preach to the poor persecuted Christians, whose lot, as witnesses to God's truth, was cast in a city both more populous and more wicked than that to which the prophet had been sent. The four scenes we have described sometimes occupy the four highest spaces on the walls of a *cubiculum;* sometimes only two are given, opposite to one another; and occasionally even the whole history is crowded together into one compendious scene, the prophet being cast out by the great fish so as to fall immediately under the booth covered with the gourd.† The fish is quite unlike any real inhabitant of the deep; it resembles only some of those marine monsters, sea-horses or cows, with which the Pagans delighted to ornament the walls both of their drawing-rooms and of their sepulchres, either as mere freaks of the imagination, or as the conventional representation of the beast in the fabulous tale of Andromeda. Even the Christians, too, used the same figure as a mere ornament in their most ancient decorations, but finally it was confined to the history of Jonas; a monstrous dragon, with a very long and narrow neck, and a large head and ears, sometimes also with horns. Perhaps it was represented in this way as a type of death, by way of distinguishing it from the real ΙΧΘΥC, or Saviour.

* See page 97. † See Plate VII.

Biblical Paintings. 245

Daniel in the lions' den is usually represented in the paintings of the Catacombs as standing naked * between two lions, with his arms outstretched in the form of a cross.† History may have been intended either as a figure of the resurrection,‡ or as a source of encouragement to the Christian flock under the extraordinary sufferings and dangers to which they were exposed at the command of idolatrous rulers. St Cyprian, writing in the midst of persecutions, § makes this use of the history, and also of the history of the Three Children (as we are wont to call them) who were cast into the fiery furnace for refusing to worship the golden image set up by Nabuchodonosor. He quotes them as signal instances of the greatness of God's mercies and the power of His protection; these men having all acquired the merit of martyrdom through the boldness of their confession, yet being delivered by His might out of the hands of their enemies, and preserved for His greater glory. By others of the Fathers,‖ these same histories find their place among the numerous symbols of the resurrection from the dead, "whence also they were received as in a figure;" ¶ and of course either interpretation is equally legitimate.

Indeed, these various interpretations, taken from the writings of men who themselves lived during the ages of persecution, are a sufficient proof of the kind of use which was then made of the Old Testament histories, and of their application to the circumstances of the day : and since it is only natural to suppose

Daniel in the lions' den, and the Three Children in the fiery furnace.

---

* Le Blant (Inscriptions, Chrétiennes de la Gaule, tom. i. 493) is only able to quote five examples of ancient Christian art in which Daniel is clothed, and all of these are of much later date than the paintings of the Catacombs. See, however, our Fig. 11 in page 73. If historical truth had been the artist's aim, the prophet should have been painted sitting, and with seven lions (Dan. xiv. 39).
† See centre of roof in Plate VI., also centre of sarcophagus in Plate XIX.
‡ S. Hieron. in Zach., lib. ii. c. ix. 864.
§ Ep. lxi. or lviii., ed. Baluz.
‖ St Irenæus, lib. v. c. 5, 2; Tertull. De Resurrect.
¶ Heb. xi. 19.

that the very same purpose animated the artist when he represented to the eye, and the preacher when he addressed himself to the ear, we are not arbitrarily imposing a sense of our own upon these paintings, but only seeking to discover, by sure rules of interpretation, what meaning was really present to the mind of their authors, and what lessons they conveyed to the minds of those who saw them. In the writings of later Fathers, such as St Augustine, St Chrysostom, and others, the history of the Three Children is used as a type of the history of the Church; at first forbidden by the rulers of this world to worship the true God, and suffering all kinds of persecution because she will not heed the prohibition, then triumphing over her enemies, and persuading even her very persecutors to become her children and protectors. And it would almost seem as if the early Christians, even in their darkest hours of trial, had enjoyed some prophetic anticipation of this blessed change, and looked upon the adoration which the infant Saviour had received from the Wise Men of the East as a kind of foretaste and first-fruits, as it were, of the homage which the whole world should one day give Him, since we find them repeatedly bringing together, in the most marked way, these two histories, the Three Children refusing to adore the image of Nabuchodonosor from the Old Testament, and the three Wise Men adoring the infant Jesus from the New. The juxtaposition of these two subjects is far too frequent to allow us to look upon it as fortuitous.* It should be mentioned that this history of the Three Children is usually represented with more truth and literal accuracy than most others; at least, we find them always " with their coats, and their caps, and their shoes, and their garments,"† just as the sacred text describes them; and these garments are always of an Oriental character, the Phrygian *tiara*, tunics, and the *saraballi*, or trousers, just as

Adoration of the Magi.

---

* They are found together, not only in the Catacombs, but also in a sarcophagus at Nismes, and other Christian monuments at Milan, &c., *Bull. Arch.* 1866, p. 64. † See Plate IX. 2.

Biblical Paintings. 247

the worshippers of Mithras or other Easterns are represented on Pagan marbles.

Another pair of subjects which seem in like manner to be studiously brought together from the two Testaments, are Moses striking the rock and the resurrection of Lazarus.* Sometimes they are found in the same compartment of a painting; sometimes roughly sketched side by side on a gravestone; still more frequently they are together on a sarcophagus. Some antiquarians consider the point of connexion between them to be the display of Divine power in bringing living water out of a dry rock, and a dead man to life out of his rocky grave; but this analogy hardly seems to be sufficiently close: any other of the miracles of Our Blessed Lord might have been selected with almost equal propriety. Others, therefore, prefer to look upon these two subjects as intended to represent the beginning and end of the Christian course; "the fountain of water springing up unto life everlasting;"† God's grace and the gift of faith being typified by the water flowing from the rock, "which was Christ," and life everlasting by the victory over death and the second life vouchsafed to Lazarus. And this interpretation seems both more probable in itself and is more confirmed by ancient authority; since Tertullian ‡ distinctly identifies the water which flowed from the rock with the waters of Baptism, which is the beginning of the Christian life, as a resurrection is unquestionably the end. St Cyprian also agrees with Tertullian, saying § that it was foretold that if the Jews would thirst and seek after Christ, they should drink with us Christians, *i.e.*, should obtain the grace of Baptism. "If they should thirst in the desert," says Isaias (xlviii. 21), "He will lead them out: He will bring forth water out of the rock for them, and cleave the rock, and my people shall drink." "And this was fulfilled in the gospels" (he continues) "when

---

* Martigny, Dict. des Antiq., *artic.* Lazare, p. 361.
† St John iv. 14.   ‡ De Baptismo, § ix.
§ Epist. lxiii. 8, tom. ii. 151, ed. Fell.

Christ, who is the rock, is cleft with the stroke of the lance in His Passion; Who, reminding them of what had been foretold by the prophet, cried aloud and said, 'If any man thirst, let him come and drink; he that believeth in me, as the Scripture saith, out of his belly shall flow rivers of living water.'* And that it might be made still more clear that the Lord spoke here about Baptism, the Evangelist has added, 'Now this He said of the Spirit, which they should receive who believed in Him'; for the Holy Spirit is received by Baptism."

Moses taking off his shoes.   Moses may sometimes also be seen in the act of taking off his shoes before approaching the burning bush; and this is treated by some of the Fathers as emblematical of those renunciations of the world, the flesh, and the devil, which all the faithful have made in Baptism;† or it might typify that reverence which is required of all who approach the Christian mysteries.

In one instance, in a fresco of the cemetery of St Callixtus, we find these two scenes in the life of Moses represented close together, almost as parts of the same picture; ‡ but the figure of Moses in the two scenes is manifestly different. In the first, where he takes off his shoes, having been called by the hand of God coming out of a cloud to go up into Mount Sinai to receive the law, he is young and without a beard; in the second, where he strikes the rock, and the thirsty Jew is drinking, he is older and bearded; and both the general look of his hair and beard, and the outline of his features, seem to present a certain marked resemblance to the traditional figure of St Peter.

These are the principal scenes from the Old Testament history of which it is necessary that we should speak; and the few which are taken from the New Testament will fall more naturally under other branches of our division. We shall have occasion also to return to one or two of those which we have

---

* St John vii. 37–39.   † St Greg. Nazianz. Orat. 42.
‡ See Plate IV.

mentioned from the Old Testament, as, for instance, Moses striking the rock, when we come to its more complete exhibition, not in paintings on the walls, but on the gilt glasses of the third and fourth centuries which have been found in the Catacombs. For the present, the interpretation given by Kügler, though not very exact, may be quoted as sufficiently intimating its general sense. "Where we find Moses," he says, "striking the rock, with kneeling figures drinking the waters,"—these are not *generally* found in the paintings, but only on the sarcophagi,—" we understand the miraculous birth of Christ, who, according to the prophet Esaias, is the Well of Salvation from which we draw waters with joy—the Spiritual Rock from which we drink."

We conclude our present chapter by observing, that we should gather even from the writings of the Apostles themselves, that nothing was likely to be more familiar to the minds of the early Christians than the symbolical and prophetical meaning of the facts of the Old Testament; so that the sight of these paintings on the walls of their subterranean chapels was probably as a continual homily set before the practised minds of the faithful of the first three centuries, and by them perfectly understood. Moreover, the constant repetition of the same subjects makes it impossible to suppose that there was no unity in their choice; and a careful study of the order and mutual dependence in which they are usually disposed, seems to reveal a certain theological knowledge in those who presided over their arrangement. Indeed, it is scarcely too much to say, that some of these artistic compositions might be made to take the place of a well-ordered dogmatic discourse. This has been noticed long since even by men who had no really extensive or intimate acquaintance with the subject, *e.g.*, by Kügler, who imagined that he saw in the order of histories chosen for the adornment of one of these chapels, an intention to set forth under typical forms the Birth, the Sufferings, and the Resurrection of Our Blessed Lord in proper succession. Lord Lindsay also writes to the same effect, when he says that " Rome seems to have adopted from the first, and steadily adhered to, a system of typical parallelism, of veiling the great incidents of redemption and the sufferings, faith, and hope of the Church, under the parallel and typical events of the patriarchal and Jewish dispensations." * This, however, is a branch of the subject to which we shall have occasion to return when we speak of the liturgical paintings, where this principle is singularly prominent.

* Sketches of the History of Christian Art, 47.

Fig. 30.—*Sculpture in the Lateran Museum, representing the ascent of Elias into heaven.*

CHAPTER V.

PAINTINGS OF CHRIST, HIS HOLY MOTHER, AND THE SAINTS.

THE three classes of paintings we have hitherto described —those which we have called symbolical, allegorical, and biblical—were all animated by the same spirit, and were, in fact, only various manifestations of the same principle. They were all cotemporaneous, therefore, and often mixed together in the decoration of the same chambers. Whereas then the genius of Christian art remained thus essentially symbolical, we cannot be surprised at the utter absence from the Catacombs of anything like real historical paintings of what was then going on in the Church. Neither the sufferings nor the triumphs of the martyrs employed the pencil of the Christian artist during the three first centuries, or at least but very rarely. Nevertheless, De Rossi enumerates scenes from the lives of the Saints and the history of the Church, as a distinct class of paintings, because there is at least one picture in the Catacomb of St Callixtus which seems to record some such event. Two men are depicted standing before a Roman magistrate on his seat of justice, or rather being led away from before it after their condemnation; and as there is good reason to believe that the two martyrs, Saints Parthenius and Calocerus, were buried in the chamber in which this painting occurs, it has been conjectured that it is a part of their history which it represents. Moreover, as these martyrs had been the guardians, during life, of the young lady whose family (we believe) gave this portion of ground for the use of the Church as

Historical paintings extremely rare in Catacombs.

a cemetery,* there was nothing improbable in supposing that the memory of their noble confession of the faith may have been thus recorded for future ages. One or two other examples, scattered here and there throughout the Catacombs, seem to invite a similar interpretation. Nevertheless, we receive it with much hesitation; the instances are so rare, and they seem so alien to the spirit and temper of the countless multitudes of paintings of a different description executed during the three first centuries. Of course, after the conversion of Constantine there was a revolution in this as in everything else; but it was not till the end of the fourth, or even the beginning of the fifth century, that paintings were executed such as those which Prudentius describes, for example, representing the various sufferings of the martyr St Hippolytus.

No real portrait of Christ, or of Blessed Mary, &c.

It is certainly more remarkable that there should not have been found here any genuine portraits, either of Our Blessed Lord, His Holy Mother, or His Apostles, which De Rossi enumerates together as forming another class of paintings. Raoul Rochette † has said very positively that there was no consecrated model in the first ages of the Church for the figures of these sacred objects of Christian devotion and worship; and although this statement may perhaps require some slight modification with regard to the two Princes of the Apostles, Saints Peter and Paul, yet in the main it is certainly true, so far as we may judge from the testimony of what still remains to be seen in the Catacombs.

Indeed, Our Blessed Lord is scarcely ever represented there at all, excepting either under the typical character of the Good Shepherd, or in the act of performing one of His miracles, or sitting in the midst of His Apostles; ‡ and in all these cases He is generally painted as a young and beardless man,§ with

---

* See page 127.   † Tableau des Catacombes, 164.

‡ We know of no other very ancient picture in the Catacombs of our Lord's Baptism, except that of which we have given a copy at p. 119. That in the cemetery of San Ponziano is very much later, of the 7th or 8th century.

§ In the mosaics, on the contrary, He is usually bearded.

nothing very marked in His appearance to distinguish Him from others of the children of men. Once, indeed, His head and bust form a medallion, occupying the centre of the roof in a *cubiculum* of the cemetery of Saints Nereus and Achilles, the same in which is a representation of Orpheus and his lyre. This painting, in consequence of the description of it given by Kügler, is often eagerly sought after by strangers visiting the Catacombs.* It is only just, however, to add that they are generally disappointed. Kügler supposed it to be the oldest portrait of Our Blessed Saviour in existence, but we doubt if there is sufficient authority for such a statement. He describes it in these words—"The face is oval, with a straight nose, arched eyebrows, a smooth and rather high forehead, the expression serious and mild; the hair, parted on the forehead, flows in long curls down the shoulders; the beard is not thick, but short and divided; the age between thirty and forty."

[margin: Kügler's description of a bust of Christ in the Catacombs.]

This description may, perhaps, remind some of our readers of the well-known letter of Lentulus to the Roman Senate, in which the personal appearance of our Lord is thus described—"His hair curling, rather dark and glossy, flows down upon His shoulders, and is parted in the middle, after the manner of the Nazarenes. The forehead is smooth and very serene; the countenance without line or spot, of a pleasant complexion, moderately ruddy. The nose and mouth are faultless; the beard thick and reddish like the hair, not long, but divided; the eyes bright, and of varying colour." We need not stop to inquire into the genuineness of this letter, nor the means which its author had of knowing the truth; for, with respect to the description given by Kügler, it must be at once acknowledged that it is too minute and precise, too artistic, for the original, as it is now to be seen. A lively imagination may perhaps supply the details described by our author, but the eye certainly fails to distinguish them.

* Kügler misnames the Catacomb, calling it of St Callixtus.

Eusebius has mentioned painted likenesses of our Lord and of His Apostles, handed down from ancient times, and similar allusions occur in St Augustine, St Basil, and others.* Nevertheless, we repeat that the monuments of the Catacombs present no authentic incontestable example of any real, or even conventional, portraiture of either. Only two members of the Apostolic College are generally distinguished from the rest, and these keep with tolerable uniformity the same type. But, ordinarily, all the saints were represented in the same way, in the act of prayer; that is, with arms outstretched in the form of a cross; and the reason of this attitude is explained by numerous inscriptions, speaking in the most distinct terms, and showing, first, that the saints were believed to be living in God, and secondly, that survivors desired the help of their prayers.

The saints generally represented as praying.

Among the innumerable *oranti*, as they are called (persons praying), which appear on the walls of the Catacombs, there is one of a woman, which is frequently found as a companion to the Good Shepherd, and which a multitude of considerations lead us to believe was intended for Our Blessed Lady, or else for the Church, the Bride of Christ, whose life upon earth is a life of prayer, even as His Holy Mother is similarly employed in heaven. The two interpretations do not necessarily exclude one another. On the contrary, both may have been present to the mind of the artist together, as there are several indications in ancient writers of a certain recognised resemblance between the Blessed Virgin and the Church. St Ambrose speaks of it distinctly;† Pope Sixtus III. (A.D. 435) set up an inscription in Mosaic in the apse of the Lateran Basilica, in which he commemorates the virginal maternity of the Church, the Spouse of Christ; and long before either of these, the

Our Blessed Lady as an orante in the Catacombs;

Euseb. H. E. ii. 25; vii. 18. St Aug. De Consens. Ev. lib. i. c. 10, St Basil, Ep. ccclx. ad Julian. Tertull. De Pudic. c. 10; and St Jerome in Joann. iv. See also Macarius, Hagioglypta, 11.

† "Multa in figura ecclesiæ de Maria prophetata sunt."—*De Instit. Virg.*, c. xiv.

famous letter, written by the Church of Lyons about her martyrs, expresses the same idea, when it calls the Church "the Virgin Mother,"* quite as though the phrase would be at once understood by all.

It has sometimes been supposed that this female *orante* denoted some martyr or person of distinction buried in the principal tomb of the *cubiculum* where the painting is found. And possibly this conjecture may be sometimes correct. But in the majority of instances, we feel certain that it is inadmissible; as, for instance, where it is manifestly intended as a companion to the Good Shepherd; and indeed, in some few instances, we find this figure engraved upon the tombstones instead of the Good Shepherd; it stands with outstretched arms between two sheep. And in many more instances it occupies a part of a ceiling in which every other compartment is filled by some person or story from the Bible, and where, therefore, it is hard to believe that any memorial of a private individual would have been allowed to remain. For these reasons, then, we more willingly believe that either the Church or the Blessed Virgin was intended; and of these interpretations, we incline rather to the latter, first, because the Blessed Virgin is to be found represented in this same attitude on some of the gilded glasses in the Catacombs, either alone or between the Apostles Saints Peter and Paul, and can be identified in both cases by her name written over her head; and secondly, because she is represented in the same way also upon a sepulchral marble of the earliest ages, in the Church of San Giovannino, at St Maximin, in Provence. The inscription on this monument runs thus,—MARIA VIRGO MINESTER DE TEMPULO GEROSALE,— which seems to refer to some legend about her ministrations in the temple, recorded in one of the apocryphal Gospels.† Moreover, it should not be forgotten

<small>in glasses, monuments, and coins;</small>

---

* Eus. Hist. Eccles. v. 1, § 40.
† Macarii, Hagioglypta, 36; Le Blant, Inscriptions Chrétiennes de la Gaule, vol. ii. 277.

that on Byzantine coins, and in works of Greek art generally, down to this very day, Our Blessed Lady is often represented in this ancient and most expressive attitude of prayer. Even if the figure were intended principally to represent the Church, it would be quite in keeping with the practice of early Christian writers to represent the Church under the symbol of the Virgin Mother of God.*

frequently also painted in the Adoration of the Magi.

Whatever may be thought of the cogency of these arguments, —and we believe that they cannot easily be refuted,—the question of Our Lady's position in the most ancient field of Christian art by no means depends upon them. If these paintings do not represent her, yet she certainly appears in more than a score of other scenes, where her identity cannot be questioned. A modern Protestant writer, indeed, laying claim, too, to a perfection of candour, boldly says that he only saw a single certain specimen of a painting of the Blessed Virgin in all the Catacombs, and that was of a comparatively late date, and that it is idle to attach much importance to so singular an exception. He is evidently referring to the Madonna in the (so-called) Catacomb of St Agnes, where she is to be seen in the *lunette* of an *arcosolium*, with her hands outstretched in prayer, the Divine Infant in front of her, and the Christian monogram on either side, turned towards her.† The presence of this monogram naturally directs our thoughts to the fourth century as the probable date of the work; but as there is no *nimbus* round the head either of Our Blessed Lord or His Holy Mother, it is necessary to fix the earlier half of that century rather than the later. De Rossi considers that

---

* See S. Clem. Alex. Pædag. i. 6. Dr Newman says on Apoc. xii. 1: "The Holy Apostle would not have spoken of the Church under this particular image *unless* there had existed a Blessed Virgin Mary, who was exalted on high, and the object of veneration to all the faithful."—*Letter to Dr Pusey on his Eirenicon*, p. 62.

† This picture, in which the Divine Infant is placed in front of his virgin mother, unsupported, and simply to show who she is, forms the original of a favourite Russian type of the Madonna which they call *Známenskaia*. See Palmer, l. c. p. 66.

Paintings of Christ, &c.   257

the style of execution indicates as nearly as possible the time of Constantine himself. This, however, so far from being the oldest or most interesting painting of the Blessed Virgin to be seen in the Catacombs, is probably one of the latest; and if the author we have referred to saw no other, he can have seen

FIG. 31.—*Fresco of the Blessed Virgin and Child in the (so-called) Cemetery of St Agnes.*

but very little of the Catacombs at all. There is quite a numerous class of paintings,—De Rossi speaks of upwards of twenty,—representations of the Magi making their offerings to the Infant Jesus, in which she is always the central, or at least the principal figure. Generally she sits at the end of the scene, with the Holy Child on her lap, and the three Magi are before her; but in three or four instances she is in the middle; and here, in order to keep a proper balance between the two sides of the picture, the number of the Magi is increased or diminished; there are either four, as in the cemetery of St Domitilla, or only two, as in that of Saints Peter and Marcellinus. It is clear, however, that three was already known as the traditional number;* for even in one of the instances we have quoted we can still trace the original sketch of the artist, designing another arrangement of the scene with three figures

<small>The Magi are always three.</small>

* It is generally said that St Leo the Great, or St Maximus of Turin, are the first witnesses to this tradition. Origen, however, seems to have had the same idea.—*Patrizi de Evangel.* iii., diss. xxvii. pars. 2da.

R

only; then, mistrusting the result, he abandoned the attempt, and sacrificed historic truth to the exigencies of his art. Paintings of this subject belong to different ages, but De Rossi assigns the two that have been specially mentioned to the first and second half of the third century respectively. He claims a much higher antiquity for the painting of Our Blessed Lady represented in Plate X. 1. He unhesitatingly says that he believes this to belong almost to the apostolic age. It is to be seen on the vaulted roof of a *loculus* in the cemetery of St Priscilla, and represents the Blessed Virgin seated, her head partially covered by a short light veil, and with the Holy Child in her arms; opposite to her stands a man, clothed in the pallium, holding a volume in one hand, and with the other pointing to a star which appears above and between the two figures. This star almost always accompanies Our Blessed Lady, both in paintings and in sculptures, where there is an obvious historical excuse for it, *e.g.*, when she is represented with the Magi offering their gifts (Plate X. 2), or by the side of the manger with the ox and the ass;* but with a single figure, as in the present instance, it is unusual. There has been some difference of opinion, therefore, among archæologists as to the interpretation that ought to be given of this figure. The most obvious conjecture would be that it was meant for St Joseph, or for one of the Magi. De Rossi, however, gives many reasons for preferring the prophet Isaias, whose prophecies concerning the Messias abound with imagery borrowed from light.† This prophet is found on one of the glasses in the Catacombs, standing in a similar attitude before Our Blessed Lord, where his identity can hardly be disputed, since he appears in another compartment of the same glass in the act of being sawn asunder by the Jews (in accordance with the tradition mentioned by St Jerome);‡ and Our Blessed

Our Blessed Lady with Isaias.

---

* The ox and the ass are found in a representation of the Nativity on a tomb bearing the date A.D. 343.—*Inscr. Christ.* i. 54.
† Isa. ix. 2; lx. 2, 3, 19; St Luke i. 78, 79.
‡ In Isaiam xv. c. 7.

Lady, as an *orante*, occupies the intervening compartment between these two figures of the prophet. Bosio * has preserved to us another fresco from the cemetery of St Callixtus, still more closely resembling that upon which we are commenting from St Priscilla; only there is no star, but in its stead the battlements, as of some town, appear behind the Woman and Child, by which it was probably intended to denote the town of Bethlehem, as was so commonly done in the sculptures, mosaics, and other works of later art. We have already said that De Rossi considers this painting, with which we are now concerned, to have been executed, if not in apostolic times, and, as it were, under the very eyes of the Apostles themselves, yet certainly within the first hundred and fifty years of the Christian era. He first bids us carefully to study the art displayed in the design and execution of the painting, and then to compare it with the decorations of the famous Pagan tombs discovered on the Via Latina in 1858, and which are unanimously referred to the times of the Antonines, or with the paintings of the *cubicula* near the Papal crypt in San Callisto, described in our next chapter, and known to belong to the very beginning of the third century; and he justly argues that the more classical style of the painting now under examination *obliges* us to assign to it a still earlier date. Next, he shows that the Catacomb in which it appears was one of the oldest,† St Priscilla, from whom it receives its name, having been the mother of Pudens, and a cotemporary of the Apostles; and still further, that there is good reason for believing what Bosio and others have said, that the tombs of Saints Pudentiana and Praxedes, and therefore probably of their father, St Pudens himself, were in the immediate neighbourhood of the chapel in which this Madonna is found; finally, that the inscriptions which are found there form a class by themselves, bearing manifest tokens of the highest antiquity. Everything, therefore, combines to satisfy him that this beautiful painting of Our

* Rom. Sott. p. 255.   † See p. 66.

Blessed Lady is the oldest which has yet been discovered, and it is needless to observe that she and her Divine Son are clearly the principal figures in it. She does not enter here into the composition of an historical or allegorical scene as a secondary personage, but herself supplies the motive, so to speak, of the whole painting. She seems also, as far as we can make out from the imperfect remains of the painting, to have been repeated in other parts of this *loculus*, both by herself, and with her Holy Spouse and Child—a group which Bosio and Garrucci also have recognised in other parts of the Catacombs. De Rossi still further tells us—and again he is able to quote Bosio and Garrucci * as having been quite of the same opinion with himself—that there are other frescoes in this same cemetery of St Priscilla, representing the Annunciation † by the Archangel, the Adoration by the Magi, and the Finding of Our Blessed Lord in the Temple; in a word, all these archæologists are agreed that this cemetery surpasses every other, both for the number, the variety, and the antiquity of the pictorial representations of Our Blessed Lady.

St Joseph. Some of our readers will be taken somewhat by surprise by our mention of any groups representing "The Holy Family," and especially of any representation of St Joseph. De Rossi acknowledges that this class of monuments is still open to some question, the paintings into which he is supposed to enter being generally in a very bad state of preservation. In the sarcophagi he certainly appears; and in the most ancient of them, as a young and beardless man, generally clad in a tunic. In the mosaics of St Mary Major's, which are of the fifth century, and in which he appears four or five times, he is shown of mature age, if not old; and from that time forward this became the more common mode of representing him. Probably the later artists followed the legend of St Joseph's age and widowhood which occurs in the apocryphal Gospels,

* Bosio, Rom. Sott. 549; Macar. Hagiogl. 174, 242.
† Hagioglypta, p. 245.

Paintings of Christ, &c. 261

especially that which bears the name of St James the Less, and those on the birth of Mary and the infancy of the Saviour. These legends had been quoted by St Epiphanius, St Gregory Nazianzen, and other writers of the fourth century; and allusions to them, or even whole scenes taken from them, occur in the artistic monuments of the fifth and succeeding centuries. Before that time Christian artists seem strictly to have been kept within the limits of the canonical books of Holy Scripture. Afterwards it was probably considered that there was no longer any danger to the integrity of the faith, and greater licence was given both to poets and artists.

FIG. 32.—*Sarcophagus found among the ruins of an ancient chamber in San Callisto.*

CHAPTER VI.

LITURGICAL PAINTINGS.

Liturgical paintings very rare.

IT might have been thought that the impenetrable secrecy which in ancient times shrouded the sacred mysteries from the gaze or knowledge of the profane would have rendered any sensible representation of them by art on the walls of the Catacombs quite impossible. And, doubtless, such representations were very rare. The paintings we are about to describe are merely exceptional; and they were executed at the end of the second century, or quite in the beginning of the third, before the invasion of the subterranean cemeteries by the heathen had taught the necessity of caution. Moreover, by a careful use of Christian symbolism, and a mixture of things natural and supernatural, simple and allegorical, the artist has contrived to produce a work which, whilst eminently liturgical in character (representing the administration of Baptism and the consecration of the Holy Eucharist), and plain enough and of the highest interest and value to us, yet to an uninitiated stranger must always have been absolutely unintelligible. The administration of Baptism, for example, is mixed up with biblical histories and allegories of various kinds; and the consecration of the Holy Eucharist is both complicated by means of the hieroglyphic sign of the fish, and also veiled under various historical scenes taken from the Old and New Testament. These paintings deserve to be examined in the most minute detail. They are to be found in that series of *cubicula* in the immediate neighbourhood of the Papal crypt,

Valuable specimen early in the third century.

Liturgical Paintings.   263

concerning which it has been already shown * that they were all made about the same time; the oldest, before the end of the second century, the latest, at no very advanced period in the third. In three of them, the paintings are too much destroyed to enable us to recognise all their details; but as far as we may judge from the fragments which remain, they were of the same subjects, and of the same general character with those of the two oldest chambers, which we propose to describe.

On the wall at the left of the door as we enter the first, is the old familiar figure of a man striking the rock, whence the water gushes forth. Next, we see a man fishing in the stream, and then another man baptizing a youth who stands in the same water. The paralytic carrying his bed on his shoulder concludes the series on that side of the chamber.† On the principal wall, or that which faces the doorway, we see a three-legged table, having on it bread and fish, with a woman standing on one side of it in the attitude of prayer; and a man on the other, clad only in the *pallium*, extending his hands, and especially his right hand, towards the table in such a way as to force upon every Christian intelligence the idea of the act of consecration.‡ This is followed by the scene already described, of seven men sitting at table with bread and fish before them, and eight baskets of loaves arranged along the floor;§ and then Abraham about to offer up his son Isaac—a scene easily identified by the ram and the faggot of wood at their side.|| These three scenes are painted, side by side, on the interval between two graves; and they are flanked at either extremity by a full-length figure of a *fossor*, with his left arm extended and a pickaxe resting on his right shoulder.¶ The painting on the third side of this chamber has perished, all the plaster having fallen to the ground and been reduced to dust. But the plaster of the small recess on the right-hand

General description of them.

* See p. 126.   † Plate XII.   ‡ Plate XIV. 3.
§ Plate XIII. || Plate XI. 1.   ¶ Plate XI. 3.

side of the doorway is still perfect, and shows us the figures of two men, not standing side by side, but one placed on a higher level than the other (probably in consequence of the narrowness of the space). One of these men is seated, and might be supposed to be teaching from a long roll, probably of parchment, which he holds in his hands; the other seems to be drawing water from a well which is already overflowing. In the second chamber, we find the rock, the fisherman, the feast of seven, the baptism, and the sitting teacher, much the same as before. On the right-hand wall, which in the former chamber was in ruins, we distinguish the raising of Lazarus from the dead; and whilst on one side of the doorway is a preacher standing, the fragments of plaster found on the other show that a *fossor* had once been represented there.

We have already said that the same subjects, with more or less of variation, appear to have been reproduced in the other chambers of this series; and such frequent repetition naturally suggests the presence of some hidden sense. Nor, indeed, is it a work of any difficulty to ascertain what that sense is. Already our readers have had the clue placed in their hands, which, if carefully used, will guide them aright through all this apparent confusion of sacramental rites, biblical histories, and scenes from common life.

Their meaning explained by Tertullian. A single author, Tertullian, who was in Rome about the time that these paintings were executed, and may very probably have often seen them, can be made to supply all the fresh guidance that is needed for their complete interpretation. In a former chapter we heard him describing Christians as little fish born in the waters of Baptism; and in his treatise upon that sacrament he speaks of those waters as flowing forth from the rock. The rock, as we know from the Scriptures themselves,[*] was Christ, who refreshes with the spiritual waters of His grace and of the faith the weary and thirsty wanderers in the wilderness of this world. There is nothing

The waters of Baptism typified by the striking of the rock;

---

[*] 1 Cor. x. 3; Isa. xxxv. 6.

in the picture to show who it is that is here striking the rock; but we must anticipate for a moment what will be brought before us in a future chapter,* and say briefly that Moses is here a figure of Saint Peter, who succeeded to him, and became "the leader of the new Israel," as Prudentius says; with him was the authority to draw forth the true living waters of sacramental grace which flow from the Rock, and are first given in Baptism, and to communicate them to the whole Church.†

The rock, then, followed by a man fishing, and another man; and the fisherman baptizing,‡ is a very striking instance of that characteristic of ancient Christian art which we have heard Lord Lindsay call "typical parallelisms." The truths of the Gospel are veiled, yet revealed, under the parallel and typical events, either of the Old Law or of common life. The pictures spoke to the Christians of those days (the second and third centuries), in a very plain and intelligible way, of the gate of all the sacraments, the beginning of Christianity, the sacrament of Baptism.

And the same mystery was again set before them in the next painting on the same wall, the paralytic carrying his bed. and the paralytic carrying his bed. Those who have ever visited the (so-called) Catacombs of St Agnes with Father Marchi, will remember that he used always to identify this painting with the sacrament of Penance, supposing it to refer to the man that was healed at Capharnaum, to whom Our Lord addressed those words, "Be of good cheer, thy sins are forgiven thee;" and, indeed, that miracle is expressly quoted in the apostolical constitutions as symbolical

---

* Chapter VII.

† St Cyprian, Ep. ad Jub., tom. ii. p. 332. Hence in the writings of the Fathers, the font of the one Baptism and its derivation from the one Rock was a favourite type of the origin and unity of the faith, the sacraments, and the Church. And the impugners of the validity of Baptism administered by heretics, had no stronger argument against their enemies than this undoubted unity of Baptism and of the Church, and the prerogative of Peter as its head. ‡ Plate XII.

of this sacrament. Nevertheless, it would have been obviously out of harmony with the prevailing tone of thought and practice among the Christians of the days of persecution that they should have represented grievous sin and repentance as a probable interlude between the sacraments of Baptism and the Holy Eucharist. It is far more probable, therefore, that all the paintings on this wall were intended to have reference to Baptism, just as all those on the next speak clearly of the Holy Sacrament of the Altar; and it is better to understand this picture of the paralytic, as representing that other miracle wrought at the pool of Bethsaida, which Tertullian, Optatus,* and others, have interpreted as typical of the healing waters of Baptism.

The next pictures denote the consecration and participation of the Holy Eucharist.

We pass on, then, to the next three pictures, which form a group by themselves, quite as intimately connected with one another as those we have been just now considering, and following from them in strict theological sequence. It is exactly the same train of thought and combination of ideas which we have found before in the ancient epitaphs of St Abercius and of Autun, in both of which there is a natural and easy transition from the waters of Baptism to the heavenly Fish of the Holy Eucharist. Moreover, we must not forget that, according to the ecclesiastical discipline of those days, these two sacraments followed one another much more closely than they do now; they were, in fact, often administered simultaneously.

There are certain details, however, in the mode of representing the symbols of the Holy Eucharist in these paintings which require a few words of additional explanation. Some persons, for instance, might take exception to that which we have called a picture of the consecration, in consequence of the insufficient clothing of the man we have supposed to be the priest. He is clad only in the *pallium*, and as he stretches out his hand over the table, his breast and arm, and one

Consecrating priest clothed in the pallium only.

* De Baptismo, c. 4; De Schism. Don. ii. 6.

whole side of his body become much exposed. There can be no doubt, however, that this simple austerity of dress, which was a characteristic of the better class of heathen philosophers, was at one time,—and especially at the time to which these pictures belong,—adopted also by the Christian clergy. The Greeks and Romans always looked on the philosopher's cloak as a guarantee of more than ordinary knowledge. Eusebius * distinctly mentions of Justin Martyr, that he "preached the Word of God in the dress of a philosopher;" but it is not quite certain that he was a priest. Before him, Aristides of Athens, and after him Tertullian, Heracles, a priest of Alexandria, Gregory Thaumaturgus, and others, did the same. Tertullian expressly defends and applauds this mode of dress in his treatise *De Pallio.*† Prudentius, who (as we know) frequented the Catacombs, must have had before his mind's eye some such painting as we are now explaining, when he described, in the beginning of his *Pyschomachia*, Faith coming down to do battle with idolatry, attired almost in this very way. He represents her as carried away by the eagerness of her zeal, and descending into the arena but imperfectly clad, with bare arms and shoulders, and other limbs uncovered.‡ St Cyprian, indeed, who lived about fifty years later than Tertullian, denounced the vainglorious immodesty of the bare breast of the heathen philosophers,§ and spoke of Christian teachers, by way of contrast, as being philosophers not in words but in deeds, not making any outward show of wisdom by their dress, but holding it in truth. But this only

* Hist. Eccl. iv. 11. See also the opening of Justin's dialogue with Trypho.

† See note at beginning of Oehler's edition of this treatise, Leipsic, 1853, tom i. 913. Also St Hieron. Ep. lxxxiii., ad Magnum. Catal. Hom. Ill. cxx. "*Humerum exertus*," is the very word used by Tertullian, c. 3.

‡ "Agresti turbida cultu,
    Nuda humeros, intonsa genas, *exserta lacertos*,
    ... nec telis meminit nec tegmine cingi,
    Pectore sed fidens valido, *membrisque retectis*."—V v. 21-25.

§ De Bono Patientiæ, § 2, 3. "Exerti ac seminudi pectoris inverecunda jactantia."

indicates a change of taste and feeling upon the subject which had come over the Christian mind between the end of the second century and the middle of the third; and, in point of fact, almost all the pictures of men, painted in the Catacombs subsequent to this date, represent them as clothed with the tunic underneath the *pallium*. Thus we seem to be provided with a very sure criterion as to the date of these paintings in San Callisto; and it is important to observe how precisely it agrees with the result to which we had been led before by a multitude of concurrent indications of a totally different kind.

The Church represented by a woman.

Another detail in these paintings which has been made the subject of some discussion, is the true meaning of the woman who stands opposite to the priest, with outstretched arms in the attitude of prayer; whether she is intended to represent some deceased lady, buried in this chamber, or whether she does not rather stand as a symbol of the Church. Looking, however, at the whole character of this series of paintings, we cannot doubt that the latter interpretation is the more correct. Just as the person represented here as receiving baptism is a mere boy, or very young man, not because the artist intended to denote some one determinate person who was really of that age, but because youth is the age of baptism, and it was even customary to call neophytes, of whatever age they might be, *infantes* or *pueri;* so, in like manner, at the table of the tremendous mysteries, a woman was represented, not because it was desired to do honour to any particular lady whose tomb might be near, but rather because, when the whole body of the faithful was spoken of, it was most usual to speak of them under this figure. Both in the Epistles of St Paul, and in the writings of the most ancient Fathers, the Church is the Bride of Christ, without spot or wrinkle. She partakes also, as we have already noticed, of the marvellous privilege of Our Blessed Lady, and, whilst still a virgin, is yet a fruitful mother, so that many things which are said of the one may be said also of the other, and a woman becomes a very natural artistic symbol for the whole Church. Thus, in the old mosaics, *e.g.*, of Sta. Sabina in Rome, put up by Pope Celestine in the earlier half of the fifth century, the legends under two female figures expressly designate them as *Ecclesia ex Gentibus*, and *Ecclesia ex Circumcisione*, *i.e.*, the Church from the Gentiles and from the Jews; and it is certainly more probable that these mosaics continued, with more or less of modification, the ancient types of Christian art, than that they invented new ones. Indeed, the tradition of this symbolical language was continued among Christian artists; *e.g.*, it occurs in liturgical illuminations of a Paschal candle in a MS. of the Barberini Library, belonging to the eleventh or twelfth century. However, whether this female figure, standing here in prayer, be really meant for the Church, for Our Blessed Lady, or for some one Christian soul, is comparatively unimportant. It is her position and occupation which command our attention, reminding us of the words of St Cyril,* "that those prayers are most prevailing which are made with the consecrated gifts lying open to view."

Of the seven men seated together, and partaking of bread and fish, we have already spoken; we will only add here, in answer to a German critic who would fain transfer the reference from the Blessed Sacrament to the eternal banquet in heaven, first, that the mere uniformity in all these paintings of the number and sex of the guests, would alone suffice to distinguish them from the representations either of the *agapæ* or of the joys of paradise. Specimens are not wanting of either of these subjects, but in both of them women appear as well as men, and in various numbers. Moreover, the position and adjuncts of this feast in these chambers seem absolutely to determine its sense. In one instance, where the two scenes are compressed into a single wall of the chamber, it stands side by side with the representation of Baptism. In another, where a type or figure of each sacrament is joined with its literal representation, as the fishing is next to the baptism, so

Answers to objections.

* Lect. xxiii. 9, Oxf. Trans. 275.

the consecration of the Holy Eucharist is next to this entertainment. To doubt, then, of its application to the Sacrament of the Altar, especially when we remember how universally the history was so interpreted by ancient Christian teachers, seems a wilful closing of our eyes against the truth, and can best be accounted for by the rejection of the ancient doctrine which the symbol expresses.

The sacrifice of Isaac typical of the holy sacrifice of the Mass.

We have seen that after the paintings of the fishing and the baptizing, there followed, on the same wall, the paralytic, which we therefore referred to the same sacrament. Here also upon this wall, is a third scene, that of Abraham and Isaac,* which, in like manner, must be connected with the Holy Eucharist; and although the same German critic, already referred to, finds a difficulty in accepting a figure of the bloody sacrifice on the cross as a suitable figure also of the unbloody sacrifice on the altar,† his scruples will scarcely be considered conclusive, even by his co-religionists. For surely the sacrifice of Isaac by his father might, in some respects, claim to be considered a more lively type of the sacrifice of the Mass than of the sacrifice on Mount Calvary; since, although, as St Paul twice repeats, Abraham "offered up his only-begotten son," yet the blood of Isaac was not really shed; he was only "as it were slain."‡ Abraham "received him from the dead for a parable."§ The offering, then, of Isaac by his father is frequently sculptured on the Christian sarcophagi of the fourth and fifth centuries, together with other biblical stories prefiguring the priesthood and sacrifice of the New Law. Here it is the pendant (so to speak) to that other picture already described, wherein the priest

---

* Both are represented as praying,—a faggot and the ram behind them alone enable us to identify them. Another fresco of the same subject was seen by Bosio.—*Rom. Sott.* 503.

† Yet it is expressly named in the Church's hymn *Lauda Sion*, "In figuris præsignatur, cum Isaac immolatur;" and in the Canon of the Mass it is named with the sacrifices of Abel and of Melchisedec.

‡ Apoc. v. 6. § Heb. xi. 17 19.

Liturgical Paintings. 271

is consecrating, "filling the place of Christ," as St Cyprian* speaks, "imitating what Christ did, offering a true and perfect sacrifice in the Church to God the Father."

Not a vestige remains of the principal subject which was painted on the remaining wall, opposite to the paintings of Baptism. Nevertheless, we may venture with confidence to supply it from the corresponding picture in the next chamber. It was, as we have already intimated, the resurrection of Lazarus, which to the Christians of that age would have seemed the most natural, and almost necessary, complement to representations of the Holy Eucharist. Not only did the language which Our Blessed Lord made use of, on occasion of that miracle, bear a very striking resemblance to parts of His discourse upon the Blessed Sacrament,† but He had also seemed to connect a resurrection to everlasting life in so special a manner with the eating of His flesh and drinking His blood, that the Fathers always speak of the one as a kind of pledge and earnest of the other. We may see from the language of Prudentius ‡ how naturally the Christian mind passed from one of these subjects to the other; as when he suddenly stops in the midst of his reflections upon the multiplication of the loaves and fishes, bearing upon their relation to the Holy Eucharist, and, as though he feared that he was in danger of revealing secrets forbidden to profane ears, abruptly addresses himself to Lazarus, as the next subject of which it would naturally become him to speak.

The series concludes with the resurrection of Lazarus.

It is to be observed that Lazarus is not here represented in the ordinary way in which he was represented during the third century, as an adult, and swathed like a mummy just emerging from the tomb, but as a youth, having the winding-sheet loosely hanging about his person, as though to mark him as an ideal and allegorical, rather than an historical personage.

It is not necessary that we should draw out at length the

* Ep. ad Corn. liv. † Cf. St John xi. 25 with vi. 58, &c.
‡ Apotheosis, v. 73.

hidden sense of that series of paintings of the history of Jonas, with which the upper part of these walls is decorated, their bearing on the trials of this present life and the hope of a future one being sufficiently obvious. There remain, however, two other figures on which we ought to make some observations. One of them is seated, apparently in the act of unrolling a volume, or, at least, holding a long roll of parchment in his hands; the other stands, drawing water from a well which is already overflowing. In the next chamber, the same figure appears twice, once standing, once sitting, but on both occasions holding a book, and seemingly engaged in the work of instruction. He wears the same ascetic dress of Pagan philosophers as the priest who was consecrating.

<small>Supplementary paintings of Doctors and *fossors* explained.</small>

Our first impulse at sight of the well with its overflowing waters is to refer it to the conversation of Our Blessed Lord with the Samaritan woman at the well,* wherein He promised to give water to them that believe in Him, such as should "become in them a fountain of water springing up unto life everlasting." And, doubtless, this would be a very beautiful and appropriate termination to a series of symbolical paintings, beginning with the stream of grace, drawn from the rock of Christ by him who was himself a rock, and now ending with the Well of Living Water and the promise of eternal life. A more careful consideration of the subject, however, has led De Rossi to adopt another interpretation. He supposes this figure to represent a Christian doctor of the faith, possibly St Callixtus himself, who perhaps devised this whole symbolical series, and is then commemorated in them, just as the mere material workmen (the *fossores*) were also represented on the same walls. He takes the drawing of the water at the well to be only an expression in art of what Origen had said in words, when he speaks of "the Well whence spiritual waters are to be drawn for the refreshment of the believers;" † and that the

---

* St John iv. 14; vii. 37, 38.
† Hom. XII. in Num. tom. ii. p. 311-314.

Liturgical Paintings. 273

reason for making use of these unusual memorials of individuals was the fact that this cemetery was the first which had ever belonged to the Church in her aggregate capacity.*

Doubtless, this same reason explains also the exceptional character of the whole system of decoration that was adopted in these chambers. They form one uniform group, adorned with the same symbols and in the same style, freely changed in their composition and arrangement, yet constant in their hidden meaning and theological sense; whereas in all the other *cubicula* of the same area there is no trace of the same system of decoration. It may well be doubted whether any private individuals would have ventured on such bold representations of the sacred mysteries for the adornment of their family vaults; neither would every artist have had sufficient theological knowledge to design them. On many accounts, therefore, they seem to bear the stamp of authority, and are certainly one of the most valuable monuments of ancient Christian art that have come down to us. *This whole series seems inspired by authority.*

Bosio and others before De Rossi have discovered in the Catacomb of St Priscilla other paintings of a liturgical character, but not so full and complicated a series. They represent the taking of the veil by some consecrated virgin, the laying on of hands for ordination, and perhaps, also, for public penance. And, as we have ourselves also before observed, many of the emblems and decorations in various parts of the Catacombs have a distinct liturgical sense and reference, even when they seem at first sight to be simply historical. Indeed, a recent English writer, who has published a work on "Ancient Christianity and Sacred Art in Italy," trying to enlist them on the side of Protestantism, or, at least, to effect a separation of them from the cause of Catholic truth, does not refuse to acknowledge that "if any one could so cast away bias and prepossession as to form for himself the ideal of a Christian church exclusively from the records of the past that meet us *A few other liturgical scenes elsewhere.*

* See pp. 83-86.

in the Catacombs, his impartial and calmly-adopted conclusion would be that, in the worship of such a church, all should revolve round a mystic centre of sacramental ordinances."

Before taking leave of this interesting series of liturgical paintings, which we have been examining, it is worth remarking how accurately they illustrate and confirm the remarks which were made in a former chapter,* on the order in which the several classes of paintings succeeded one another in the development of Christian art. We are sure that these chambers were excavated in the very earliest period of the third century, if not in the end of the second; and there can be little doubt that the paintings were executed at the same time, and the same subjects were painted in all of them. But in the latest of the *cubicula*, they are represented only by means of the biblical stories, without any admixture of scenes merely allegorical or hieroglyphical. In a yet later *cubiculum* near the tomb of St Eusebius, the same substantial idea is still there, in that picture of the Good Shepherd and His Apostles, and the various attitudes of the sheep, described in page 237; but it is reduced to an expression less secret, and in more literal conformity to the text of the histories and parables. The rock is there, whence flowed the waters of Baptism, and by its side on the next wall is the symbol of the Holy Eucharist; but it is merely in a representation of the two Apostles bringing the bread and fish to Our Blessed Lord before the miraculous multiplication. It is, therefore, rather an accurate representation of an historical fact, than a mysterious symbol, though, of course, we do not doubt that it was with a mystical intent that it was painted there.

* See page 196.

CHAPTER VII.

GILDED GLASSES FOUND IN THE CATACOMBS.

THERE are, in many of the great museums of Europe, collections more or less extensive of articles found in the Catacombs of Rome. Rings, coins, *terra-cotta* lamps with Christian emblems upon them, and various other objects of domestic use or ornament, have been from time to time discovered in the Christian cemeteries. They have been found stuck into the cement which surrounds the *loculi*, and must have been placed there at the time of burial, and by surviving friends who desired thus to express their own affection, and to distinguish the grave of their departed relative from those around it. In some few instances the instruments of martyrdom were buried with the martyr; and although many of the articles exhibited under this appellation are undoubtedly fictitious, still there seems no reason why we should doubt the genuineness of some of the *ungulæ*, or iron-claws, and of the *plumbatæ*,* or scourges loaded with lead which are to be seen in Christian museums, and which correspond exactly to the instruments of torture described in the Acts of the Martyrs, and other ancient records. The Vatican Library contains the largest collection of these Christian antiquities; but very rarely has any account of the locality in which they have been discovered been preserved, and thus they have lost much of their interest and historical value.

Another class of objects, however, have an interest and value

<small>Various articles found in the Catacombs.</small>

<small>Gilded glass.</small>

* R. S. ii. 164.

of their own, and tell their own story; although here also, in many instances, we have to regret the absence of information as to the locality in which they were discovered. These are the fragments of glass, ornamented with figures and letters in gold, of which the largest collection is to be seen in the Vatican Library. Smaller collections may be found in the Kircherian Museum at the Roman College, and in the museum of the Propaganda. The British Museum possesses about thirty specimens, the museums of Paris, Florence, and Naples, not so many. Among private collections, Mr C. W. Wilshere's in this country is probably one of the best; it contains about twenty specimens, the more important of which are at present in the loan collection of the South Kensington Museum.

Description of glasses found in the Catacombs. These glasses are, the greater part of them, evidently the bottoms of drinking cups. Their peculiarity consists in a design having been executed in gold leaf on the flat bottom of the cup, in such a manner as that the figures and letters should be seen from the inside, like the designs on the glass bottoms of the ale tankards so popular at Oxford and Cambridge. The gold leaf was then protected by a plate of glass, which was welded by fire so as to form one solid mass with the cup. These cups, like the other articles found in the Catacombs, were stuck into the still soft cement of the newly-closed grave; and the double glass bottom, imbedded in the plaster, has resisted the action of time, while the thinner portion of the cup, exposed to accident and decay by standing out from the plaster, has in almost every instance perished. Boldetti informs us that he found two or three cups entire, and his representation of one of these is given in Padre Garrucci's work.* Even the bottoms of these glass cups have frequently perished in the attempt to detach them from the plaster, and the impression left in the cement is often all that remains to show the loss sustained by Christian archæology.

The discovery of these glasses is coeval with that of the

* Vetri ornati di figure in oro.— *Tav.* xxxix. nn. 7 a, 7 b, first edition.

Gilded Glasses found in the Catacombs. 277

Catacombs themselves. Bosio found five or six fragments of them during all his researches on the Via Appia and Via Ardeatina, and then found an equal number of whole unbroken specimens in a single gallery on the Via Salaria; and when Aringhi published the drawings and descriptions of these, he added an account of a few others that had been discovered since. Buonarruoti's work contains an account of about seventy specimens, which were all that were known in his time. Boldetti added about thirty more. Padre Garrucci, however, has obtained accurate drawings of all the specimens now extant in the various museums of Europe, so that in his publication we have a full collection of about 340, twenty of which, however, only exist in the pages of Boldetti, Olivieri, and other authors. Modern exploration has not brought to light many new specimens. In the course of twenty-three years of labour in the Catacombs, De Rossi has only come upon two fragments, and two or three have been brought to light by the excavations recently made at Ostia. Until 1864 not a single specimen had been discovered except in the neighbourhood of Rome, but in that year a very remarkable fragment of a gilded glass plate was found at Cologne in excavating the foundations of a house near the Church of St Severin; and in 1866 another, though of a different workmanship, was discovered, together with some charred bones, in a rough stone chest about thirty inches in length, and fifteen in width and depth, in a similar excavation near the well-known Church of St Ursula and her companions. This last specimen is now in the Slade Collection in the British Museum; and a woodcut of the other is given in page 290.

<small>Their discovery by Bosio and others in Roman Catacombs.</small>

<small>Two found at Cologne.</small>

These two exceptions scarcely seem sufficient to overthrow the general opinion of archæologists that Rome was the only place where this kind of glass was manufactured. Garrucci has, indeed, adopted a further conclusion, and considers the art to have been confined to the Roman Christians. It is, however, exceedingly improbable that the Christians should

<small>The art of making them known only in Rome;</small>

have been acquainted with any ornamental art which was unknown to their Pagan cotemporaries. Besides, several of the figures represent gladiatorial combats and scenes from Pagan mythology, such as no Christian artist of the early ages would have thought of depicting, nor can either the figures or the inscriptions which accompany them be in any way adapted so as to bear a Christian signification. How, then, it may be asked, are we to account for the fact of these glasses scarcely ever having been found except in Christian sepulchral crypts? We acknowledge the fact, but deny the inference; for it is no less a fact that these glasses have never been discovered in any Christian building or sepulchre *above ground*, and yet we know that from very early times, and more especially after A.D. 312, the Christians possessed many places of burial which were not subterranean. That no such glasses have come down to us from antiquity, except those found in the Catacombs, is to be ascribed to their extremely fragile nature, which the peculiar circumstance of their having been imbedded in mortar alone preserved from destruction. Cavedoni conjectures, with much probability, that vessels of glass thus ornamented have been destroyed in great quantities for the sake of the gold which they contained, and this conjecture is confirmed by one or two instances recently found, in which some of the gold leaf has been scraped away with an instrument forced in between the plates of glass.* The Jew " dealers in broken glass," who plied their trade in Trastevere, even in the days of Martial,† may have had some share in producing the scarcity of specimens of this kind of manufacture.

and practised in the third and fourth centuries. It is difficult to determine precisely the period to which these glasses are to be assigned. Olivieri discovered one in the cemetery of St Callixtus, "in the middle of which was

* Cavedoni, Osservazioni, &c., p. 6, &c., quoted in *Bullettino*, 1864, p. 82.
† Transtyberinus ambulator,
Qui pallentia sulphurata fractis
Permutat vitreis.—*Epig.* i. 42.

represented a heap of money, and in the centre of the heap, on the top of all the rest, was to be distinguished the head of Caracalla."* Another glass bears the name of Marcellinus, who was martyred under Diocletian in A.D. 304.† From an examination of the style of dress, and of the mode of arranging the hair, as also from the orthography of the legends and other indications, Padre Garrucci considers them all anterior to the time of Theodosius; and De Rossi speaks more precisely, assigning them to a period ranging from the middle of the third to the beginning of the fourth century.

The subjects depicted on them are more varied than those painted on the walls of the Catacombs. A few are, as we have already mentioned, scenes from Pagan mythology: Hercules, Achilles, and Pagan gods and goddesses. Others represent boxers contending for the prize, charioteers, and hunting scenes; a ship-builder with his men variously employed; a money-coiner, a tailor, and a druggist, each in his shop. Domestic scenes from the nursery and the schoolroom are also here to be met with; a father and mother, with one or more of their children in front of them; or still more frequently, a husband and wife, standing side by side, sometimes with hands joined over the nuptial altar, which is generally presided over by Christ, either represented by His monogram ☧, or else in His own person crowning the married couple. In one instance, it seems to be an angel instead of Christ, who is assisting at the union; but it is quite possible that this may be a Pagan scene, and the winged figure may be intended for Cupid. Five or six specimens exhibit the seven-branched candlestick, the ark containing the rolls of the law, and other Jewish symbols; but the great majority are manifestly Christian.

Subjects depicted on them.
Pagan.
Social and domestic.
Jewish.

Three of these, of which two are in the possession of Mr Wilshere, have one or two figures in the centre, and, grouped around these, a number of subjects from Holy Scripture.

Most frequently Christian.

* Garrucci, Tav. xxxiii. n. 5.   † Ib., Tav. xix. n. 3.

Description of some of these. Thus in one * we have Christ with the rod of power changing the water into wine; Tobias with the monster fish; Christ with the rod of power enabling the paralytic to carry his bed; and lastly, with the same rod of power protecting the Three Children in the flaming furnace of Babylon. Another, also in the possession of Mr Wilshere,† has the Apostles Peter and Paul in the centre, and the six compartments around them contain successively figures of the Three Children; a man, supposed by Garrucci to be the prophet Isaias, with a roll of a book taken out of a chest, and a symbolical figure of the sun; then a female figure praying, possibly the Virgin, whose maternity the prophet saw in vision; next a man, probably the prophet Isaias, being sawn asunder by two executioners; then another man with a rod and a serpent in front of him, probably Moses and the brazen serpent, which Our Lord tells us was a type of Himself; and lastly, Moses striking the rock. These and other scriptural subjects, such as the Fall, Noe in the Ark, the sacrifice of Isaac, the destruction of the dragon by Daniel, and the history of Jonas, are found sometimes singly, and sometimes together. Our Lord is frequently represented as the Good Shepherd, or as multiplying the loaves, or changing the water into wine; but in this latter miracle the number of water-pots is invariably represented as seven instead of six, apparently to signify that the symbolical meaning of the miracle as a type of the Holy Eucharist was principally in the artist's mind.

Figures of Saints. The Blessed Virgin is represented sometimes alone, with her name over her head, praying between two olive-trees; sometimes with the Apostles Peter and Paul on either side of her; sometimes accompanied by the virgin martyr St Agnes. St Agnes is found on several glasses with similar variations. Other saints, as St Lawrence, St Vincent, Hippolytus, Callixtus, Marcellinus, Sixtus, Timotheus, &c., are found more

---

* Garrucci, Tav. i. n. 1.   † Ib. l. c. n. 2.

rarely. But the favourite subject is evidently the representation of the two great Apostles Saints Peter and Paul.

Those who have passed a summer in Rome will not easily forget the enthusiasm with which the Romans still keep the *festa* of their great patrons. Even the vast basilica on the Vatican appears full of citizens in gala dress, when they listen with proud satisfaction to the glorious hymn: —

<blockquote>
"O felix Roma! quæ duorum Principum
Es consecrata glorioso sanguine,
Horum cruore purpurata cæteras
Excellis orbis una pulchritudines."
</blockquote>

Feast of Saints Peter and Paul

The sermons of St Leo the Great, and the poems of Prudentius, show us with what solemnity the festival was observed in the fourth and fifth century. "The people flock together," sings the latter, "for more than ordinary joys. Tell me, my friend, what this may be? They run to and fro through the whole of Rome, and shout for joy, because to us this festal day of the Apostles' triumph has come again, this day enobled by the blood of Peter and of Paul."* These festivities were then, as now, apt to run into excess, and hence St Jerome, while thanking Eustochium for her childish presents of sweetmeats, adds the caution, "It is the feast and birthday of Blessed Peter . . . and therefore we must take all the more care that we keep this solemn day not so much with the abundance of our food, as with the gladness of our souls. For it is very absurd to propose with over-eating to honour a martyr, who you know pleased God by his fasts."† St Augustine laments the dishonour done by scenes of riot to the saints, "whom drunkards now persecute with their cups, as much as the furious Pagans used to pursue them with stones;"‡ and he specially mourns over the scandal given by the wine-bibbing in "the basilica of St Peter,"§ where *agapæ* were celebrated in the portico for the benefit of

at Rome in fourth century.

---

* Peristeph. xii. † Ep. xxxi., ad Eustochium.
‡ Enarr. in Ps. lix. § Ep. xxix., ad Alypium, § 10.

the poor. Paulinus of Nola tells us how the *agapæ* thus degenerated, how "the table of Peter receives what the teaching of Peter denounces," and at the same time he draws a graphic picture of a *festa* in the fourth century. "Among the crowds attracted thither by the fame of St Felix," he says,*—and with one alteration we may fairly transfer his description to Rome on the 29th of June,—"there are peasants recently converted who cannot read, and who, before embracing the faith of Christ, had long been the slaves of profane usages, and had obeyed their senses as gods. They arrive here from afar, and from all parts of the country. Glowing with faith, they despise the chilling frosts ;† they pass the entire night in joyous watchings; they drive away slumber by gaiety, and darkness by torches. But they mingle festivities with their prayers, and, after singing hymns to God, abandon themselves to good cheer. They joyously stain with odoriferous wine the tombs of the saints. They sing in the midst of their cups, and by their drunken lips the devil insults St Felix. I have therefore," continues the good bishop, "thought good to enliven with holy pictures the whole temple of St Felix. It may be, when the sight of them strikes their astonished minds, these coloured representations will arrest the attention of the rustics. Inscriptions are placed above the pictures, in order that the letters may explain what the hand has depicted. While they point them out to one another, and read by turns these pictured objects, they forget their eating till a later hour. The enjoyment of the sight beguiles their hunger, better habits are formed in these gazers, and studying these sacred histories, chastity and virtue are engendered by such examples of piety. . . . And as they spend the day in gazing more and more, their potations become less frequent, and only a short time remains for their repast."

* Poema xxvi. (*aliter* xxxv.); De Felice, Natal., carm. ix. v. 541, *seqq*.
† The *contadini* who spend the vigil of Saints Peter and Paul on the steps and under the colonnade of the Piazza di San Pietro are not in danger of frost.

Gilded Glasses found in the Catacombs.

Whether the same idea of restraining the potations of the Roman Christians, by depicting figures which could only be seen to advantage when the glass was empty, suggested the use of these gilded cups, we shall not pause to inquire. It is at any rate certain that the feast of Saints Peter and Paul was observed as a general holiday in Rome during the fourth century, very much as Christmas is now amongst ourselves, and the representation of the two apostles on eighty glasses out of the three hundred and forty published by Garrucci, is a strong argument of their having been intended in some way or other to commemorate that day. The inscriptions, where they occur, with the figures of the apostles, confirm this supposition, for they are all of a convivial character. We give a few examples—DIGNITAS AMICORVM PIE ZESES CVM TVIS OMNIBVS BIBAS. DIGNITAS AMICORVM PIE ZESES CVM TVIS OMNIBVS BIBE ET PROPINA. CVM TVIS FELICITER ZESES. These may be translated—"*A mark of friendship,*[*] *drink,*[†] *and* [*long*] *life to thee, with all thine. Mayest thou live* [*long*]." "*A mark of friendship, drink, and* [*long*] *life to thee, with all thine, drink* [or, *live*] *and propose a toast.*" "*Mayest thou live happily with thine own,*" or, more freely, "*Life and happiness to thee and thine.*" A more religious inscription has:—HILARIS VIVAS CVM TVIS OMNIBVS FELICITER SEMPER IN PACE DEI ZESES; that is, "*Joyfully mayest thou live with all thine; happily mayest thou live for ever in the peace of God.*" Doubtless in Rome many a pious pilgrim followed the practice which St Monica learned in Africa, of whom St Augustine records, with the playful fond-

Figures of Saints Peter and Paul on glasses.

---

[*] DIGNITAS AMICORVM appears to have been equivalent to the phrase *Digni amici*, with which a Roman host was accustomed to pledge his guests before drinking their health. Perhaps it would have been more exactly rendered by "*Here's to our friendship.*" The phrase is evidently alluded to by St Augustine in the passage quoted below, where *dignationem* stands for the honour paid to the saints by St Monica with her cup of wine.

[†] PIE, ZESES, for πιε, ζησῆς, Greek words in popular use in Rome. BIBAS may be understood as it stands, or as written for VIVAS. The latter is more in conformity with the spelling on the inscriptions in the Catacombs, in which VIXIT is usually written BIXIT.

ness of filial affection, that she used to bring to the festivals "a small cup of wine, diluted according to her own abstemious habits, which for courtesy she would taste ('*unde dignationem sumeret*'). And if there were many shrines of the departed saints to be honoured in that manner, she would carry round that one same cup which she used everywhere; and this, even when it had become not only very watery, but unpleasantly lukewarm, she would distribute to those about her by small sips, for she sought there devotion, not pleasure."*

<small>Ancient portraits of these Apostles.</small>

A question here naturally arises as to the representations of the Apostles, how far they may be considered to be real likenesses, or whether they were purely conventional, invented and perpetuated merely by Christian art. We have the testimony of Eusebius that he had "seen representations of the Apostles Peter and Paul, and of Christ Himself, still preserved in paintings;" and he adds, "that it is probable that, according to a practice among the Gentiles, the ancients were accustomed to pay this kind of honour indiscriminately to those who were as saviours or deliverers to them.† Moreover, it cannot be denied that there is a certain uniformity of type about the figures of these Apostles on most of the glasses of which we are speaking, so that they might often be distinguished, even if there were no legends over their heads.

The oldest representation of them now extant is probably that on a bronze medal preserved in the Vatican Library.‡ This medal is about three inches in diameter; it is executed in a fine style of classical art, and the heads are finished with great care. This was found by Boldetti in the cemetery of Domitilla, and has every appearance of having been executed in the time of the Flavian emperors, when Grecian art still flourished in Rome. The portraits are very life-like and natural, bearing a strong impress of individual character. One of the heads is covered with short curly hair, the beard clipped short and also curled, the features somewhat rough and common-place. The features

<small>* Conf. vi. 2.   † Hist. Eccl. vii. c. 18.   ‡ See Plate XVII. 1.</small>

Gilded Glasses found in the Catacombs. 285

of the other are more noble, graceful, and strongly marked, the head is bold, and the beard is thick and long. This valuable medal confirms the tradition preserved by Nicephorus * of the personal appearance of the two Apostles, the first being that of St Peter, and the latter that of St Paul; and, as we have already said, these characteristics are in the main retained in most of the glasses, excepting a few which are of very inferior execution. The two Apostles are represented side by side, sometimes standing, and sometimes seated. In some instances Christ is represented in the air (that is, from heaven, as it were), holding over the head of each a crown of victory; or, in other instances, a single crown is suspended between the two, as if to show that " in their death they were not divided." This crown becomes sometimes a circle surrounding the labarum or ☧, which is often supported on a pillar, thus symbolising "the pillar and ground of the truth," which is "that very great, very ancient, and universally known Church founded and organised at Rome by the two most glorious Apostles Peter and Paul."† For there certainly seems to be good ground for Mr Palmer's conjecture,‡ that in some of these glasses the Roman Church is intended to be symbolised in the persons of her founders and patrons, rather than the Apostles themselves to be represented personally. In this way we can account for their being placed on either side of the Blessed Virgin, § of St Agnes, or of other saints, who have their hands uplifted in prayer, whilst the Apostles are not in the same attitude, and moreover, are made to appear of very diminutive stature. It can never have been intended to represent St Agnes as superior to the chiefs of the Apostles, or

Variously represented on glass.

sometimes symbolical of Roman Church.

---

* See also St Jerome, Comment. in Ep. ad. Galat. i. 18, tom. vii. p. 329, ed. Migne. It is a curious coincidence also that in the apocryphal Acts of the Apostles, edited by Tischendorf, it is said of Dioscorus, the shipmaster, who had followed St Paul to Rome, and was mistaken for the Apostle and beheaded in his stead, that he was bald, "καὶ αὐτὸς ἀναφαλαντὸς ὑπάρχων," p. 4.   † S. Irenæus, Hær. iii. 3.
‡ Early Christian Symbolism, p. 21.   § See Plate XVIII. 1.

as making intercession for those who had "finished their course" nearly a century and a half before her. Rather, we understand St Agnes, St Peregrina, and the rest, even our Blessed Lady herself, as praying for the Roman Church which these Apostles had founded, and through it for the Church at large. St Agnes was always accounted a very special ornament and glory of the Roman Church, and we have certain proof of the Roman Christians of the fourth century asking her prayers in the inscription by Pope Damasus, still to be seen at the entrance of her church *fuori le mura*—

UT DAMASI PRECIBUS FAVEAS PRECOR, INCLYTA VIRGO.

She was also represented alone* upon these glasses almost more frequently than any other saint excepting the two Apostles of whom we have been speaking.

St Peter under the type of Moses; The relative positions of these two Apostles, in ancient works of art, have been a subject of frequent discussion ever since the days of St Peter Damian. It seems impossible, however, to establish any theory upon them. St Peter is generally at the right hand, but by no means always so; and if any one attempts to prove from this that the Roman Christians looked upon the two Apostles as in all respects equal and co-ordinate, he is met by the fact;—first, that Our Lord Himself is found once standing on the left of St Paul; St Agnes, too, in the place of honour, where she appears with the Blessed Virgin; and husbands, often placed on the left of their wives: moreover, that Pagan artists, when they placed Jupiter between Juno and Minerva, observe the same indifference as to the relative position of the two goddesses.† And secondly, that the primacy of St Peter is distinctly attested in some of these glasses by another symbol which can hardly be misunderstood. We mean those in which he appears under the type of Moses striking the rock. The rock, of course, at once suggests the passage of St Paul: "They drank of that

* See Plate XVIII. 2.   † *Bullett.* 1868, 43.

Gilded Glasses found in the Catacombs. 287

spiritual rock that followed them, and that rock was Christ;" but we should hardly have ventured to affirm that the figure striking the rock was St Peter, if his name had not, in two instances at least, been unmistakably given at his side. One of these glasses has been long known to antiquarian visitors to the Vatican Museum,* and within the last few months a second, preserved in the same place, but whose surface had become corroded and opaque, has been cleaned and rendered transparent by Professor Tessieri. It does not differ in any essential respect from the other, yet there is just sufficient difference to indicate the hand of another artist.

FIG. 33.—*Bottom of a Gilded Glass found in the Catacombs, and lately cleaned, and restored to the Vatican Museum.*

These invaluable glasses supply us with a key to many of the paintings in the Catacombs and sculptures on Christian sarcophagi, where the same scene is so frequently repeated. They show us that St Peter was considered to be the Moses

* See Plate XVII. 2.

of "the new Israel of God," as Prudentius speaks, and they explain the reason why the rod, the emblem of Divine power, is never found except in three hands, those of Moses, Christ, and Peter. It belongs primarily, and by inherent right, to Christ, the eternal Son of God. By Him it was of old delegated to Moses, of whom God testified, "He is most faithful in all my house."* For a few years the rod of power was visibly wielded by the Incarnate Word; and when He withdrew His own visible presence from the earth, "afterwards," to use the words of St Macarius of Egypt,† "Moses was succeeded by Peter, to whom is committed the New Church of Christ, and the new priesthood." We understand, also, that it

also in sculpture on sarcophagi, is not without reason that in the sarcophagi the figure striking the rock is almost invariably found in immediate juxtaposition with the Prince of the Apostles led captive by the satellites of Herod Agrippa, and there is frequently a studied similarity in the features of the principal figure in both scenes. The most striking example of this is in the large sarcophagus which stands at the end of the principal hall in the Lateran Museum. In one of the four compartments into which the front of that sarcophagus is divided, we have an epitome of St Peter's life. First, he stands with the rod of power, already given to him by his Divine Master, who is warning him of his fall, symbolised by the cock at his feet. Next, he is taken prisoner by the satellites of Agrippa, but he still bears the rod, for "the Word of God is not bound," and no worldly violence can wrench the rod of jurisdiction from him to whom Christ has given it.‡ Lastly, he appears under the symbol of Moses,

---

* Num. xii. 7 ; compare Heb. iii. 5, 6.   † Hom. xxvi. c. 23.
‡ There must have been some special cause for the frequent repetition of this scene. The most reasonable explanation is, that St Peter's imprisonment and miraculous deliverance, after which "he went into another place" (Acts xii. 17), was the occasion of his coming to Rome, where the same scene was enacted again and again in the apprehension and martyrdom of so many of his successors. The parallel event in the life of St Paul (his imprisonment and deliverance at Philippi) is nowhere reproduced in early Christian art. See Palmer's "Symbolism," p. 18.

Gilded Glasses found in the Catacombs. 289

using the rod to bring from "the spiritual Rock" the streams of grace, at which the Israel of God slake the thirst of their souls. We have already seen that the same idea runs through the paintings in the earliest *cubicula* of the Catacombs. All sacramental grace is there represented as flowing from that one stream over which Peter presides. Early in the fifth century, St. Augustine expressed the same idea when, writing to Pope Innocent I., he said, "We do not pour back our streamlet for the purpose of increasing your great fountain, but we wish it to be decided by you whether our stream, however small, flows forth from that same Head of rivers whence comes your own abundance."* And in his reply the Pope says of St Peter, "from whom the very Episcopate, and all the authority of this name (of the Apostolic See) sprung . . . that thence all other churches might derive what they should order; whom they should absolve; whom, as bemired with ineffaceable pollution, the stream that is worthy only of pure bodies should avoid; just as from their parent source all waters flow, and through the different regions of the whole world the pure streams of the fountain well forth uncorrupted."†

and in frescoes in Catacombs.

Among the glasses delineated by P. Garrucci may be noticed a great number of very small size. These had been supposed to belong to glass cups of small dimensions; but a careful examination of them, especially since the discovery which we have mentioned of the fragments of a glass plate at Cologne, has proved that they once formed parts of similar *patenæ*. It will be observed that they rarely contain a whole subject at once. Thus one of them will contain the figure of Adam, another that of Eve, while the tree and the serpent coiled round it will be represented on a third. The Three Children are represented each on a separate glass, and so are the three Magi. Our Lord, or St Peter, as the case may be,

Large *patenæ* with small medallions let into the glass.

* S. Aug. Epist. clxxvii. vol. ii. p. 938, ed. Gaume.
† Inter Epist. S. Aug: 181; ib., p. 949. See Note C. in Appendix, on the *Chair of St Peter*, and its connexion with the Baptismal Font on the Vatican.

T

is represented about a dozen times standing alone with a rod in his hand, while on other glasses are to be seen the paralytic carrying his bed, Lazarus as a mummy at the door of his

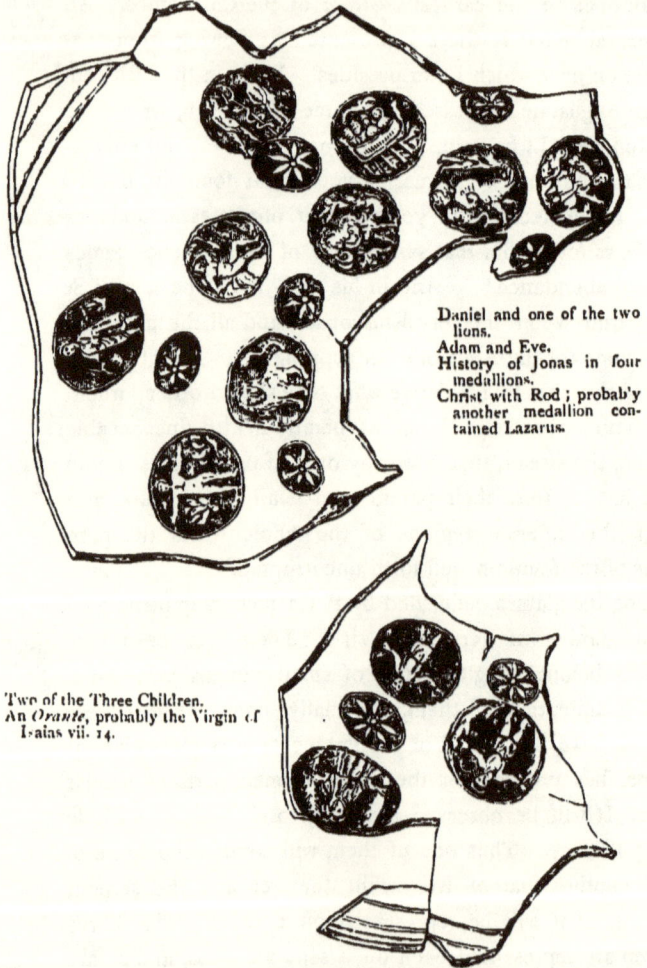

Daniel and one of the two lions.
Adam and Eve.
History of Jonas in four medallions.
Christ with Rod; probab'y another medallion contained Lazarus.

Two of the Three Children.
An *Orante*, probably the Virgin of Isaias vii. 14.

FIG. 24.—*Fragments of a Glass Patena found at Cologne.*

sepulchre, and the rock with the stream issuing from it. It is true that sometimes these small glasses have been taken out of the series to which they belong. Thus, one published by

Garrucci in Tav. iv. 9, which is in the Vatican, was found in the plaster round a child's grave, in the cemetery of St Priscilla, surrounded with a circle of iron with a ring by which it had been hung round the neck as a medal; and yet the subject is one of the three Magi. But the general use of these small glasses is proved by the fragments discovered at Cologne, of a flat plate about ten inches in diameter made of clear glass, into which have been inserted, while in a state of fusion, a number of small medallions of green glass exactly similar to those found separately in Rome, and which together form a series of scriptural subjects. These medallions, being of double glass, have resisted the ravages of time and accident which have destroyed the more thin and fragile glass of the *patena*. De Rossi has seen in the plaster of *loculi* in the Catacombs the impression of large plates of this description, which have probably perished in the attempt to detach them from the cement.*

We have alluded to the probable use of these glasses at the *Agapæ*, and the subjects on many of them suggest their having been also used on other festive occasions, as marriages, birthdays, &c. It is however a more interesting question to consider whether it is not possible that some of them may have been used as patens or chalices in the celebration of the Holy Eucharist. The well-known passage in which Tertullian scoffs at the Roman Pontiff for painting on his chalice the figure of the Good Shepherd,† would lead us to suppose that the chalices of the second and third century must have been frequently of similar material and workmanship to the glasses of which we are treating. The celebrated *Graal* or *Sacro Catino*, preserved at Genoa, which is supposed to have been the chalice used by our Saviour at the Last Supper, and in search for which so many romantic adventures were encountered by legendary knights, is of glass, and of hexagonal form; but it

Glass chalice.

---

* *Bullett.* 1864, pp. 89-91.
† "Ipsæ picturæ calicum vestrorum, si vel in illis *perlucebit* interpretatio," &c.; and again, "pastor quem in calice depingis."—*Tert. De Pudicit.* 7, 10.

would not be safe to deduce any archæological argument from so doubtful a relic.* The *Liber Pontificalis* says of St Zephyrinus, that "he made it a constitution of the Church, that ministers should carry *glass patens* into the church in front of the priests, while the bishop celebrated mass with the priests standing before him, and that in this manner masses should be celebrated, care being taken for what belonged to the rights of the bishop, that the clergy only should take away for all present the Holy Loaf (*coronam*) consecrated by the bishop's own hand, and that the priest should receive it to administer it to the people." About twenty years afterwards, St Urban "made the consecrated vessels all of silver, and set apart twenty-five silver patens." From these notices later writers, such as Honorius of Autun, have affirmed that "the Apostles and their successors celebrated masses in wooden chalices; Pope Zephyrinus in glass; but Urban, Pope and martyr, ordained that the Holy Sacrifice should be offered in gold or silver chalices and patens."† The passages, however, do not bear out so absolute a limitation of the period of glass chalices to the few years between Zephyrinus and Urban. It is not said that the latter Pope forbade the use of chalices of less precious materials; it is merely stated that he provided sacred vessels of silver, and especially a number of patens corresponding to the number of the city *tituli*. The history of St Sixtus II. and St Laurence shows that the treasures of the Church were constantly liable to confiscation, and it would have been as impossible to ensure the sacred vessels being always of the precious metals in Rome, during the ages of persecution, as it is now for those Christian communities which groan under the bondage of Mohammedanism.‡ When hap-

* See Didron, "Christian Iconography," vol. i. p. 270, note, (Bohn's trans.) † De Gemma Animæ, i. 89.

‡ The present writer once received a visit from a Coptic priest, who begged earnestly to have given him for a chalice one of the ale-glasses which he saw on the table of the Nile-boat saloon. Glass chalices are universal throughout Egypt in the Coptic churches.

pier days came, and the munificent gifts of gold and silver chalices displaced the glass vessels, it was not at all unlikely for some of the latter to be put up as tokens of affection and distinction on the tombs of the departed, and hence it is quite possible that some of our glasses may be fragments of chalices.

The *patenæ vitreæ* which St Zephyrinus required, belong to a different category. They were not for the use of the celebrant bishop or priest; but in conformity with that ancient practice which required all the priests in cathedral cities on Sundays and great festivals to assist at the bishop's mass, St Zephyrinus ruled that the priests of the several *titles* should be attended on such occasions by a minister with a glass *patena*, in which a requisite number of consecrated hosts (made then in the form of the Roman circular biscuit *ciambella*, and hence called *corona*) should be placed at the bishop's mass, and taken by the priests to be administered to the faithful in the different parishes, who thus signified their union with the bishop by "being all partakers of that one bread" consecrated by his hands. "Take heed," says St Ignatius of Antioch, "that you have but one Eucharist. For there is one flesh of Our Lord Jesus Christ, and one chalice in the unity of His blood. One altar, as there is but one bishop, with the priests, and the deacons, my fellow-servants."* Now, the fragments of the two large *patenæ* discovered at Cologne, correspond exactly to the kind of glass paten here mentioned. The scriptural subjects, and the absence of any allusions to secular feasting, accord well with so sacred a purpose, and we may therefore fairly presume that those other smaller glasses of which we have also spoken may also be remains of the *patenæ* used to convey the Blessed Sacrament from the Pope's altar to the parish churches in Rome. Padre Garrucci thinks this not improbable, although he does not admit that any of our Cata-

<small>Glass *patenæ* and their use.</small>

---

* S. Ign. ad Philadelph. c. 4; compare ad Smyrn. c. 8:—"Let that be deemed a sure Eucharist which is [administered] either by the bishop, or by one to whom he has entrusted it."

comb glasses ever formed portions of Eucharistic chalices. The *patena* found near the Church of St Ursula differs from the other discovered two years before, in having the subjects depicted in gold and colours on the surface of the glass, instead of being within medallions of double glass. The drawing is also in a better style of art.

FIG. 35.—*Sarcophagus still to be seen in Cemetery of San Callisto.*

CHAPTER VIII.

CHRISTIAN SARCOPHAGI.

IN the course of the preceding chapters we have frequently had occasion to mention the sarcophagi, or stone coffins, in which some of the more illustrious of those buried in the Catacombs were laid to rest. The use of sarcophagi comes down from the remotest Egyptian antiquity, and, as we have already remarked, it prevailed in Rome before the practice of burning became general. Examples of Pagan Roman sarcophagi may be seen in almost every museum, and the most extensive collection of Christian sarcophagi is to be found in the great hall of the Lateran Palace. It was arranged by Padre Marchi, and additions have been made from time to time under the direction of the Commendatore De Rossi. Before examining this interesting collection of early Christian sculpture, it is worth while to inquire into the Christian use of this mode of burial, in order that we may gain some general idea as to the date of the specimens before us.

We have seen that the Catacomb of St Domitilla,* which bears every mark of having been constructed in the time of the Flavian emperors, appears originally to have been intended solely for the reception of those buried in sarcophagi. The *loculi*, cut through the plaster which covers the walls of the first portion of this cemetery, are manifestly later additions; while the wide recesses, in which the sarcophagi once stood, prove the original design of the sepulchre. In fact, the body of St Petronilla lay here in a stone sarcophagus, in which it

Christian use of sarcophagi

dates from Apostolic times.

---

* See page 71.

was translated to St Peter's by Pope Paul I. In 1474, King Louis XI. of France restored the altar of this saint, and in consequence the sarcophagus was exposed to view; and there is a letter of Pope Sixtus IV. to the king, in which he describes it as having four dolphins at the corners. The inscription,

AURELIAE PETRONILLAE FILIAE DVLCISSIMAE,

is said to have been engraven by the hand of St Peter himself, whose daughter, in the Gospel, this saint of Cæsar's household was. The sarcophagus of Linus, the immediate successor of St Peter, is related by Severano* to have been found in the time of Urban VIII., during the restoration of the Confession of St Peter. The Christian use of sarcophagi, then, appears to have been coeval with the introduction of Christianity. There were, however, several reasons which made this mode of burial far from general among the Christians.

They were not, however, in very general use.

In the first place, the sarcophagus was an expensive article, and the mass of the Christian community was composed of the poor. The conveyance of a heavy stone coffin from the city to the cemetery required the presence of a considerable number of workmen, and must have attracted more attention to the Christian cemeteries than was generally desirable. Consequently we find, at a very early period, the *sepolcro a mensa*, which is nothing else but a sarcophagus cut out of the living rock; and the later form of this kind of sepulchre was, as we have seen, the *arcosolium*,† which has been described as " an excavated sarcophagus, with arched niche above."

Christian subjects not sculptured on sarcophagi during ages of persecution.

Even when the Christians did bury their dead in sarcophagi, they do not appear, until the ages of persecution had passed away, to have ornamented them with sculptures of a distinctive Christian character. Out of the four hundred and ninety-three dated inscriptions, described by De Rossi as belonging to the first four centuries, only eighteen are found on sarcophagi, and of these not more than four bear dates anterior to the time of

* See page 65.   † See fig. 4, 5, in page 30.

Constantine. These are ornamented with genii, or griffins, or pastoral or hunting scenes; and the earliest dated sarcophagus, with a distinctively Christian subject sculptured upon it, is one from the Catacomb of Saints Peter and Marcellinus, upon which is represented the Nativity with the ox and ass, and which bears a consular date corresponding to A.D. 343.

This tardy development of Christian sculpture cannot be explained by the supposition that the Church forbade or discouraged the representation of sacred subjects and symbols, for if such had been the case, the same rule would have applied to painting, and we have seen that no restriction was placed upon the Christian artist even from the apostolic age. A simple explanation of the contrast presented by these two branches of Christian art is to be found in the consideration of the widely different circumstances under which the painter and the sculptor pursued their respective callings during times of persecution. The Christian artist, concealed in the bowels of the earth, prosecuted his labours without fear of danger; while the sculptor would be unable to execute Christian subjects in his workshop without drawing a dangerous attention to his work. Hence upon the sarcophagi, prior to the time of Constantine, we find Christianity, if represented at all, veiled under forms which were not unknown even to the Pagans; while upon those belonging to the period which followed the peace of the Church, we notice at once the reproduction in marble of the same series of sacred subjects which we have seen reduced to a regular symbolical system in the subterranean fresco-paintings of the second and third centuries. In fact, no sooner was peace given to the Church than Christian art sprang up everywhere, and sarcophagi of the fourth century, adorned with Christian sculptures, have been found in Arles and Saragossa as freely as in Rome, Ravenna, or Milan.*

* A great number of Christian sarcophagi, discovered in the neighbourhood of Arles, may still be seen in the museum of that city. There appears to have been a very considerable school of Christian sculpture there.

Subjects selected by Christians from the Pagan shops.

From the difficulties in the way of anything like the formation of a Christian school of sculpture during the ages of persecution, it is evident that those who wished to procure sarcophagi must have had recourse to the shops of the heathen; and an examination of the fragments which remain of these ages proves, that they took considerable pains to select those which did not directly offend against the Christian religion by representing idolatrous rites, or false gods, or scenes clearly peculiar to Paganism. Sarcophagi with such scenes sculptured upon them are sometimes indeed to be met with in the Catacombs, but they have either been carefully defaced with a chisel, or turned against the wall; and when used to close *loculi*, the sculpture has been turned towards the inside of the tomb. For instance, a bacchanalian scene sculptured on a sarcophagus was found in the cemetery of St Lucina, turned against the wall, while the rough side was exposed to view, and on this side was inscribed the name of the deceased, IRENE. The sarcophagi usually found in Christian cemeteries are ornamented either by wave-lines,* or by scenes of pastoral life, agriculture, the chase, and (more rarely) comic figures. Figures with their hands raised in prayer, *oranti*, were not unknown on Pagan tombs. A shepherd with a sheep on his shoulders is also to be found among heathen subjects. These were at once expressive of thoroughly Christian ideas, and were consequently in great request, as the numerous examples of them testify. Sometimes, other subjects appear less susceptible of a Christian interpretation. Cupid and Psyche are represented side by side with a Good Shepherd, who is overturning a basket of fruit, an omen of evil rather than good.† It is however fair to add, that this sculpture was found with signs of plaster upon it, and had been buried beneath the floor of the chamber. Another, found in the crypt of St Lucina, represents the story of Ulysses and the Syrens, and it is probable that the monogram of TYRANIO was

Pastoral scenes.

Ulysses and Syrens.

---

* As in Fig. 15, page 109. † Fig. 32, page 261.

Christian Sarcophagi. 299

a disguised form of the Cross.* This is not the only instance of the representation of this fable on Christian tombs; and in the fifth century, St Maximus of Turin explained the ship of Ulysses to be a type of the Church, the mast being the Cross, by which the faithful are to be kept from the seductions of the senses, " for in that Christ Our Lord was fastened to the Cross, so let us pass through the ensnaring perils of the world with as it were closed ears; thus shall we be neither held back by the pernicious hearing of the world's voice, nor swerve from our course to the better life and fall upon the rocks of voluptuousness."† Both these fragments of sarcophagi may be seen in the Catacomb of St Callixtus.

The Good Shepherd at each end of one of the sarcophagi in that Catacomb, which still contains the well-preserved body of a man, was probably taken from the Pagan shops. The dog at his feet is foreign to Christian art.‡ Yet the chamber was probably not made before the fourth century, and another sarcophagus in it is covered with subjects wholly biblical. In the Lateran Museum a good specimen of a Pagan Good Shepherd, adapted to Christian purposes, may be seen about the middle of the hall, on the right-hand side. It represents three shepherds, one holding a sheep by his tail, the second with a sheep on his shoulders and another at his feet, while the third leans on his staff and watches three sheep feeding on the mountain-side, a fourth lying at his feet. This sarcophagus bears the inscription :—

ΕΝΘΑΔΕ ΠΑΤΛΕΙΝΑ
ΚΕΙΤΑΙ ΜΑΚΑΡΩΝ
ΕΝΙ ΧΩΡΩ
ΗΝ ΚΗΔΕΤΣΕ ΠΑΚΑΤΑ
ΕΗΝ ΘΡΕΠΤΕΙΡΑΝ
ΓΛΥΚΕΡΗΝ
ΑΓΙΑΝ ΕΝ ΧΡΩ

" Here Pauline lies in the place of the blessed whom Pacata buried [for she was] her sweet and holy nurse in Christ."

---

* Fig. 28, page 232.
† S. Maxim. Hom. i. De Cruce Domini. See also Philosophumena, vii. c. 1, Clark's edition, vol. i. p. 267. ‡ Fig. 35, page 294.

Bosio says that it was dug up out of the cemetery of St Priscilla on the Via Salaria, and he infers from the inscription that that cemetery was a celebrated resting-place of saints.* The sarcophagus, with Orpheus and a fisherman sculptured upon it, of which a lithograph is given in Plate XX. at the end of the volume, belongs to the same category.

Sarcophagi in the Lateran. That nearest the entrance.

Since sculpture cannot be said to have existed as a Christian art before the time of Constantine, we may safely attribute all the sarcophagi, with distinctively Christian subjects sculptured upon them, to the fourth and fifth centuries; and having thus determined an approximation to their date, we may pass on to examine some of the more remarkable specimens. We will commence with the large sarcophagus which stands at the end of the hall in the Lateran, and which is usually the first to attract the attention of visitors. A lithograph is given of it at the end of the volume.† This sarcophagus was recently found above the tomb of St Paul, when the excavations were made for the construction of the magnificent Baldacchino which now covers the high altar in his basilica on the Via Ostiensis. That basilica was rebuilt by Theodosius towards the close of the fourth century, and this sarcophagus appears to have been placed there about that time. The unfinished faces of the busts in the centre, doubtless intended for the man and woman to be buried in it, and other heads in the same incomplete condition, show that some circumstance prevented the execution of the original design. It has been suggested that the invasion of the Goths under Alaric was the cause, and this would fix the date at A.D. 410.

The Holy Trinity.

Beginning at the right hand of the upper part of the sarcophagus, we have three bearded figures, representing by their unity of operation the Three Persons of the Ever-Blessed Trinity. The Eternal Father, as the source and fountain of Deity, is symbolised by the figure in the chair, veiled, as the episcopal chair was, in token of His supreme

* Bosio, Rom.-Sott. p. 513.   † Plate XIX.

dignity. In front of Him is a figure who represents the
Eternal Word, by whom all things were made, in the act of
creating Eve from the side of the sleeping Adam. Behind the
seated figure stands a third, to represent the Holy Ghost, who
co-operates in the work of creation. In the next group we The Fall.
see the serpent with the fatal apple in his mouth, which he
offers to our common mother, while between the guilty pair is
Our Lord, here represented without a beard, because it was in
the depth of the shame of the fall that He was revealed as the
promised seed who should be born of the woman, and the Incarnation is expressed by the signs of youth. He gives to Adam
a sheaf, for " in the sweat of thy brow shalt thou eat bread ;"
while to Eve he gives a lamb, a type of domestic labour in
spinning, and also of the Lamb of God whom the second Eve
was to bring forth to atone for all the evil that the first Eve
had brought upon mankind. Immediately below we see two The Epiphany.
other groups, evidently intended to contrast in some way with
those already described. Here the Eternal Word is again
represented, but this time not according to His divine nature
by which He is co-equal with the Father, but He is the Word
made flesh, an infant on His mother's knee. The Holy Ghost
is represented just as before, for it was by the operation of the
Holy Ghost that Mary conceived the Second Person of the
Blessed Trinity in her virginal womb. Her chair is not veiled,
to distinguish the most blessed of creatures from the unap-
proachable Creator; and to mark the twofold generation of
Christ, that which is invisible by which He was born of the
Father before all worlds, and that which was made manifest by
which He was born of His mother in the world. The universality of His kingdom is typified by the three Magi, the
representatives of the whole Gentile Church. And finally, the
application of the universal redemption to the individual is set
forth by Christ giving sight to the blind, while He holds in Our Lord
His hand a roll, either to signify His divine mission, or to the blind.
show that it is His doctrine which alone can enlighten the

Eucharistic types. eyes of the darkened understandings of men. Turning now to the upper portion of the other side of the sarcophagus, we see our Lord with the rod of His power changing the water into wine, and multiplying the loaves, the well-known patristic symbols of the Holy Eucharist, in which the wine becomes His blood, and the bread His flesh, which He gives for the life of the world. And then, as a type and foreshadowing of the power of the Holy Eucharist even upon the mortal body, according to the promise, "He that eateth My flesh, and drinketh My blood hath everlasting life, and I will raise him up in the last day," we have a third group, mutilated indeed, but with enough remaining to show that it represents the raising of Lazarus.

St Peter. Beneath this Eucharistic series, as we may call it, we see St Peter, having had already committed to him the rod of power, which Our Lord held in the former series, and yet receiving from his Master the solemn warning, "Before the cock crow thou shalt deny Me thrice." The uplifted hand of Our Lord, and the cock at St Peter's feet, express this with sufficient clearness, while the rod in the Apostle's hand shows that his fall would not deprive him of his great prerogatives, but that, being converted, he should "confirm his brethren." The next group represents the apprehension of St Peter; the bearded face and general similarity of expression identify the Apostle, and distinguish him from his Divine Master. The Jewish caps mark the satellites of Herod Agrippa, and it is worthy of note that, though they have power to lead the Apostle whither he would not, yet he still retains the rod, for "the Word of God is not bound," and imperial soldiers, who repeated the scene over and over again in the person of Peter's successors, have never been able to wrest from him the rod of power with which he rules the Church as Vicar of Christ. Another reason, which probably led to the very frequent representation of this scene in St Peter's life, is that his imprisonment and miraculous deliverance was the immediate cause of his coming to Rome and founding the Church there; and thus Roman

Christians would see in the apprehension of St Peter the symbol of "the Holy See of Blessed Peter, through which," in the words of St Leo, Rome "was made a priestly and royal city, and the head of the world, extending her sway more widely by the religion of God than ever she had done by earthly domination."* The next group is a mutilated representation of Moses striking the rock, of the waters flowing from which the people of Israel are drinking. We have seen that the glasses found in the Catacombs enable us to interpret this as a symbol of St Peter, and in him the Christian priesthood, touching with the rod of power the Rock from which the spiritual Israel draw grace for all their needs. The remaining group, beneath the busts of the persons for whom the sarcophagus was intended, represents Daniel in the lions' den, protected by God under the figure of an old man, while the figure offering to Daniel a basket of food represents the prophet Habacuc, whom "the angel of the Lord took by the top of his head, . . . and set him in Babylon, over the den, in the force of His spirit. Then Habacuc cried, saying: 'O Daniel, thou servant of God, take the dinner that God hath sent thee.'"† This group is met with very frequently both in painting and sculpture. It is found in the earliest known Catacomb, and it may be seen in the subterranean church of San Clemente, among frescoes of the tenth century. The continuator of the *Liber Pontificalis* mentions Gregory IV. having adorned altar frontals with gilded representations of Daniel in the lions' den. The writings of the early Fathers inform us that the Christians saw in Daniel the type of the Christian martyr, sometimes like Daniel unharmed by the savage beast to which he was exposed in the arena, but always victorious over those who could at most only destroy the body, and consoled in the dungeon, in which he awaited his martyrdom, by the Christian

Daniel among the lions.

---

* Serm. i. in Nat. Apost. See Corn. à Lap. in Act. xii. 17.

† Dan. xiv. 32–38. In the Protestant version it is called "The Story of Bel and the Dragon."

priest who strengthened him for the conflict with the heavenly food of the Holy Eucharist. Thus St Cyprian applies the history: "For since all things are God's, nothing will be wanting to him who possesses God, if God himself be not wanting to him. Thus a meal was divinely provided for Daniel: when he was shut up by the king's command in the den of lions; and in the midst of wild beasts who were hungry and yet spared him, the man of God was fed."*

Sarcophagus with Jonas. On either side of this sarcophagus are two small statues of the Good Shepherd. Eusebius tells us that statues of Our Lord, under this form, were set up by Constantine at Constantinople, but in Rome early Christian sculpture is nearly always confined to *bassi rilievi*. A remarkable exception will be noticed before we leave this museum.

The first sarcophagus on our left, as we pass up the hall, is one whose lid is ornamented with sea-monsters, and bears the inscription—MARIVS . VITELLIANVS . PRIMITIVAE . CONIVGI . FIDELISSIMAE . AAIKCBBIN ⳩. " Marius Vitellianus to his most faithful wife Primitiva. Hail, innocent soul; dear wife, mayest thou live in Christ." † This lid, however, in all probability, belongs to another sarcophagus, since in Bosio's time this latter was used as the cistern for a fountain in the Medici Gardens, on the Pincio, whither it had been removed from the crypt of St Peter's. The central group, immediately beneath the inscription, again represents the smitten rock and the apprehension of St Peter; while on the one side is Our Lord calling Lazarus as a mummy out of the tomb, close to which stands Martha; her sister Mary kneels at the feet of Our Lord, and the disciples stand around. On the other side is a Good Shepherd watching over two sheep in a temple-like house, probably intended for the Church. But the most striking subject on the sarcophagus is the history of Jonas, who is

* S. Cypr. De Oratione, 21.
† Such at least is the interpretation adopted by De Rossi, who follows Maffei in understanding the congeries of letters at the end as the initials of *Ave anima innocens kara conjux bibas in Christo.—Bullett.* 1868, 10.

represented first as being cast out of a ship, the large sail of which is filled with the wind from the conch-shell of the winged figure above. The sea-monster opens his enormous jaws to receive Jonas, and a female bust in the sky apparently indicates the calm which succeeded. The same monster is next represented as vomiting forth the prophet upon the dry ground, upon which crabs, lizards, and snails are seen crawling about. Close to this scene is the reclining figure of Jonas asleep under the grateful shade of the gourd. The sculptor has filled every bit of available space with figures, and the same water in which float the sea-monsters is made to bear up a little square box, intended for the Ark, in which Noe sits and receives the olive-branch from the dove, which is made, perhaps not without meaning, to come from the place of refreshment where the prophet reposes. At the water's edge, on either side, are represented fishermen—in one case hooking a fish which a boy is assisting him to land, and in the other, giving the basket of fish to the boy. A water bird is also looking out for prey, and may be intended to convey the warning, that others, besides those whom Christ has made " fishers of men," are on the watch for those who are born of the waters.

On the same side of the hall is another sarcophagus, upon the lid of which are two shepherds, each taking care of three sheep rather larger than themselves. Every one of the sheep holds a circular roll of bread in his mouth, evidently a figure of the Holy Eucharist, which (we have already said) was formerly consecrated in bread made in the shape of a *corona*. The sarcophagus itself is ornamented with sacred subjects, the first of which is the sacrifice of Cain and Abel. The invisible God is represented by the bearded figure seated on a stone, which possibly has reference to the rude altar of patriarchal times; Cain, as the eldest, offers his fruits first, while Abel follows with his lamb. In the next group, the Fall is again represented, but Eve has taken the apple, and the promised Saviour, beardless, as in all representations of the Incarnation,

Sarcophagus with Cain and Abel offering sacrifice.

U

holds the sheaf in His hand, but extends it towards the seated figure, as though to imply that the bread obtained by the sweat of Adam's brow is to be offered to God, if His blessing is to be expected upon the labour of man. He does not here give the lamb to Eve, Abel's offering, perhaps, sufficiently con-

<small>St Mary Magdalene.</small> veying the lesson. The central figure is a female with an open box in her hand, the "alabaster box of precious ointment" which Mary poured on Our Lord's head, and of which He said, "Wheresoever this Gospel shall be preached in the whole world, that also which she hath done shall be told for a memory of her."* The remaining subjects are the paralytic carrying his bed, Our Lord giving sight to the blind, changing the water into wine, and raising Lazarus from the tomb.

<small>Sarcophagus from *S. Paolo fuori le mura.*</small> Proceeding still further along this side of the Museum, the visitor will hardly fail to notice a very finely sculptured sarcophagus, in the centre of which are the busts of two men, whose refined and intellectual expression of face contrasts strongly with the rude grotesquesness of most of these sculptures. It is impossible to say who these two men were; but the sarcophagus, which probably once contained their remains, formerly stood beneath the altar in the tribune of *S. Paolo fuori le mura*, and the relics of the Holy Innocents were placed within it. Sixtus V. removed it with the relics to a chapel built by him in Sta. Maria Maggiore. The upper series of figures represent Mary kissing Our Saviour's hand in gratitude for having restored her brother Lazarus to life; Peter warned of his denial before the cock should crow; and Moses receiving the law from a hand stretched out from heaven. Another outstretched hand checks the uplifted arm of Abraham as he is about to sacrifice his son Isaac, who kneels with his hands <small>Pilate washing his hands.</small> bound behind his back. The sacrifice of the true Isaac is not found among the subjects selected by early Christian art, but the article of the Creed, "crucified under Pontius Pilate," is set forth here with sufficient clearness in the group which

* St Matt. xxvi. 13.

represents the servant with the ewer and basin standing ready to wash the hands of the irresolute governor, who, seated on his veiled judgment-seat, turns away his head in token of his repugnance in condemning the innocent blood. Our interpretation of Moses as the figure of St Peter is confirmed by this sarcophagus, on the lower portion of which we see that Apostle in the hands of Herod's satellites, still pointing to the stream which flows from the rock above his head; while Christ, or possibly St John, is represented as also engaging the attention of the satellites, either in allusion to His own apprehension in the Garden, or else to teach that He suffers still in the persecution of His Church. Again, we see Daniel in the lions' den, and the prophet Habacuc, while, on the opposite side, Our Lord gives sight to the blind, and multiplies the loaves and fishes. In the centre, however, is a group which has somewhat puzzled the learned. Bosio makes the old man under the tree to be Moses giving the law to the people, and the head which appears between the branches of the tree to be that of Zaccheus climbing up in order to see Our Lord.

_{St Peter.}

On the same side of the hall is a sarcophagus, with the nearest resemblance to the later representations of Our Saviour's Passion to be found in early Christian art. It is

_{Sarcophagus with the *labarum*.}

FIG. 36.—*Sarcophagus in Lateran Museum of fourth or fifth century.*

divided into five compartments by twisted Corinthian pillars, the pediments above which are decorated with scenes from the vintage. In the central compartment is the *labarum*, surrounded with a crown of immortality, and supported on a cross, on each of the arms of which is a dove pecking at the crown, thus symbolically representing the hope of an immortal crown with Christ, which feeds the soul, although here below its only resting-place is His Cross. The guards appointed by Constantine to keep watch over the sacred standard are represented below by two soldiers; and we may see here a type of the Christian army, who, whether they sleep or wake, live or die, find rest beneath the Cross. Two of the side compartments represent Our Lord witnessing a good confession before Pontius Pilate, above whom hangs a crown, the reward of those who confess Christ before men. On the other side a soldier places a crown on the head of Our Saviour, but it resembles rather the crown of glory which is the recompense of the crown of thorns endured for Him on earth. The last compartment contains a representation of Our Lord carrying His Cross under the guard of a soldier, but there are none of the traces of suffering with which later artists, following the sacred narrative, have familiarised our imagination, and the crown above points to the reward for bearing the Cross after our suffering Master. Above this sarcophagus is let into the wall a fragment of another, which represents a number of persons, some listening with devout attention to one who is reading to them, while others of the same company are partaking of the *agape*.

Representations of the Passion.

Sarcophagus under canopy.

Perhaps the finest specimen of Christian sculpture among all the sarcophagi in the Lateran Museum is that which stands under a canopy supported by two beautiful columns of Pavonazzetto marble, and is placed in this position to show how the sarcophagi were arranged in the ancient basilicas; for this, as well as the one last described, were found in the crypt of St Peter's. The front of the sarcophagus is sculptured with figures in high relief, divided into groups by eight richly ornamented pillars. The groups at the two extremities are Abraham's sacrifice, and Our Lord before Pilate, who is washing his hands. The rest of the figures are the Apostles

Christian Sarcophagi. 309

grouped around Our Lord, who is seated in the centre as in glory, the vault of heaven beneath His feet being expressed (as in Pagan monuments) by the veil which a female figure holds above her head. De Rossi remarks that the grace and refinement of the faces of Our Lord and the Apostles would incline us to ascribe this work to the age of Septimius Severus,* rather than to that of Constantine, did not the ⳩ on one of the sides indicate the latter as its actual date. The two principal figures among the Apostles are manifestly intended for St Peter and St Paul, and the characteristics of each Apostle, which we have noticed on the gilded glasses, are easily to be discerned here. St Paul is on the right, distinguished by his baldness from St Peter, who receives, with hands reverently veiled, the new law from the Mediator of the New Testament, just as heathen magistrates were wont to receive from the emperors the book of the constitutions whereby they were to govern the province committed to their charge. Often, on similar representations, Our Lord is represented as giving the volume to the Apostle, but saying nothing. In others, again, the roll bears the inscription, DOMINVS DAT LEGEM, or PACEM, sometimes one, and sometimes the other, whence the Bishop Eribert was led to engrave on the Book of the Gospels provided for the cathedral of Milan the words "LEX ET PAX." Here again we see Peter represented as the Moses of the new dispensation, and every such discovery increases the probability that in all other representations also of Moses, the chief Apostle was really meant to be understood. The two sides of this sarcophagus are covered with sculpture. On one is represented the denial of St Peter, with a basilica and a baptistery in the background, the latter of which (no doubt by an intentional anachronism) is surmounted with the ⳩. On the other side is a similar kind of background, but in front is the smitten rock, and, apparently, the "*Noli Me tan-*

Our Lord in glory surrounded by the Apostles.

Saints Peter and Paul.

Denial of St Peter.

---

* Sickler, Almanach aus Rom. pp. 173, 174, actually assigns to it that date.

gere," although this latter group may be intended to represent the gratitude of Mary for the resurrection of her brother.

Sculpture of Elias ascending to heaven, and leaving his pallium to Eliseus.

On the visitor's right, as he ascends the staircase at the end of the hall, he will notice a spirited sculptured representation of the ascent of Elias into heaven in the fiery chariot.* The sons of the prophets are gazing with eager astonishment at Eliseus, who reverently, and with veiled hands, receives from the ascending prophet the cloak or *pallium*, the symbol of the double portion of the Spirit which rested upon him. In Elias, St Ambrose and other Fathers saw a figure of Our Lord; and Rupertus explains further: "When Elias was on the point of being translated, he laid his *pallium* on Eliseus; because Christ Our God and Lord, when about to pass out of this world unto the Father, gave to the Apostles both His office and His Spirit." † "Eliseus," says the Venerable Bede, "took the mantle of Elias, and with it struck the waters of Jordan, and when he invoked the God of Elias, they were divided, and he passed over. The Apostles took up, the Church founded by them took up, the sacraments of her Redeemer, and with them is spiritually enlightened, cleansed, and consecrated; and she also invoked the name of God the Father, and learned how to conquer the torrent of death, and despising the hindrance of it, to pass over to eternal life." ‡ This history forms the subject of a painting which may still be seen in the Catacomb of SS. Nereus and Achilles. It is carved also at the end of a sarcophagus near the door of the sacristy of St Peter's, containing the bodies of Popes Leo II. III. and IV.; and on two or three other sarcophagi, copied in the works of Bosio, Bottari, and others. It would certainly have reminded Roman Christians of the *pallium*, the symbol of jurisdiction worn by the Bishops of Rome, and given by them to metropolitans as from the very body of St Peter,—"*de corpore Sancti Petri.*" § It is worthy of notice, in connexion with this subject,

---

* See Fig. 29, p. 251. † Rupert. Abb. De Trin. v. c. 15.
‡ Hom. in Ascen. Dom. § See Note F in Appendix.

Christian Sarcophagi. 311

and also with the roll given to St Peter by the ascended Saviour in the last sarcophagus, that the most ancient part of Filocalus' catalogue of the Popes commenced thus:—
"*Passus est Dominus noster Jesus Christus duobus Geminis consulibus viii Kal. Apriles, et post Ascensum ejus beatissimus Petrus episcopatum suscepit, ex quo tempore,*" &c. *

"Our Lord Jesus Christ suffered on the 25th March, the two Gemini being consuls, and after His Ascension the most blessed Peter undertook the episcopacy, after which time," &c.

Above the translation of Elias is a fragment of a small sar- The Nativity. cophagus representing the Nativity, with the ox and ass and the Magi; and below is a rude *intaglio* of the raising of Lazarus, on a marble covering of one of the *loculi*, with an inscription to DATVS. But our readers will easily be able to interpret for themselves most of the other sculptures in this museum.

As we pass out of the great hall into the upper corridor, Sarcophagus of Junius around which De Rossi has arranged the inscriptions from Bassus. the Catacombs, we may observe a number of casts of a sarcophagus similar to some that we have described, and yet possessing certain remarkable features peculiar to itself. Many of our readers will have seen the original in St Peter's crypt, where it stands on the right hand of the passage leading to the subterranean chapel, and bears the inscription:—

 IVN · BASSVS VC QVI VIXIT ANNIS · XLII MEN . II . IN IPSA
  PRAEFECTVRA VRBIS
 NEOFITVS IIT AD DEVM · VIII KAL SEPT EVSEBIO ET
  YPATIO COSS

"Junius Bassus, who lived forty-two years and two months. In the very year in which he was Prefect of the city, he went to God, a neophyte on the 23d of August, A.D. 359."

The noble family of the Bassi is mentioned by Prudentius as having been among the first of patrician rank to embrace the Christian religion;† and the death of this very Junius

* Rom. Sott. ii. 307.   † Contra Symmachum, i. 558.

Fig. 37.—Spandrils of the Tomb of Junius Bassus, A.D. 359.

Bassus is recorded by a cotemporary writer * as having taken place soon after his appointment as Præfect of Rome. The sarcophagus is of white marble, handsomely carved in the Corinthian style; and besides the representations of Adam and Eve, the sacrifice of Isaac, Daniel among the lions, and Our Lord in glory delivering the law to His Apostles, we have, on the upper portion, a group in which is represented the apprehension of Our Saviour in the garden; and again His condemnation by Pilate. The apprehension of St Peter appears on the other side, the Apostle being distinguished from his Lord by the beard, thus confirming our explanation of a similar scene on other sarcophagi. The lower portion also contains in the centre Our Lord's entry into Jerusalem; and, at one extremity, Job comforted by his friends, while his wife, with her handkerchief to her nose, illustrates the complaint of the afflicted patriarch, "My wife hath abhorred my breath." † The other extremity contains the representation of a person bound and led away, which, from the baldness of the head, and the sword in the hand of one of his guards, we may consider

* Ammianus Marcellinus. † Job xix. 7.

Christian Sarcophagi. 313

to be intended for St Paul being conducted to the place of his execution on the Ostian Way. The spandrils of the five arches which make up the lower portion are ornamented with figures which form perhaps the most interesting feature in this sarcophagus. The subjects indeed have been explained before in other sculptures, but here it is a lamb who occupies the place of the Three Children in the furnace of Nabuchadonosor. A lamb with a rod touches the rock from which another lamb drinks. Again, a lamb with the rod multiplies the loaves; a lamb imposes his foot upon the head of another lamb, while a dove pours down a stream of light upon the latter, signifying the seven-fold gift of the Holy Ghost in the sacrament of Confirmation or of Holy Order. Further on, a lamb approaches reverently to receive the law; and lastly, a lamb with the rod brings forth Lazarus from his tomb. These six subjects prove incontestably the symbolical character of the subjects represented on these sarcophagi, and teach us that, whether in the hand of Moses, or of Peter, or of the Lamb, the divine rod is the power of Christ, by whom the miracles of grace in the sacraments of the Church are still worked.* {Symbolical figures of the Lamb working miracles.}

Our account of the Christian sculptures in the Lateran Museum will not be complete without some notice of the statue of St Hippolytus, which stands at the upper end of the hall, and which is pronounced by Winckelmann and other critics to be the finest known specimen of early Christian sculpture. This statue was discovered, A.D. 1551, when some excavations were being made near the basilica of San Lorenzo *fuori le mura*, and must have stood either in the subterranean cemetery of St Hippolytus, or in a basilica close by. It bears {Statue of St Hippolytus.}

---

* These six subjects, three of which are shown in Fig. 37, are more clearly to be distinguished in Bosio, Rom. Sott., p. 45, than on the sarcophagus itself, which has probably suffered some damage during the last two hundred years.

It is interesting to observe the comparative frequency of the different scriptural subjects introduced into the sculptured sarcophagi. The following list is taken from Burgon's Letters from Rome, Letter xx., with one or two corrections in the description. He counted fifty-five sarco-

every mark of having been executed during the third century, for, though the head and arm are modern restorations, yet the classical dignity of the figure is greatly superior to statues of the age of Constantine; while the *Canon Paschalis*, engraved on one of the sides of the chair in which the saint is seated, would hardly have been considered worthy of commemoration many years after the martyrdom of St Hippolytus. We have no intention of taxing our readers' patience with an account of the long disputes concerning the proper time for the observance of Easter, which occupied so much serious attention during the early ages of the Church. It is well known, however, that the Roman Church always strenuously opposed those who followed the Jewish reckoning, and who, from their keeping Easter on the 14th day of the lunar month, received the name of *Quartodecimans*. Still, during the first and second centuries the Church had, as was natural, adopted the Jewish mode of determining the Paschal full moon; but the blind fury of that unhappy people against Christianity prejudiced the minds of Christians against anything coming from them; and since, at the beginning of the third century, the Church possessed men in no way inferior to the Jewish rabbis in scientific knowphagi, and we have placed side by side with his numbers those which result from an examination of the forty-eight sarcophagi illustrated by Bosio, thirty of which were found in the crypts of the Vatican:—

	Lateran.	Bosio.		Lateran.	Bosio.
History of Jonas,	23	11	Fall of Adam and Eve,	14	10
The Smitten Rock,	21	16	Woman with Issue of Blood,	8	9
Apprehension of St Peter,	20	14	Christ's Entry into Jerusalem,	6	8
Miracle of Loaves,	20	14	The Good Shepherd,	6	9
Giving Sight to Blind,	19	11	Noah in Ark,	5	6
Change of Water into Wine,	16	8	Christ before Pilate,	5	6
Raising of Lazarus,	16	14	Giving of the Law,	4	6
Denial of St Peter,	14	8	Three Children in Fire,	4	3
Daniel in Lion's Den,	14	7	Moses taking off his Shoes,	2	2
Paralytic Healed,	12	7	Elias taken up to Heaven,	2	3
Creation of Eve,	11	2	Nativity, with Ox and Ass,	1	4
Sacrifice of Isaac,	11	9	Crowning with Thorns,	1	1
Adoration of Magi,	11	8			

Mr Burgon, in his contemptuous remarks about the symbolical meaning of these sculptures, seems to show himself entirely ignorant of the method of interpreting Holy Scripture universal among the Fathers of the fourth and fifth centuries, to which these sarcophagi belong.

ledge, it was fitting that the Christian bishops, and especially the Bishop of Rome, should sanction some authoritative method for determining the great Christian festival.

Hippolytus was the first to form a table, in which, by doubling the Greek periods of eight years, he endeavoured, with the help of seven such periods, of sixteen years each, to obtain a formula by which the difference between the lunar and solar years should be corrected, and the true Easter determined for ever. There is, in accordance with this mode of calculation, engraved on the opposite side of the chair to that upon which the *canon* itself is found, a table for 112 years. Unfortunately, St Hippolytus' method laboured under the fatal defect of an error of three days in every sixteen years; and hence the praise lavished upon the first attempt to form an independent Christian calendar died away, and fresh calculations became necessary. We learn this from a work which has been ascribed to St Cyprian, and which bears the date of A.D. 243, and whose author, curiously enough, ascribes St Hippolytus' error of three days to his having calculated from the creation of the world instead of from the 4th day, on which the moon was created! We may therefore conclude that this statue belongs to the early part of the third century, while the errors of Hippolytus' canon still remained unknown, and the renown of its author caused it to be considered a fitting tribute to his memory.

St Hippolytus professes that his table will show Easter in the past as well as in the future. He therefore gives some of the more remarkable Paschal solemnities, such as the Exodus, which he makes out to have taken place on April 2d, or April 5th, if Daniel's computation is to be followed. The Paschal solemnities in the desert, in the time of Joshue, Ezekias, Josias, and Esdras are also determined. The Pasch in the year when Christ was born, and also in that wherein He suffered, are marked as being of the greatest interest to all Christians.

316   *Roma Sotterranea.*

The list of the works of St Hippolytus commences with the titles of two works, of which only the last four letters can now be deciphered. Critics have exercised their ingenuity in supplying the remainder, but no certainty can be arrived at. The Paschal Canon, and other matters inscribed on this statue, are given with explanations in Migne's edition of the works of St Hippolytus, to which we must refer those of our readers who desire to investigate further this interesting monument of early Christian art.

FIG. 38.—*Glass in the Vatican Library*,
Representing Christ between Sts. Peter and Paul; also Christ as the Lamb, and the faithful as Lambs—Jews and Gentiles coming from Jerusalem and Bethlehem (*Becle*) to Mount Sion, whence flow the four Evangelical Streams, united in the Mystical Jordan.

BOOK V.

THE TESTIMONY OF THE CATACOMBS.

CHAPTER I.

THE TESTIMONY OF THE CATACOMBS TO THEIR CHRISTIAN ORIGIN.

IN the preceding chapters our information has been princi- *Scope of this* pally drawn from the historical records which have come *portion of the work.* down to us from antiquity, and of which an account has been given in the second part of the Introduction.* We have also taken our readers into the subterranean cemeteries, and confirmed our historical conclusions by the inscriptions and other monuments still remaining there. An important branch of our subject, however, still remains comparatively untouched, and this is what we may call the Testimony of the Catacombs themselves,—understanding by this expression, not the evidence to be drawn from the dates and names inscribed on the stones and walls, but the conclusions to be deduced from a careful examination of the subterranean galleries, and the method of their construction. This appears at first sight a dry and uninviting subject, but the results are too important to be passed over in silence, and the striking and incontro-

* See page 17.

vertible confirmation which they give to many of our historical conclusions, will amply repay the reader for the pains it will cost him to master the details.

<small>The Catacombs used by none but Christians as burial-places.</small>

The first question which we would ask of these long dark silent subterranean streets of tombs is, whether they are able to afford us any clue as to their own origin. The ignorant assertions of Burnett and Misson do not deserve a serious refutation. The former was foolish enough to publish his opinion that all the tokens of Christianity found in the Catacombs were the forgeries of a few monks in the fourth and fifth centuries, while the latter put forth the no less untenable theory that they were used "as marks of distinction to prevent the graves of the faithful from being confounded with those of the infidels." The exclusive use of the Catacombs by the Christians has now, however, been universally admitted, and the only serious argument that was ever adduced against it, viz., the presence of a few Pagan inscriptions in these Christian cemeteries, has been found to tell in the opposite direction,

<small>Pagan inscriptions accounted for.</small>

for it is now ascertained that in every instance these Pagan inscriptions have some marks which prove that they were not originally intended for the position in which they have been found, but like the stone on which the copy of the inscription to Pope Eusebius was written,* have been appropriated by Christians, and used for their own purposes. It is not enough, however, to establish the exclusively Christian use of the Catacombs as burial-places. We are able also to prove them to have been originally excavated by the Christians for that purpose, and this by the testimony of the Catacombs themselves.

<small>Padre Marchi the first to vindicate the Christian origin of the Catacombs</small>

Until within a very recent period it was the generally received theory that these subterranean excavations had been made by the Pagan Romans in order to extract materials for building; and that the Christians, finding them convenient as places of concealment where their martyred brethren

* See page 171.

Christian Origin of the Catacombs. 319

might rest undisturbed, had taken possession of them, and adapted them by additional excavations to the purposes of burial and worship. This theory was not, as we shall afterwards see, destitute of some apparent support from ancient documents, and was accepted by Baronius, Severano, Aringhi, and other writers upon the subject. Bosio himself is silent upon the origin of the Catacombs, and Boldetti, with all his knowledge acquired by personal observations, only ventures to claim a Christian origin for a few particular cemeteries. Padre Lupi went somewhat farther, and showed that the additions made by the Christian *fossors* exceeded in extent the original works of the Pagan excavators; but Bottari, D'Agincourt, and Raoul-Rochette, all maintained the heathen origin of the Catacombs. Padre Marchi was the first to enunciate the proposition, that the Christians themselves had originated all those subterranean cemeteries which are known by this name. The weight of authority was strong against him, but he defended his proposition by proofs taken not so much from the works of learned authors, as from the cemeteries themselves. His investigations have been continued by the brothers De Rossi, and their patient labours have thrown so much additional light upon the subject, that the Christian origin of the Catacombs may be regarded as now firmly established. In order to understand the proofs of this conclusion, it will be necessary to give a brief notice of the geological strata in which the Catacombs have been excavated, and a portion of the carefully compiled Geological Summary in Murray's "Handbook to Rome," will perhaps be more satisfactory to our readers than any attempt of our own to condense the more diffuse account given by Michele De Rossi.

against a widely-received opinion to the contrary.

"By far the greatest part of the surface of the Roman Campagna, in the environs of the capital, is formed of materials of igneous origin. They may be classed under two heads, very different in their mineralogical characters, as they are in the mode in which they have been deposited, their age, &c.

Volcanic strata of soil around Rome.

The more ancient, which appears to have immediately succeeded the Tertiary marine deposits, or even to have been co-temporaneous with them, and to be the result of submarine volcanic action, consists, in the more immediate vicinity of Rome, and within the city itself, of a red volcanic tufa, formed by an agglomeration of ashes and fragments of pumice :

Tufa litoide. it has been designated by the name of *tufa litoide* by the local geologists: and was, and still is, much used for building purposes. It forms the lower part of most of the Seven Hills on the left bank of the Tiber, constituting the Tarpeian rock beneath the Capitol, the lower portion of the Palatine, Quirinal, Esquiline, and Aventine. .... It is extensively quarried at the foot of Monte Verde, outside the Porta Portese, for building stone..... No trace of the craters which produced this older tufa can now be discovered.

"A certain interval appears to have occurred between the latter deposit and the more modern volcanic rocks of the Campagna, during which the land seems to have been raised, and several parts of it covered with fresh-water lakes or marshes. It is to this period that belong the strata of cinders, ashes, &c., which form the more immediate surface, which are often very regularly stratified, and certain impressions and leaves of land plants, and here and there a bed of calcareous gravel and marls, with land and fresh water shells, and sometimes of fossil bones..... But the greater part of these more recent volcanic rocks have been deposited on dry land; the

Pozzolana. beds are in general horizontal; the deposits of *pozzolana* or volcanic rocks, so extensively used for making mortar, belong

Tufa granulare. to this period of subaërial volcanoes, the red *tufa granulare*, in which the Catacombs or early Christian cemeteries are hollowed out, and probably the more compact varieties of tufa known under the name of *peperino*, quarried at Albano and Marino."*

Such being the nature of the soil in the vicinity of Rome,

* Murray's *Handbook of Rome*, 1868, p. 321.

Christian Origin of the Catacombs.

the confidence of Padre Marchi in the old theory of the Pagan origin of the Catacombs was first shaken by his observing that they were excavated in the *tufa granulare* rather than in any other kind of rock. The *tufa litoide*, called by the ancients *lapis ruber* and *saxum quadratum*, affords numerous examples of ancient quarries, but not one instance of a Catacomb; while the *pozzolana*, esteemed so highly by Vetruvius as fulfilling all the conditions of the best sand for making cement,* and extensively quarried for that purpose, appears to have been carefully avoided by those who originated the Catacombs. The *tufa granulare*, from the quantity of earth which enters into its composition, would never be used for cement when the true *pozzolana* was procurable, while it is far too soft to be of any use as stone for building. Yet it is in this very stratum that have been excavated those vast systems of galleries which we call the Catacombs. The extreme improbability, therefore, of the Pagan Romans having constructed these galleries for no conceivable purpose is the first argument in favour of their Christian origin; for the *tufa granulare*, useless for other purposes, was admirably adapted for the reception of the dead. It is easily worked, of sufficient consistency to admit of being hollowed out into galleries and chambers without at once falling in, and its porous nature causes the water quickly to drain off from it, thus leaving the galleries dry and wholesome, an important consideration when we think of the vast number of dead bodies which once lined the walls of the subterranean cemeteries. Some of the Catacombs have been constructed in a rock still more unserviceable for building purposes than the *tufa granulare;* as, for instance, the Catacomb of San Ponziano on Monte Verde, and that of San Valentino on the Via Flaminia, where the stratum is a mere marine or fluvial deposit, com-

Catacombs excavated in tufa granulare

a proof of their Christian origin.

---

* Vetruvius, Arch. iii. 7, "ut ea sit idonea neque habeat terram commixtam . . . et quæ manu confricata fecerit stridorem erit optima . . . item si in vestimentum candidum ea conjecta fuerit, postea excussa vel icta non inquinaverit neque ibi terra subsiderit, erit idonea."

posed of earth, sand, shells, and pebbles, vegetable and animal fossils, &c., requiring solid substructions of masonry to resist its tendency to fall in. Such excavations could only have been made for the purpose of sepulture, and since the Christians alone used them for that purpose, we conclude that none but the Christians had any part in originating them.

Their general form contrasted with that of the sand-pits another proof,

The manner in which the Catacombs are constructed affords another proof of their exclusively Christian origin; especially when we contrast them either with the *arenifodinæ* or sand-pits, which have been excavated both in ancient and modern times for the purpose of obtaining pozzolana, or with the *lapidicinæ*, as the ancient stone-quarries were called. In both these cases the object has been to extract the largest possible quantity of material with the least possible difficulty. Hence the passages are made as wide as possible, the arch of the roof springing from the floor, thus affording space for carts to be introduced to carry away the sand or stone. The same reason causes the excavators to avoid sharp angles, and to make the passages run in curved lines. Entirely different is the construction of the Catacombs. In them the walls are vertical and the roof is very slightly arched and often quite flat; the passages are narrow, so as rarely to admit of two persons walking abreast; they run generally in straight lines, and they cross each other often at very sharp angles. Only the narrowest kind of hand-carts can be used by those who are now occupied in clearing them out, and hence the slowness and expense of the work. The latter consideration, indeed, might not have weighed with the Pagan Romans, who had an almost unlimited supply of slave-labour; but the comparison of a Catacomb with an undoubted ancient *arenifodina*, such as may easily be made at Santa Agnese, of a portion of which a plan has already been given,* will be more convincing than any description of the great difference between the two kinds of excavation.

There are not, however, wanting instances in which *arenariæ*

* See Fig. 2 at page 29.

Christian Origin of the Catacombs. 323

have actually been converted into Christian cemeteries, and these exceptions, which prove the rule, afford us the most convincing proof of the Christian origin of all the other Catacombs. We have one remarkable instance in a portion of the first floor of the cemetery of St Hermes, in which the form and proportions of the galleries and of the *loculi* do not

which is only strengthened by apparent exceptions to the rule; such as the Cemetery of St Hermes,

FIG. 39.—*Part of Wall of Gallery of St Hermes.*

in appearance differ greatly from the general type; but a closer examination shows that their walls, instead of being cut in the rock, are constructed of masonry. The roof is of tufa, slightly arched, and often sustained by brick-work; the niches of the *loculi* are regularly formed in the two walls, and closed in the usual manner, with the exception of the uppermost range, the slabs at the mouth of which are laid obliquely, as

FIG. 40.—*Section of Gallery in St Hermes.*

in the section above (Fig. 40). The gallery is of the usual height, but when the brick-work is cleared away its breadth is on an average two or three times that of an ordinary Catacomb; the section of the walls and roof forms a tolerably regular semi-ellipse. At the crossing of the galleries the span of the arch becomes greater, and the walls more inclined, and sometimes the roof is supported in the middle by a thick wall containing *loculi*, while the walls are strengthened at the base by brick-work, but contain no tombs. This instance

FIG. 41.—*Section of Gallery supported by Brickwork.*

which show the difficulty of converting an *arenaria* into a Catacomb.

is sufficient to show the alterations necessary in order to convert an *arenaria* into a Christian cemetery; whereas if the theory of Raoul-Rochette were true, we ought to find in the Roman Campagna numbers of subterranean excavations destitute of tombs, with the narrow, straight galleries of the Catacombs. None such have been discovered, and we therefore conclude that the marked contrast between the Catacombs and the *arenariæ* proves that they had a different origin; for, although a Catacomb might easily be so amplified as to resemble an *arenaria*, nothing could convert an *arenaria* into a Catacomb except a process which whould tell its own story as plainly as in the instance just described.

How the theory of their Pagan origin came to be accepted.

It may, however, not unreasonably be asked, if the Catacombs themselves bear so conclusive a testimony to their Christian origin, how came the theory of their having been originally excavated by Pagans to be so generally received by learned men? This question must be satisfactorily answered before our readers can feel confidence in the arguments by

Christian Origin of the Catacombs. 325

which we have proved our case. The fact is, that, as we have already hinted, learned men formed their theory of the origin of the Catacombs rather from a supposed historical tradition than from the examination of the cemeteries themselves. This tradition rested on the words in ancient documents which describe the burial-places of certain martyrs and others as *in arenario*, or *juxta arenarium*, or *in cryptis arenariis*. Thus, it is stated in some copies of the *Liber Pontificalis* that Lucina buried Pope Cornelius in her own property *in crypta juxta cœmeterium Callisti in arenario;* the Acts of Saints Hippolytus, Eusebius, Marcellus, and their companions relate that "St Stephen, the bishop, collected their remains, and buried them on the Via Appia, at the first mile from the city of Rome, in the very *arenarium* in which they were wont to assemble;"* the Acts of Saints Nereus and Achilles tell how "Auspicius carried off their bodies, and buried them in the property of Domitilla *in crypta arenaria*, on the Via Ardeatina;"† the Acts of Saints Marcus and Marcellianus likewise mention those martyrs having been buried "two miles from the city in the place which is called *Ad arenas*, because there were the sand-pits (*cryptæ arenarum*), from which the walls of the city were built;"‡ the Acts of St Susanna represent her as buried *in cœmeterio Alexandri, in arenario in crypta juxta S. Alexandrum*. Other copies have: *juxta corpora SS. Chrysanti et Dariæ via Salaria in arenario;*§ on the same Via Salaria Nova, St Crescentianus, martyr, was buried *in cœmeterio Priscilla in arenario;* ‖ on the Via Labicana, about three miles from Rome, the bodies of the Quatuor Coronati were buried with other saints *in arenario;* ¶ and lastly St Tertullinus "was led out to martyrdom to the second milestone on the Via Latina, and St Stephen buried his body at the same place, *in crypta arenaria.*"** These passages from ancient documents certainly

Passages in ancient records which seem to identify the burial-places of Christian martyrs

---
* See Bosio, Rom. Sott. p. 193. † Ib. p. 192. ‡ Ib. p. 186.
§ Ib. p. 481 ; and Bolland. Acta SS. August. ii. p. 625.
‖ Aringhi, Rom. Sott. tom. ii. p. 219.
¶ Bosio, p. 319. ** Ib. p. 300.

establish a connexion between the *arenariæ* and *some* at least of the Catacombs; and when we recall the passage where Cicero describes the murder of the young Asinius, *in arenarias quasdam*, outside the Esquiline gate,* or the still more famous saying of Nero, when in his last extremity he was urged to conceal himself for a time in these subterranean caverns (*in specum egestæ arenæ*), and he refused to be buried before he was dead (*negavit se vivum sub terram iturum*);† we cease to be surprised at the theory of the Pagan origin of the Catacombs, which appear to be so identified with the ancient sand-pits.

<small>with Pagan sand-pits.</small>

A careful examination, however, of the ancient documents proves that the eight passages quoted above are the *only* instances to be found in which Christian burials are said to have taken place in *arenariæ*. It is true that if we include the accounts of martyrs buried at Nomentum and other places beyond the circle of the Roman Catacombs, a few more examples may be collected. But, confining ourselves within a range of five or six miles from Rome, we find that there is no mention of *arenariæ* in connection with any of the cemeteries on the Via Ostiensis, Portuensis, Aurelia, Cornelia, Triumphalis, Flaminia, Salaria Vetus, Nomentana, or Præ-nestina. On the Via Tiburtina, indeed, Constantine is said to have built a basilica, *in Agro Verano super arenariam cryptam;* and Bosio sees reason to think that the saints buried there were Saints Narcissus and Crescentius, companions in martyrdom with St Lawrence. Thus we have, at the most, nine different sepulchres of martyrs in *arenariæ* or *cryptæ arenariæ*. The latter expression occurs three times, viz., as the locality of the sepulchre of Nereus and Achilles, on the Via Ardeatina; of St Lawrence, on the Via Tiburtina; and of Tertullinus, on the Via Latina. During the recent restoration of the basilica of *San Lorenzo fuori le mura*, there were unusual facilities for examining the rock in the neighbourhood

<small>Examination of these passages, of which there are at most nine in number.</small>

<small>The term *cryptæ arenariæ* does not imply pozzo-lana-pits.</small>

---

* *Pro Cluentio*, 14.   † Sueton. *in Neron*. 48.

of that basilica. Every one might convince himself that it is composed of a material quite different from pozzolana. It is, in fact, what is vulgarly called in Rome *capellaccio*, and is utterly useless for building purposes. And yet in this rock lies the whole Catacomb of St Cyriaca. The same must be said of the rock in which is formed the Cemetery of Domitilla. The sepulchre of Tertullinus is not yet identified, and therefore cannot be examined, but the other two examples are sufficient to prove that the expression *crypta arenaria* merely denotes an excavation made in a sandy kind of rock, and does not necessarily imply the existence of an *arenarium* or sand-pit proper. As to the sepulchre of Saints Marcus and Marcellinus, Padre Marchi justly observes that it is not said that those martyrs were buried *in cryptis arenarum*, but *in loco qui dicitur Ad arenas*,* and, therefore, merely in the neighbourhood of "the pits from which the walls of the city were built."

There remain then five passages in ancient documents which mention martyrs being buried *in arenario*, a term certainly denoting a pozzolana-pit. The first of these, relating to Pope Cornelius, is not found in all the MSS. of the *Liber Pontificalis*, but as there really is a stratum of pozzolana in that Catacomb at a lower level than the stratum in which his crypt was made,† some excavations there may have led later copyists to add the expression *in arenario*, in order, as they probably thought, the more distinctly to identify the spot. Of the four remaining passages, three describe localities which can be identified, and which correspond exactly with the description, for there is in each of them excellent pozzolana precisely at the same level with the galleries of the Catacomb. De Rossi has not yet succeeded in finding any good pozzolana in the cemetery of Marcellinus and Peter, which is supposed by Bosio to be the locality indicated by the fourth

Five remaining passages:—
1. Pope Cornelius;

2. *Quattro Coronati*;

* Compare *Ad Catacumbas*, and similar appellations of places.
† See Map accompanying this volume, E*h*, F*h*.

passage, which describes the burial of the *Quatuor Coronati;* but the artists employed to draw the plan of that Catacomb for Bosio's work seem to have penetrated into a portion of the ancient *arenarium,* for their drawing represents some passages resembling those of pozzolana rather than the galleries of Catacombs, and in their description they speak of "a large grotto without tombs, like a stone quarry;" and again, " a wide place where the tombs have been destroyed to get out the pozzolana."* It will be more satisfactory to our readers if we examine carefully the three passages mentioned above, in order that we may thoroughly satisfy ourselves whether they do in truth prove or disprove the theory to which they apparently gave rise.

3. SS. Chrysanthus and Daria;

First, there is the *arenarium* in which were buried the martyrs Chrysanthus and Daria, on the Via Salaria Nova. The *Liber Pontificalis* states that Pope Adrian I. "restored the basilica of S. Saturninus, on the Via Salaria, together with the cemetery of SS. Chrysanthus and Daria." Now these saints were not only buried *in arenario,* but the Emperor Numerian " ordered them to be led out on the Via Salaria, and put down *in arenario,* .... and there to be both of them blocked up alive with earth and stones." This *arenarium* was identified and described by Bosio and Marangoni; and it may still be observed that, in one part of the Catacomb, the galleries widen out into the form of an *arenarium,* and the *loculi* are diminished in number, so that there are only two tiers of them, one above the other. This has evidently been done in order to avoid weakening the walls, which are sloping and of good pozzolana. In fact, as we pass from the Catacomb into the *arenarium* proper, we find even these attempts to convert the latter into a cemetery disappear, and there are evident traces of the Christians having blocked up the passages in order to prevent access to a region unfitted for sepulture; while in the immediate vicinity of one of

* Bosio, p. 591, D.

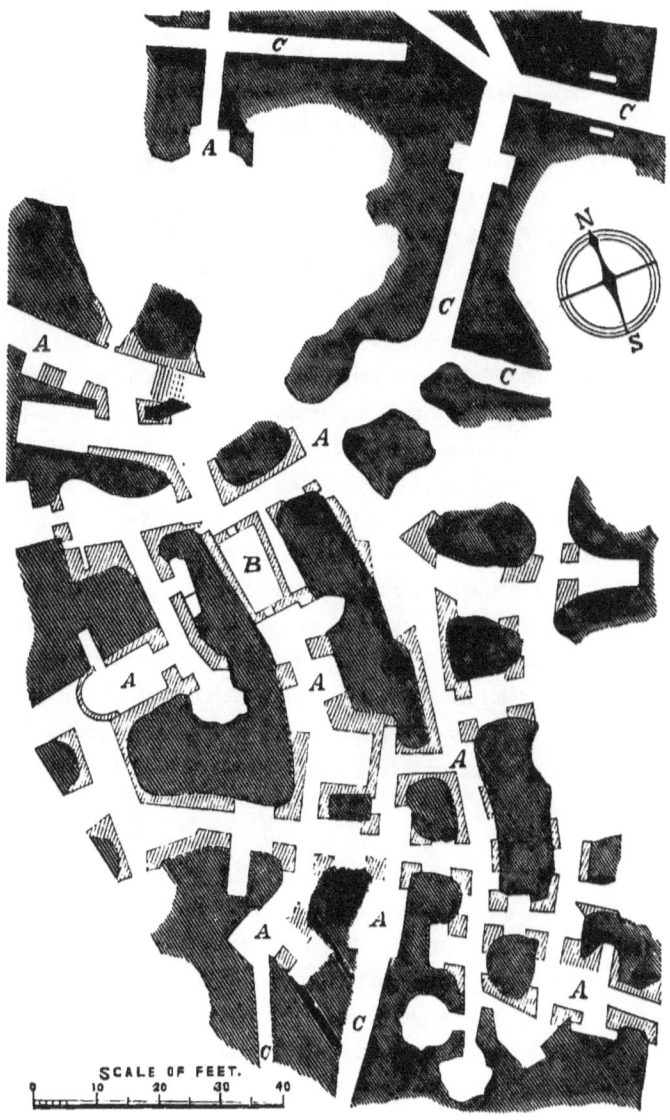

FIG. 42.— *Plan of part of Catacomb of St Priscilla.*

the galleries thus blocked up, a flight of steps leads down to a lower level, where we find a Christian Catacomb of the ordinary type. We have, therefore, here another instance of the Christians having made an attempt, as at St Hermes, to utilise the *arenarium*, but it appears that they found it more convenient to abandon that attempt, and to construct entirely new galleries, even at the cost of descending to a greater depth into the bowels of the earth.

4. S. Crescentianus in cemetery of S. Priscilla;

The second passage to be examined is that which relates how the martyr Crescentianus was buried *in cœmeterio Priscillæ in arenario* on the same Via Salaria Nova. Every one who has visited the central and more ancient part of that Catacomb has remarked how greatly it differs from the usual type. Numerous pillars, of various sizes; long walls of solid masonry, sometimes straight, sometimes broken into angles, both concealing and sustaining the tufa and the tombs in the galleries; the graves often interrupted by pillars of brickwork;—all these peculiarities show the immense labour that was required to convert the original excavation into its present form. The plan on the preceding page will render this more unmistakably evident, for the masonry is represented by light shading, the tufa rock being shaded darkly, so that the original excavation is at once distinguished from the form into which it was afterwards converted. The wide passages of the *arenarium* are to be traced in the portions marked A, while the Catacomb galleries are marked C. The shaft B was originally a pit for extracting pozzolana from the *arenarium*, but was afterwards modified so as to form a large *luminare*. Here, then, is actually a Catacomb having its origin in an *arenarium*, but the examination of its plan is sufficient to prove the impossibility of many of the Christian cemeteries having been so constructed.

5. Saints Hippolytus, Eusebius, &c., on Via Appis.

Lastly, we must examine the passage of the Acts of Saints Hippolytus, Eusebius, Marcellus, and their companions, which relates their burial by Pope St Stephen "on the Via Appia, at the first mile from the city of Rome, in the very *arenarium* in which they were wont to assemble."* De Rossi will not undertake to say that he has identified this *arenarium* with the same certainty as the two just described; but it is a significant fact that one of the largest staircases in the cemetery of St Callixtus leads directly from the surface of the soil to the third *piano* of the Catacomb, which is on the same level with pozzolana pits, and close to the spot where passages connect them with the cemetery. Later excavations have also revealed the existence of a very narrow secret passage leading directly to the sand-pits themselves from the surface of the ground. This staircase stops suddenly short at the roof of the *arenarium*, so that a person descending by it would require a movable ladder, or some other assistance supplied by those below, to enable him to reach the floor.† These facts prove a connexion between the Catacomb and the *arenarium*, which will be more fully examined in our next chapter; and, if De Rossi is right in supposing this *arenarium* to be the one in which Christians were wont to assemble for worship during a time of persecution, its connexion with the Catacomb is sufficient to account for St Stephen being said to have buried the martyrs in *arenario*, when in fact he buried them in the cemetery adjoining.

The examination of these instances, so far from leading us to suppose that an *arenarium* was the ordinary matrix of a Catacomb, suggests the very opposite conclusion, since the difference between the one and the other is so marked as to strike the

These apparent exceptions thus prove the rule.

---

* The ancient Acts quoted by Bosio relate the baptism of Adria, Paulina, Neo, and Maria, and how afterwards these holy women took up their abode with the priest Eusebius, and the deacon Marcellus, and others, in the same crypt where Pope Stephen was concealed, and every day and night they used to persevere in prayer, and fastings, and the voice of psalmody. When St Paulina suffered martyrdom, Hippolytus, a monk, by command of St Stephen, buried her body in the *arenarium* where they used frequently to meet together, and afterwards, Hippolytus and the rest being martyred, their bodies were also buried in the same *arenarium*. —*Bosio*, p. 193.

† A section of this staircase is given in our next chapter. It is marked X^4 in the plans which illustrate that chapter.

most ordinary observer, and yet these and two others are all the examples of their connexion which have been noticed by the explorers of the last three hundred years.* We argue, therefore, thus :—The ancient documents in four or five passages seem to speak as though the martyrs had been buried in sand-pits. In five cemeteries out of twenty-five or thirty, an *arenarium* is found more or less closely connected with the cemetery, and of these, three are discovered to be identical with three of those mentioned in the ancient records. We consequently conclude that what is mentioned so seldom by ancient writers, and found so seldom by modern explorers, could not have been the normal condition of things, but, on the contrary, that these instances were deemed worthy of special mention as being exceptions to the general rule, and thus these examples form one of the most convincing proofs of the Christian origin of the Catacombs generally.

* In fact, what Bosio calls the "*singularity*" of the portion of the cemetery of St Priscilla, and of that near St Saturninus described above, has been commented upon by nearly every writer on the subject, from Bosio's time to the present day.

FIG. 43.—*Gilded Glass in the Louvre Collection representing St Callixtus.*

CHAPTER II.

MODE OF THEIR CONSTRUCTION AND DEVELOPMENT.

WE have seen how the Catacombs bear witness to their Christian origin, and furnish a reply to the difficulties that have been urged against this now established fact. It remains for us to examine them still more carefully, and to extract from them, if possible, an account of the mode of their construction, the successive additions and modifications which they received from time to time, the traces to be found in them of the relations in which these Christian cemeteries stood at various periods to the Roman laws, and of the condition of the Roman Church in times of persecution and of peace. We have already traced these various relations in our historical chapters, and if we find those observations borne out by the testimony of the Catacombs themselves, we shall be repaid for having mastered the somewhat dry and uninviting portion of our subject which now lies before us, for we shall have examined an independent and perfectly unexceptionable witness to the truth. *Scope of this chapter.*

We have already noticed some of the circumstances which determined the locality of the early Christian cemeteries.* The laws obliged them to be outside the walls, and convenience required that they should not be too far away from the city. The ancient documents give us a radius of from one to three miles from the wall of Servius Tullius as the zone within which most of the cemeteries were situated, and it is precisely *Locality of Christian cemeteries. Distance from the city.*

* See page 56.

within this zone that we see, in the present day the entrances to all the principal Catacombs. Between the third and fifth mile from the walls, no Christian sepulchre has been found; at the sixth only one, that of St Alexander; while beyond the seventh mile from the city, tombs are again met with, but these belong rather to the towns and villages of the Campagna than to Rome itself.

On high ground.

A further cause which determined the situation of the Christian cemeteries was the geological condition of the soil within the limits stated above. Had they been excavated in deep valleys, they would have been constantly exposed to the danger of being flooded by the neighbouring streams, or at any rate by the filtration of water, which, besides impeding access to the cemeteries, would have greatly accelerated the putrefaction of the bodies, and corrupted the air, in spite of the careful closing of the *loculi*. The cemetery of Castulo, on the Via Labicana, is an instance of this. Being in a somewhat low situation, it is now quite inaccessible, from the water and the clay with which the galleries are filled, and it bears signs of having been from the first an exceptional excavation. The pains taken by St Damasus to prevent the water damaging the tomb of St Peter on the Vatican are commemorated in his usual manner :—

> " Cingebant latices Montem, teneroque meatu
> Corpora multorum cineres atque ossa rigabant.
> Non tulit hoc Damasus, communi lege sepultos
> Post requiem tristes iterum persolvere pœnas.
> Protinus aggressus magnum superare laborem,
> Aggeris immensi dejecit culmina Montis.
> Intima sollicite scrutatus viscera terræ,
> Siccavit totum quidquid madefecerat humor,
> Invenit Fontem, præbet qui dona salutis.
> Hæc curavit Mercurius Levita Fidelis."

" The waters used to surround the hill, and with their gentle flowing used to drench the bodies, ashes, and bones of many [saints]. Damasus did not suffer this [to go on],—that those buried after the law common to all should be disturbed in their rest, and again suffer sad punishment. So at once he set himself to conquer the formidable difficulty, and cut away the ridge of an immense bank of the hill. He diligently dived into the

Mode of Construction and Development. 335

very bowels of the earth, and drained the whole of that which the damp had moistened. He discovered the spring, which [now in the baptismal font] conveys the gifts of salvation. Mercurius, his faithful deacon, had charge of these works."

The Christian cemeteries were thus restricted to the high ground, and there in fact we find them; and this circumstance alone was sufficient to prevent any line of communication having existed, either between the various Catacombs, or between them and the churches within the city. We have already remarked how the Christian cemeteries were almost always excavated in the *tufa granulare*, rather than in any other stratum of rock. Another characteristic, depending to a certain extent upon the geological formation, is, that the different levels, or *piani* of excavation in the same cemetery, are quite distinct from each other. Hardly ever does a gallery lead gradually down from a higher to a lower level; the descent is made by a flight of steps. The preservation of the horizontal plane throughout each *piano* was a wise precaution against danger to the roof or to the floor of the galleries and chambers, for, if the horizontal plane had been departed from, it would have been almost impossible for the *fossors*, unaided by scientific instruments, to have avoided running one gallery into another. An accident of this kind on the same plane would cause but little damage, but the safety of a whole chamber, or even of a whole gallery, would have been imperilled by the excavation of another, either close above or close below it. Hence the principal levels are separated by a very wide interval, and if between them small galleries are sometimes found, these are a later work of very limited extent, and resemble those little rooms which are to be seen between the first and second stories of large houses in Rome, and which are called *mezzanini*.

The section on the next page will convey a general idea of the depth below the surface at which the different *piani* are excavated. It is a section of the crypt of St Lucina, imme-

Cemeteries in tufa granulare:

the galleries of each piano horizontal.

Different piani one below another.

diately beneath the vast ruined monument already described.* The floor of the gallery Φ is not more than twenty feet below the surface of the soil, and in some places not above ten; so that had it been continued on the same plane, it must have run out into the open air, in consequence of the slope of the hill. This *piano* is consequently very small, and it is in fact the only

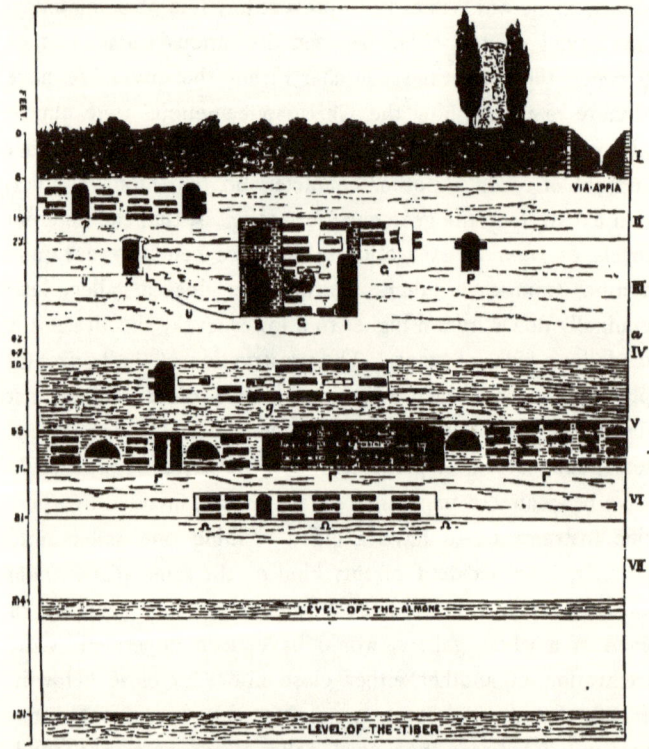

FIG. 44.—*Section of the Cemetery of St. Callixtus.*

specimen of a gallery being excavated so near the surface. The stratum in which this gallery was formed is composed of a friable *tufa granulare*, of a gray colour, and full of amphigene, a kind of garnet, and here and there black augite. This is marked II.; and the stratum I. above it is made up of earth and stones, ruins of ancient monuments, and other mate-

Geological strata.

* See page 123.

Mode of Construction and Development. 337

rials. Stratum III. is composed of a less solid kind of tufa without those crystals, and this was the favourite stratum of the Christian *fossors*, in which we find the most ancient and most important *piano* of galleries. The section shows how P, X, and U were excavated, with the roof of those galleries coinciding with the junction of this with the stratum above. By this means the *fossors* secured a more solid kind of rock for the ceiling, and the difference of colour, and the sparkling of the crystals in the rock which forms the roof, when compared with that in which the *loculi* are cut, frequently arrests the attention of those who visit this Catacomb. About the point *a*, this stratum insensibly merges into the pozzolana proper, although between them there is sometimes a thin stratum of stones and cinders in fine volcanic sand, with crystals and bits of mica. This occasionally has become solidified by the action of water into *tufa litoide*. Stratum V. is pozzolana proper, and here a low and narrow gallery has been excavated, marked *g* in the section, which would terminate here if it were simply a vertical section of the galleries beneath this ruined monument. De Rossi, from whose work this (Fig. 44) is copied, has, however, added below the line which crosses stratum V., a section of another portion of the Catacomb of St Callixtus, the principal *piano* of which is very nearly of the same level with U and X the principal *piano* here, but whose position may be found on De Rossi's map by the reference L *c*, 1, 2, and I *b*, 1.* By this means we have a comparative view of another lower *piano* in the pozzolana, marked Γ Γ Γ; and in stratum VI., which is composed of *tufa granulare* again, we have a still lower gallery, Ω Ω Ω, so deep that the air becomes less easy to breathe, and a limit is put to the excavation by the water which almost always inundates the gallery at this level. The rock VII. beneath this is impervious to water, and has not been examined. The levels of the Tiber, and of a little stream

* These are situated too far to the north to be included in the map accompanying this volume.

which crosses the Via Appia, called the Almone, are given from Father Secchi's measurements of the trigonometrical base on the Via Appia.

Formation of the Catacomb of St Callixtus. Having obtained a general idea of the mode in which the various *piani* of galleries were constructed, we may proceed to inquire into the manner in which the galleries and chambers on the same *piano* were formed; and as the necropolis of St Callixtus is the only Catacomb of which a full and scientifically accurate plan has yet been published, we will confine our observations to this great cemetery. The first impression conveyed by a glance at the map accompanying this volume, is that of an inextricable confusion; but, as we have already remarked, a more careful examination, aided by the various colours which distinguish different parts of the map, enables us to recognise a certain order in the disposition of the galleries within each of these divisions, so that we are prepared to acquiesce in Michele De Rossi's assurance that each of these *Distinct areæ.* portions originally formed a separate cemetery, the *area* of which was defined and protected by the Roman law. The measurements of these *areæ*, reduced to Roman feet, singularly confirm this observation, since it can hardly be an accident that they should form such round numbers as 100, 125, 150, 180, and 250 feet. But the fact is put beyond all reasonable doubt by a minute examination of the galleries themselves, and of the points at which those of one *area* now communicate with those of another. It would be impossible for us, in a work of this size, to follow De Rossi through his careful analysis of each gallery and chamber, and almost of every tomb, by which he demonstrates the truth of his conclusion; and we shall therefore content ourselves with the results of De *Area of St Cecilia and the Popes.* Rossi's examination of a single *area*, for the minute analysis of which we must refer our readers to a separate chapter. We shall select the *area* which includes the tombs of the Popes and of St Cecilia, which have been already described, and which history teaches us to regard as the most important of

Mode of Construction and Development. 339

all the ancient cemeteries, being in fact the *cœmeterium* administered by the Pope's archdeacon. It would, of course, be unfair to conclude that the architectural characteristics of this *area*, and its successive developments, formed a type which was universally followed in the construction of other cemeteries. The circumstances of the soil, the wealth of the proprietor, or the architectural notions of the persons who superintended the excavation, doubtless varied in the different Catacombs. Nevertheless, since the laws affected all Christian cemeteries alike, and the necessities for increased accommodation or for concealment came at the same periods upon the whole Christian population, the account which we are about to give of this great and important cemetery, will enable us to trace the leading features of the changes and successive developments of other Catacombs.

The great necropolis, which forms what is called the Catacomb of St Callixtus, is bounded by the Via Appia and the Via Ardeatina, and the tract of ground between these two public ways was anciently traversed by two small cross roads which connected them, and which we will call Via Appio-Ardeatina. It will be seen by the map that most of the staircases which led into the hypogæa were either parallel or at right angles to one or other of these roads, and that the different *areæ* into which the necropolis is divided, each with its own staircase, have a clearly-defined frontage along them. Confining our attention to the *area* of St Cecilia (marked III. in the map), we will proceed to trace its architectural development from its first construction to its latest transformation. *Public and private roads.*

A plot of ground, measuring 250 Roman feet along the small cross-road, and extending back 100 feet *in agro*, was secured by its Christian proprietor as a burial-place with the usual legal formalities. The plan of the excavation was then determined, and, as occasion required, was carried out in the manner indicated in Fig. 45, which is drawn on a scale of $\frac{1}{1000}$. *First period of excavation.*

The two parallel galleries, A and B, each with its staircase communicating with the surface, appear to have been excavated about the same time, and extended the full length of the *area*. The gallery C connecting them appears from the marks of the pickaxe in its walls to have been commenced from the corner AC. The ambulacra, A and B, were also united by the two

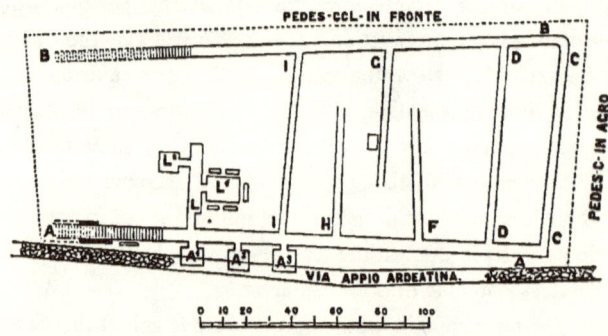

FIG. 45.—*First Period of Excavation.*

other galleries D and I; and the original design appears likewise to have provided for the passages F, G, H, which, however, were not, during this first period, completed to their full extent. The gallery I, with the papal crypt L^1, and the chamber L^2, belong to this period, as also do the *cubicula* A^1, A^2, A^3, whose painted walls have been described in a former chapter.*

How it can be distinguished. Our readers will here fairly ask, upon what grounds do we thus positively assert that such and such a gallery belongs to this or that period of excavation, and pretend to give the exact dimensions of the *area* as gravely as though we were in possession of the original legal documents which defined them. To the latter question we reply, that this *area* is at once marked off from the adjacent *areæ* of the Catacomb by its floor being about five feet lower in level than theirs. With respect to the period in which the different galleries were

* Chapter VI. of Book IV.

Mode of Construction and Development. 341

formed, it may certainly be taken as an axiom, that when the *loculi* in the walls of an *ambulacrum* are broken through in order to afford an entrance into a gallery, this portion of the gallery at least is of a later date than the ambulacrum into which it enters, and did not form part of its original plan. Thus, in Fig. 46, which represents the outside wall of the gallery C, the entrances to C^1 and C^2 have been broken through three or four *loculi*, which have been strengthened afterwards by masonry. It is therefore evident that the

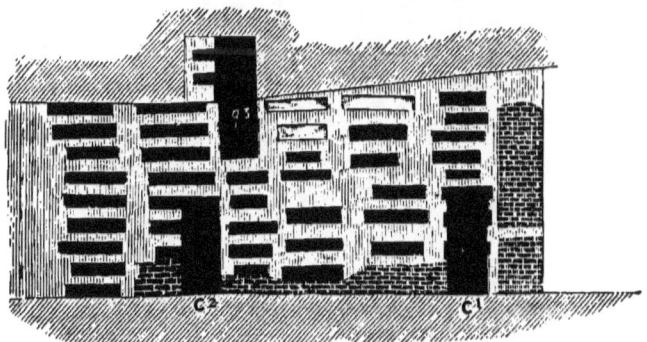

FIG 46.—*Outer Wall of Ambulacrum C.*

galleries C^1 and C^2 were not contemplated in the original plan of the gallery C, and were constructed at a much later date. This observation, however, only affects the outside walls of B and C, and enables us to exclude from the original plan all those passages which now branch out from them; but it does not account for our representing F and H as stopping short of B, and G, in the same manner, as not having originally extended so far as to fall into A. Our grounds for so representing these galleries will appear from an examination of the woodcut on the next page, which gives the elevation of the whole of the inner or left-hand wall of the *ambulacrum* A, as it exists at the present day, and shows the relative sizes and positions of the entrances into the cross galleries D, E, F, G, H, I, and L. Now it is obvious that the entrance D could never have been constructed of the height of 15 feet, which it

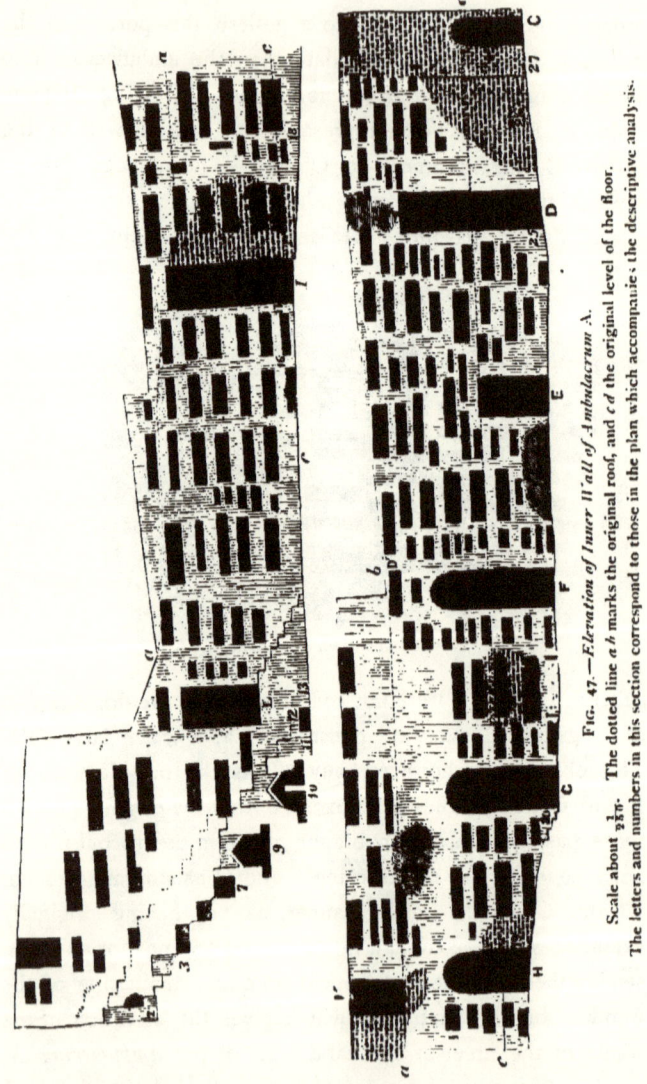

FIG. 47.—*Elevation of Inner Wall of Ambulacrum* A. Scale about 1/80. The dotted line *a b* marks the original roof, and *c d* the original level of the floor. The letters and numbers in this section correspond to those in the plan which accompanies the descriptive analysis.

now reaches, and it can be proved that the original level of the floor of the *ambulacrum* must have been that indicated by

Mode of Construction and Development. 343

the dotted line *cd*. This level would give the entrance to D a height of about 7 feet, that to F a somewhat lower elevation, but still sufficient for practical purposes; while the entrance to G, being yet lower, was in all probability not excavated until the floor of the *ambulacrum* A had been lowered, and the gallery E could not possibly have been constructed until after that had been done. A similar examination of B would prove in like manner that F and H did not fall into that *ambulacrum* until after its floor had been lowered; but we have said enough to show that our plan has not been arbitrarily drawn, and for further details we must refer our readers to the descriptive analysis.

The lowering of the floor of the galleries marks what we may call the second period of excavation. The necessity of providing more space for graves, and the confidence in the consistency of the rock which practice had given the *fossors*, led them to adopt this method of enlarging the cemetery. They appear to have commenced with the *ambulacrum* B, and to have continued the work along C until they reached A. In this latter gallery, however, the change of level was by no means uniform, and was never carried out to the extent contemplated when the chambers A^4, A^5, A^6, were constructed.

Second period —lowering the floor of the galleries.

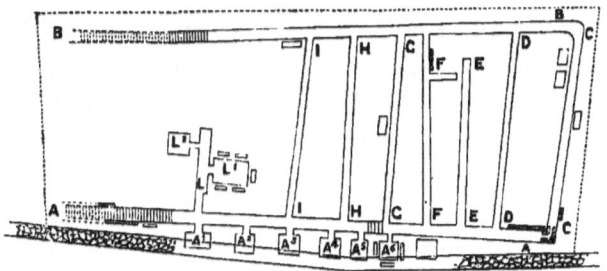

FIG. 48.—*Second Period of Excavation.*

These *cubicula* were evidently excavated in anticipation of a much greater depression of the floor of the *ambulacrum*, for we now enter them by descending some steps, whereas we have to ascend in order to reach A^2 and A^3 from the gallery which is there at its original level. A reasonable explanation of this variation is, that the *fossors* had presumed too much upon the strength of the rock, and finding themselves obliged to support the wall by the mass of brickwork which now forms the corner 27 C,* they deemed it more prudent to abandon the design of reducing the whole gallery to the same level with B and C. This work, together with the completion of the galleries F, G, and H, and the construction of a new one E, marks the termination of the second period of excavation, when the plan of the cemetery must have been such as it is represented in Fig. 48.

Third period. We now come to a third period in the construction of this cemetery. The further enlargement of the *ambulacra* having proved dangerous, the *fossors* were compelled to attempt the construction of another system of galleries at a lower level. In order not to endanger the existing hypogeum it was necessary to go to a considerable depth, and we find a staircase leading from the cross gallery H, and consisting of thirty-four steps. They had hardly, however, penetrated below the former level, when they found that they had passed through the *tufa granulare*, and were in a stratum of very friable pozzolana. The very walls of the staircase had to be protected with brickwork; and, at length, finding it impossible to get out of this stratum, they pushed a narrow passage in a horizontal direction, which is represented in Fig. 49 as H^2; but, not meeting with any kind of rock adapted for their purpose, they abandoned the design, and the few *loculi* constructed here are formed entirely of brickwork. We have already remarked how this and other similarly fruitless attempts to excavate sepulchral galleries in the pozzolana go to prove the exclusively Christian origin of the Catacombs. The tiles used in this staircase, and the galleries immediately adjacent, all bear the stamp of the imperial brick-kilns of Marcus Aurelius,

Attempt to make a lower *piano*

* See Fig. 47.

Mode of Construction and Development. 345

and must, therefore, have been made between A.D. 161 and about A.D. 170. 180. It is true that we cannot from this circumstance alone determine positively the date of the work; but it is unlikely that *all* the bricks of a building should bear the same date, if the building itself had been constructed at a period far removed from the time of their manufacture. If this be admitted, we have a proof of this cemetery having been in use

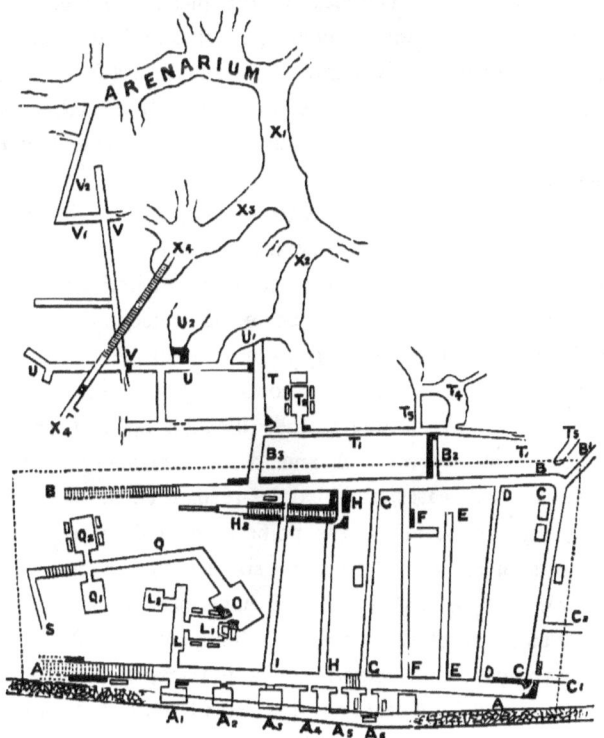

FIG. 49 — *Third Period. Connexion with Arenarium.*

for a considerable time before A.D. 197, when it was committed by Pope Zephyrinus to his deacon Callixtus.

It was during this period that an alteration was made at the farther end of the papal crypt L1, in order to form a passage into O, the crypt where St Cecilia was buried near to the

Construction of crypt of St Cecilia.

tombs of the Popes. This crypt bears evident marks of having been originally of much smaller dimensions than at present, and was probably of the form represented in the plan, in which we also see a gallery Q, and two *cubicula* Q_1, and Q_2, the entrance to which was originally through the crypt of St Cecilia. All the chambers and galleries, whose architectural history we have hitherto been tracing, are distinguished by the fineness and whiteness of the plaster on their walls, especially in the more ancient portions, and also by the absence of *arcosolia*. The graves are simple *loculi;* or when, as in the instances distinguished on the plan by a small oblong, they are table-tombs,* they are always *loculi a mensa* and not *arcosolia*.

Necessity for concealment.

Our readers will not have forgotten that, towards the middle of the third century, the Christians began to be disturbed in the hitherto peaceful possession of their cemeteries.† It was no longer possible for them to claim the protection of the law, and hence it became necessary to provide for the preservation of the tombs of the saints by concealing their entrance from public view. Accordingly, they blocked up and partially destroyed the staircases A and B. The evidences of this remain in both cases, and may be recognised in the section of A, Fig. 47, where, at the point numbered 11, we see the ancient staircase stop short about six feet from the floor, while the tombs, 7, 9, 10, could only have been excavated after

Cemetery connected with arenarium.

the demolition of the staircase. The entrance B was still more completely destroyed, and a passage, B^3, was opened and supported by masonry in the outside wall of the *ambulacrum*, in order to enable the Christians to enter their cemetery through an *arenarium*, $X_1 X_2 X_3$, which was situated in convenient proximity. We see from the plan that there were several entrances from the *arenarium*, some of which have been closed with masonry. These various passages provided means of escape even when their enemies had tracked the

* See Figs. 4 and 5, page 30.   See pp. 54-88.

Mode of Construction and Development. 347

Christians into the Catacomb itself; and, while the satellites of the tyrant, led perhaps by some traitor, were penetrating into the cemetery by one passage, the faithful, only separated from them by a few feet of rock, might be silently passing out at another. Even when the Pagans had set guards at all the entrances into the *arenarium*, the Christians had still a way of escape through an exceedingly narrow and steep staircase, which leads directly from the *arenarium* to the open air. This staircase, marked X4 in Fig. 49, to which allusion has already been made,* and of which a section is given in Fig. 50, was clearly never intended to reach farther than the roof

Secret staircase.

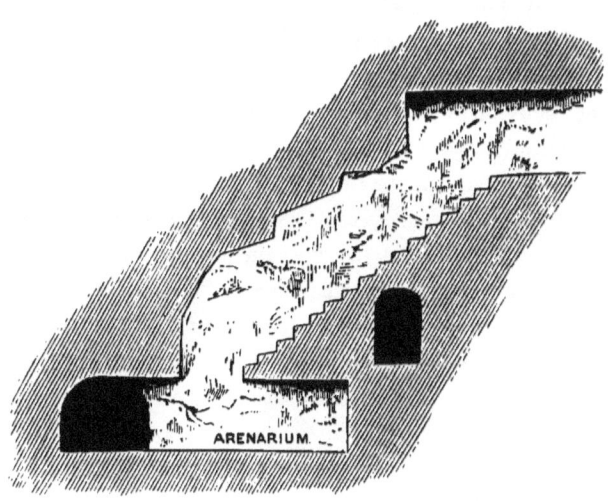

FIG. 50.—*Secret Staircase into Arenarium.*

of the *arenarium*, and must have been useless either for ingress or egress, except to those who had friends below to assist them with a movable ladder, or some other means of connecting the lowest step with the ground. In none of the galleries uniting the cemetery with the *arenarium* do we meet with *arcosolia*, the introduction of which we have already noticed as a sign of a later period than we have as yet reached.

* *Supra*, p. 331. It is marked Ac^2 on the large map.

A second *area* incorporated with the original cemetery.

We have seen how the original limits of the *area* were transgressed, in order to put the cemetery in communication with the *arenarium*. Indeed, the legal protection being removed, there was no longer any reason for observing the legal limits; and, since the adjacent *areæ* on either side of the little crossroad appear to have been in the possession of Christians, this cemetery, which was, as we have seen in other parts of this work, the most important of all that belonged to the Roman Church, was enlarged by the addition of other *areæ*, which were so connected with it as to form one necropolis. The first *area* thus added was that on the opposite side of the Via Appio-Ardeatina, marked V on the large map. The plan opposite, which is drawn on a scale of $\frac{1}{500}$, being double the size of those previously given, represents this *area* in its present condition, with its dimensions determined partly by the gallery S^1, viz., 150 by 125 Roman feet. At first it was connected with our cemetery by the gallery S, but when the steps, of which traces still remain, leading from Q into the latter gallery were destroyed by subsequent works, a new entrance was effected through the chamber A^1 into *a*, which had been the main *ambulacrum* of this second *area*. The most striking peculiarity of the latter is the group of large chambers, a^2, a^3, a^4, a^5, a^6, and a^7, situated opposite to each other on either side of the *ambulacrum*. These evidently formed the earliest and most important part of this hypogeum; and, since the *arcosolia* which they now contain are coated with a plaster of an inferior kind to that which covers their walls, we may safely adopt De Rossi's opinion that these *cubicula* were not originally intended for sepulchral crypts at all, but for wine-stores. In times of danger, the Christian proprietor of the vineyard above put them at the disposal of the Church for places of assembly, the original entrance being turned into a *luminare*, and they were then fitted with marble benches, which still remain, and lighted by wide *luminaria*.* When once connected with

Characteristics of this second *area*.

* See the illustration, Fig. 6, p. 31, which represents a similar arrangement.

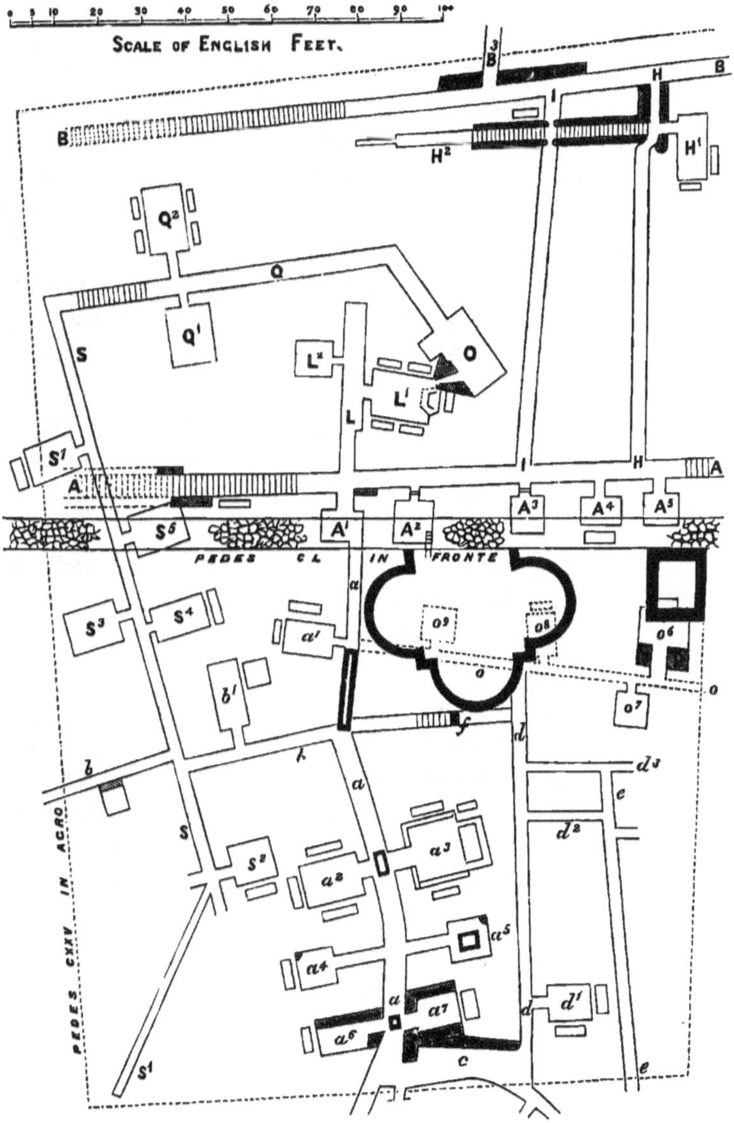

Mode of Construction and Development. 349

FIG. 51.—*Fourth Period. Union with a Second Area.*

N.B.—The shaded parts represent masonry below ground. The black parts represent two buildings on the Via Appio-Ardeatina, and *luminaria*. The *cubiculum* a^3 contains the sarcophagus of St Melchiades. For description, see Note G on Atlas.

the cemetery by the galleries S and *b*, the *area* gradually became intersected by galleries, and filled with *loculi*, and the frequent occurrence of *arcosolia* in both galleries and chambers oblige us to refer the construction of these to a later date than the third period of excavation. De Rossi sees sufficient grounds for supposing that the three-apsed building, situated nearly in the middle of the frontage of the *area*, is one of the *fabricæ* constructed by St Fabian.*

Fourth period. Arcosolia. The fourth period in the architectural history of this cemetery is marked by the appearance of *arcosolia*, which are sometimes found adorned with slabs of marble. The chambers, H^1, P^1, and Q^3†, are thus identified with this period, and the formation of Q^4, with its *arcosolia* and *luminare*, necessitated the demolition of the steps which led from Q up into the gallery S. From what has been already said of the second *area*, it is evident that many of the passages and chambers in it belong to this period, for they abound in *arcosolia*, and many of the *cubicula* are adorned both with paintings and marble, which are never found together in earlier constructions.

Fifth period. Galleries filled with earth. We now approach an epoch which has left its traces in almost every portion of Roma Sotterranea. History has informed us that in the last terrible persecution which the Church endured under Diocletian, not only were the faithful forbidden to enter the cemeteries, and hunted out when they evaded the tyrannical edict, but the cemeteries themselves were confiscated, and handed over to the possession of heathen.‡ In order to prevent the profanation of the sacred sepulchres, the Christians had recourse to an expedient, the labour and expense of which proves its extreme necessity. They filled up with earth all the principal galleries, and thus rendered the cemeteries inaccessible either to friend or foe.

Evidence of this. The evidence of this extraordinary fact is deduced, not only

---

* See p. 86.   † See Fig. 52, which illustrates the fifth period.
‡ See above, p. 90.

Mode of Construction and Development. 351

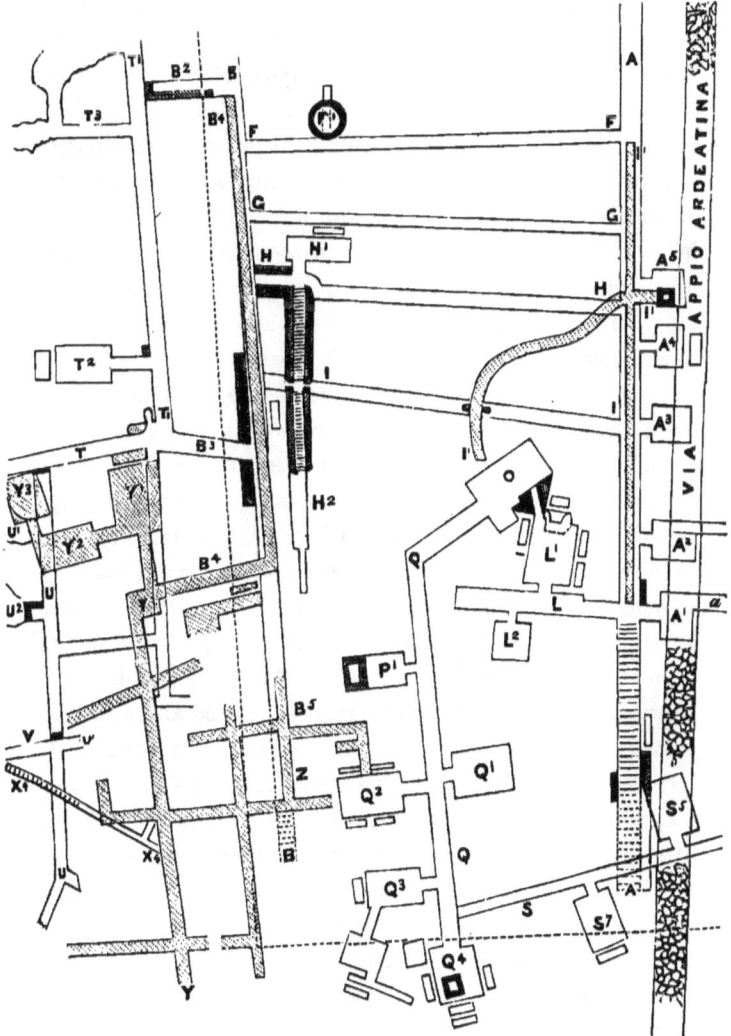

FIG. 52.—*Fifth Period. Galleries made when the ancient ones were filled with earth.*

N.B.—These galleries are distinguished by the light shading. Brickwork is denoted by darker shading. *Luminaria* by black squares. F¹ is a well which still contains water.

from the condition in which most of the Catacombs are found at the present day,* but, still more convincingly, from the discovery of a series of galleries, the floor of which in many parts must have been the surface of the earth with which the older galleries had been thus filled. Fig. 52 is a plan of part of the cemetery whose history we are tracing, and in it these galleries are represented with a light shading to distinguish them from those whose direction they sometimes follow. Thus, along A runs the narrow gallery I^1, one branch from which crosses H and I in an irregular curve, while the other terminates in a shaft immediately above A^5. Along B runs a similar gallery, B^4, which opens into Y, and the *cubicula*, Y^1, Y^2, and Y^3. B^5 and Z are excavated at a higher level, and have no connexion with the more ancient *ambulacra*. We shall confine our remarks to the little gallery I^1, and we must refer the reader back to the elevation, in Fig. 47, of the wall of A. The dotted line, $a\,b$, was stated to have been the original line of the roof of the *ambulacrum*, and it is evident that the *loculi* above that line could never have been constructed while the floor of A was at its present level, or even at its more ancient level marked by the dotted line $c\,d$. Moreover, the doorway which may be noticed above the entrance to H, shows that $a\,b$ was the level of the floor of the gallery in whose wall that doorway was opened. This will be more clear from the opposite Fig. 53, which is a transverse section of A at the point where H falls into it. Here we can observe the difference in width between the original *ambulacrum* and the gallery I^1, cut through its roof, and now destitute of any floor. The latter gallery could only have been made at a time when A was filled up with earth, and it was only by means of this artificial floor that Pomponio Leto and his companions were able to write their names on the ceiling of

* The great work of the Commission of Sacred Archæology is the removal of this earth, which, except in the important crypts cleared by St Damasus, conceals the galleries now as effectually as in the year A.D. 303.

Mode of Construction and Development. 353

this narrow gallery, where they now appear twenty feet from the ground. Fig. 53 also gives us a longitudinal section of the branches of I¹, which crossed that gallery a little above the roof of H. A bridge of brickwork has recently been

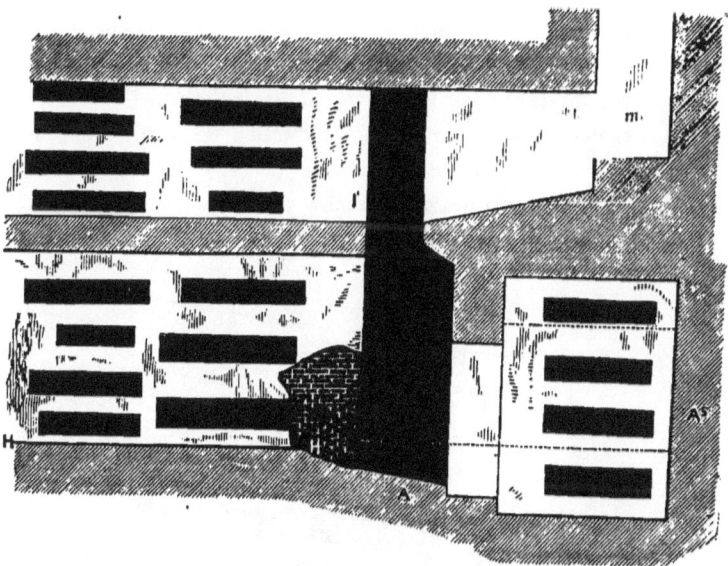

FIG. 53.—*Section of Galleries A and H, and of* I¹.

thrown across the *ambulacrum* to supply the place of the earth which has been removed, but it is worthy of notice that I¹ does not break through the roof of H, nor into the chamber A⁵, which it could hardly have failed to do, unless those excavations had been filled with earth when I¹ was in use.*

This earthing-up of the galleries marks a fifth period in the history of our cemetery, to which we may, without hesitation, assign the date of the Diocletian persecution, A.D. 303.

A sixth period commences with the cessation of persecution,

* Fig. 53 also illustrates our remarks upon the depression of the original level of A, which is now entered from H by a sharp incline. That it was not lowered, however, so much as had been anticipated, appears from the floor of A⁵ being considerably below the present level of A, from which it is entered by steps.

Z

Sixth period. Peace of the Church.
Excavation of small galleries.

when the faithful eagerly sought access to the tombs of the saints. The staircase A was re opened and restored, although at a somewhat higher level, shown by the dotted lines in Fig. 47, and thus an entrance was effected into the crypts of the Popes and of St Cecilia. The earth, however, was not removed from other less remarkable portions of the cemetery, and hence it became possible to excavate the little galleries just described. An inscription in one of them bears the date, A.D. 321; the shafts (as *m* in Fig. 53) for extracting the earth prove them to have been made in a time of peace, while the inscriptions and other characteristics show them to have belonged to a period anterior to the age of St Damasus.

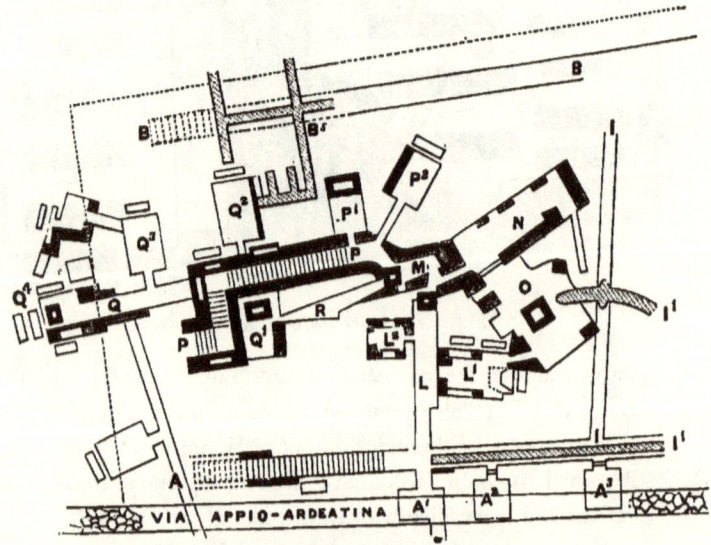

FIG. 54.—*Last Period. Works of St Damasus.*

N.B.—The *luminaria* and masonry, which reaches the surface, are represented black. Subterranean masonry by daik shading. Galleries of sixth period by lighter shading.

Last period. Works of St Damasus.

The last epoch in the architectural development of the subterranean cemeteries is marked by the extensive alterations of the indefatigable Pope Damasus. The restored staircase A proved insufficient for the crowd of pilgrims who came from

Mode of Construction and Development. 355

all parts of the world to satisfy their devotion at the tombs of the martyrs. St Damasus therefore constructed the staircase by which we now descend directly to the crypts of the Popes and St Cecilia. It is marked P in the accompanying plan, from which it will be seen that it occupies a large portion of the gallery Q. In fact, the brickwork which sustains it blocked up some of the *cubicula*, and reduced the dimensions of others. The raising of the floor and ceiling of the chamber A^1, and the passage through it into the second *area*, probably belongs to this period; and also the chamber P^2, and the vestibule M, with its *luminare*, and passage R, leading to Q^1, of which the former entrance had been stopped up. The enlargement of the crypt of St Cecilia and its *luminare*, and the adornment and lighting of the papal crypt, which could not be enlarged without "disturbing the ashes of the saints," were certainly carried out under the special direction of St Damasus.

We have confined our attention to the successive developments of this one *area*, and therefore have not alluded to a third *area* * intimately connected with the second *area* by the *ambulacrum* o,† which is continued throughout its entire length. The dimensions of this third *area* are exactly the same as that of the second, and its architectural characteristics prove it to have been not of an earlier, and probably of a later date. The *arcosolium* appears frequently, and the *luminare*, but the *loculo a mensa* never. At the same time the disguised figure of the Cross, and the double, and often triple chambers for purposes of sacred assembly, prove it to have been occupied before the age of persecution had ceased. In fact, the dated inscriptions of this *area* (among which is the celebrated one of the Deacon Severus) range from the latter part of the third century to the tenth year of the fourth.

A glance at the large map shows how this last *area* is connected with the cemetery of St Soteris, comprising the four

A third *area*.

Other *areæ*.

* Marked VI. in the large map. † See Fig. 51.

areæ VII. VIII. IX. X., which were once, in all probability, separate cemeteries, and the peculiarities of which have been noticed in a previous chapter.*

Labyrinth connecting the different *areæ*. We have thus traced the successive development of the most important group of sepulchral galleries in the Catacomb of St Callixtus, from its first commencement as a private cemetery, to its final embellishment by St Damasus as the centre of the vast necropolis with which, in course of time, it had become united. We have also called our readers' attention to the striking manner in which the most remarkable facts of the history of the Catacombs, already deduced from documentary sources, have been at each successive period confirmed and illustrated by the testimony of the Catacombs themselves, as represented by this particular cemetery which we have examined. This testimony would be still further strengthened if our space permitted us to examine with equal minuteness the other *areæ*, and especially that scarcely less important and ancient one which contains the tomb of St Cornelius. Our account, however, of the architectural history of the Catacombs, and even of this particular cemetery, would be incomplete if we were to omit all mention of that vast and bewildering labyrinth of galleries which fills the ordinary visitor with astonishment, and which it is impossible, even on an accurately-drawn map, to reduce to any regular system. We have already described these galleries, which are found at two different depths below the surface, the horizontal plane of each *piano* of which is pretty generally observed. From the characteristics already mentioned,† we may safely conclude that both *piani* of this labyrinth belong to an age posterior to the regular construction of the *hypogeum* within the legal limits of the separate *areæ*. The union of these into one vast necropolis was not effected without difficulty, owing to the widely different levels at which their principal galleries had been excavated; and the attentive observer who traverses a portion of

* See p. 128. † See p. 176.

Mode of Construction and Development. 357

this labyrinth on his way from the tomb of St Cecilia to that of St Cornelius, will not fail to recognise the points of junction, and will appreciate the ingenuity with which the *fossors* accomplished their task.

We must again repeat that we by no means venture to affirm that the successive architectural changes which we have traced in the Catacomb of St Callixtus, are to be found in all the subterranean Christian cemeteries of Rome. No doubt each of these had its own characteristics, and possibly its own architect; but yet we are quite justified in supposing that the cemetery which we have examined, placed at so early a period under the immediate care of the Pope, and committed by him to the Archdeacon of Rome, must have furnished a pattern, followed with more or less exactness by those who had the charge of less important cemeteries. We may, therefore, sum up the testimony of the Catacombs as to their successive development, in the following general remarks. *Application to Catacombs generally.*

When the Roman Christians of the apostolic age commenced the excavation of subterranean cemeteries, the work was comparatively new. It was carried on in a rock the consistency of which was unknown, within the narrow limits of a legal *area*, and for the use of a people as yet few in number. Consequently, they did not think of constructing spacious chambers with ceilings of perilous dimensions, neither did they contemplate the construction of more than one *piano*, nor again did the necessity of economising space lead them to excavate galleries dangerously near to each other. Hence the most ancient part of a Catacomb is found to consist of a gallery, extending as far as the limits of the *area* permitted. Small *cubicula* were then constructed as circumstances might render necessary, with entrances from this gallery; and when this single gallery became insufficient for the wants of the community, other galleries and *cubicula* were excavated at considerable intervals from each other. *Summary of the process of the gradual development of a Catacomb from its commencement;*

As time went on, certain further modifications became

through divers modifications necessary to obtain increased accommodation; necessary. The galleries having been increased in length and number, the necessity of great economy of space was forced upon the attention of those who had the charge of the cemetery, and the experience which had been gained by the *fossors* of the consistency of the rock enabled them to practise this economy in various ways. Thus we find more *cubicula* on either side of the galleries, and these latter are made more lofty by lowering the floor, so as to receive many more tiers of *loculi;* while, in new excavations made during this period space was economised by the galleries being made narrower than before. The *loculi* themselves were made smaller, and space was saved by their being formed wide at the shoulders, and narrow at the feet. The *fossors* also found it practicable to cut galleries with a comparatively thin wall of rock between them, and at the angles of their intersection, where the friability of the *tufa* would not admit of full-sized *loculi* being cut, these portions were turned to account by being made to receive the bodies of infants. Even these expedients failing at length to supply sufficient space, the *fossors* conceived the idea of excavating another *piano* either above or below the first. The decorations of this period also show that the *fossors* had become more accustomed to the material in which they were working. The most ancient ornamentation had been formed entirely of stucco and brickwork, but now we find cornices, columns, pilasters, brackets, and even chairs,* cut out of the solid rock. The shape of the *loculi* was in time diversified by the introduction of the *arcosolium*, and the chambers themselves varied in many instances from their former rectangular shape, and are found of an hexagonal or octagonal figure, and sometimes with *apses* at one or more of the sides.†

or to avoid the search of persecutors; A later period shows signs of the protection of the laws having been removed, and the cemeteries no longer manifest the same careful observance of the limits of the geometrical *area*. The shafts communicating with the open air, constructed during

* See Fig. 7, page 32.   † See examples in Area X in Atlas.

Mode of Construction and Development. 359

this period, are not square apertures for conveying light and air into the *cubicula*, but are round pits, generally situated just above the crossing of the galleries, and were evidently made principally for the removal of earth. The *fossors*, no longer confined within certain prescribed limits, constructed at this period very large crypts and wide *arcosolia*, and, at the same time, to satisfy the requirements of a large Christian population, we find a multitude of poor miserable galleries full of *loculi*, but destitute of all ornament. It is also during this period that we meet with studied contrivances for concealment from persecution. The regular staircases were demolished, and instead of them were constructed secret passages leading into caves and sandpits. As a last resource, many of the galleries were filled with earth in order more effectually to conceal the tombs of the saints, and preserve them from the profane insults of the Pagan occupiers of the confiscated cemeteries. Finally, in this period we notice indications of the gradual abandonment of the practice of subterranean interment. [until its abandonment as a burial-place.] Many of the galleries terminate in portions which contain no *loculi*, or in which the *loculi* are marked in outline on the wall, but have never been excavated; and even in some of the spacious crypts we find the spaces for *arcosolia* sketched out, but the *arcosolia* themselves have not been constructed. Of course, in the more celebrated historical crypts, more striking characteristics are to be discerned, but the foregoing remarks apply to the Catacombs as a whole.

CHAPTER III.

ANALYTICAL DESCRIPTION OF THE PLAN OF THE MOST IMPORTANT AREA OF THE CEMETERY OF ST CALLIXTUS.

N.B.—*The reader should open the Plan while studying this Chapter, and should refer also to the elevation in Fig.* 47, *p.* 342.

Staircase A. THE staircase which originally formed the entrance to the principal gallery of this area was thoroughly and minutely examined by the brothers De Rossi in May 1865. The inclination of the steps enabled them to determine with accuracy the upper portion of the flight, of which nothing now remains, but the original position of which is indicated by the dotted lines. The first remains appear about ten feet below the surface of the soil, and extend to a depth of about thirty-nine feet underground. The plan indicates a wall of brick-work and *tufa* on each side of the staircase for a short distance, but the greater part of the length is excavated out of the living rock. As we have before remarked, there are evidences of two flights of stairs constructed at different periods. The original flight had steps covered with slabs of marble, and walls coated with very fine stucco, and adorned with narrow bands of a bright red colour. This flight of steps, however, bears signs of having been demolished and interrupted in many portions of its length; and hence another flight was constructed on foundations composed of masonry resting on such of the original stairs as remained entire. This flight of stairs is indicated by the dotted line in Fig. 47, to which we must refer our readers, as well as to the plan at the end of this analysis. The numbers and letters are alike in both, being those used by De Rossi.

A 2. Wall resting on a step of the earlier staircase.
A 3. Similar construction on three steps.

About half-way down the stairs, on the left, we find a large Staircase A 4. *sepolcro a mensa* divided so as to contain three bodies. It is shaped like that of St Cornelius, and lined with white stucco, but the filling up of the niche above the *mensa* is of rough masonry covered with coarse plaster, as also are the materials used to stop the *loculi* which are on either side of the staircase. These are, therefore, of later construction than the original *ambulacrum* to which the steps lead.

Three or four *loculi* have been cut in the staircase itself, A 7. evidently between the period of its demolition and that of the construction of the later staircase upon its ruins. And near its A 9. lower extremity, two large sepulchres have been constructed, each between four and five feet in depth, and so wide as to appear like small galleries passing beneath the staircase. In the sides of one of these sepulchres are three *loculi* closed in the usual manner, while the other is so divided as to contain nine bodies each in a separate niche. The mouths of these A 10. sepulchres are covered with tiles placed roof-wise, so as to bear the weight of the staircase afterwards built over them. The last few steps of the original flight, indicated by dotted lines, A 11. have been entirely destroyed, evidently with the design of not leaving even the least remains of them on the side walls, so that any one attempting to enter the cemetery would have had to make a leap of some five feet in order to reach the floor of the *ambulacrum*. In the vertical wall thus left a sepulchre for several bodies was afterwards found, the ruins of which still remain.

The second staircase is about thirty-three inches above the A 13. first, and this difference in level necessitated the construction of a flight of steps in order to reach the *cubiculum* A_1 on the right, and likewise to enter the gallery L on the left.

The *ambulacrum* which we have now entered was cleared Ambulacrum of earth at the beginning of 1856, but it had been visited by A. Boldetti and other explorers, who have left memorials of their visits in the galleries leading out of it. As we pass along between chambers A_2 and A_3 we notice that the walls are A 16. much ruined, almost up to the roof; but that immediately Its roof. under this they are in good preservation for the space of two *loculi*, and that here they do not spring from the same base-line as do the lower portions of the wall. The *loculi* of this higher portion are smaller than those at a lower level, and both the roof and walls are plastered and ornamented with paintings, which cannot be distinguished when we stand on the ground. This upper portion, of which a section is given on page 353, must therefore have been excavated when the whole of the lower part of the *ambulacrum* was filled with earth, and this earth, which formed the floor of the small gallery above, enabled the companions of Pomponio Leto to write their names, *Parthenius* and *Gallus*, on the roof of the gallery.

Its floor. Turning our attention from the roof of the gallery to its floor, we observe that we have to ascend two steps in order to enter the chamber A_2, and at the door of chamber A_3 a similar

Ambulacrum ascent indicates a corresponding depression of the level of the A 17. floor. On the opposite side of the gallery the same peculiarity strikes us even more forcibly, for while the roof of the gallery I is horizontal throughout, the floor, for about half its length, rises gradually from the point where it meets the *ambulacrum*

A 18. A. When, however, we reach the door of chamber A_4, we find the floor of this chamber at the same level with the *ambulacrum*, showing that this chamber was constructed subsequent to the depression of level. At the entrance to the

A 19. gallery H, the level of which is about two feet higher than that of A, there are to be seen traces of two steps, which have now become worn into an inclined plane. The difference of level is shown in the section on page 353, which proves that H must have been formed before the floor of A was lowered. Almost opposite to H is the entrance to the chamber A_5, which is entered by descending two steps, as may be seen in the above-mentioned section. This *cubiculum*, therefore, was constructed after the floor of the *ambulacrum* had been lowered, and in anticipation of a more considerable depression than was actually carried into effect. The same section shows the narrow gallery above the *ambulacrum* A, and the traces of the original roof of that *ambulacrum*. It also represents a portion of the small gallery $I_{,,}$ the shaft for removing the earth from which falls exactly on a line with the wall of the chamber A_5. The modern bridge, which now crosses the *ambulacrum* A, had no counterpart in the ancient remains, and was only constructed by the Commission of Sacred Archæology to enable the gallery I_1 to be traversed, now that

Analysis of the Cemetery of St Callixtus. 363

the earth which formed its floor has been removed from the galleries A and H.

We next descend five steps, now worn into an inclined plane (see page 344), and reach the entrance to the gallery G, which is formed at the lowered level of A, and the way into which would not have been practicable when the floor of the latter was first made. This opening, therefore, of the gallery G was constructed after the level of A had been lowered. Nearly opposite to G is the entrance to the *cubiculum* A_6, the floor of which is very slightly below that of the *ambulacrum*, of which we have reached the lowest portion, so that here we see the design carried into effect, which the lower level of A_5 has shown us had been intended also there, but not carried out. The state of the walls of the *ambulacrum* is so ruinous in this part as to have required them to be sustained by modern masonry. The entrance to the gallery F was first opened at the higher level, and then lowered to the new level, as appears from its great height, and also from the *tufa* not having been entirely cut away from the lower portion of its walls. Close beside A_6 is a large sepulchre A 23, marked in the plan, resembling a *sepolcro a mensa*, except that it is too near the ground, and seems to have been closed like a simple *loculus*. The entrance to the gallery E must evidently have been constructed after the depression of the floor of A; while D, like F, bears evident signs of having been cut away to meet the lower level after its original construction. As we approach the corner AC, the left wall is observed to be strengthened for a considerable portion of its height by constructions of *tufa* and brick-work, while the corner itself is entirely filled up with a solid pillar of the same materials, having merely a narrow passage through it, along which only one person could pass at a time. Along the whole length of A, numerous inscriptions have been found in fragments which have fallen from the *loculi*, and they are for the most part in the Greek language.

Returning again to the foot of the staircase, we enter the *cubiculum* A_1, the original floor of which was thirty-three inches lower than it is at present, and from the line where the fine white stucco, with red lines upon it, now ends, we are able to determine the corresponding elevation of the roof.

Ambulacrum A 20.

A 23.

A 26.

A 27.

Cubiculum A_1.

The left wall of the original chamber is entirely gone, and was removed in order to enlarge the chamber, and to make room for the entrance through it into the second and third *areæ* of the necropolis, which being at a higher level, required the elevation of the floor of this chamber. Both the door and *loculi* are quite in ruins.

Cubiculum A_2. A_2 is approached by two steps, and is lined with stucco, on which are painted the frescoes in Plate XII. 1 ; XIV. 2. An examination of the stucco at the lower part of the walls shows that the original floor must have been lowered about eight inches. Near the door on the right hand is a square pedestal or seat made of *tufa*, and covered with a slab of terra-cotta, and to the left is a little staircase leading to a higher *piano* of the cemetery, but evidently much more modern than the chamber.

Cubiculum A_3. The chamber A_3 is square like the last, and similarly decorated. The floor is about eleven inches above the level of the *ambulacrum*. This chamber is called by the guides the *Capella dei Sacramenti* from the liturgical paintings on the walls. See Plate VII.; XI. 1 ; XII. 2, 3 ; XIV. 3. See also page 263.

Cubiculum A_4. The succeeding chamber, A_4, is decorated in the same way, but the stucco is of an inferior quality. The roof is so low as to be hardly six feet two inches above the floor, which is of coloured marbles arranged in a geometrical pattern. De Rossi has, however, ascertained that the original floor is beneath this pavement, and that in consequence of the *ambulacrum* A not having been lowered to the depth once contemplated, this original floor was raised so as to be on a level with the *ambulacrum*, thus accounting for the unusual lowness of the ceiling. This, as well as A_3, has a *loculo a mensa* in the wall directly opposite the door ; the side walls are also pierced by two *loculi*, one above the other. Above the *loculo a mensa* two *loculi* for children have been irregularly cut at a later period. The explorers of the fifteenth century had penetrated into this chamber, and left their names, *Parthenius, Gallus, Matthias, Thomas*, which are now barely visible.

Cubiculum A_5. The *cubiculum* A_5 resembles the preceding in its form and decorations, and there is reason to suppose that the floor, which is now two steps below the *ambulacrum* A, had been raised like that of the chamber A_4, since the original ceiling has been removed, and a new one made at a sufficient elevation to admit of an additional range of *loculi* all round the chamber. This later portion is covered with a very inferior kind of plaster, and has a barrel-roof, instead of the flat or cruciform vaulting found in all the preceding *cubicula*. See dotted lines in Fig. 53.

A_6 resembles the other chambers in form and decoration, but on either side the lower tomb is a *loculo a mensa*, with the sepulchre lined with marble and forming a *bisomum*, although in each case they have been closed like a common *loculus*. The end of the chamber, however, is entirely occupied with one large *sepolcro a mensa* divided for two bodies, each division being lined with marble. The iron bars which supported the *mensa* are still to be seen. At a later period it became necessary to strengthen this wall with masonry, and to this period must be assigned the two marble pilasters which now stand on either side of the sepulchre, and the vertical slab of Grecian marble which once covered the whole space between these pilasters. The marble pavement still remains upon the floor. Within this chamber was found the epitaph— *Cubiculum A_6.*

SERGIVS ALEXANDI
CAECILIE FAVSTAE
COIVGISVEBENE
MERIENTI FECIT.

The staircase and *ambulacrum* B is parallel to A, and very wide and lofty, but it has suffered not only from the changes made in ancient times, but from the carelessness with which the possessors of this property in the last century adapted it for the purposes of a wine-store. Both tombs and walls were recklessly destroyed to make receptacles for the butts of wine, and the gallery was entered from a modern staircase made beneath the three-apsed chapel which we have noticed above the second *area*. This staircase has now been blocked up, and the point where the ancient steps must have reached the surface of the soil is marked in the plan by the dotted lines. *Staircase B.*

A wall closing up the staircase at about half its length. *B 29.* From this point the upper portion of the staircase was deprived of half its width in order to make a space for the narrow flight of steps B_5, which lead down to the galleries Z and Y. Near this wall the staircase B retains traces of the same fine stucco, with its ornament of thin red lines, which we observed on the walls of A. Almost immediately below this wall the steps have been demolished, as we observed had been done in the case of the parallel flight, and evidently at the same period; the traces of them, however, remain on the side walls. Here was found the remains of a small sarcophagus, ornamented with dolphins, and bearing the inscription ΛΟΓΓΑΙΑΝΟC · ΚΑΤ · ΠΡΟΗ ΕΙΔΩΝ ΑΠΡΙΑ; and another inscription in Latin to HASELLICA, apparently on a step of the staircase.

Staircase B 32. A small opening on the left leads into a rectangular cham-
$B\ B_4$. ber coated with coarse plaster, and almost destroyed by a modern passage which passed close above it. The entrance to the gallery B_4, cut through so many *loculi*, shows the damage done to the sepulchres in B in its formation, although a point was chosen with special care that the damage might be as small as possible. The wall on the right is all in ruins. On the left wall may be observed a line of *loculi*, near the roof, evidently belonging to a different period to those below them, from which they differ in size and arrangement. These indicate the existence of a gallery, similar to I_1 in the *ambulacrum* A, excavated when B was filled with earth, and probably communicating with B_4 after the staircase was blocked up, since it has no other outlet apparent; and must have been on the same level with that gallery. From the entrance of B_4 to the bottom of the flight, the steps are well preserved and covered with slabs of terra-cotta.

Ambulacrum The *ambulacrum* itself is paved with large tiles, all of which
B. bear the stamp OPUS DOLIARE EX PRÆDIIS DOMINI N ET FIGL NOVIS, that is, according to Marini, from the imperial manufactory of Marcus Aurelius. As we approach the entrance to the gallery B_3, communicating with the *arenarium*, we notice the wall on either side of that entrance is sustained by masonry of *tufa* and brick-work, and that the entrance itself has been cut through some of the *loculi*; an evident proof of its having been made at a later period than the *ambulacrum*. The masonry, however, does not reach the present roof, because at the time

that it was built the roof had not been raised to its present
elevation by the excavation of the small gallery B_4.

On the right hand, now at a somewhat high elevation, is a *Ambulacrum* *sepolcro a mensa*, 37, which is important as proving the present B 37. floor of the *ambulacrum* to be at a considerably lower level than when it was originally constructed. And a practised eye will at once perceive that the adjacent entrance into I was B I. originally opened at a level which corresponded to that required by the tomb. The entrance to H, on the contrary, is little B H. more than six feet high, and could not therefore have been made use of when the floor of the *ambulacrum* was nearly four feet above its present level. From the arrangement of the *loculi*, however, it appears that an entrance into H was contemplated in the original design, although not carried into effect until after the depression of the pavement of B. The masonry on either side of H, and other signs, show that H was once continued in a direct line into B, but was at a later period moved about twenty inches to the left.

On the left the wall is much broken, and on the right we see that the gallery G was commenced originally from this end, B G. although it appears to have been only commenced and not proceeded with until the *ambulacrum* was deepened. The small gallery in the roof is very discernible at this point. The entrance to F shows the same traces of having been opened B F. after the level of B had been lowered, which we observed in the entrance to H. The passage B_2, cut through three *loculi*, and B B_2. even now of a very moderate height, could not have been made until after the deepening of the *ambulacrum*. Immediately above this door we perceive in the roof the termination of the small upper gallery. From the holes high up in the left wall, it would seem that the *fossors* began at the high level to open a way into the gallery E, but never carried out their design, probably because the wall was afterwards filled with *loculi*.

The entrance into D was made at the high level, and then, B D. as at the other end, excavated so as to suit the reduced level of B. The wall above this entrance is modern, and belonged to the wine-stores constructed here in the last century. The opening into T_5 is also modern. It is worthy of notice that the point where B and C meet is not a sharp angle, as is usually B C.

the case in the meeting of catacomb galleries, but a curve. This peculiarity is an additional work of antiquity, for it suggests the thought that at the period when these galleries were first formed, the work of the *fossors* had not yet settled into a system. Few *loculi* appear to have been cut in this corner, and those few at a later period, so that

Gallery B₁. Which connects this *area* with a neighbouring *arenarium*, need not, and did not, belong to the earlier periods of this part of the cemetery, even though its entrance did not occasion the demolition of any *loculi*. After a few steps we come upon a modern opening which leads into the *area* of St Sotere, excavated at a higher level than that which we are now describing.

Gallery B₂ Appears hardly to have been formed and filled with *loculi*, when it was perceived that its direct leading into B endangered the discovery of the whole cemetery. It was accordingly half blocked up by a thick wall, and then entirely closed at the point where it fell into T₁.

Gallery B₃ Led into the *arenaria* through T, and B₄, and B₅, into Y and Z, the latter being entered by the steps cut through the upper part of the original flight B.

Ambulacrum C. The *ambulacrum* which unites A with B was cleared out in 1863, and is wide and very lofty. The marks of a change of level are not very apparent in the gallery itself, but having been proved to the very ends of A and B, the same change must necessarily have been effected in C. The *loculi* in this gallery are large, arranged in order, and with numerous niches for lamps, &c. Some of the large tiles, bearing the stamp of the manufactories of the emperors M. Aurelius and Commodus,

C 49, 50. remain still in the *loculi*. Two large *loculi* are to be seen on the right immediately after turning the corner out of B₁, and

C 52. further on in the left wall is a *sepolcro a mensa*. These being near the floor, are marked in Fig. 48 as having been constructed subsequently to the deepening of the gallery. Above the *sepolcro a mensa* is an opening in the wall near the roof made by excavators of the last century, who were making their way from a higher set of galleries in the *area* of St Eusebius, and through this opening must have fallen into the *ambulacrum* C several fragments of inscriptions belonging to that *area*, and differing entirely in character from the other inscriptions found here. One of these has the ⚓, of which no other instance

Analysis of the Cemetery of St Callixtus. 369

occurs in this *area;* and of another the remainder has been found in a gallery of the *area* of St Eusebius.

The entrance to C_2 is cut through *loculi*, and therefore of Gallery C_2. later date than the *ambulacrum;* the gallery is full of earth, and unexplored; but above the entrance, we see in the section on page 342 another passage which must have crossed C when the latter was full of earth, and which is continued almost until it meets D. The passage is in direct communication with the area of St Eusebius, and appears to have been deepened considerably after its first construction, either by modern excavators or by graves having been made in its floor. See the section of it q_3 in Fig. 48.

Another doorway leads into the gallery C_1, which apparently C_1. belongs to the same system of passages as C_2, and bears marks of having been formed about the same time. The fragments of inscriptions found in these two galleries are of a character similar to those in the *ambulacrum* itself.

D is a lofty gallery, excavated, as we have seen, during the D. first period of the *area*, and afterwards deepened like the *ambulacra* A, B, which it connects. Many inscriptions, the majority of which are in Greek, have been found in this gallery, which was explored in the winter of 1862-63.

E was excavated, as we have seen, subsequently to the E. depression of the level of A_1, and throughout its whole length is never more than six feet high. Many of its *loculi* are closed with *tufa* constructions.

F was opened at the high level of A, and then cut away to F. correspond to the depressed level at which it enters B. The little passage F_1 was evidently excavated after the lowering of the floor, for it carefully avoids breaking into E.

It was afterwards demolished in part, in order to make way Well F_1. for a well of ancient construction, but still holding water. The well is furnished with foot-holes, in order to admit of a man descending to clean it, as may be seen in all other ancient wells connected with the Catacombs.

G, on the contrary, commenced from B at the high level, and Gallery G. was continued so as to fall into A after the level had been lowered.

H commenced from A at the high level, and fell into B after H.

2 A

the floor of that *ambulacrum* had been lowered. Its floor was paved with marble. The change in its direction near its conjunction with B we have already noticed, and careful observation shows that change to have been made at the same time with the sinking of the staircase H_2. The pavement here is composed of tiles of the date of Marcus Aurelius. The staircase H_2 is at first excavated in *tufa* with *loculi* in the walls, it is then flanked with thick walls of *tufa* and brickwork, in which some *loculi* have been scooped out. About half-way down the staircase, on the left, is seen a doorway in the wall, with an arch turned over it, but walled up, apparently a gallery commenced, and speedily abandoned. On the right is seen a half-open *loculus*, within which, instead of a skeleton, was found a little terra-cotta sarcophagus containing the body of an infant. The upper portions of the *loculi* in this place are not flat, but somewhat arched, and the roof of the staircase breaks into the gallery I, which is half blocked up by the masonry sustaining it. The staircase, after all, remained useless, for it was found impossible to use, for sepulchral purposes, the gallery into which it leads. The tiles are in many cases stamped with the mark of the manufactory of M. Aurelius.

Staircase H_2.

Cubiculum H_1. The *cubiculum* H_1, whose entrance is immediately opposite to H_2, differs from all the chambers we have hitherto described, in the very inferior plaster with which it is lined, in the barrel roof, and especially in the double *arcosolia*, which are here met with for the first time in this *area*. These circumstances justify De Rossi in assigning to it a later date than that of the staircase H_2.

Gallery I. The gallery I was originally excavated at the high level of A and B, as we have seen from the openings into both those *ambulacra*. It was afterwards cut away so as to correspond with the new level, and thus it is found at present, with its floor sloping downwards from the middle each way towards A and B, while the middle portion itself remains still at the higher level. The walls are much damaged by the rude attempts to convert it into a wine cellar in the last century, and scarcely any inscriptions have been found in it. The opening by which the majority of visitors pass into this gallery from the crypt of S. Cecilia is quite modern, but a little farther on, on the left hand, we may, by climbing to the top of a heap

Analysis of the Cemetery of St Callixtus. 371

of rubbish, penetrate into the little crooked gallery I_1, which Small Gallery here crossed this gallery when it was filled up with earth, in I_1. its way from A_5 to the crypt of S. Cecilia, where it seems to have terminated. It contains a number of small *loculi*, all open, above one of which is traced on the mortar the sign of the cross thus ✢. There are signs of an intention of excavating two branches of this little gallery along I, in a similar manner to those which we have noticed along A and B, but the intention appears never to have been carried into effect. The modern constructions along the part of the gallery I, usually traversed by visitors, are the work of the Commission of Sacred Archæology, and were rendered necessary by the rude staircase which had been made into the crypt at this point, at the time when it was used as a cellar.

We now enter L, the first gallery which branches off from the Gallery L. *ambulacrum* A, and which still retains some traces of the fine smooth plaster with which it was originally coated. We have already seen how the construction of another flight of stairs into A rendered it necessary to make the steps by which we now descend into L. At the bottom of these steps, we notice, on the right hand, traces of the original wall having been cut away in order to widen the passage; and similar traces may be observed beneath the *luminare* which now gives light to that which originally formed the end of this gallery, proving that the crypt of S. Cecilia was originally entered through the Papal crypt. Slight traces also appear of the deepening which this passage must have undergone when the original level of A was lowered.

At the entrance to L_1 we see in the pavement and on the Papal Crypt walls traces of the original level having been about a foot L_1. higher than it is at present. The door of this crypt, which is the central and most important in the Catacomb, as having been the burial-place of the Popes of the third century, is five feet wide, and constructed of brick-work. The plaster which covers it is covered with *graffiti*, the majority of which are at a higher level than would naturally have been chosen by those who wished to write on the wall, so that these *graffiti* would seem to have been upon the plaster at the time when the pavement was lowered. Others being cut off in the middle must have been written previous to the widening of the door, and consequently to the construction of the arch above it which is covered with three coats of plaster, two of them decorated with painting. The crypt itself is now almost entirely reconstructed with modern masonry, for the ruinous condition in which it was found when cleared of earth in 1854 rendered this absolutely necessary for its safety. It is impossible to determine whether the original chamber has *loculi* in its walls, or what was the nature of its roof, so many successive works have succeeded each other in this important crypt. See the description, pp. 130–150.

The earliest modification of this chamber appears to have been the slight lowering of the level of the floor, the traces of which remain in the lowest range of *loculi*, and especially in the large sepulchre at the end of the crypt, which had its parapet made in the best style of imperial lateritial work. At the same period with this parapet was formed the little passage leading into the crypt of S. Cecilia, as the form of the parapet itself shows, and as is proved still more convincingly by the brickwork of the passage being of the same kind as that which covers the parapet. This was afterwards covered, first with white plaster, then again with rough mortar, in order to attach to it slabs of marble, and lastly, the roof was lined with mosaic. Above the large sepulchre, which must originally have been a *loculo a mensa*, we cannot see any traces either of other *loeuli*, or even of plaster. In front of it are two steps, the lower of which has four holes, in order to receive the pillars that supported the *mensa* of the altar which here stood out, with the episcopal chair behind it. A fragment of marble in the corner shows the chamber to have been once lined with similar slabs.

The right-hand wall, when it was first discovered, contained nothing but its eight large *loculi*, two of which, close to the floor, had space for marble *sarcophagi*. Among the rubbish was found the *mensa* of a tomb, with a vine sculptured on its edge in very low relief; and on the edge of another was carved the inscription OΥΡΒΑΝΟCE. . . . Between the two sets of *loculi* stood a pillar, of which the base is still in its position, and a wall forming a *sarcophagus* jutting out into the chamber in front of the *loculus* makes a continuation of this base. Remains of a similar arrangement on the left hand wall justify

Analysis of the Cemetery of St Callixtus. 373

the restoration of De Rossi, while in the roof above the broken column, which is here in its original position, is the shaft of a second *luminare*, now blocked up. The wall near the entrance is formed of masonry, with traces of an inferior kind of plaster. The base and mark in the wall of a small column still remain at the left hand side as we enter, while above the door is the space for the oblong tablet of a large inscription. In the wall, on the other side, is a niche for a lamp, or for the vessel in which was burned the hallowed oil of which St Gregory the Great speaks. A similar niche is right in front of the entrance in the left wall of the gallery L. The papal crypt had a barrel roof, greatly occupied by the large *luminare*. The pavement was of marble, and covered tombs made beneath it, the inscription upon one of which is still in its place, ΔΗΜΗΤΡΙϹ ΚΑΤ · ꜩ ΙΓ · ΚΑL · ΙΟΤΝ—*Demetrius, buried on the 20th of May*. See De Rossi's restoration of this crypt, Plate XV.

The chamber L_2 has its three principal walls entirely covered Cubiculum L_2. with a thick wall of brickwork, which has considerably reduced the size of the *cubiculum*. The arches in these walls have been much destroyed, and the *loculi* of the primitive walls behind them have suffered also. Still, enough remains to show that they were covered with fine white smooth plaster, that the roof was vaulted in the cruciform manner, and, like the walls, adorned with fresco. The central figure in the roof is that of Orpheus, Plate XI. 2. All the characteristics of this chamber are those of the very earliest portions of the *area*.

The vestibule M is constructed entirely of masonry, and De Vestibule M. Rossi confesses himself unable to account for its peculiar form. Its walls are lined with plaster covered all over with *graffiti*. Here were found a number of polygonal paving-stones of basalt, evidently having formed part of the pavement of the cross road which we have called the Via Appio-Ardeatina.

The portico to the crypt of S. Cecilia is excavated in the Portico N. tufa, and sustained by brick arches. The inscriptions on the *loculi* found here apparently belong to the period of S. Damasus. At the end of N a narrow passage runs close behind the crypt of S. Cecilia. That crypt itself is entered by two steps, above Crypt of S. which are arches in brickwork. But behind the right hand Cecilia O. wall of the entrance we see these *loculi* which mark the position of the gallery Q, before the works of Pope Damasus had completely transformed this portion of the Catacomb. Entering the crypt, we notice on the left, opposite to the tomb of S. Cecilia, a piece of brickwork forming the segment of a circle, which, when complete, was the pit in which the little gallery I, lost itself. This pit, and the end of the gallery afterwards incorporated into the crypt, were distinct from it when first constructed. The chamber itself, therefore, must have been of the restricted dimensions represented in the plans of the third and fourth periods of excavation in pages 345, 349.

Cubiculum P_1. The chamber P_1 has its entrance almost blocked up by the staircase P, which has been already described, page 355. The walls of the chamber are in a very ruinous state, and the *loculi* broken. It is not easy to determine whether the *arcosolium* at the end of it was made within a pre-existing recess, or whether the brickwork and marble with which it has been adorned were later additions; but it is certain that before these portions were added, with the inscription to *Dasumia Quirica* which occupies the lunette, there was a simple *loculus*, closed with a slab of marble, which these constructions afterwards covered. Above the door was found in 1854 the inscription of the year 290:—

VIBIV · FIMVS R · VII KA SEP
DIC · IIII · ET · MAX · COS.

Vibius Fimus died (recessit) August 26th, when Diocletian for the fourth time and Maximinus were Consuls.

P_2. The *cubiculum* P_2 is in a most ruinous state; the left wall being quite broken away, and the left only sustained by masonry, the plaster has nearly all fallen. From its position this chamber appears to have been constructed about the same time with the staircase P. The passage leading to it is sustained by masonry.

Gallery Q. The gallery Q has now been occupied by the staircase P, but formerly formed a communication between the gallery S and the crypt of S. Cecilia. The tombs formerly excavated in its floor have been destroyed by the constructions which support the staircase P; but within one of these tombs, near the entrance to Q., were found two *plumbatæ*, or leaden balls covered with a shell of bronze, and each fastened to a bronze chain. It is possible that these might have been weights for

Analysis of the Cemetery of St Callixtus. 375

scales, but history records instances of even these weights being used as implements of torture, and the burial of these in the Christian's tomb certainly favours the supposition that they had been the instruments of his martyrdom. The walls of this gallery are strengthened by masonry in order to sustain the staircase P. On the left wall, among this masonry, may be seen traces of a flight of broad steps in the tufa leading up to S. These steps must have been demolished before the entrance to Q_3 could have been made, otherwise it would not have been of sufficient height to have admitted any one into that chamber. The entrance to S was afterwards closed with a wall when the staircase P was made, although the outline of a door was traced on this wall, as if it had been at one time contemplated to reopen that passage. Q 78.

The plaster near the entrance to Q_1 is covered with *graffiti*, most of them in Greek, and apparently belonging to the third century. The chamber itself, together with the others in this gallery, was cleared out in 1855. The right hand wall of it, cut in the tufa, is now in ruins, but preserves the traces of rather large *loculi*. Part of the left wall is in ruins, another part filled with ancient masonry, and the remainder with the whole lower end of the chamber is faced with a solid wall of stone and brick-work, with four pieces of marble jutting out like brackets about seven and a half feet from the ground. This brick-work forms a solid arch, which fills half the roof of the chamber. The other half is taken up by the *luminare*, which together with the passage R, giving access to this chamber when the substructions of P had blocked up the original doorway, show that this chamber was one of the important shrines of the Catacomb. The *graffiti* and the inscriptions confirm this evidence. *Cubiculum* Q. Passage R.

On the opposite side of the gallery is another chamber Q_2 with a barrel roof, the *luminare* in which formerly received light from that of Q_1 but was blocked up by the building of the staircase P. Nevertheless, a window was opened over the door, in order to compensate to some extent for this loss, and at the same time the chamber was coated with plaster, which is consequently not of so fine a kind as that of which some remains are to be seen in Q_1. The *loculi* are large, and those near the ground are sunk below the floor. On the left side is an *arcosolium*, but its arch is of the same construction as the masonry *Cubiculum* Q_2.

at the door, so that its antiquity is not greater than that of the staircase P. Some remarkable sarcophagi were found in this chamber, as also in Q_1. They are described in page 298.

Cubiculum Q_3. We have seen that the entrance to Q_3 was formed after the demolition of the stairs 78, leading to S. At the end of this chamber is seen a large *arcosolium* once covered with marble. The parapet of this tomb is so high that it would have been impossible to have used the *mensa* as an altar, if the priest had stood on the present pavement. This is a proof of the floor having been lowered; in fact, we descend a step on entering it. The inconvenient height of the *mensa* of the *arcosolium* was remedied by a little step covered with a slab of *giallo antico* marble which now stands in front of the tomb. A small passage in the left hand corner leads into another chamber, with a little gallery stretching out of it, in which is an *arcosolium*, so arranged as to avoid falling into Q_4 which must have been in existence before these appendices to Q_3 were made.

Q_4. The chamber Q_4 has two *arcosolia* in its right hand wall, one lined with marble, and the other with fine white plaster. In the left wall are *loculi*. A massive wall for the support of the staircase fills up a considerable part of the chamber on the left, and the roof is pierced by a large *luminare*.

Gallery S. It appears from the marks of the pickaxes of the *fossors* in the walls that the gallery S was first commenced at the end where it was united to the gallery Q, although it is somewhat higher than the level of that gallery, and corresponds to that of the adjacent *area*, with which it was connected by the passage *b*. (See plan on page 349.) On the plaster of the *loculi* are *graffiti* in Greek, *e.g.*, ΘΗCCTPEEIC · ΜΝΗCΘΗ ΖΗCΗ and ΑΤΤΙΚΕΙΑΝΟC. Some of the *loculi* have been broken through in order to make an entrance to *b*, which proves that the gallery S existed previous to its being made the means of connecting the two *areæ*. The *cubicula* S_2, S_3, S_4, are all constucted with barrel roofs, and contain *arcosolia*. Immediately beneath the cross road is the entrance to the *cubiculum* S_5, of similar construction, in the left wall of which only one *loculus* appears, evidently from a fear of weakening the rock beneath the staircase A, which must, therefore, have been in use when this chamber was made. Opposite the entrance to S_5 is the way into another gallery, S_6, leading into the labyrinth, clearly of

Cubicula S_2, S_3, S_4

Cubiculum S_5

Analysis of the Cemetery of St Callixtus. 377

much later date than the gallery from which it branches off. The *cubiculum* S_7 is similar to the others along this gallery, but its roof is damaged by a passage from the labyrinth having broken into it. In a *loculus* on the left is the inscription MOTCIKIA still in its place.

The gallery T is a continuation of B_3, and connects that Gallery T into passage with the *arenarium*. Its floor slopes continually to-*arenarium*. wards the level of the *arenarium*, and its roof is cut in steps, sinking as much as nine and a half feet in a very short space. The galleries T_1 and T_3, and others which branch off from it, are narrow and low, as is also the chamber T_2, which contains a large *loculus a mensa*. The *loculi* in U are large, and con- U. tained several fine inscriptions in Greek and Latin, *e.g.*, EICTEP-KOPI; KAI · ΝΑΤΑΛΕΩC; AGATEMERIS · SPIRITVM · TVVM · INTER · SANCTOS. U_1 and U_2 are branches of the *arenarium*, but contain a few *loculi*. Some of the *loculi* in the gallery V are still intact, but most of them are destroyed, as V. also in V_1. V_2 leads into the *arenarium*, which is evidently V_1, V_2. more ancient than this gallery which here opens into it.

The vast gallery of the *arenarium*, with its branches X_1, X_2, *Arenarium* X. X_3, needs no description, and the secret passage X_4, leading X_4. into it, has already been described, page 347.

The gallery Y, with its dependencies, is low and narrow, Y. and at the level of the galleries excavated above the earth which filled up the main *ambulacra*. Three *cubicula* Y_1, Y_2, Y_3, are of the rudest description; while Z is merely a continua- Z. tion of the *hypogeum* entered through B_5, and a portion of it breaks into the roof of the chamber Q_2.

The reader who has had patience to study this analysis will easily perceive how fully it justifies the account of this *area* given in the last chapter, and will be able to estimate the magnitude of De Rossi's labours in thus analysing every portion of this vast necropolis.

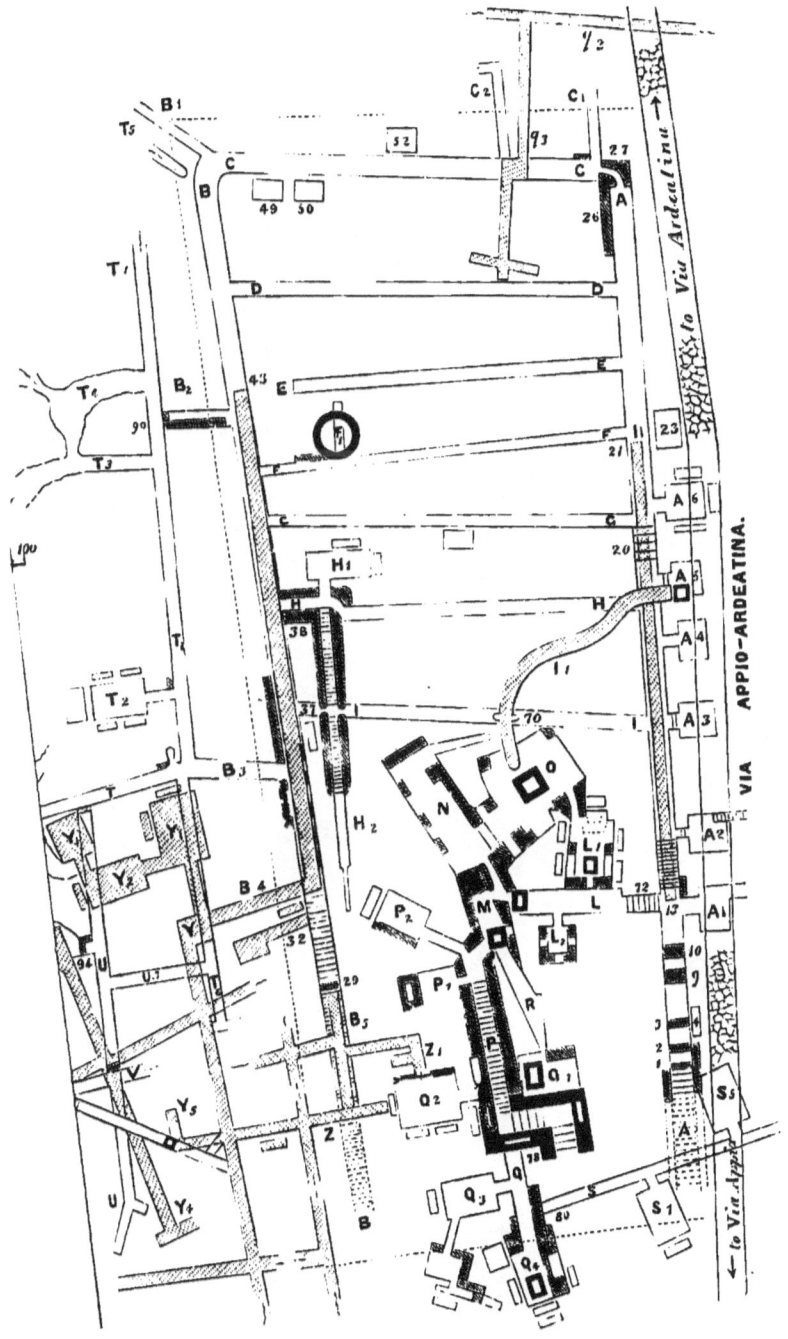

APPENDIX.

Note A (page 15).

THE discovery of the tomb and body of St Hyacinth by Father Marchi deserves to be told in detail, as showing how innocently a false tradition may be created about the possession of such or such a relic by any particular church.

On the evening of Good Friday, March 21, 1845, one of the men employed in digging in the Catacombs, came to F. Marchi, in the Roman College, with a slip of paper in his hand, on which were these words,—" DP. III. IDUS SEPTEBR YACINTHUS, MARTYR,"— which he said he had just copied from a stone that was still inclosing a grave in a chapel of the Catacomb of St Hermes (or Sta. Basilla, as it is sometimes called). This excited not a little surprise in the learned Father, who knew from ancient calendars, martyrologies, and other sources, that the two brothers, St Protus and St Hyacinth, had suffered martyrdom together under the Emperor Valerian, and that they had been buried in this Catacomb on the 11th of September; but he imagined that their bodies had been long since removed to other churches. Arringhi * states that they were translated from the church of San Salvatore, in Trastevere, to that of San Giovanni dei Fiorentini, under Clement VIII., in the year 1592. However, when Father Marchi visited the spot on Monday morning, in company with a painter and an architect to draw illustrations of the chapel, he satisfied himself that it was indeed a grave that had never been opened; he observed also that the chamber in which it was, was only one of five chambers, all connected together, receiving light from a very large *luminare*, and having a double approach by staircases from two opposite sides, just as he had before noticed in the principal churches in the Catacombs of St Agnes, St Helen, and St Prætextatus. In a

[marginal note: Discovery of tomb of St Hyacinth in 1845;]

* Arringhi, ii. p. 235.

word, the place had every arrangement necessary for accommodating a large number of the faithful, just as one would expect at the tombs of such famous saints as St Protus and St Hyacinth. Moreover, turning over the heaps of earth which encumbered the pavement, he found a fragment of marble, with the words, SEPULCHRUM PROTI M(*artyris*), and this placed it beyond a doubt that here had certainly been the burial-place of those two glorious martyrs, and that one of them still lay in his original tomb.

and of the tombstone of St Protus.

But because this discovery contradicted the popular belief and the claims of the Church of San Giovanni dei Fiorentini, F. Marchi rightly judged it advisable to proceed with unusual care and circumspection; he therefore left the grave exactly as it was, and spent the next three weeks in a diligent investigation of every record he could discover which could throw light upon the history of the two brothers; paying frequent visits to the chapel, however, in the meantime, accompanied by cardinals, bishops, prelates, and others, whose devotion or curiosity led them to the spot. The result of his historical researches was most satisfactory. He found that about a century after their martyrdom, the chapel in which they had been buried was so blocked up with earth, that Pope Damasus was obliged to repair it, and that, according to his usual habits, he took the opportunity at the same time of putting up an epitaph of verses in their honour; also that Pope Symmachus, in the beginning of the sixth century, had again restored the chapel, and that the bodies of the martyrs were still there at the end of the seventh century.

History of relics of St Protus.

The next trace of them belongs to the middle of the ninth century, when it is recorded that Leo IV. placed under the high altar of the church of SS. Quattro Coronati, the heads of St Protus, St Sebastian, Sta. Prassede, and others, together with the bodies of fifty-seven martyrs, taken either from the cemeteries or from other churches. Now, we know that Paschal I. had translated the body of Sta. Prassede to the church dedicated to her honour, and that Gregory IV. had translated that of St Sebastian to the basilica now known by his name, but before that time called after St Peter and St Paul, whose bodies, as we have seen, once found a temporary resting-place there; and although we do not know who had translated the body of St Protus, yet we are certain that it had been done at some time prior to this, for Leo would never have removed the head only, and left the rest of his body in the Catacombs, since the motives assigned by his predecessors for removing the martyrs bodies from the Catacombs at all was, "*ne remanerent neglectui*," that they should not remain exposed to neglect and irreverence in the midst of such a chaos of ruins. Leo's act can only be explained by supposing that some church was already in possession of the whole body, and that he did not choose to deprive them of more than a part; and this church can have been no other than that already spoken of, the church of San Salvatore in Trastevere, for from hence it was undoubtedly transferred to the church of the Florentines at the close of the sixteenth century.

The reader will observe that there is no mention in this account of Pope Leo's proceedings, of either the whole or part of the body of St Hyacinth; yet if this had been within his reach, it is impossible that he should have overlooked it, when he went out of his way so far as even to rob other churches, in order to enrich his own with all the precious relics he could find.

How then could the Florentines assert that they had the bodies of both the brothers? They were told so by the church of San Salvatore, where an inscription in the pavement under the high altar expressly said, "*Sub hoc lapide requiescunt sanctorum corpora gloriosissimorum Proti et Hyacinthi.*" But this inscription was not older than the fourteenth or fifteenth century, and between this and the eighth or ninth century there was abundance of time to confound the memory of the original translation of the relics. Moreover, there was in the same church another inscription, or rather half of it,* half of the epitaph written by Pope Damasus, and in this Hyacinthus was named as well as Protus, and everybody knew that both had suffered together, and that they had been buried in the same chapel, and that the body of St Hyacinth was not to be heard of anywhere else. It was but natural, therefore, that they should conclude that as they certainly had the body of the one brother, so also they had that of the other. [St Hyacinth's relics *supposed* to be with those of St Protus. Why?]

But was not the mistake discovered when the relics were removed to San Giovanni? Christopher Castelletti, who has left us an account of the translation, says that they dug beneath the stone until they came to a large marble case; that they opened this, and found no entire bodies, for that other churches had been enriched at various times with some portions of them; but he adds that there were a great many bones. There were legs, arms, ribs, one jawbone with teeth, and several loose teeth. This account exactly confirmed all that F. Marchi had been able to discover from an examination of the history. Here is no mention of two bodies. On the contrary, there is a conjectural explanation why two bodies could *not* be found. Nor does there appear to have

---

* The other half was, and is, in the church of the Quattro Coronati; and F. Marchi conjectures that the inscription had been divided at the same time as the body. There seems no other way of accounting for ha'f of it being in San Salvatore, and the other half in the Quattro Coronati.

been any head at all, only a single jawbone and some loose teeth, which might have been accidentally left when Leo IV. separated the head of St Protus from its body.

Why they were not removed with those of St Protus.

Still the question remained, why did not those who originally extracted the body of St Protus, extract also the body of St Hyacinth? But this, too, was soon answered, when F. Marchi came on Saturday, the 19th of April, with the Pope's Sacristan (an Augustinian bishop) and other dignitaries, and with two or three of the excavators, to open the grave itself. One of the restorations effected by Pope Damasus, or by Pope Symmachus, had been an entirely new pavement, made of *tufa* and Roman cement, which in that damp place, under the open *luminare*, had become as hard as any stone. St Hyacinth's grave had been excavated in the very lowest tier of graves in the wall. Still the whole of it had been above the level of the *original* pavement, but now it was half above, and half below, the upper and more modern pavement, so that it was not until some portion of this had been broken, that the excavators were able to remove the marble slab, and expose the interior of the grave. Moreover, the crumbling, insecure nature of the soil was such, that it was manifest the whole wall on that side would inevitably give way, now that its last stay had been removed. And so it happened; not immediately, indeed, but within a few days, so that the whole chapel is again a mass of ruins; and it was through a fear of this disaster that former generations had left the grave undisturbed.

Discovery of relics of St Hyacinth.

We must not omit to mention the interior of this grave, because it brings to light two or three interesting features in the history of the Catacombs, which we have not had a convenient opportunity of mentioning elsewhere. At first sight it appeared to be full of mud, and the uninitiated began to fear that after all their care they were only to be rewarded with disappointment. F. Marchi, however, soon explained to them, that where the rain-water came pouring down a *luminare*, it brought much of the soil of the Campagna along with it; but that though it penetrated the lower graves, and filled them with mud, yet this only destroyed the unformed bones of infants, not those of a full-grown man, such as St Hyacinth was. He immediately began to divide the mud, therefore, with a piece of cane, and soon brought to light the bones of a man; only, instead of being in their natural condition, they were partly burnt to a cinder, and all had manifestly been subjected to the action of fire. We cannot account for this, since the genuine Acts of the martyrdom are lost.

Lastly, when these bones were removed into broad daylight, and were being examined by a professor of anatomy in the Pope's

Palace, F. Marchi observed several gold threads, crossing and recrossing one another, lying amid the earth and about the bones ; and when these had been collected and submitted to a professor of natural philosophy, he declared it certain that the body had been wrapt up in some very precious material ; whether it was what we call cloth of gold, or whether it had been stuff or silk embroidered with gold, he could not say, as only these threads had survived. This is a valuable confirmation of what we already knew, not only from the testimony of Eusebius and others in individual historical cases, but also from Bosio, Boldetti, and other *collaborators*, who had observed the same phenomena in many graves of martyrs which they had opened. Boldetti especially mentions one, in which all the bones of the skeleton were perfect excepting a broken skull, and the fragments of the cloth of gold only covered this one spot of the whole body. The relics of St Hyacinth now rest under one of the altars in the newly-restored basilica of St Paul *fuori le mura*.

Whilst these pages are passing through the press, another historical monument of early Church history has been recovered ; and although on this occasion we are not indebted to De Rossi for the discovery, yet we certainly are for its identification, and the most interesting commentaries by which he has illustrated it.

<small>Discovery of another historical monument in 1868.</small>

In the month of August 1866, a tablet of the Acts of the *Fratres Arvales* was discovered in the vineyard of Signor Ceccarelli, about five miles from Rome, on the Via Portuensis ; the same place where the first large discovery of monuments of this heathen sodality had been made in the sixteenth century. Further examination brought to light, in the same place, about thirty more considerable fragments ; and it was shrewdly noticed by Henzen, the learned Prussian antiquarian (under whose direction the excavations were being made, at the joint expense of the court and the archæological societies of his country), that these fragments were not mixed together promiscuously, but that a certain chronological order might be observed in their arrangement ; thereby showing clearly that they must have originally belonged to some building on the very spot where they were now found. The walls to which they had been attached had perished ; and large portions of the tablets themselves had been carried away ; but the fragments which remained had lain for centuries precisely where they had fallen. Several other fragments, however, were found on the top of the hill ; and these were not arranged in any kind of order. Moreover, there were found amongst them fragments of Christian epitaphs of the fourth century. This discovery was wholly unlooked-for, as there had been no previous knowledge of the existence of a Catacomb in this neighbourhood. As the work of excavation proceeded, small columns, bases, and capitals, were brought to light, all of which seemed to indicate the same age and style of architecture as we were already familiar with in the ruins of the Hospital of Pammachius at Porto, and other monuments of the fourth century. At last, a piece of marble was turned up, the fragment of an architrave, bearing only three letters complete, STI, but these of unquestionably Damasine character. The presence of a Christian monument was now certain; and by and bye the entrance to a Catacomb was detected, and lastly the Catacomb itself. On the staircase by which we descend to it, we find monograms, of the form *d* in Fig. 27, represented in page 230; and in the first gallery there is a painting of a Good Shepherd, quite of the usual kind, excepting that on the dress there is a *crux gammata* (see Fig. 27, *k*, page 230), such as we see on the tunic of the *fossor* Diogenes, belonging to the age of Damasus.* On the wall of a small *cubiculum* is a much later painting, of our Blessed Lord sitting in the midst of four saints, each holding a crown in the hand, and having the name written at the side, just as in the case of St Cornelius and Cyprian (Plate V.) The first of these names it is impossible now to decipher; of the second, we can only see SCA . . . TRIS; the two others are plain, SCS + FAVSTINIANVS, SCS + RVFININ (*Rufinianus*). De Rossi at once conjectured that the obliterated name must have been of SIMPLICIVS, and that he had before him some memorial of Saints Simplicius and Faustinus, who were drowned in the Tiber in the persecution of Diocletian, and buried in the cemetery of Generosa *super Filippi*, or, as it is somewhat differently expressed in the Acts, *juxta locum qui appellatur Sextum Philippi viâ Portuensi*, and of their martyred sister, St Beatrice, who was afterwards buried near them.

The owners of the vineyard kindly made some excavations under his directions, and soon brought to light ruined walls of a small Christian oratory, once adorned with mosaics, and two or three more fragments of the Damasine inscription, which gave VSTINO . VIATRICI. This, of course, confirmed De Rossi's confidence in the truth of his conjecture; but the subject presented many and unusual difficulties, which he has only now succeeded in clearing up, in the first number of the *Bullettino* for this year.

We will state both the difficulties and their solution as briefly as we can, for they are worth attending to, as illustrating various points which have been often insisted upon in this volume. First, how could a Christian cemetery have been excavated under the

Identification of Cœmeterium Generoses ad Sextum Philippi.

* Inscr. Christ. i. 594.

very temple and grove of a heathen sodality in the days of Diocletian? and secondly, how can the position of this cemetery, so near to Rome, be reconciled with the description of the cemetery of Generosa given above, *juxta Sextum Philippi;* since we have the testimony of Ethicus, a Christian writer of the fifth century, that the farm called *Sextum Philippi* (which he tells us was also called *prædium missale*) was seven or eight miles further down the river, near the island now called *Isola sacra?*

As to the first difficulty, it is well known to all who have studied the subject of the *Fratres Arvales*—so important in its bearing upon disputed questions of Roman chronology during the Imperial period—that when Marini published his great work upon them, all the fragments of their tablets which had been discovered ranged between the reigns of the first emperors and that of Gordian, about A.D. 238. Marini expressed an earnest hope that tablets of a later date would one day be discovered, but that hope has never been realised. De Rossi—observing that the last writer who mentions these *Fratres* is Minucius Felix, a cotemporary of Gordian, and the last magistrate who enumerates the title of Priest of this Pagan college among his dignities, belongs to the very same age, —conjectured, with his usual sagacity, that the college must have been either abolished or incorporated with some other, or, at least, fallen into disrepute and neglect, about that time. This he announced in a paper published in the *Annali dell' Istituto di Corrispondenza Archeologica* in 1858, and the recent discovery singularly confirms the statement, for the latest date which has been found is of the year 225. There is nothing, therefore, strange or improbable in the supposition that, at a time when entrance to the usual Christian cemeteries was forbidden by the Emperor Diocletian, a new place of burial should have been provided here where the bodies of the martyrs Simplicius and Faustinus had been recovered from the Tiber. This account of the origin of this cemetery is the more certain, because, although it is singularly perfect (never having been disturbed apparently at any time, excepting for the translation of the relics of the Saints by Pope Leo II.*), yet not a single Christian epitaph has been found more ancient than the days of Diocletian, nor any vestige of the more primitive signs and symbols. On the other hand, the use of the monogram is frequent, and there are several epitaphs with consular dates of the age of Damasus. Moreover, it is important to observe that this Catacomb is connected with an *arenarium,* like those mentioned in this volume at p. 332; and this we have pointed out (p. 88) as

Sts. Simplicius, Faustinus, and Beatrice buried under deserted grove of a heathen temple.

---

* Lib. Pontif. *in loc.* He translated them to the Church of St Bibiana.

This discovery confirms our History of the Catacombs, and the Acts of these Martyrs.

one of the characteristics of those parts of the Catacombs which belong to the times of persecution. The numerous openings of this *arenarium* on the side of the hill would have rendered the secret construction of a small cemetery here a matter of no great difficulty, even in the days of Diocletian, and there is absolutely no reason to suppose that it was used extensively at any time. On the contrary, it is but a small Catacomb even now, and seems to have had one central shrine, as it were; the tombs of the martyrs that have been named. Over these, Pope Damasus raised a little oratory or basilica, so arranged that through a window in the *apse* the worshippers could look in upon the sacred graves. A small gallery was also excavated, which would lead them directly from the oratory to this *cubiculum*, whilst the adjacent galleries were blocked up, as we have seen in the neighbourhood of the tomb of St Eusebius (p. 168), to prevent the pilgrims from going astray and losing the object of their pious search. For these saints were once held in great veneration; their festival was kept on the 29th of July; special lessons and prayers in their honour may be seen in the office-books of Gelasius and St Gregory the Great; and their names even have a place in the Litanies in the most ancient MSS. both of England and France.*

The second or topographical difficulty may be dismissed more summarily. The Acts of Saints Simplicius and Faustinus, and the inscription on the front of the old marble sarcophagus, which may still be seen in the precincts of St Mary Major's, connect their place of burial with some place known as *Filippi*, or *Sextum Philippi;* and a geographer of the fifth century describes this spot as being several miles farther down the river. A careful examination, however, of all the passages in which this place—deriving its name from Philip—is mentioned, had already led Bosio to suspect that the name belonged to a considerable tract of country, viz., all the low land which stretches out towards the sea, beyond the height on which this cemetery has been excavated, and which is the last spur of Monte Verde and the whole range of hills on that side of the Tiber. If we accept this simple explanation of the term, there is no longer any inconsistency between the locality of the cemetery just discovered and the descriptions of it in ancient monuments. On the contrary, there is a special fitness in the word used in one of those descriptions, which speaks of the cemetery as being *super* Filippi. This is a subject, however, which need not further be discussed in this note. But the discovery of another Catacomb, agreeing so exactly in all its phenomena with

* Mabillon, Analecta, t ii. p. 670.   Martene de Div. Off., p. 630.   Morini de Pœnit. in App., p. 65.

the general theory of their history, as laid down by De Rossi and explained in these pages, was too important a fact to be altogether omitted.

Note B (page 22).

The "Acts of the Martyrdom of St Cecilia," published by Bosio in 1600, and republished by Laderchi in 1722, were taken from a late MS. in the possession of her church in Trastevere. The Greek version of Metaphrastes was made from an older MS., of which Latin copies also are extant; and it will be worth while to set side by side a passage of the Acts as it stands in each of these two versions. The additions in the later MS. which we have *italicised* are very significant. — Two versions of the Acts of St Cecilia compared.

Almachius ordered Cecilia to be brought before him, and he asked her, What is your name? She answered, Cecilia.	Almachius the *Prefect* orders *Saint* Cecilia to be brought before him. And he asked her, What is your name? She answered, Cecilia, *among men; but, what is much more distinguished, I am a Christian.*
A. said, Of what condition are you?	A. said, Of what condition are you?
C. answered, I am free, noble, and of senatorial descent (*clarissima*).	C. answered, I am a Roman citizen, distinguished, (*illustris*),* and noble.
A. said, I ask you about your religion.	A. said, I ask you about your religion, *for we know that you are noble by birth.*
C. answered, Your questioning then took a very foolish beginning, to expect two answers to be included in one enquiry.	*Saint* Cecilia said, Your questioning took a very foolish exordium, to expect two answers to be included in one enquiry.
A. said, Whence have you so great presumption in answering?	*The Prefect* A. said, Whence have you so great presumption in answering?
C. said, From a good conscience, and a faith unfeigned.	*Saint* C. said, From a good conscience, and a faith unfeigned.
A. said, Do you not know what power I have?	A. said, Do you not know what power I have?

* The vagueness of this word marks a later date than the exact specific words used n the other version.

	The Blessed C. said, And do you not know whose spouse I am? *A. said*, Whose? *Saint C. said*, Of our Lord Jesus Christ. *A. said*, I know you to be the wife of Valerian.
C. said, You know not what power you have; for if you question me about your power, I will manifest it to you by most true assertions.	*Saint C. said*, O Prefect, you know not yourself what power you have; for if you question me about your power, I will manifest it to you by most true assertions.
A. said to her, Tell me what you know.	A. *the Prefect* said to her, If you know anything, tell me. *I shall be delighted to hear a discourse from your mouth.*
C. said to him, The power of man is as when a bladder, &c.	*Saint C. said*, In proportion as you are delighted, so shall you be judged. Nevertheless, listen. The power of man is as when a bladder, &c.

It is clear from the prologue to these Acts that their compiler lived at a time subsequent to the triumph of Christianity; yet it is difficult to believe that he had not access to the genuine official documents of the trial, or at least faithful copies of them, when he wrote this detailed account of the examination, for in its older and simpler form it has all the preciseness of the legal forms of a criminal process.

Note C (page 68).

THE CHAIR OF ST PETER.

"The Chair of Peter" used in a double sense. The term *Cathedra Petri* has, in the course of ages, gathered round it so many associations of the supreme authority in the Catholic Church, that we are apt to regard it solely in its moral and, of course, most important signification, and to forget that within the bronze seat supported by the colossal figures of the four Doctors of the Church there is an ancient chair which Roman tradition asserts to have been actually used by the Apostle St Peter. Among the Essays of the late Cardinal Wiseman is a learned and interest-

Appendix. 389

ing paper which exposes the absurdity of Lady Morgan's amusing blunder in confusing this venerable relic with an ancient chair at Venice, and so pretending that on the Chair of St Peter was to be found the Mussulman formula. The Cardinal, however, was obliged to be content with descriptions and drawings of the true chair, which were two hundred years old, as the relic had never been seen by man since Alexander VII. had placed it in its present position. Commendatore De Rossi has been more fortunate ; for, at the eighteen hundredth anniversary of the martyrdom of the Apostles, in 1867, Pope Pius IX. commanded this venerable relic to be exposed for the veneration of the faithful, and full opportunities were given for a close and scientific examination of it from every point of view. The illustration given here is carefully copied

The real Chair has been recently exposed.

from a photograph taken during the exposition of the Chair, and will assist our readers in following the description of it which we proceed to give.

I.—DESCRIPTION OF THE CHAIR.

The Chair has four solid legs composed of yellow oak, united by horizontal bars of the same material. In these legs are fixed the

It is composed of two kinds of wood.

iron rings which make the whole a *sella gestatoria*, such as that in which the Sovereign Pontiff is now carried on state occasions, and such as those which the Roman senators began to use in the time of Claudius. The four oak legs were evidently once square, but they are much eaten away by age, and have also had pieces cut from them as relics. These time-worn portions have been strengthened and rendered more ornamental by pieces of dark acacia wood, which form the whole interior part of the chair, and which appear to have hardly suffered at all from the same causes which have so altered the appearance of the oak legs. The panels of the front and sides, and the row of arches with the tympanum above them, which forms the back, are also composed of this wood. But the most remarkable circumstance about these two different kinds of material is, that all the ivory ornaments which cover the front and back of the chair are attached to the acacia portions alone, and never to the parts composed of oak. Thus the oak framework, with its rings, appears to be of quite a distinct antiquity from that of the acacia portions with their ivory decorations.

Ornamented with ivories, also of two kinds.

These ivory ornaments themselves, again, are of two distinct kinds of workmanship. Those which cover the front panel of the chair are square plates of ivory, disposed in three rows, six in a row, and have the Labours of Hercules engraved upon them, with thin *laminæ* of gold let into the lines of the engraving. Some of them are put on upside down, and their present use is evidently not that for which they were originally intended. The other ivories, on the contrary, fit exactly the portions of acacia which they cover, with the architecture of which they correspond, and they appear to have been made on purpose, and never to have been used for ornamenting any other article. They consist of bands of ivory, not engraved, but sculptured in relief, and represent combats of beasts, centaurs, and men, and in the middle of the horizontal bar of the tympanum is a figure of a crowned emperor, holding in his right hand a sceptre which is broken, and in his left a globe; he has a moustache, but no beard, and De Rossi conjectures he may be intended for Charlemagne or one of his successors. Two angels, one on either side, offer him crowns, and two others bear palms. The style of the carving and of the arabesques corresponds to the age of Charlemagne. The Labours of Hercules are of a much more ancient date, but De Rossi does not think them as old as the first century.

The tradition of its antiquity presents no archæological difficulties.

Before passing on to consider the historical notices of this venerable relic, it may be well to observe, that although a more accurate description of the Chair of St Peter than Cardinal Wiseman was able to obtain from the works of Torrigio and Febeo prevents our

Appendix. 391

adopting his hypothesis that this was the ivory curule-chair of the Consul Pudens, yet the most rigid criticism has nothing to object against the traditional antiquity of the oak frame-work of this chair. When the inner part of acacia was added, and adorned with bands of ivory, the ancient ivories which cover the front appear to have been put on, and it is not at all uncommon to meet with copies of the gospels, reliquaries, and other valuable works of the early medieval period, which are ornamented with ivories representing subjects of Pagan mythology. At that time Paganism was dead in Europe, and its treasures of art were transferred to innocent and often to sacred uses; but when the struggle between the infant Church and the dominant power of heathen idolatry was still raging, the Christians, as we have seen in our Chapter on Sculpture, were extremely cautious in their admission of scenes of Pagan mythology, and would not have been likely to allow them to remain undefaced on so sacred an object as the Chair of St Peter. On the other hand, all that the Cardinal urges as to the introduction of the use of the *sella gestatoria* by the senators, precisely in the reign of Claudius, is most valuable, as showing what was regarded in those days as a special honour, and therefore one antecedently probable to have been conferred by a convert of senatorial rank upon the Chief Pastor of the Church, to whom, in the words of the *Liber Pontificalis,* "the chair was delivered or committed by our Lord Jesus Christ."*

2.—HISTORICAL NOTICES OF ST PETER'S CHAIR.

In order to prove satisfactorily from historical sources that the *Cathedra Petri* relic now venerated as the Chair of St Peter was so regarded from used in a literal the earliest ages of the Roman Church, it will be necessary not only to trace a chain of testimonies up to apostolic or quasi-apostolic times to the *cathedra Petri,* but also to produce good evidence that the expression *cathedra* or *sedes Petri* is to be understood not merely in a metaphorical and moral, but also in a literal and physical sense. For instance, when we read in the pages of Bede † that Ceadwalla, king of the West Saxons, converted by St Wilfrid, went to Rome to be baptized, and died there A.D. 689, and that Pope Sergius I. put up in St Peter's an epitaph which stated—

"King Ceadwalla, the powerful in war, for love of God left all, that he might visit and see Peter and Peter's Chair, and humbly receive from his font the cleansing waters,"

we might reasonably think that as "Peter" is put metaphorically for his successor Pope Sergius, so "Peter's Chair" might not im-

* "Hic [Clemens] ex præcepto Beati Petri suscepit Ecclesiam, et Pontificatum gubernandum, sicut ei fuerat a Domino Jesu Christo cathedra tradita, vel commissa."—*Lib. Pont.*, c. iv.   † H. E. v. 8.

probably be a metaphorical expression for Rome, the seat of his jurisdiction; and hence we could not from such passages as this conclude that any certain reference was intended to a visible material chair, such as that of which we have given a description.

by Ennodius, A.D. 500.

Our first authority, then, shall be one who leaves us in no doubt upon this point. Ennodius of Pavia, who flourished at the end of the fifth and beginning of the sixth centuries, introduces Rome as rejoicing in having become Christian, and puts into her mouth the following words: "*Ecce nunc ad gestatoriam sellam apostolicæ confessionis uda mittunt limina candidatos; et uberibus, gaudio exactore, fletibus collata Dei beneficio dona geminantur.*"* "See now the dripping thresholds send forth the white-robed [neophytes] to the *sella gestatoria* of the Apostle's Confession; and amid floods of joyous tears the gifts conferred by the kindness of God are doubled," *i.e.*, in the two sacraments of Baptism and Confirmation. In this passage Ennodius brings vividly before us the scene presented by the Baptistery of the Vatican, when the newly baptized, with joyful emotion, passed at once from the font to receive Confirmation from the Bishop seated in the *sella gestatoria*, which appears to have been then a conspicuous object at St Peter's shrine.

Inscription in Baptistery.

This passage is illustrated by some lines from the Codex of Verdun, a fragment of the fourth or fifth century—

"*Istic insontes cælesti flumine lotas
Pastoris Summi dextera signat oves.
Huc undis generate veni quo Sanctus ad unum
Spiritus ut capias te sua dona vocat.*"

"In this place the right hand of the Chief Pastor seals the sheep who have been washed in the heavenly stream. O thou who hast been born again in the waters, come to that one place whither the Holy Ghost calls thee to receive His gifts."

The lines preceding these in the same Codex were written at the entrance of the Baptistery—

"*Sumite perpetuam sancto de gurgite vitam
Cursus hic est fidei, mors ubi sola perit.
Roborat hic animos divino fonte lavacrum,
Et dum membra madent, mens solidatur aquis.
Auxit apostolicæ geminatum sedis honorem
Christus et ad cælos hunc dedit esse viam:
Nam cui siderei commisit limina regni
Hic habet in templis altera claustra poli.*"

"From this sacred font draw everlasting life; for this is the stream of faith in which death alone is destroyed. Here the washing of the font of God gives strength to souls, and while the limbs are moistened, the mind is made strong in the waters. Christ has added double honour to the Chair of the Apostle, and given him to be the way to heaven; for he to whom He committed the portals of the kingdom above, has here in the churches another gate of heaven."

* Apolog. pro Synodo, *apud* Sismond. Opp. tom. i. p. 1647.

Appendix.

From these lines we gather that the Baptistery of the Vatican in which they were inscribed, was "an honour doubled by Christ to Peter, and to the Chair of the Apostle," and that there was in that Baptistery a distinct place where the neophytes were sealed and enriched with the gifts of the Holy Ghost by the hand of the Supreme Pastor. Now, comparing this with the passage of Ennodius, we perceive that the *sedes apostolica* is not mentioned only in its moral, but also in its literal and material sense; and that in the fifth century at least there was solemnly preserved in the Baptistery of the Vatican a *sella gestatoria*, upon which, or in front of which, the Pope used to sit when he conferred the Sacrament of Confirmation.

A remarkable testimony to the same fact is the evident allusion to it in the inscription which St Damasus put up in this Baptistery which he had built— *By St Damasus in fourth century;*

"UNA PETRI SEDES UNUM VERUMQUE LAVACRUM."

Again, in the inscription on the tomb of the immediate successor of Damasus, we read that Pope Siricius—

"FONTE SACRO MAGNUS MERUIT SEDERE SACERDOS." *

Now, the usual place for the Bishop's throne was in the *apse* of the basilica, and therefore if it is recorded that Siricius "was counted worthy to sit as High Priest at the Sacred Font," it is clear that "in the Sacred Font," *i.e.*, in the Baptistery, was placed the chair to which the Bishop of Rome owed his pre-eminent rank as the *Sacerdos Magnus*, and, in fact, the magnificent Baptistery of St Damasus is described by Prudentius as "the Apostolic Chair."

With these authorities to guide us, we read the epitaph of Ceadwalla in an entirely new light, and we cannot doubt that the "Chair of Peter" which he is described as leaving home to see, was none other than the famous *sella gestatoria* which the Saxon king could not fail to visit when he received the sacrament of regeneration in "Peter's Font."

Our next authority shall be St Optatus of Milevis, who published the first edition of his work against the Donatists during the pontificate of St Damasus, and the second during that of St Siricius. The Donatists boasted of having in Rome a bishop of their sect. Optatus opposed to them the line of Roman pontiffs from Peter to Damasus, and to Siricius, "all occupiers," as he pointed out, "of the same Chair;" and proceeded—"In fact, if Macrobius"(the Donatist bishop) "be asked where he sits in Rome, can he say, In the Chair of Peter?" (*in cathedra Petri*) "which I am not aware that he *and St Optatus.*

* Gruter Inscr. pp. 1163, 10, and 1171, 16.

has ever seen with his eyes, and to whose shrine he, as a schismatic, has not approached."* The Chair, therefore, on which Damasus, and afterwards Siricius, sat as pontiffs, was in the time of St Optatus regarded not only morally, but materially, as the Chair of St Peter, and was seen by the eyes of those who approached *ad Petri memoriam*, *i.e.*, to his basilica on the Vatican.

Now, it is impossible that this Chair could have been so generally regarded in the fourth century as having belonged to the Apostle St Peter and his successors, unless there had been at the time an ancient tradition to that effect. Before St Damasus placed it in the Baptistery of the Vatican, it must have been preserved elsewhere, perhaps in the very crypt of St Peter's Tomb, or in the Basilica of Constantine. At any rate, before the Diocletian persecution, and in the course of the third century, Catholics professed, in the presence of heretics who did not attempt to deny it, the same tradition which St Optatus opposed to the Donatists concerning the Chair in which the successors of St Peter presided over the Church. This comes out with striking clearness in the Poem against Marcion, usually appended to the works of Tertullian, and which from internal evidence clearly belongs to the third century. Towards the end of Book iii., this ancient author enumerates the Bishops of Rome, and commences the list with these lines :—

> " *Hac cathedra, Petrus qua sederat ipse, locatum*
> *Maxima Roma Linum primum considere jussit.*"

" In this Chair in which Peter himself had sat, he ordained Linus first to sit with him [as bishop] established in Great Rome."

St Cyprian.
These words certainly suggest the idea of a material chair, and this literal sense becomes still more certain when we recall the language of St Optatus and Ennodius. In fact, with the light thrown upon the expression *Cathedra Petri* by the passages of those authors, it is impossible to avoid observing, that in many of the works of the early Fathers in which that expression occurs, its force is immensely increased if we suppose them to have used it with a full knowledge that the very chair of the Apostle was preserved in Rome as the visible witness to, and symbol of, the apostolic foundation of her line of Pontiffs. Thus, when St Cyprian wrote of the Roman See being vacant by the martyrdom of St Fabian, " *cum locus Fabiani, id est locus Petri et gradus cathedræ sacerdotalis vacaret*," † the force of the expression is greatly increased if we understand him to have had in view the venerable chair, " in which Peter himself had sat," and on which his successors, down to St Fabian, were enthroned.

* St Optat. ad Parmen. ii. 4. † Epist. 59.

Appendix. 395

The celebrated passage of Tertullian, *De Præscript.* c. 36, loses Tertullian. all its significance if we regard him as ignorant of the existence of this venerable relic. He invites all heretics to test their doctrines by the living tradition of the Apostolic Churches : " *Percurre ecclesias apostolicas, apud quas ipsæ adhuc cathedræ apostolorum suis locis præsident.* . . . *Si Italiæ adjaces, habes Romam,*" " Go through the Apostolic Churches, where the very chairs of the Apostles still preside in their places. . . . If you are near Italy, you have Rome." The Church of Jerusalem preserved the *ipsa cathedra* of St James ;* Alexandria venerated the *ipsa cathedra* of St Mark ; † and Tertullian's long residence in Rome must have familiarised him with the *ipsa cathedra* " in which Peter himself had sat."

Another passage of the same work of Tertullian states : " *Romanorum* [*ecclesia*] *Clementem a Petro ordinatum edit.*" "The Church of the Romans proclaims Clement to have been ordained by Peter."‡ Yet the ancient catalogues place both Linus and Cletus before Clement. At any rate, this passage of Tertullian shows the antiquity of the account afterwards inserted in the *Liber Pontificalis*, that Linus and Cletus had governed the Roman Church while the Apostles were living, and that Clement had been ordained St Clement by Peter himself as his successor, and had been enthroned by him ordained by in his own Chair. This tradition forms the subject of one of the St Peter. frescoes recently brought to light by Father Mullooly in the subterranean Church of San Clemente. It is true that a full account of it is found in the apocryphal Clementines, but it does not therefore follow that the whole story is fabulous, for these pages abound in examples of valuable historical truths, having been buried under a mass of doubtful and sometimes fictitious stories.

We have now traced up the testimonies to this celebrated relic, Summary of from the fifth century to the age when men were living who had evidence to the conversed with the contemporaries of the Apostles themselves. Chair. All this time it was regarded by Christians in various parts of the world as the very pledge and symbol of apostolic succession and of true dogmatic teaching. It was the object of a festival, celebrated alike by St Ambrose at Milan and St Augustine in Africa ; and the relic itself was deposited by St Damasus in the Basilica of the Vatican, where it remained throughout the fifth and at the beginning of the sixth century : and there is every probability that it is directly alluded to in the epitaph of Ceadwalla at the close of the seventh century. During the middle ages the mention of it becomes merely incidental, principally in accounts of the enthronizations of the Pope, and in liturgical books ; so that instead of this Chair of St Peter having been an invention of the credulity of the barbarous

* Euseb. H. E. vii. 19, 32.   † Vales. *in ibid.*   ‡ c. 32.

ages, it barely maintained during those ages the veneration paid to it from apostolic times, and was never adduced, as in earlier days, as an important weapon for the confusion of heretics. We learn from incidental notices, that every year, on the 22d of February, it used to be solemnly carried to the High Altar of St Peter's, and that the Pope was then seated in it. The historians of the Vatican relate, that it was translated from one chapel of the Basilica to another, until Alexander VII., two centuries ago, enclosed it in the bronze monument, where it remained concealed from the eyes of all until the summer of 1867. It is impossible, or, to say the least, in the highest degree improbable, that a new chair could have been surreptitiously substituted for that mentioned by Ennodius, and placed by St Damasus in the Vatican Baptistery. The *sella gestatoria* exposed for veneration in 1867 corresponds exactly with Ennodius' description, for the rings which render it *gestatoria* are fixed in a portion clearly distinguishable from the more modern additions to the Chair; wherefore we conclude that from a historical and archæological point of view, we are justified in regarding as true the venerable title which a living tradition has never failed to give to the Chair of St Peter.

3.—ANOTHER CHAIR OF ST PETER IN THE CEMETERY OF OSTRIANUS.

Where was the Chair of St Peter whence came the *olea* at Monza.

It is by no means clear that "the oil from the chair in which Peter the Apostle was first enthroned" was taken by the Abbot John from the Vatican, where undoubtedly the venerable relic which we have described was to be seen in the days of St Gregory the Great. On the contrary, it appears among *olea* taken from various shrines on the Via Salaria Nova, and the care with which the index of the oils at Monza is grouped on the papyrus MS. makes us hesitate long before admitting that a mistake has been made in this instance. Between the Via Salaria Nova and the Via Nomentana there was a lane, beside which was situated a crypt, where, according to Bede, the bodies of the martyrs Papias and Maurus, who had been baptized in prison by Pope Marcellus, were buried, and the place was called "*Ad Nymphas B. Petri, ubi baptizabat,*" or, as we read in the *Mirabilia Urbis Romæ*, "the cemetery of the Font of Peter." Now, since all the other *olea* of the Abbot John are noted down in the precise order in which he must have collected them as he passed from one shrine to another, we cannot avoid the conclusion that when he stopped to collect the *olea* at "the Font of Peter" on his way from the Via Salaria to the Via Nomentana, there must have been at that cemetery a Chair which was venerated as the "*sedes ubi prius sedit Petrus Apostolus.*" The

Appendix. 397

Hieronymian Martyrology marks January 18 as "*Dedicatio cathedræ S. Petri apostoli, qua primum Romæ sedit.*" This same day is marked as the Feast of St Peter's Chair at Rome in the martyrologies of Ado and Bede, and in other ancient records, and it is never said *ubi primus* or *prior*, but always the adverb *prius* or *primum*, so that the reference is evidently not to the line of Roman Pontiffs of whom he was the first, but to some other chair in which he afterwards sat. All ancient authors record two journeys of the Apostle to Rome, one in the time of Claudius, and another in the reign of Nero; and these two journeys afford an easy explanation of his having had two well-remembered places of abode, and two chairs treasured up with affection and veneration by his children in the gospel. The antiquity of the cemetery of Ostrianus has been shown already,* and the description of one of its crypts by Bosio reads, as De Rossi observes, extremely like an account of the very spot in which this chair was venerated. But all trace of the chair itself has disappeared, and no legend, or even fable, is left to perpetuate its memory. The supposition of its existence is only offered as the simplest way of accounting for many strange associations which seem to have hung about this crypt, which, though insignificant in size, was yet styled *cœmeterium majus;* and of unravelling the otherwise inextricable confusion in which the history of the two Feasts of St Peter's Chair is involved.

4.—THE TWO FEASTS OF ST PETER'S CHAIR.

The establishment of the Roman Church by St Peter as the perpetual seat of his divinely-received primacy was never disputed until the sixteenth century; when the straits to which the clear teaching of Holy Scripture and the Fathers reduced Protestant controversialists, impelled some of the more unscrupulous of them boldly to assert that St Peter was never at Rome at all, that he never made it the seat of his apostolic jurisdiction, and never watered with his blood the foundations of that long line of Pontiffs whose history is the history of Christianity. "It was," says the Abbé Guèranger, "in order to nullify, by the authority of the Liturgy, this strange pretension of Protestants, that Pope Paul IV., in 1558, restored the ancient Feast of St Peter's Chair at Rome, and fixed it on the 18th of January. For many centuries the Church had not solemnised the mystery of the pontificate of the Prince of the Apostles on any distinct feast, but had made the single feast of February 22 serve for both the *Chair at Antioch* and the *Chair at Rome*. From that time forward the 22d of February has been kept for the *Chair at Antioch*, which was the first occupied by the

Feast of January 18.

Feast of February 22.

---
* Pp. 67, 68.

Apostle."* And in fact all the martyrologies from the eighth century downwards mark that day as "*cathedra Petri in Antiochia,*" or "*apud Antiochiam,*" or "*qua sedit apud Antiochiam.*" De Rossi, however, observes that ancient documents anterior to the eighth century make no allusion to Antioch in connexion with the feast of February 22. Thus the Gregorian Liturgy simply marks that day as "*cathedra S. Petri,*"† and in one MS. of that book it is expressly added *in Roma*. In the times of St Leo the Great this day was celebrated in the Vatican Basilica with a large concourse of bishops, and was called "*dies Apostoli;*" while in the Bucherian Calendar, which marks the greater feasts of the Roman Church restored after the Diocletian persecution, we find it noted as "*natale Petri de cathedra.*" The sermon attributed to St Augustine on this festival makes no mention of Antioch, but states : " The institution of to-day's solemnity received from our forefathers the name of the Chair (*cathedræ*), because Peter, the first of the Apostles, is said to have received on this day the chair of the episcopate. Rightly, therefore, do the Churches venerate the feast of that see (*sedis*) which the apostle undertook for the salvation of the Churches."‡ St Ambrose in his sermon for this feast merely expounds the gospel, without any allusion to the special object of the festival. Ptolemæus Silvius in the fifth century registers the Feast of St Peter as on the 22d of February; and the Gothic-Gallican sacramentary assigns to the same day a Mass, the collect of which begins : " O God, who on this day didst give blessed Peter to be after Thyself the head of the Church," &c. § The same Mass however, in the later edition of this sacramentary, reformed in the eighth century, was transferred to the 18th of January. ‖

February 22, St Peter's Primacy.

We gather from these authorities that an ancient tradition existed in the Church that the famous words, " Thou art Peter, and upon this rock," &c., were addressed by our Lord to his chief Apostle in the month of February, and that the 22d of that month was especially dedicated to the celebration of the institution of the primacy of St Peter, and that in Rome this festival was made still more marked by the solemn enthronisation of the supreme Pontiff in the very Chair which the Apostle himself had once used. This is confirmed by the words of the Gothic Liturgy, which declare : " God committed the keys of heaven to a man compacted of the earth ... and set on high the throne of the supreme See. The

---

* *Liturgical Year.* Christmas, vol ii. p. 331. Jan. 18. Duffy, 1868.
† S. Greg. Magn. Opp. iii. p. 312, ed. Maur.
‡ S. Aug., Serm. 15, De Sanctis.
§ Mabillon, *Liturgia Gallicana*, p. 226. " Deus qui *hodierna die* beatum Petrum post te dedisti caput ecclesiæ, cum te ille vere confessus sit et a te digne prælatus sit," &c. ‖ Ibid., p. 121.

Appendix. 399

episcopal Chair of blessed Peter, this day exposed, [for veneration] is the witness." * It is equally clear that there is no mention of Antioch, as connected with this feast, until the eighth century. Two difficulties, however, remain to be cleared up, viz., How did the dea of Antioch become connected with the feast of February 22? and also, How did the Feast of St Peter's Chair in Rome, on the 18th of January, find its way into the martyrologies of the eighth and ninth centuries?

The latter question appears to be satisfactorily answered by the supposition of the Chair, which, we have shown, was venerated at the cemetery of Ostrianus. This Chair did not, indeed, like that in the Vatican, symbolise St Peter's primacy, but it did symbolise his first coming to Rome, whatever may have determined the particular day on which that chair was venerated. The other question it is impossible to determine with any certainty, but the suggestion of De Rossi commends itself as probable, viz., that the copyists of the ancient Roman Calendar, finding the 18th of January marked as "*cathedra S. Petri qua primum Romæ sedit*," and not understanding why another Feast of St Peter's Chair at Rome should be kept on February 22, inserted the words "*apud Antiochiam*" in order to explain the anomaly. The Feast of St Tecla, with the title of *discipula Pauli Apostoli*, who went to Antioch in Pisidia to hear St Paul, and a certain St Gallus, a martyr of Antioch, being celebrated on the same day, may have led to the insertion of the word which has perplexed so many antiquarians, and which receives no explanation from any records of the Church of Antioch which have come down to us.†

January 18, his coming to Rome.

Note D (page 102).

The treatise of St Augustine, *De Curâ pro Mortuis Gerendâ*, was written about A.D. 421. St Paulinus of Nola had written to him, saying that a certain widow had pressed him to allow her son Cynegius to be buried in the Church of St Felix; and that he had consented to her petition, thinking that these desires of pious souls could not be altogether foolish (*non esse inanes motus animorum religiosorum et fidelium pro suis ista curantium*); that it was, in fact, one mode of asking for the help of the saints, &c. He asks,

St Augustine on the benefit of being buried near the Saints.

* Mabillon, l. c., p. 298.

† Mr Wright has lately published a valuable Syriac martyrology of the fourth century, from a MS. of the year 412, in which the martyrdom "in the city of Rome, of Paul the Apostle, and of Simon Peter, the Prince of the Apostles," is commemorated on the 28th of December (*Journal of Sacred Literature and Biblical Records* for January 1866). St Gregory of Nyssa and St Sophronius of Jerusalem assign the same date to the festival of the two Apostles.

however, for the opinion of St Austin—Does it profit a man's soul that his body should be buried after death near to the shrine of some saint? (*apud sancti alicujus memoriam.*)

St Austin answers, first, that there are many whom it does not profit at all, viz., those whose lives were so good that they need no such help, and those who were so bad that they cannot be benefited by it. Next, he quotes 2 Macch. xii. 43, and adds, that even if this had not been written in the Old Scriptures, the authority of the Church would have been of no small weight in this matter, which always provides that the recommendation of the faithful departed should have its place among the prayers which the priest pours forth to God at His altar. Then he enters into the *rationale* of the thing, and says, quoting St Matt. x. 28-30, that even the absence of any burial at all cannot bring any real loss to the soul; that all that concerns a funeral is more for the consolation of the survivors than the good of the deceased; nevertheless, that it is a part of religion to respect the bodies of the dead, which have been the instruments and temples of the Holy Ghost; and that if it be an act of religion to bury the dead, the choice of a place for the burial can hardly be altogether indifferent. He conceives the benefit of being buried near the shrine of a saint to be this: that, when we call to mind the place of our friends' burial, we may commend them to the saints near whom they lie, that being received by them as by patrons, they may be helped by their prayers with God; but without those prayers of ours he does not think the place would be of much use. (*Adjuvat defuncti spiritum, non mortui corporis locus, sed ex loci memoriâ vivus* [*matris*] *affectus.*) The Church prays for all who have died in the communion of the Catholic Church, under a general commemoration, without any mention of names, that those who have no children or parents, friends or relatives, to perform this work of piety in their behalf, may receive it at the hands of the Church as the common mother of us all.

"*How* the martyrs help men is a question," he says, "which passes the powers of my understanding. Nevertheless, that they do so is certain. Whether they themselves are present by virtue of their own power at one and the same time in so many different and distant places, either at their shrines, or wherever else they are felt to be present; or whether they remain in a place suited to their deserts, far removed from all converse with mortal things, yet praying in general for all the needs of their petitioners (just as we pray for the dead, to whom nevertheless we are not present, and we neither know where they are nor what they do), and Almighty God, who is everywhere present, neither confounded

Appendix. 401

and made one with us, nor yet removed to a distance from us, hearing their prayers, gives these consolations to those to whom He thinks it right to bestow them amid the miseries of this life, by means of the ministry of angels everywhere dispersed, and thus, by His wonderful and ineffable power and goodness, commends the merits of His martyrs wherever He pleases, when He pleases, and as He pleases, but especially by means of their shrines, because He knows it to be expedient to us for the building up of our faith in Christ, for confessing Whom they have suffered—This is a matter higher than I can reach, more abstruse than I can penetrate; and therefore I dare not define which of these two it is, or whether both perchance may be true, viz., that these things sometimes happen by means of the very presence of the martyrs themselves, sometimes by means of angels assuming their persons. I would rather inquire of those who know; for some one perhaps may know, though not he who seems to himself to know and is really ignorant; for they are the gifts of God, who gives some things to some men, and others to others, according to the testimony of the apostle (1 Cor. xii. 7–11)."

After this full and explicit discussion of the question by the great Doctor of the West, it is hardly necessary to quote any other witnesses. The reader, however, who desires it, will find similar testimony in St Ambrose's sermon on the death of his brother, and in his epitaph upon him; in a sermon of St Maximus of Turin (Hom. lxxxi.); and in several epitaphs collected by Le Blant, *Inscriptions Chrétiennes de la Gaule*, &c., tom. i. pp. 396, 471; ii. p. 219.

Note E (page 184).

The *Liber Pontificalis* attributes to St Felix, Pope about the year 270, the institution of the law that Mass should be celebrated on the sepulchres of the martyrs. Baronius, however, and others are of opinion that the practice had been universal and long established, before there was any legislation on the subject. The testimony of the fourth and fifth centuries is very explicit and abundant as to the practice of those days. St Ambrose speaks of the martyrs Gervasius and Protasius in this way. He says that he had intended to be buried there (under the altar) himself, because it seemed to him fitting that the priest should rest where he was wont to offer the holy sacrifice whilst alive; but that he yields the place to the martyrs to whom it is due, for that those triumphant victims ought to be where Christ is the victim (*ubi Christus hostia*

[marginal note: Mass said over the relics of the Martyrs from the earliest ages.]

est); only He who died for all lies *upon* the altar, they who were redeemed by His passion lie below it;* in which last words he seems to intend a reference to the language of the Book of the Apocalypse, VI. 9-11. That which St Ambrose testifies about Milan, Prudentius testifies about Spain; the sepulchres of St Eulalia at Barcelona, and of St Vincent at Valenza; also, as we have seen, of St Hippolytus in Rome.† St Jerome‡ also, about the tombs of Saints Peter and Paul, in the same city; and he appeals at the same time to the practice of all the bishops throughout the world.

<small>or on altars near their graves.</small>
We need not suppose, however, that the altar was always immediately over the grave, though doubtless this was the more usual practice. Prudentius speaks as though, in the case of St Hippolytus, the altar was only *near* his tomb ("*Propter* ubi apposita est ara dicata Deo"); and both Bosio and Boldetti seem to have found instances in which the altar was placed in the middle of the chamber, not on a tomb in the walls, just as we have seen that it was, at one period, in the Papal crypt.

Neither were the *mensæ* of these altar-tombs always fixed and immovable. On the contrary, in three or four instances they have been found with massive bronze rings inserted in them, by which they could be lifted off, and a sight of the martyr's relics obtained.§

St Martin of Tours is said to have been the first saint, *not a martyr*, whose tomb became an altar.‖ When altars were multiplied in churches, it was a rule universally observed that the altar must contain some relics, and there still remain many indications of the ancient practice in the prayers and ceremonies of the Liturgy.

<small>Traces of this practice in the present *Ordo Missæ*,</small>
The prayer in the mass immediately after the *Confiteor*, when first the priest goes up to the altar, contains these words: "We beseech Thee by the merits of the saints whose relics are here"—"Oramus te per merita sanctorum *quorum reliquiæ hic sunt*"—and the priest kisses the altar. Moreover, the little recess in the altar-stone, in which these relics are placed, is called the *sepulcrum*, in manifest allusion, as it would appear, to the ancient practice of which we have been speaking; and the act of depositing the relics in this *sepulcrum* is so essential a part of the consecration of an altar, that should they by any accident be removed or lost, it is not sufficient to replace them by others,—the whole altar must be consecrated afresh.

<small>and in the consecration of an altar.</small>
The details of the prayers and ceremonies appointed for the consecration of an altar, and especially for this portion of it, recall in the most striking manner the burial of the saints and martyrs of

---

* Epist. xxii. 15.   † Peristeph. Hymni III. V.
‡ Adv. Vigilant.   § Rom. Sott. i. 169, 285.
‖ Greppo. Dissertations sur l'Histoire du Culte des Reliques, p. 16.

old. The bodies of the dead were often carried to the cemetery in which they were to be deposited on the eve before the day of burial; and so, in like manner, the relics about to be placed in the *sepulcrum* of an altar are brought to the church on the previous evening, in some vessel prepared and blest for the purpose. Three grains of incense are enclosed in the same vessel with them, like the spices and perfumes with which the bodies of the saints were so frequently buried; and ecclesiastics keep watch before them all night, reciting the office of the saint whose relics they are. Then, in the office of Consecration the next day, these relics are carried in solemn procession, and among the hymns and prayers used on the occasion, the vision of St John, already referred to (Apoc. vi. 10), holds a conspicuous place. Finally, the consecrating bishop closes the sepulchre, and secures it with mortar, in the very same way in which the *fossors* formerly closed tombs in the Catacombs. The *rapprochement* between these two functions cannot be accidental. It is clearly the result of an unbroken tradition. It prevails in the Greek Church as well as the Roman.

It has been pretended by some writers that the doctrine of the Church underwent some change when the *arcosolia*, or tombs of the martyrs, became also altars for the celebration of the Holy Eucharist. It has even been recently asserted that none of the Fathers before St Cyprian knew anything of a sacrifice in which, or an altar on which, the Body of Christ was offered. Dr Dollinger, however, has shown in his commentary on the *Philosophumena*, that St Hippolytus, who lived before St Cyprian, clearly taught this same doctrine, and that the same may be said also of many Greek Fathers who lived immediately after St Cyprian, and who certainly did not borrow their doctrine from the Latin writings of the Bishop of Carthage. The earlier Greek Fathers, indeed, avoided the expressions which were in use as designating Pagan altars. They either spoke of "the holy table," or they used the word that had been introduced to designate the Jewish altar, which also was quite unknown to the Greeks. They did not use Βωμός or ἐσχάρα, but θυσιαστήριον. It is not till a constitution of the Emperors Theodosius II. and Valentinian in the fifth century, that the first of these words is used in speaking of a Christian altar. The Christians of the Latin Church, on the contrary, had no hesitation in designating their altars by the names *ara* and *altare*, though they had been hitherto used in a Pagan sense. In fact, the expression, "holy table," would have conveyed the same meaning to the Latin-speaking heathens as the word *ara*. When the Christians were reproached by the heathens for having no temples or altars like other religions and nations, they admitted the charge in the sense

[marginal notes:] Doctrine of the Christian sacrifice in writings of St Hippolytus, &c.

Names used for the altar.

in which the heathens used those terms, and with good reason. Nevertheless, Origen speaks of the altars to be met with in Christian Churches; and although Cæcilius, in Minucius Felix, speaks of Christians having no public altars visible to the Pagans, yet St Cyprian gives the Pagan Demetrius clearly to understand that they had their altars *in secret*. Compare also the language of St Paul in his Epistle to the Hebrews (xiii. 10), "We have an altar whereof they have no power to eat who serve the tabernacle."

Note F (page 310).

Origin of the Pallium.
The oldest writers confess that the *pallium* had been in use from time immemorial, and that its origin was lost in antiquity. The most natural and probable account of it, however, is certainly that to which reference is made in the text, and which is supported with great skill and learning in the treatise, *De Pallii Origine*, published in Rome in 1856 by Monsignore Vespasiani.

He observes that the scholars of the most famous heathen philosophers used to adopt the dress, as well as the principles, of their masters, and that the handing on of the mantle, or upper garment of the master served to designate his legitimate successor. It may easily be shown that among the early Christians also, a certain religious meaning and value was attached to the wearing the mantle of any great saint or doctor, as though a more intimate and immediate communion were thereby established with the original owner of the mantle. Thus, the great St Athanasius gave his to St Antony; and when St Paul, the hermit of Egypt, prayed St Antony to bring it to his cell, and to wrap his body in it for burial, St Antony took the hermit's mantle from off his shoulders, and ever afterwards wore it on all great occasions of solemnity. When St Ignatius, Patriarch of Constantinople, was habited in the episcopal vestments, we read that "they reverently put on him the venerable cloak of St James, the brother of our Lord, which had lately been brought from Jerusalem, and which Ignatius received with the same respect and veneration as though he had recognised in it its former apostolic owner."

But other examples are still more important as involving the principle of succession to office by him to whom the mantle was transferred. Thus, we read that Metrophanes, who occupied the see of Byzantium in the time of Constantine, took off his *pallium*, and laid it on the altar, charging that it should be preserved and delivered to his successor. And still more distinctly, Liberatus the Deacon, in his history of the Nestorian and Eutychian heresies, testifies as an essential part of the ceremony of consecrating and enthroning the Patriarchs of Alexandria. "It is the custom at Alexandria," he says, "for him who succeeds to the deceased bishop, to keep a vigil by the corpse of the deceased, to lay the dead man's head upon his own head, and then, having buried him with his own hands, to take the *pallium* of St Mark and to place it on his own neck, after which he is held legitimately to occupy his place." Thus, the *pallium*, or mantle of St Mark, was religiously handed on from one of his successors to another in the see of Alexandria, and its possession was accounted an important token of the legitimate possession of that dignity and office.

The origin of the Roman *pallium* seems to have been precisely the same. The oldest writers agree in referring its first use to the immediate successor of St Peter, and say that it implied the possession of plenary jurisdiction, *i.e.*, of succession to the jurisdiction enjoyed by St Peter. Moreover, it has always been described, and is still described, as *pallium de corpore S. Petri*. It is always blessed on the feast of his martyrdom,—the very day, that is, on which its first transfer was made, if not materially, yet morally,— and, when blest, it is laid upon the apostle's tomb.*

It is always assumed by each successive Pontiff at the altar above that tomb, and used to be delivered to archbishops or their procurators only at the same place. When it was conferred upon any one, it was always given as to a person holding the place of the Pope for the time being, acting as his deputy and representative within certain limits. Thus, Pope Vigilius sends it to Auxanius, holding the see of Arles, as a fitting ornament to one "acting in *our stead*." Pelagius sends it to another occupant of the same see, as "our vicar." St Gregory the Great sends it to many, but the same condition is always implied, and generally expressed.

This sculpture, then, of Elias giving his mantle to Eliseus, seems really to typify, if it does not sometimes directly represent, our Lord giving His commission to St Peter, and St Peter, not deeming himself worthy to receive it, holds forth his hands under the cover of his cloak, just as it has been mentioned in the text that he is always represented as receiving the Book of the Law from our Blessed Lord with the same outward token of reverence.

This note has been abridged from an article contributed by the writer, to the *Rambler* of July 1856.

* It used to be laid upon his Chair, until that relic was inclosed in bronze, and elevated to the position described in Note C.

DESCRIPTION OF THE ATLAS OR LARGE MAP, AND PARTICULARLY OF AREA V.

The following notes upon some other portions of the cemetery of St Callixtus may be added to the short explanations given in the Atlas itself, as a kind of supplement to the Analysis of Area III. They are intended to explain the Section, Fig. 44, page 336, and also the Plan, Fig. 51, page 349 :—

Area I. The most ancient portion of Area I is the staircase Dg 1, leading to a gallery about 37 feet beneath the surface of the ground. This gallery,
Fig. 44. which in Fig. 44 is marked U, leads to the doorway X, which is the
U. entrance to the *cubiculum duplex*, the frescoes on whose walls have been
X. described as probably belonging to the first century. The gallery was originally continued at the same level, but the same reasons which we have noticed in page 343, led here also to that level being depressed, so that a
B. flight of steps now leads from U to a lower level, BGI. B may be found
Dh 1. in the Atlas as Dh 1, a gallery leading to three *cubicula*, while another short gallery, G, at right angles to it, springs from the foot of the same staircase, and by an entrance opposite to I leads to the crypt of St Cor-
Dh 3. nelius, Dh 3. The traces of another staircase, afterwards destroyed, are
Crypt of St to be found at Dh 2, and Dh 4 is the vast ruined monument of which some
Cornelius. notice is given in page 123. The long gallery of the third *piano* is connected with g in Fig. 51.

Pagan tombs. Between Area I and the cross-road is a small *hypogeum*, Dh 5, apparently of the age of Alexander Severus, which marks the limits of the *area* on this side. On the other it is equally limited by another *hypogeum*, Ch 4, which does not appear to be more ancient than the end of the third century. Another small sepulchral cell, which may have been a Christian chapel, and which stands immediately opposite the present entrance to the Catacomb enclosure, is marked Ch 1. A small Pagan *columbarium* may be noticed near the Via Appio-Ardeatina, Ag 1.

Area III. Areæ III. and IV. have been fully described in our Analysis. It will suffice to mention that Be 1 is the staircase A, and Be 3 the staircase B of the Plan ; Be 2 is the staircase by which we now enter the crypt of St Cécilia, which is marked Be 5, and that of the Popes, Be 4. Be 6 is the passage leading to the crypt Be 7, or Q^1, in which were discovered several
Area IV. sarcophagi. Bf 1 and Bf 2 are described in the Analysis as Q^3 and Q^4; and Ce 5 and Ce 6 as A^1 and A^2; while Ae 1, 2, is the secret passage described as x^4, and of which an account is given, page 347.
Area V. An enlarged plan of Area V. is given in page 349, where its connexion with Area III. is explained ; and the three-apsed building above ground, Ce 1, together with the square building Ce 3, are stated to be remains of ancient Christian oratories of the time of St Fabian. Ce 4, Cf 1, Cf 2,

Appendix. 407

Cf 3, are there marked respectively o^7, a^1, a^6, and c. It may be worth Description while to describe that Area according to those letters, observing that the of Fig. 51. gallery S^1 is represented in this Atlas as transgressing the limits of the *area*, which is an error of the artist.

The wide though irregular gallery *a* was originally entered by a stair- *a*. case, now demolished, but of which the remains still exist in the long *luminare* which may be seen on the Plan. It terminated anciently at *Cf* 3, where it now breaks through *loculi* and passes the limits of the *area*. Along this *ambulacrum* are several *arcosolia*, some of which are decorated with frescoes, and on the right and left are the entrances to *cubicula*.

a_2 is a chamber containing three large *arcosolia*, formerly lined with a_2. marble, and having figures on the ceiling which represent classical personifications of the seasons, &c., without any distinctively Christian allusion. This ceiling is evidently much more ancient than the *arcosolia*, and confirms De Rossi's opinion that this and the opposite chambers were originally intended simply for secular purposes.

a_3 is a large chamber whose walls were once lined with marble, which a_3. still remains on the bench which goes round three of its sides, and also on the pavement, where is the inscription, PAVLVS EXORCISTA DEP. MARTVRIES VI. A deep and wide recess at the end of the chamber once contained an immense sarcophagus, probably that of St Melchiades, the cover of which, shaped like the roof of a house, still remains. Its corners are decorated with *bassi relievi* of a shepherd and sheep. The remains of frescoes on the ceiling of the chamber resemble those of a_2 in style and subject, except that here we see the Good Shepherd and the Raising of Lazarus. Both *cubicula* are well lighted by the same wide *luminare* as in Fig. 6, page 31.

The two chambers, a_4, a_5, are of a date posterior to the *arcosolia* in a_4, a_5. a_2, a_3, and each have in one corner a small table of *tufa* similar to that described in the crypt of St Cornelius, page 184.

A long narrow chamber, on the principal *arcosolium* of which are two of a_6. the *graffiti* to Sophronia mentioned page 132. This and the opposite a_7. chamber are much filled up by modern constructions deemed necessary for the safety of the *hypogeum*.

A gallery, *b*, unites *a* with the gallery S, connecting this *hypogeum* with *b*. Area III. It contains several large *loculi*, one of which is marked on the Plan as closed by a wall. Nearly opposite this, and just before the gallery passes the limits of the *area* into the labyrinth, is an *arcosolium* beautifully painted, although the *lunette* has been almost destroyed by graves. The ceiling has an *orante*, and on either side Daniel and Jonas are painted in separate compartments.

De Rossi calls *c* a subterranean piazza. Over the door which leads from *c*. it into a *cubiculum* are to be seen the names of the first visitors of the Catacombs in the fifteenth century, see page 2. Out of this piazza extends *d*, a gallery in a very ruined condition, and which falls into the *ambulacrum* *d*. *o* by a rapid descent near the point of junction. This portion of *d*, however, seems to have been of a later period than the rest of the gallery. Only one

d_1. *cubiculum* is entered from this gallery, and this is elaborately painted—the lower portion of the walls have a lattice-work pattern, and the upper portion fruit, flowers, birds, and *putti*. A head of Oceanus is on the ceiling, the *luminare* of which is adorned with the bust of a man holding a book, with his name in white letters below. His face seems to have been originally painted on canvas, which has been removed, so that now we have only the faint outlines of his features. The chamber was originally designed for a single *arcosolium*, which was decorated with frescoes, and had above it a painting of the Good Shepherd, which is now all but gone.

d_2, d_3, e The galleries d_2 d_3 and e are still unexcavated.

f Is a small gallery with large *loculi* in it, and contains a staircase leading to a lower *piano*, which is also reached by the little staircase in A^2.

o Is an *ambulacrum* which extends throughout the whole length of Area VI., taking its rise from the foot of the staircase, Ce 2. It was afterwards continued to meet the gallery d, and pushed forward until it fell into a. The *cubicula* o^9, o^8, o^7, o^6, are poorly constructed, apparently after the

o^7. time of Diocletian. In o^7 are written on the walls the names of visitors of the fifteenth century, Ce 4.

Area VI. The staircase Ce 2 is remarkable for its leading both to the higher and lower *piano* of the *area*, which were apparently excavated at nearly the same period.

Crypt of St Eusebius. Turning to the left in the lower *piano*, we come at once to the crypt of St Eusebius, De 1, described page 167. Further on still we come to two more *cubicula* on opposite sides of the gallery, of which the one marked

Calocerus and Parthenius. Dd 1 is the crypt of Calocerus and Parthenius, mentioned page 175. Between these two crypts a gallery crosses the *ambulacrum*, which afterwards breaks through the wall of gallery C in Area III., as shown in Fig. 46, q_3.

Area VII. Continuing our course along the *ambulacrum*, we pass into Area VII., the centre of which De Rossi has discovered in the *cubiculum* Dd 4, which was once the principal staircase of this *area*, and of the three others which appear to have been constructed subsequently. The last of these (Area VIII.) had afterwards a staircase of its own, De 2. Opposite to the door of Dd 4 is a gallery which leads us to the *cubiculum duplex* of the Deacon Severus. See page 93. The remaining areæ are not yet sufficiently excavated to enable us to give a detailed account of them.

INDEX.

ABERCIUS, St, Epitaph of, 217.
Acts of Martyrs, their value, 21 (see *Cecilia* and *Perpetua*).
Ad religionem meam pertinentes, meaning of, 61.
Agapitus, St, deacon and martyr, 144.
Agnes, St, on glasses, 286 (see *Catacomb*).
Alaric, Rome taken by, 103.
Alexander, St, Pope, martyrdom and burial, 81; cemetery of, 81, 334.
Alexandria, Catacomb paintings of, 221.
Allegorical (see *Paintings*).
Almanac (see *Filocalus*).
Altar in Papal crypt, 135; in crypt of St Cornelius, 184; over relics, 401; consecration of, 402; doctrine of, unchanged, 403; words used for, 403.
Anacletus, St, Pope, erected *memoria* of St Peter, 64.
Antherus, St, Pope, his work, 18; his epitaph, 137, 142.
Apamea, coins of, representing Noe, 241.
Apostles, paintings of, 237; sculptures of, 308 (see *Peter and Paul*); Catacombs in age of, 63, 64, 74, 75.
Arcosolium, 30; age of, 350.
Arenarium, sometimes connected with Catacombs, 28, 323, 327, 329-331.
Aringhi, his edition of Bosio, 7.
Arvales, Fratres, 385.
Asclepiodote, epitaph, 207.
Augustine, St, on cemeteries, 90; on milk as symbol of Eucharist, 228; on fish and bread, 215; on intercession of martyrs, 400.

Aurelian, edicts of, 54, 89.
Authors on Catacombs, modern, 1; ancient, 17.
Autun, epitaph at, on Eucharist, 218.

BAPTISM of Christ, 119, 252; sacrament of, 264, 265; symbols of, Noe, 240; Jonas, 243.
Baronius, Cardinal, 3, 156.
Basilicas over tombs of martyrs, 96.
Bishops, burial of, 138; in Rome, 140.
Boldetti on Christian antiquities, 11.
Boniface IV. translates relics from Catacombs, 107.
Bosio, his life and labours, 5-8.
Brandea, a kind of relic, 23.
Bruttia Crispina, 70.
Buonarrotti on gilded glasses, 12.
Burnet, his ignorant remarks on Catacombs, 11, 318.
Burning of dead not Christian, 59.

CAIUS, St, Pope, 145.
Callixtus, St, deacon to Pope Zephyrinus, 83-86; cemetery of, 83, 110-185, 336-378; identified, 117; distinct *areæ* in, 120, 122; maps of, 121; first *area* of, 126, 130, 338-355; second *area*, 127, 348; third *area*, 127, 355.
Calocerus and Parthenius, their epitaph and tomb, 145.
Canon of Council of Elvira on sacred pictures, 191.
Catacomb, the name, 109.
Catacomb of St Agnes, 27, 29, 31.
—— St Alexander, 81.
—— St Balbina, 128, 129.
—— St Callixtus (see *Callixtus*).
—— St Commodilla, 65.
—— St Domitilla, 69-74.

Catacomb of Generoses, 384-386.
—— St Hermes, 323.
—— St Hippolytus, 98.
—— Ostrianus, or Fons Petri, 67, 396.
—— St Prætextatus, 76-81.
—— St Priscilla, 66, 330.
—— St Sebastian, 108, 112-117.
—— St Soteris, 128.
Catacombs, discovery of, 1; early visits to, 2; general description of, 25; locality of, 25, 331; number and names of, ix., 27; Christian origin of, 28, 56, 317-332; excavated on high ground, 334; in *tufa granulare*, 319, 325; in various *piani*, 337; within certain prescribed limits, 47, 120, 340; at first small, 61; used for worship, 54, 348; for hiding-places, 89, 346; martyrdoms in, 87, 88; disuse of for burial, 95, 103; frequented as shrines, 31, 97, 104; described by St Jerome, 97; by Prudentius, 98; damaged by indiscreet devotion, 96, 100, 102; repaired by Popes, 97, 104, 105, 354; relics translated from, 106; finally abandoned, 108, 359; rediscovered, 33; history of, 63-109; Jewish, 58.
Cecilia, St, her tomb, 151, 158, 160; her family, 160, 164; her history, 152, 163; her Acts verified and corrected, 162; various versions of them, 387; her body translated by Paschal I., 154; found incorrupt in sixteenth century, 154; statue of, 157; crypt of, 151-166; its original form, 346, 371.
Cemetery, the term of Christian origin, 29 (see *Catacomb*); gradual development of a, 338-359.
Cemeteries protected by Roman law until the middle of third century, 45, 83; invaded by Pagans, 54, 88; proscribed by Valerian, 55; restored to Christians, 87; confiscated by Diocletian, 90; restored, 90, 146; ecclesiastical administration of, 91-93, 101; all extramural, 56.
Cerealis et Sallustia cum xxi., *graffito*, 185.
Chairs of *tufa* in Catacombs, 31, 128.

Chair of St Peter in Vatican, its description, 389; its history, 391; in cemetery of Ostrianus, 396; two Feasts of, explained, 397.
Children, Three, in paintings, 245; on glasses, 280, 290; in sculpture, 313.
Christ, paintings of, 119, 252; symbols of, *e.g.*, Orpheus, 199; the Good Shepherd, 199, 234; the Fish, or ΙΧΘΥC, 207-212; monogram of, 230.
Christians did not burn their dead, 59 (see *Cemeteries*); Roman, legal position of, 34; at first regarded as a Jewish sect, 40; persecuted by Nero, &c., 42; their cemeteries protected, 45; persons of noble rank, 35; even of the imperial family, 36.
Christian art, 186-316 (see *Glasses, Paintings, Sculpture, Symbols*); antiquity of, 187, &c.; can be traced to Apostolic times, 188, 197; growth of, 190; checked by persecution, 191; early history of, 196; not formed entirely on Pagan models, 198; classes of, 200.
Chrysanthus and Daria buried *in arenario*, 328.
Ciacconio, his researches, 4.
Columbaria, Pagan, 57; never Christian, 60.
Cornelius, St, Pope, his account of the Roman clergy, 92; his family, 177; his epitaph, 117, 118; why in Latin, 177; his sepulchre, 175-185; near an *arenarium*, 327; painting of, with St Cyprian, 181.
Clement, St, Pope, 17; basilica of, 74.
Confraternities, burial, 49; some of them Christian, 53.
Cross disguised, 127; various forms of, 229, 230.
Crypt (see *Catacomb, Cecilia, Cornelius, Popes*, &c.); of St Lucina, 27, 122-126, 336, 337, 356.
Cupid and Psyche, 261.
Cyprian, St, painting of, 182.

D'AGINCOURT, damage done to Catacombs by, 13; on Christian art, 186.
Damasus, St, Pope, his love for the Catacombs, 96, 102; value of his

inscriptions, 20, 97; his inscription to St Agnes, 286; his inscription in baptistery of Vatican, 390; his inscription in cemetery *ad Catacumbas*, 114; his inscription at tomb of St Cornelius, 179, 180; his inscription at the tomb of St Eusebius, 105, 167-174; his inscription at tomb of St Januarius, 80; his inscription at tomb of St Marcellus, 174; his inscription at tomb of St Peter and St Paul, 334; his inscription at tomb of Papal crypt, 118, 147; his inscription at tomb of Sixtus II., 144; his labours, 354, 355.
Daniel in paintings, 73, 245; in sculpture, 303, 307.
De Rossi, Gio. Battista, his method of research, 15; his chief sources of information, 16; his reconstruction of early history, 93.
De Rossi, Michel Stefano, brother of the Commendatore, his success in mapping the Catacombs, 121; his analysis, 360.
De Winghe, his sketches in Catacombs, 4.
D. M., meaning of, on Christian epitaphs, 59.
Domitian, Emperor, his Christian relatives, 39, 42.
Domitilla, St, 39, 69; her cemetery, 69-74; bronze medal found in, 284; sarcophagi in, 295.

ECCLESIA FRATRUM, significance of, 53.
Edict, first, against cemeteries by Valerian, 54, 87; revoked by Gallienus, 87; renewed by Aurelian, 89; by Diocletian, 90; of Milan, 90, 95.
Eleutherius, St, Pope, 64, 163.
Elias taken up to heaven, in sculpture, 250, 310.
Ennodius of Pavia on St Peter's Chair, 392.
Epitaphs of Popes, 137; episcopal, very rare (see *Eusebius* and *Damasus*); of St Abercius, 217; of Autun, 218.
Eucharist, Holy, symbolised by fish and bread, 215-224; by milk, 225-229; doctrine of, illustrated by paintings of second and third centuries, 222, 266-271; constitution of St Zephyrinus concerning, 292; represented in sculpture, 302, 305.
Eusebius, St, Pope, remarkable incident in life of, 172; epitaph of, 167; broken and recopied, 171; its interpretation, 172.
Eutychianus, St, Pope, his epitaph, 137, 143.
Evelyn, John, his visit to the Catacombs, 10.

FABIAN, St, Pope, 17, 137, 142.
Fabretti on inscriptions, 11.
Faustinianus, an inscription, 82.
Felix, St, Pope, 401.
Felicissimus, deacon and martyr, 144.
Fidentibus in Domino, significance of, 62.
Filocalus, Furius Dionysius, his almanac, 19; his inscriptions, 170.
Filippi ad Sextum, cemetery of, 386.
Flavius Clemens, 37 (see *Domitilla*).
Flavius Sabinus, 37.
Fratres Arvales, the, 385.

GARRUCCI, Padre, S.J., on gilded glasses, 12, 277; on Jewish Catacomb, 58.
Glasses, gilded, found in Catacombs, 275-294; two recently found at Cologne, 277, 289; date of, 279; subjects on, 280; their probable use, 283, 291, 293.
Good Shepherd, in paintings, 274, 234-238; in sculpture, 299; statues of, 304; Pagan examples of, 261, 298, 299.
Graffiti of three kinds, 131; in Papal crypt, 130, 144; in crypt of St Cecilia, 161; in crypt of St Cornelius, 184.
Gregory the Great, Pope, on burial of St Peter and St Paul, 115, 116; on relics, 23.
Gregory of Tours, St, on a martyrdom in Catacombs, 88.
Hippolytus, his cemetery, 98; his *festa* in fourth or fifth centuries, 99; his statue, 313; his Paschal Canon, 314.
Hyacinth, St, his body discovered by Padre Marchi, 15, 379.

ITINERARIES of seventh century, 22, 23, 111, 112.

JANUARIUS, St, tomb of, 79, 80.
Jerome, St, on Catacombs, 97; on the ivy or gourd of Jonas, 243.
Jews protected by Roman laws, 41; occupied Trastevere, 278.
Jewish Catacombs, 58.
John and Paul, Saints, buried within the walls, 106.
John III., Pope, directs mass to be said in Catacombs, 105.
Jonas, history of, in paintings, 243, 244; in glasses, 290; in sculpture, 304, 305.

KALENDAR of St Hippolytus, 314.

LAMB, a symbol of Christ, Figs. 37, 38; of Christians, 103, 225.
Lazarus, raising of, in paintings, 247, 271; in sculpture, 302, 304, 306, 313.
Leo III., Pope, his care for cemeteries, 107; his decorations in crypt of St Cornelius, 183.
Leo IV., Pope, translated relics from Catacombs, 107.
Liber Pontificalis, account of, 20.
Linus, St, Pope, his sepulchre, 65.
Liturgical paintings, 262-274.
Loculo a mensa, 30.
Lucius, St, Pope, his epitaph, 137, 143.
Lucina, St, probably Pomponia Græcina, 124; crypt of, 122, 126, 337; frescoes in, 103, 185, 201, 224, 225.
Luminare, 31, 127, 129, 165, 348.

MABILLON *de cultu sanctorum ignotorum*, 12.
Macarius, his *Hagioglypta*, 4.
Magi, adoration of, in paintings, 246, 257; in sculpture, 301, 311.
Malmesbury, William of, 22, 62.
Marangoni, his labours in Catacombs, 12.
Marcellus, St, Pope, 90.
Marcellinus, St, Pope, 90, 93, 279.
Marchi, Padre, S.J., his labours and writings, 14; the first to insist upon the Christian origin of Catacombs, 318.
Mark, St, Pope, buried in St Balbina, 95, 129.
Martyr vindicatus equivalent to *canonizatus*, 143.
Martyrs, vast number of, 148; they assist us by their prayers, 400; desire of Christians to be buried near to, 102; this practice defended and accounted for by St Augustine, 399.
Martyrologium, Hieronymianum, 17; Bedæ, Adonis, &c., 21.
Melchiades, St, Pope, recovered the confiscated cemeteries, 90, 91; the last Pope buried in Catacombs, 95, 146; his tomb, 146, 349.
Merivale, Mr, not correct as to early Christian burial, 59.
Misson, his rash assertions, 11.
Monogram (see *Christ*).
Monza, papyrus MS. at, 23.
Moses, in paintings, 247; taking off his shoes, 248; when striking the rock typifies St Peter, in paintings, 248, 265; in glasses, with name *Petrus*, 286; and in sculpture, 302.

NICOLAS I., Pope, visited Catacombs, 108.
Nimbus, use of, in determining dates of pictures, 193.
Noe in the ark, in paintings, 240-242; in sculpture, 305; not copied from Pagan coin, 241.

OLEA from shrines taken away as relics, 23
Optatus, St, fresco of, 166.
Ordo cænarum, its resemblance to the Christian Kalendar, 53.
Orpheus, type of Christ, in painting, 199, 373; in sculpture, 300.
Ostrianus, cemetery of, 67, 396.

PALLIUM, origin of, 310, 404.
Paintings, determination of date of, 192; by *nimbus*, 193; by letters on dress, 195; by choice of subject and treatment, 195; Gnostic, 199; allegorical, 233-238; Biblical, 239-250; of Christ, 252, 253; of the Blessed Virgin Mary, 254-260; of St Joseph, 260; of Isaias, 258 (see *Moses, Magi*, &c.); liturgical, 262-274; symbolical, 202-231.
Panvinius, Onophrius, on Christian cemeteries, 12.
Papyrus MS. at Monza, 23.
Paschal I., St, Pope, his translation of relics, 107; of St Cecilia, 155.
Paul, St, the Apostle, his tomb, 65.
Paul I., Pope, his translation of relics, 106.

Index. 413

Perpetua, St, Acts of, 226.
Peter, St, his tomb, 64, 113, 116, 139 (see *Chair*); represented as Moses, 286-289 (see *Moses*).
Peter and Paul, Saints, burial and translation of, 113-116; feast of, 281; Damasine inscription to, 114; figured on glasses, 281; symbolised the Roman Church, 285.
Philosophumena, its testimony to Catacombs, 83, 85.
Policamus, painting of, 165.
Pomponia Græcina, 39.
Pomponius Bassus, 124; sarcophagus of, 311.
Pomponio, Leto, 2, 352, 362.
Pontianus, St, Pope, 142.
Popes, early register of burial of, 19; at first buried in Vatican, and then at San Callisto, 86; epitaphs of, 137; officially known to Pagan governors, 19; crypt of, 130-150,
PP. for *Papa*, in use in third century, 93; *PP. Rom.*, 183.
Prayers for dead, 131; to departed saints, 132.
Prætextatus, Catacomb of, 76-81; discovery of, 77; paintings in, 78, 79; martyrdom of St Sixtus II. in, 143.
Priscilla, Catacomb of, 66; sepulchre of Pudens and his family, 66; ancient painting of Blessed Virgin in, 258.
Ptolomæus Silvius, 398.

QUIRINUS, St, tomb of, 80.
Quirinus, a Bishop of Siscia, 165.
Quattro Coronati buried *in arenario*, 325, 327.

RECORDS, ancient, of *Roma Sotterranea*, 17.
Relics, different kinds of, 23 (see *Cecilia, Peter*, &c.)
Restutus M. Ant. inscription, 62.
Roma Sotterranea, the name, 1; of Bosio, 7.
Roman Academy, the, 2.
Roman burial-grounds adapted for Christian cemeteries, 46; burial confraternities, 48; their rules, 50.
Roman Church symbolised by St Peter and St Paul, 285 (see *Christians*).
Roman clergy in time of St Cyprian, 92.

Roman *festa* in fifth century, 98, 281.
Roman laws regarding burial, 44, 45.
Rome taken by Alaric, 103; by Totila, 105; by Vitiges, 104; by Astolphus, 106.
Rosatio, a Pagan ceremony, 129.

SABINUS, the deacon, his epitaph, 102.
Sebastian, St, cemetery of, 108, 112-117.
Sentia Renata, epitaph of, 60.
Sergius I., Pope, his epitaph to Ceadwalla, 391.
Sergius II., Pope, translates relics, 107.
Severano, Padre, editor of Bosio, 7.
Severus the deacon, his *cubiculum*, 93.
Sfondrati, Cardinal, finds the body of St Cecilia, 155.
Siricius, St, Pope, inscription by, 180.
Sixtus II., St, Pope, his martyrdom, 77, 87, 143; inscription to, 144; prayers to, 132.
Sophronia, graffiti of, 132.
Soter, St, Pope, 141.
Soteris, St, cemetery of, 113, 128, 355.
Stephen, St, Pope, confused with St Sixtus II., 144.
Sylvester, St, Pope, buried in a *basilica*, above ground, 95, 107, 146, 308.
Symbolism, 203; rules for interpreting, 204.
Symbols, anchor, 204; sheep and dove, 205; fish, 207; fish and dove, 212; fish and bread, 213; Good Shepherd, 234; Noe, 240; Jonas, 243.

TERTULLIAN, his testimony to the condition of Christians at end of second century, 19, 36, 37, 41, 43, 51, 84; on cemeteries, 52, 54; styles the Church *Jerusalem*, 134; explains symbols of dove and ark, 242; milk, 226; the rock, 247, 264; fish, 211; the paralytic, 266; the use of the *pallium* by Christians, 267; the custom of painting the Good Shepherd on chalices, 291; T in Greek and Latin regarded as a form of the Cross, 230.

Theodelinda, Queen, relics sent to, 23.
Tituli or parishes of Rome, 91.
Tufa granulare, 319, 321; *litoide*, 319; chairs, &c., cut in, 32, 358.

URBAN, St, Pope, 141, 163, 164, 182.

VALERIAN, his edicts against Christian cemeteries, 54, 87.

Vatican, *Memoria* of St Peter in, 64, 65; Popes buried there, 64; Christian museum of, 13, 275 (see *Chair*).
Vigilius, Pope, restored Damasine inscriptions, 105, 170.
Volcanic *strata* around Rome, 319.

ZEPHYRINUS, St, Pope, entrusted the first public cemetery to Callixtus, 83, 85; buried there, 141.

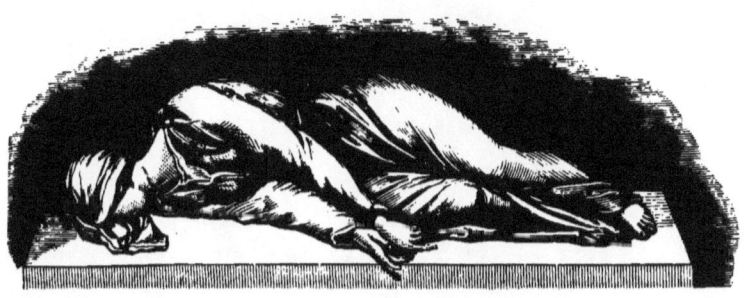

Maderna's Statue of St Cecilia.

N.B.—It was not observed until too late that in Fig. 17, page 157, the artist had supplied from his imagination a view of the features of St Cecilia. The present figure, by the same artist, is a faithful representation of Maderna's statue.

BALLANTYNE AND COMPANY, PRINTERS, EDINBURGH.

HIC CONGESTA IACET QVAERIS SI TVRBA PIORVM
CORPORA SANCTORVM RETINENT VENERANDA SEPVLCRA
SVBLIMES ANIMAS RAPVIT SIBI REGIA CAELI
HIC COMITES XYSTI PORTANT QVI EX HOSTE TROPAEA
HIC NVMERVS PROCERVM SERVAT QVI ALTARIA XPI
HIC POSITVS LONGA VIXIT QVI IN PACE SACERDOS
HIC CONFESSORES SANCTI QVOS GRAECIA MISIT
HIC IVVENES PVERIQ SENES CASTIQ NEPOTES
QVIS MAGE VIRGINEVM PLACVIT RETINERE PVDOREM
HIC FATEOR DAMASVS VOLVI MEA CONDERE MEMBRA
SED CINERES TIMVI SANCTOS VEXARE PIORVM

DAMASVS EPISCOPVS FECIT

HERACLIVS VETVIT LABSOS PECCATA DOLERE
EVSEBIVS MISEROS DOCVIT SVA CRIMINA FLERE
SCINDITVR IN PARTES POPVLVS GLISCENTE FVRORE
SEDITIO CAEDES BELLVM DISCORDIA LITES
EXEMPLO PARITER PVLSI FERITATE TYRANNI
INTEGRA CVM RECTOR SERVARET FOEDERA PACIS
PERTVLIT EXILIVM DOMINO SVB IVDICE LAETVS
LITORE ETINACRIO MVNDVM VITAMQVE RELIQVIT
EVSEBIO EPISCOPO ET MARTYRI

DAMASVS EPISCOPVS FECIT
HERACLIVS VETVIT ABSOS PECCATA DOLERE
EVSEBIVS MISEROS DOCVIT SVA CRIMINA FLERE
SCINDITVR IN PARTES POPVLVS GLISCENE FVRORE
SEDITIO CAEDES BELLVM DISCORDIA LITES
EXTEMPLO PARITER PVLSI FERITATE TYRANNI
INTEGRA CVM RECTOR SERVARET FOEDERA PACIS
PERTVLIT EXILIVM DOMINO SVB IVDICE LAETVS
LITORE TRINACRIO MVNDVM VITAMQVE RELIQVIT
EVSEBIO EPISCOPO ET MARTYRI

Plate IV

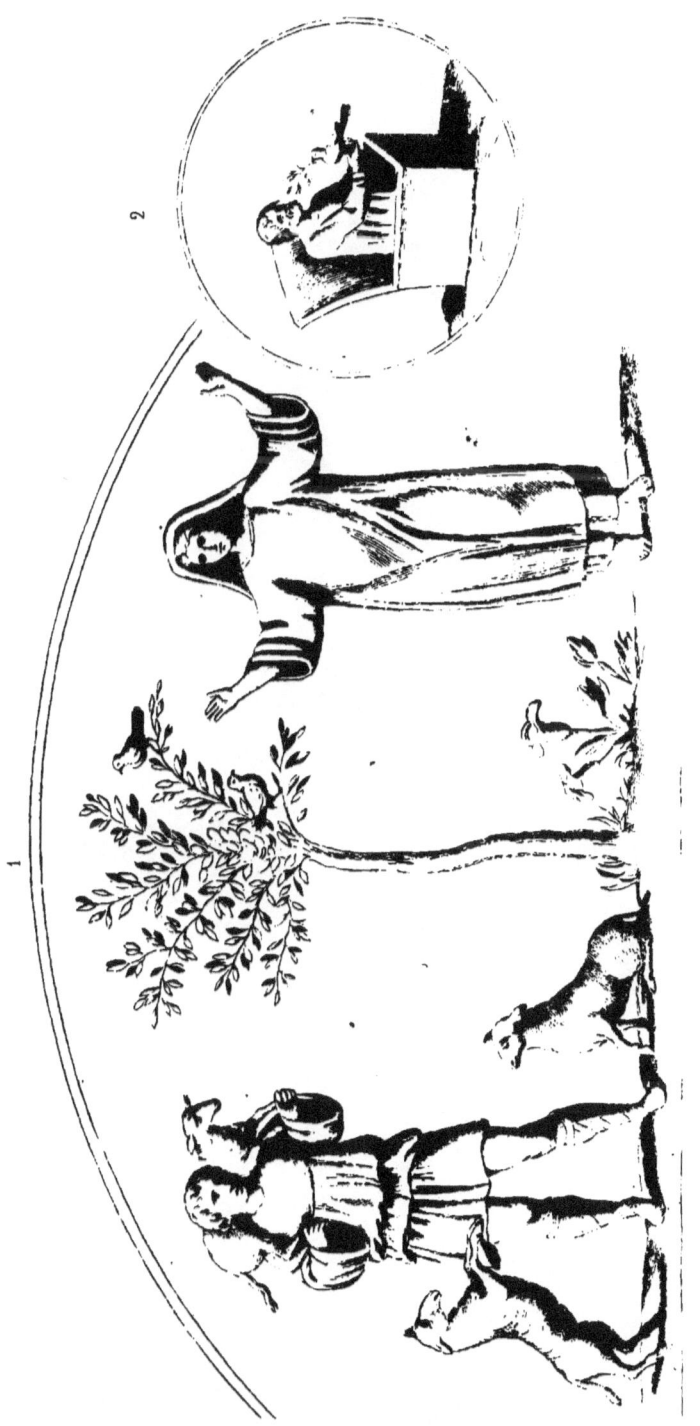

Plate X

1

2

Plate XV.

Plate XVI.

Plate XVII.

1

2

Plate XIX

Plate XX

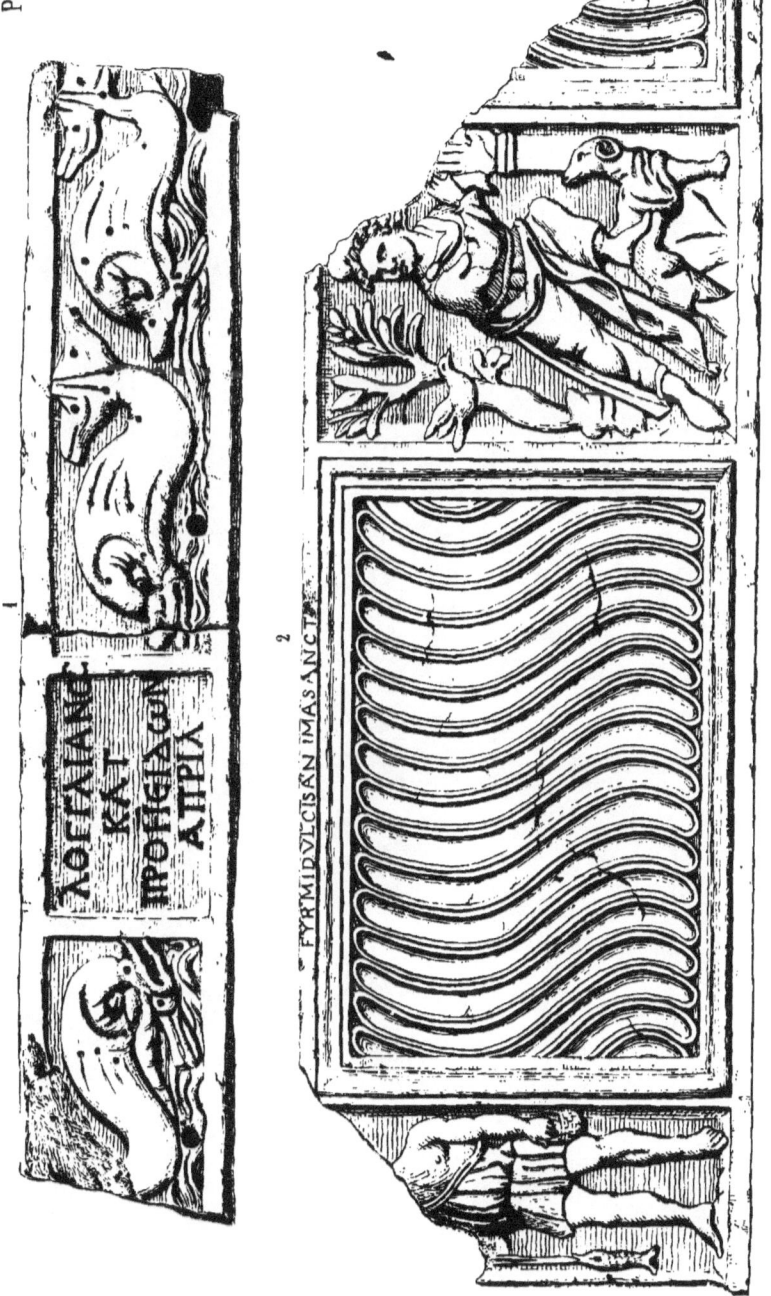

www.ingramcontent.com/pod-product-compliance
Lightning Source LLC
Chambersburg PA
CBHW051846300426
44117CB00006B/287